PROFESSOR McDONALD'S
CONVEYANCING OPINIONS

PROFESSOR McDONALD'S CONVEYANCING OPINIONS

Compiled and edited by

CHARLOTTE WAELDE

Lecturer in the Legal Practice Unit,
University of Edinburgh

T&T CLARK
EDINBURGH
1998

T&T CLARK LTD
59 GEORGE STREET
EDINBURGH EH2 2LQ
SCOTLAND

British Library Cataloguing-in-Publication Data
A catalogue record for this book is available from the British Library

ISBN 0 567 00524 0

Typeset by Fakenham Photosetting Ltd, Fakenham, Norfolk
Printed and bound in Great Britain by MPG Books Ltd, Bodmin, Cornwall

CONTENTS

STAMP DUTIES AND VAT

CREATION OF THE NEW FEUDAL ESTATE

THE FEU CHARTER

DESCRIPTIONS

RESERVATIONS

PREFACE

Professor A. J. McDonald produced the first edition of his *Conveyancing Manual* in 1982. The *Manual* – now called *Professor McDonald's Conveyancing Manual* – is in its sixth edition. It has become not only a well-established textbook for LLB and Diploma students but also an essential first source of reference for busy practitioners.

Soon after the *Manual* first appeared, solicitors began to seek Professor McDonald's opinion on a wide range of conveyancing matters. The number of memorials and opinions rose year on year during the 1980s and 1990s, and would have gone on increasing had Professor McDonald not insisted that the time had come for him to retire. One of the results is that an enormous database of vital information has been created, containing opinions on almost every aspect of conveyancing law and practice. The purpose of this collection is to make available just a few of those opinions for students and practitioners.

The layout of the book follows very broadly the layout of the *Manual*. Many of the opinions cover more than one topic; a brief headnote outlines the contents of each opinion. This is followed by a synopsis of the memorial. The opinion restates the opinion that the Professor gave, with minor amendment to the text to ensure anonymity. An end note refers to the section of the *Manual* to which the opinion is linked. In some cases there has been a change in the law since the date of the opinion (which can be found at the beginning of each opinion), and suggestions are given as to the relevant legislation or cases to which the reader might like to refer to update the substance of the opinion. Particular note should be taken of the Requirements of Writing (Scotland) Act 1995 and the Contracts (Scotland) Act 1997, both of which were enacted after the majority of the opinions were given.

This compilation would not have been possible without the generous permission of those who requested the opinions. I would like to thank Thorntons, WS, for providing access to the opinions and not least for providing desk space and the use of a photocopier!

The compilation stands as a tribute to Professor McDonald; to his sharp intellect, to his intimate knowledge of and love for the law and practice of conveyancing, and to his phenomenal capacity for hard work. His contribution to this branch of the law will help shape the thinking of students and practitioners alike for many years to come.

Charlotte Waelde
September 1998

TABLE OF CASES

TABLE OF STATUTES

TABLE OF STATUTORY INSTRUMENTS

TEXTBOOKS AND ARTICLES

THE ROLE OF SOLICITORS

1 The role of solicitors in heritable property transactions
Negligence of solicitors - survey reports

Date: August 1990

Memorial
Various properties were sold in a small new housing development. Three different sets of solicitors, referred to here as 'A solicitors', 'B solicitors' and 'C solicitors', acted for three different sets of purchasers. After purchase, the properties flooded. Questions arose as to the import of the survey and the content of the missives drawn up by the agents, in particular as to whether the missives should have contained specific clauses relating to planning permission and building warrants.

It was suggested by the agents ('the agents') acting for the insurers that the purchasing solicitors should have sought unqualified planning permission in the missives, rather than planning permission referring to a possible risk of flooding. In addition, it was argued that a clause should have been introduced to allow for purchasers to resile from the missives in the event that the planning permission produced referred to such a risk.

The specific question was whether the solicitors involved had followed good practice or whether had they been negligent.

Opinion
I have now had an opportunity of considering in detail the three files which you sent me with your original letter, and your further letters containing the information which I requested.

Notwithstanding the purported difference between the case of C solicitors and the other two cases, which the solicitors comment on in their correspondence with you, all three cases undoubtedly involve the same general principles.

Survey reports
Two points arise here.
1 *The solicitor's duty to advise on obtaining survey.* I think it is now generally accepted that, in any case of sale and purchase of heritage, it is the duty of a solicitor to advise the purchaser to obtain a survey report. If the client objects, the solicitor should warn him of the risks of proceeding either without a report or simply on a valuation by a building society surveyor for loan purposes. The 6th edition of my *Conveyancing Manual*, para 28.18 and subsequent sections, substantially repeated in the context of chapter

34, explains in some detail the various types of survey report available and the pros and cons of each such report.

In the present claims, A solicitors obtained a survey report before missives were concluded, and were in my opinion perfectly entitled to rely on it in the context of the content of their offer. That report, dated February, deals generally with the situation of the property and its description, services including roads, and an opinion on the suitability of the property for loan purposes which, for that purpose, the surveyors value at £xx. There is no reference whatsoever in their report to any possibility of flooding and nothing to put A solicitors on their guard in that respect. Compare the report from the same firm produced for B solicitors during April, where the question of flooding is specifically dealt with and recommendations are made as to suitable protective works. If that recommendation had been included in the case of the A solicitors' report, I have no doubt that appropriate clauses would have been inserted in his contract.

In the case of C solicitors, their offer was made initially subject to a satisfactory survey, but that was deleted in the qualified acceptance. However, a survey report had clearly been obtained before missives were concluded, although admittedly it was only a valuation for mortgage purposes prepared for the building society. None the less, the terms of the report were known to the client and discussed with the client by C solicitors, as the note of November, on file, discloses. The copy survey report on file contains no reference to any possible risk of flooding, and indeed Question 7 is answered positively in the negative as regards evidence of flood damage. Likewise Question 11, 'Any unusual hazards', is answered 'No'. The disclaimers at the foot of page 1 and the note of Applicants underline the risk of relying on building society reports, and possibly as a result the solicitors may not be able to shelter behind it.

In the case of B solicitors, no survey report was apparently obtained before concluding missives; but, when the planning permission was exhibited to them shortly before settlement, a report was immediately instructed (I assume, because of the reference to potential flooding in the planning permission), and as a result reported thereon. In the report, it was indicated that the builder was actively working on the formation of soil bunds to give adequate protection; and the surveyors simply suggest that some form of written guarantee should be obtained from the builder to ensure satisfactory completion of the work 'to prevent any future damage'. I take that to mean that, in the opinion of the surveyors, if the works were duly completed, any risk of flooding would be excluded.

By that time, of course, it was far too late to incorporate any specific provision in the missives as to flooding, or as to protective works, and there was nothing more at that stage which B solicitors could have done. None the less, I think there is a potential claim for a failure of duty in not ensuring that a survey report was first obtained before concluding the bargain. However, judging from the report of February by the surveyors, any preliminary report from that firm would not have produced the requisite warning, and so no specific clauses would have been included in the contract.

2 *The relationship between surveyor and solicitor*. It is an open and unre-solved question as to whether or not, and if so to what extent, a surveyor when instructed should investigate the planning position and the question of building warrants and their implementation. It has always seemed to me that, unless the surveyor effectively investigates these matters, he cannot properly advise on value or on suitability for loan. That being so, it is cer-tainly arguable that a solicitor, when making an offer following on the obtaining of a survey report, is entitled to rely on the content of that report, and, unless there are adverse comments therein, it is unnecessary for the solicitor to make special provision in the contract. So, in this case, where A solicitors obtained a survey report from the surveyors which made no ref-erence to flooding, I really do not think that they can be faulted for not making special provisions in the contract in that respect since there is nothing to draw their attention to it in the surveyor's report.

Provisions in the missives
This is the crucial question, and I am bound to say that I find it very difficult to state with confidence exactly where the line lies. Undoubtedly, it is essential in any such contract that the purchaser's solicitor should ensure:

(*a*) that planning permission has been or will be obtained and will be deliv-ered or exhibited to the purchaser at or before settlement. Whether or not it is permissible to accept the selling solicitor's letter of obligation in this respect is a different question; and
(*b*) that a building warrant has been obtained and that a completion cer-tificate will be delivered at or before settlement. In this case, I think there is no doubt that a letter of obligation is *not* an acceptable alterna-tive to delivery of a completion certificate.

I would make two points here, however, which to some extent affect the claims by A solicitors:

(i) it really does not matter to a purchaser whether he obtains the actual planning permission, building warrant and completion certificate or merely copies thereof, provided he is satisfied the copies are genuine. The essential to the purchaser is not the formal document itself but the fact that the necessary permission has been granted; and
(ii) if the contract fails adequately to provide for production or delivery of planning permission, building warrant or completion certificate, that may be bad conveyancing but it will not entitle the purchaser to any remedy against his solicitor by way of damages if, in the end of the day, planning permission, building warrant and completion certificate were in fact duly obtained and exhibited. It follows that, while it is obviously prudent for the purchaser's solicitor to include obligatory clauses in the missives requiring the seller to deliver these documents to the purchaser at or before settlement, the purchaser will not suffer any loss if the doc-uments are not actually so delivered, provided the permissions were in fact granted in the terms which he anticipated.

The agents, however, go further and maintain, in all three cases, that the

3

solicitor had a positive duty to obtain the planning permission and the building warrant (or copies) before even concluding missives. If they had done so, they would have seen the note on the planning permission as to the risk of flooding. This would have put them on their guard, and the clients would then have had an opportunity not to proceed with the contract. Undoubtedly this is so but it does, I think, fail to take account of market conditions and in particular of the pressure on the solicitor to conclude a bargain on behalf of the potential purchaser in situations where, in the great majority of cases, the obtaining of copies of the planning permission and building warrant before concluding missives is unnecessary and of no benefit to the client.

In each of the claims against A, B and C solicitors, the agents take the view that the solicitor in each case was aware that the subjects comprised a new house in a small housing development, and in that situation they maintain that a reasonably competent solicitor would have included in the offer a stipulation for exhibition, prior to conclusion of the missives, of 'clear and wholly unqualified planning consents and building warrants in respect of the development'. In my view, that is unrealistic for two reasons: (*a*) planning permission is virtually never granted unconditionally; and (*b*) in any event, the seller, particularly a builder or developer, will never accept conditions of this kind in an offer, and any such condition will simply be deleted.

In my experience, in the great majority of cases, a builder or developer will not agree to anything more than was agreed to in this case – that is, an undertaking that planning permission, building warrant and completion certificate have been or will be obtained and exhibited at or prior to settlement.

In the case of building warrant, my experience is that conditions in such terms are invariably accepted by the purchaser without further qualification because, under the Building Acts, all the requirements of the Building Regulations which apply to a particular building, and which are therefore notionally incorporated in the warrant, must be fully complied with before the completion certificate is issued; and accordingly, at least in a straightforward dwellinghouse development of this kind, there really could be nothing in the building warrant application which could cause any problems to a purchaser, provided he ensures that the completion certificate is issued before he pays over the price.

In the case of planning permission, however, there are invariably conditions under which the permission is granted. In certain situations, these may be of critical importance to the purchaser. So, in purchasing land for a commercial development, it is essential to qualify the contract in such a way that, if and when planning permission is granted, it is not granted subject to a condition which is unexpected or objectionable to the purchaser. In a standard clause suggested by the Styles Committee of the Law Society of Scotland for insertion in contracts dependent on planning permission, which is quoted by Halliday, *Conveyancing Law and Practice in Scotland*, para 15–106, the contract is made conditional upon the obtaining of planning permission and building warrant. Three alternative provisions are then suggested to ensure that the purchaser is protected against unpleasant surprises in the planning permission or the warrant. The first two are relevant here. It is suggested:

(*a*) that the permission and warrant should be to the client's entire satisfaction. Clearly that would hardly have been appropriate here because, at the date when the contracts were being negotiated in each case, planning permission and building warrant had already been obtained; or

(*b*) that the permission and warrant should be free of unduly onerous conditions. It would have been possible to qualify the contract in each case here with this second alternative provision; but, as it turns out, that would not in fact have protected the purchaser because there is no *condition* in the planning permission (and I assume no such condition in the building warrant) which requires the builder to take action to protect against flooding. There is merely the warning note on the planning permission which is not the same thing, and would *not* fall within the terms of this proviso.

The clause suggested by the Styles Committee is intended for a contract where planning permission and building warrant have not yet been applied for and so there is no question here of requiring exhibition of the planning permission before concluding the bargain.

The only other clause suggested by Halliday dealing with planning is again not entirely appropriate to the present situation and is dealt with in para 15–136, Note 2. That is very close to the situation which we have here, although admittedly not exactly the same. The clause suggested by Halliday simply requires the seller to *produce evidence before the date of entry* that all necessary planning and building consents and warrants have been obtained and complied with. There is nothing in that style of offer, or in the clause in Note 2, to cover the situation where a building has been erected within, say, the preceding ten years. Admittedly, in each case, the present building was in course of erection but, in each of the three cases, what the builder was selling in effect was a completed building according to certain specifications, covered by planning permission and completion certificate. According to Halliday's clause, it is sufficient protection to the purchaser simply to require evidence that permission and building warrant had been obtained and complied with.

Against that background, was it necessary for the purchasers' solicitors in this case to insist on seeing the planning permission *before* concluding the bargain?

In practically all cases it would have served no useful purpose to the purchaser to see the existing planning permission. Here the development was well advanced at the date when each of the contracts was entered into; the layout plan was already approved; the road pattern must have been visible on the ground; and the siting and types of building were dealt with in the sale particulars. None the less, there are occasionally, but only very occasionally, conditions in a planning permission which could, just conceivably, adversely affect the purchaser of a dwellinghouse in a development of this kind. But the risk is so remote that, in my view, a reasonably competent solicitor would not have felt it necessary to insist on seeing the planning permission before concluding the bargain.

5

He might have thought it appropriate to insert a condition in the offer on the lines of one of the alternative clauses suggested by the Styles Committee: that the planning permission was free of unduly onerous conditions, or alternatively Halliday's Note 2 clause in C Style para 15–136. I would have been content to conclude a bargain with that qualification; and I would have been content if the qualification had required production of the planning permission, containing the onerous condition, at latest before the date of entry. I would not have insisted, given that provision in the missives, on seeing the actual planning permission or a copy thereof before concluding the bargain.

The reason is that, for practical purposes, the important matter to the purchaser is that planning permission has been granted for the development as he sees it and that there are no adverse conditions attached. But even if a qualification to this effect had been included in each of the three bargains in this case and if it had been accepted by the builder (which it probably would not have been, on normal practice), this would not have protected the purchaser or allowed him to escape from the bargain, because the planning permission did not contain any onerous condition and therefore, notwithstanding the note thereon, the purchaser could not have resiled.

On the other hand, it is undoubtedly the case that, if the solicitor in each case had insisted on seeing the planning permission or a copy before proceeding to conclude, he would have seen the note on the planning permission and that would have put the purchaser on his guard.

On balance, I am inclined to the view that the reasonably competent solicitor could not have been expected to require more than the qualification in the missives that the planning permission was free from unduly onerous conditions; and, if the bargain had contained such a qualification, the reasonably competent solicitor would not have been negligent.

It necessarily follows that although in the present case none of the contracts contained any such qualification, it would not have assisted the purchaser in each case if the contract had contained such a qualification, because the planning permission did not contain an unduly onerous condition. It simply contained a note with a warning as to the possibility of flooding.

I am not clear, in law, as to the status of a mere note on the planning permission, but it certainly is not a *condition* thereof, as the planning permission in this case quite clearly demonstrates. The permission, as granted, contains six *conditions*, specifically so referred to in the permission, numbered 1–6, and the reasons are given for each of them. Below the reasons and after the date of the permission there are three notes. Clearly, notes 1 and 3 are *not* conditions under which the permission was granted and indeed would not be competent as conditions. I think it necessarily follows that note 2 is in the same category and is not in any sense a *condition* under which the planning permission was granted.

The agents, however, maintain that a copy of the planning consent should have been obtained before completion of the contract; they also maintain that, thereafter, the solicitor in each case should have investigated the risk of flooding referred to in note 2 on the planning permission. I agree that, if the planning permission had been obtained before conclusion of the bargain, this would have been incumbent on the solicitor in each case.

This then leads us to a further point. If, as the agents suggest, the solicitors in each case had started to investigate the flooding risks, the developer, I presume, would immediately have quoted regulation G3 of the Building Regulations, subject to which the building warrant in each case was granted. I have not seen a full copy of the building warrant but I assume, from the tone of the correspondence on the files, that one of the building warrants contained any specific provisions as to flood prevention. In addition, the builders would have produced the letter by the builder to the Environmental Health Department which, following on a telephone conversation with that department, confirmed that a small embankment would be formed at the bottom of plots 1 and 2 to protect them from any flooding danger from the burn. Copies of this letter and the relevant plan were sent to C solicitors with a letter. The inference to be gleaned from this correspondence is that, while there may have been some risk of flooding not apparently sufficiently serious to require any special provision in the planning permission or in the building warrant, it was being taken care of by the construction of the protective works.

In these circumstances, it seems to me by no means certain that a purchaser would automatically have been put off by the reference to the possible risk of flooding in the note to the planning permission; but of course that is mere speculation.

It follows from the foregoing that, when the agents maintain, as they do in the case of B solicitors in particular, that, after conclusion of the bargain but before settlement, no attempt was made to explore the flooding risk further, I do not think this is relevant. If the contract did not provide an escape clause which would allow the purchaser to resile from the bargain on this ground, it was fruitless to pursue the question of a flooding risk after the missives were concluded. Admittedly, as a matter of professional practice, the solicitors should probably have communicated more information to their respective clients, but that would not have allowed the clients to take any effective action since the missives did not so provide.

The building warrant and Building Regulations
Under the Building (Scotland) Acts 1959–70 the local authority are placed under a positive statutory duty to issue a building warrant if, but only if, they are satisfied that the operations authorised by the warrant will be carried out in accordance with the Building Regulations. The regulations which now apply are the Buildings Standards (Scotland) Regulations 1981, as amended by the Building Standards (Scotland) Amendment Regulations 1986, a copy of which you kindly provided. I refer in particular to reg G3, which states quite specifically that 'the site of every building ... shall, so far as is reasonably practicable, be ... treated to the extent necessary to prevent any harmful effects on any part of the building from ... flood water'. As you know, the regulations are voluminous and detailed. Not all of them, of course, apply to dwellinghouses but a substantial portion of the regulations do so apply. The amendments in 1986 are also substantial and detailed.

7

So far as reg G3 is concerned, there seem to be two possibilities: (*a*) that the local authority, having considered the problem, thought that no special treatment or protection was necessary against flood water. If the local authority building officers, who are the experts in this particular area, took this view, I cannot see how a solicitor could be negligent for failing to take a different view; or (*b*) that the local authority failed properly to consider the question of flood risk and made no appropriate requirement in the building warrant. I think this is one point that would have to be checked because there does not seem to be any copy of the building application among the papers. Further, I am not clear as to the originating cause or the import of the telephone conversation(s) and letter(s) between the Environmental Health Department and the developer regarding flooding and flood protection; and that is certainly something which would have to be explored. But in any event, if the local authority have failed to impose the necessary requirement on the developer to protect against flooding, they have failed in their statutory duty, and, in my view, a solicitor is entitled to rely on the local authority not to issue a building warrant where there is a failure to comply with the regulations. I think this must be the case.

There are an enormous number of regulations which apply to the construction of dwellinghouses from the foundations to the roof. I do not think that the solicitor could possibly be required to take upon himself the responsibility for checking and ensuring that all these detailed regulations were imported into the building warrant in each case and were complied with. Instead, I think the solicitor is entitled to assume that, insofar as the building regulations impose requirements on the builder or developer, the local authority will see to it that they are applied in the building warrant, and will not issue a completion certificate unless and until all the relevant regulations have been complied with by the builder. For example, part C of the 1981 Regulations deals with foundations and prescribes detailed specifications for individual cases. If, in a particular development, inadequate foundations were approved by the local authority in the building warrant and if, as a result, the building subsided after the issue of a completion certificate, I cannot believe that the court would hold a solicitor liable in negligence on that account. If that is so, I cannot see any difference in principle between reg C2 dealing with foundations and reg G3 dealing with flooding.

Summary
To sum up thus far, it seems to me that the three claims fail on the following grounds.

1 So far as the terms of contract are concerned, Halliday, who is the recognised expert, nowhere suggests that, prior to conclusion of the bargain, the purchaser's solicitor should see the planning permission; nor does he suggest that the purchaser's solicitor should require a clear and unqualified planning permission and building warrant to be exhibited. Instead, Halliday apparently would be content, justifiably in my view in a contract of this type, with a requirement in the contract that the planning permission should contain no unduly onerous conditions, that being the most appropriate of the various alternative suggestions by Halliday for this

particular case. But, as stated above, even if all the contracts had contained a condition in these terms as recommended by Halliday, the client would have had no redress against the builder and could not have resiled because the note as to flooding was not a condition of the planning permission. Therefore, any reasonably competent solicitor concluding a bargain with a provision in these terms could not be held liable in negligence.

2   Each of the three solicitors was entitled, in my view, to assume that the local authority would properly apply the building regulations, which apparently they failed to do. The solicitors cannot be held liable in negligence for the failure of the local authority. Alternatively, if the local authority considered the point but thought that no special flood protection precautions were required, that must, I think, exonerate the solicitor, who cannot be assumed to be expert in such matters.

3   In the case of A solicitors, I think the solicitor was entitled to rely on the surveyor's report and cannot be held responsible for the surveyor's failure to draw attention to the risk of flooding. In the case of B solicitors, the same may apply but, in that case, the survey report was instructed by the building society and I am not sure whether the solicitors were aware of the full terms of it when completing the bargain. In any event, there is the doubt about disclaimers. None the less, the surveyor's report obtained by the building society made no reference to the flooding risk. In the case of C solicitors, there appears to have been no survey, and, depending on the advice tendered by the solicitor to the purchaser prior to conclusion of the missives, there may be liability in this case on the grounds that he should have advised his client to obtain a survey report. Of course he may have done so and the client may have ignored that advice, in which case C solicitors are exonerated on this ground.

The following further points, which may or may not be significant or helpful, occurred to me on reading the files.

(*a*) In the agents' claim against B solicitors, they criticise B solicitors for having settled the transaction during April although, before that date, they had become aware of the potential flooding risk. That is of course the case; but it is also the case that, given the terms of the missives, there was no effective action which the purchaser could legally have taken either then to resile from the bargain or to claim compensation from the builder, given the terms of the missives in his case. Accordingly, while B solicitors may be criticised for failing to bring home to the purchaser the significance of the potential flooding risk, there was nothing they could have done about it to protect their client and that part of the letter is really irrelevant.

(*b*) In the case of the agents' claim against C solicitors, they make a similar criticism but the same applies as in the case of B solicitors. In fact, in C solicitors' case, they did go over the copy planning permission with its note and the survey report (which I have not seen); and there is a note on C solicitors' file, dated December and flagged, which seems to indicate that the planning permission was discussed with the client. There is a note to the effect that the surveyor had made no comment thereon, and therefore 'it should be okay. Happy to let matters rest there'. I think that is the import of the note. At the same time, C solicitors had in their possession, and no doubt discussed with the purchaser, the letter of August from the builder to the Environmental Health Department indicating proposals for flood protection.

(c) On the question of the duties of a surveyor, I was interested to read the final paragraph on page 2 of the surveyors' letter of June on C solicitors' file. According to the surveyors, it was well known locally that the site was prone to flooding and in their view a prudent *valuer* should have made a cautionary comment in the survey report, *even if he was not in possession of the local knowledge*. I would certainly have thought that, in a site of this nature where there clearly was a potential for flooding, the surveyor should have pursued some inquiries with the local authority and would then, on the face of it, have been given quite a bit of information, and he should have seen the note on the planning permission. A prudent surveyor would probably also have inquired as to what special requirements, if any, were imposed on the builder under the building warrant in relation to flood protection. If that duty lies on the surveyor, is the solicitor not entitled to rely on the surveyor's report without himself in parallel having to make equivalent inquiries?

(d) I presume that the buildings insurance position has been explored by each owner. My own buildings policy covers me against flooding and I think this is fairly standard. But of course that part of the policy may be voided in these cases on the *uberrimae fidei* rule, although the surveyors' reports would certainly make it difficult for the insurance company to establish *mala fides*.

(e) With reference to building regulation G3, I suggested that there might be a liability on the local authority for failing to require the builder to provide adequate flood protection. The letter of August from the architect to the Environmental Health Department would seem to indicate that the local authority were concerned with the question of flooding and, that being so, I would have thought that the building warrant should have imposed on the builder a duty to provide specified flood-protection works. I think that should be investigated. If the Environmental Health Department were sufficiently concerned to phone the architects and, in response, the architects provided proposals for flood protection, failure to provide for flood protection in the building warrant was negligence on their part which would sound in damages at the instance of each of the affected owners. Alternatively, if the local authority can show that, in their considered view at that time, no further protective works were necessary, that in itself might be sufficient to exonerate the solicitors concerned. You doubted whether such an action would be competent and I think you may well be right; but I enclose as a matter of interest an excerpt from the 1989 *Current Law Year Book* where, in not dissimilar circumstances, a local authority were sued for damages for negligence under the Buildings Acts, although exonerated on technical grounds which would not I think apply here. So, if the solicitors are liable, they may in turn have a claim against the local authority. That claim would be extinguished by the short prescription if not pursued in time.

To focus the issue more concisely, I would answer the questions posed thus:

In relation to planning clauses in missives in contracts of this kind I think the normal practice, almost universally, would go no further than to require production of planning permission at latest by date of entry. The fact that this was a small building development favours that view because, in such cases, it is exceedingly unlikely that the planning permission will throw up anything to the disadvantage of the purchaser who is contracting at a time when the development is well advanced.

It would have been possible to attempt to incorporate a right to resile but in my experience it would have been unsuccessful and the builders' solicitors would not have accepted any such clause in the missives. This is standard practice in ordinary transactions, but particularly so when dealing with builders.

In any event, the recommended formula quoted above would not have served to protect, and there would seem to me nothing special in this case which would have required an ordinary competent solicitor to devise clauses for unknown risks because, at the time when the missives were being framed, the flooding risk had not been drawn to anyone's attention.

I am bound to say that, in my view, a prudent solicitor would like to see the planning permission before concluding missives if he could persuade the builders to produce it, in case it might contain some disadvantageous *conditions*, but, in developments of this kind, that is exceptionally unlikely.

Further reading
Smith v *Bush* [1990] 1 AC 831.

Manual, para 1.3.

2   The role of solicitors in heritable property transactions
Negligence of solicitors – examination of title

Date: August 1991

Memorial
A garage was disponed to the memorialists. The description in the disposition referred to a plan in the progress of titles. The missives stated: 'The subjects of sale are those contained in our clients' titles which are in your possession.' It subsequently transpired that a strip of ground which the memorialists had understood to be included in the sale, and had indeed been occupied by them under a lease prior to purchase, was not included in the disposition.

The question was whether the agents acting for the memorialists had been negligent in the purchase of the garage.

Opinion

On the facts it is difficult to see how the solicitors who acted for the purchasers of the garage could escape liability for failing to notice that the subjects in the title, which are perfectly clearly designated on the plan attached to the disposition, differed, to a material extent, from the subjects as defined on the plan attached to the lease in favour of the purchasers.

In so stating, I am assuming that the purchasers instructed their solicitors to purchase the *existing* business and the *existing* premises, all as occupied by them, under whatever title, and that the solicitors clearly understood that this was the purchasers' intention. Given the terms of the lease and the fact that the purchasers were in occupation of the larger subjects, this would seem self-evident, but it is something which will have to be established in support of a claim.

On that assumption, there would seem to be no excuse for the failure on the part of the purchasers' solicitors to notice the discrepancy. Admittedly, in their offer, no attempt is made to identify the subjects of purchase except in the most general terms but, in the qualified acceptance, the sellers' agents state specifically that, for the avoidance of doubt, the subjects of sale are those contained in the sellers' titles, which were then in possession of the purchasers' agents. According to the memorial, the additional area of ground not included in the sellers' title was held by them on a lease which the purchasers' agents had never seen and so the purchasers' agents could not have been misled into thinking that the reference in the qualified acceptance to 'our clients' titles' was intended to include both the subjects as defined in the 19XX feu disposition and the subjects as defined in the lease of the additional strip. Again, however, that is a fact which ought to be established because, if the lease which is referred to in the memorial was in the possession of the purchasers' agents at the date of the qualified acceptance, they might have an argument that they were justified in thinking that the reference in the qualified acceptance to the sellers' titles included a reference to the subjects both in the feu disposition and in the supplementary lease.

The term 'titles' is of flexible meaning and could be taken to include, in certain circumstances, subjects occupied on lease. But even if that were so, the purchasers' solicitors clearly failed in their duty to acquire *title* to the whole subjects of purchase in that the disposition in favour of the purchasers simply conveys the subjects as in the 19XX feu disposition and nothing more. Again, therefore, it seems to me a fairly safe assumption that the purchasers' agents were totally unaware of the additional twenty-foot strip held on lease by the sellers and were simply misled into thinking that the subjects in the 19YY lease, which was the basis of the purchasers' occupancy at the date of the contract of sale and purchase, coincided with the subjects in the feu disposition which, on close examination, they clearly do not. On that basis, the purchasers' solicitors simply took a disposition of those subjects and nothing more without, apparently, making any further inquiry as to the missing twenty-foot strip.

I think it may be appropriate in this context to refer to para 33.4(1) of [the 6th edition of] my *Conveyancing Manual*. That chapter deals with examination of title and states: '*Description*. Does this correspond exactly with the contract; and does it correspond exactly with what the purchaser imagines he has purchased? In all but the simplest case, this requires a physical check on the ground with the client, or possibly by a surveyor.'

It would seem to me fair to say that any professional practitioner should be expected to be aware of his duty to the client in this particular aspect of the sale and purchase of heritable property. Apparently, however, no effort was made on the part of the purchasers' solicitors to confirm with the purchasers that the subjects as described in the 19XX disposition were the *whole* subjects which the purchasers thought they were acquiring. That seems to me an *elementary* and basic component in the examination of any title, as stated in the passage quoted from the *Manual*. The subjects as described in the 19XX feu disposition are crystal clear and even the most cursory check as between the title plan and the subjects in occupation of the purchasers on the ground would have disclosed the error, whether that examination was made by the solicitors or a surveyor or the purchasers themselves. In addition, there is a plan attached to the lease, which was the basis of the purchasers' occupancy, and the discrepancy clearly shows when the lease plan is compared with the feu disposition plan.

I am therefore driven inescapably to the conclusion that the purchasers' solicitors in this case were negligent.

Whether or not the purchasers have any alternative remedy seems to me very doubtful. I did wonder whether the sellers' agents, in their qualified acceptance which states that, for the avoidance of doubt, the subjects of sale are those contained in the title, might be said to have induced the purchasers' solicitors into an error in thinking that the subjects in the title were in fact the *whole* subjects in occupation under the 19YY lease. If so, and since the missives are still in operation under a non-supersession clause, there might have been some comeback against the sellers themselves. On reflection, however, I have come to the view that, whatever the motives of the sellers' solicitors may have been in inserting that qualification into the qualified acceptance, it is so clear and unambiguous in its terms that it could not in any sense be construed as misleading or as a misrepresentation of intention. Accordingly, the sellers' intention was perfectly clear. The subjects of sale were as described in the 19XX title and nothing more. That fact is stated in plain and unambiguous terms in the missives. There cannot therefore be any room for mutual error or misrepresentation on the part of the sellers. The qualification should have put the purchasers' agents on their guard and it was up to them to satisfy themselves that the subjects in that title, as so described, were the subjects which their clients thought they were acquiring.

In the result, the sole responsibility for the mistake lies with the purchasers' solicitors and I can see no alternative remedy available to the purchasers except an action of damages against them for negligence.

Manual, para 1.3.

AUTHENTICATION

3   *Execution by various types of person*
Execution of deed by company – error in name – whether title
unmarketable – procedure to cure defect

Date: July 1994

Memorial
A 1982 disposition conveyed a property to M Company (X) Limited,
whereas the correct name of the company was M Co (X) Limited. The
question was whether the use of the word 'Company' instead of 'Co' invalidated the title.

Opinion
Although I would hesitate to say categorically that the disposition is invalid,
I cannot state with any degree of assurance that it is undoubtedly valid and
unchallengeable, for it contains a patent and significant error in that the
name of the company does not coincide with its registered name.

This is a question which commonly arises and which I always answer by
referring to Halliday, para 4–04. Halliday's view is that minor errors in the
names of individuals do not necessarily invalidate, provided that there is
sufficient identification. But the separate legal persona created by the
incorporation of a company exists *only* in the company whose name is
registered. So a deed intended to be granted by or in favour of that
company but reproducing the company name inaccurately is granted by or
to a body which has no legal entity. In the result, according to Halliday, a
supplementary corroborative deed is necessary in all cases. See also his
Opinions at p 205.

There almost certainly are cases where an error is of such a minor nature
(for example, by inserting a full stop instead of a comma) that the court
would not treat the deed as invalid, under the *de minimis* rule. The error in
this case, however, seems to me almost certainly too significant for the
court to dismiss it on that footing. The Companies Act 1981, later repro-
duced in the Companies Act 1985, s 26 (3), may *seem* to indicate that the
abbreviation of the word 'Company' to the expression 'Co' can be disregarded, but that provision must be read in context. It applies only for the
purpose of determining whether one name is the same as the other in
relation to the registration of a company name; and it only applies to this
particular type of abbreviation where the word company is the last word of
the name. It has no relation to validity.

In the present case, 'Company' is written out in full instead of the
abbreviation 'Co' which is the registered name; and the word 'Company'

is *not* the last word of the name. So, even for the special purposes of the 1985 Act, s 26 (3), and the provisions in the earlier Act, the variation here between the name used and the registered name would not fall to be disregarded under that subsection. In the 1985 Act, in addition, there is a provision in s 27 which permits certain minor deviations from the registered name, in more general terms than s 26, but it does *not* authorise the interchangeability of Company and Co. In any event s 27 applies only in cases where, by a provision of the *Act*, the company is required or is entitled to include certain words in its name, which is not the position here.

Professor Halliday was, of course, aware of these provisions in the passage referred to but, significantly, makes no reference to them in that context. I think it is fair to say that in his writings generally, which are, of course, very highly thought of and extensive, his approach was always pragmatic and he was generally disinclined to engage in or put forward purely theoretical and academic arguments, especially in his *Conveyancing Law and Practice in Scotland*.

In all the circumstances, and given in particular the firm and unqualified statements as to the company name and the need for absolute accuracy in reproducing the same made by Professor Halliday in the passage quoted above, it would certainly be unsafe, in my view, to assume that the disposition in question is valid.

The result is that the only safe approach is to treat the deed as invalid. This in turn means that the disponers conveyed the property to a non-existent entity and, as a result, the apparent subsequent infeftment in name of 'M Company (X) Limited' achieves nothing and a company under that name is not infeft because it does not exist. Accordingly, the property still remains vested in the disponers, if the company is still in being, failing which the property will have passed to the Crown as *bona vacantia*.

On the face of it, since more than ten years have passed since the recording of the 1982 disposition, it might be said that the error in the company name had been cured by the running of the positive prescription. But it seems to me that there is an insuperable difficulty in this argument when it now comes to taking a title *from* the M Co (X) Limited, except on the footing that they are granting that conveyance on an *a non domino* basis, in which case it would have to be supported by indemnity for the next ten years. This would certainly suggest that some investigation would have to be made into the history of the disponers. In particular, if that company has gone into a creditor's liquidation or been wound up by the court, there is a potential risk that the liquidator might still claim the property for the benefit of its creditors. I think this last point underlines the risk.

Manual, para 2.21.

CAPACITY

4 Trustees
Death of partners – transfer of title – procedure to be followed

Date: August 1990

Memorial

A farm was run by a partnership. The partners were Mr A, Mrs A, Mr B, Mrs C and Mr D. Two partners died and two partners resigned. There were two securities over the partnership property, both granted by the partners of the original partnership. The question arose as to how the title to the partnership property should be transferred into the name of one remaining partner.

1 Would a notice of title using resignation documents of the other partners suffice?

2 Would the security holders have to discharge the existing securities in return for fresh securities, or would a deed of variation suffice?

3 The farm was not to be included as a partnership asset in the newly constituted firm. Would it be appropriate to show it in the books, but with a specific note that it was not a partnership asset? Would that be effective as against any party claiming legal rights in the estate?

Opinion

1 The subjects in this case were originally conveyed to five parties, as then partners of the firm. This reflects the long-standing feudal rule that a partnership as such – although in Scotland having a separate persona – cannot sustain the feudal relationship; and so any heritable property belonging to the firm must be conveyed to, and the title taken in name of, one or more persons as trustees for the firm, the firm being the beneficial owner thereof. It is common practice in such cases to convey heritable property purchased by a firm to the partners of the firm at the time of the conveyance; but, to satisfy the feudal rule, the title is taken in their name, *not* as beneficial owners in their capacity as partners or otherwise, but in their joint names as trustees for the firm. It is perfectly competent, however, and quite common practice, for the title to a heritable property belonging to a firm to be taken in name of a trustee who is not a partner. The existence of the partnership, and the acquisition by the partnership as beneficial owner of a heritable property, is something quite separate and distinct from the trusteeship created in terms of the relevant disposition. It follows that, where heritable property belonging to a firm has been conveyed to certain partners of the firm as trustees therefor, the fact that one of these parties

16

resigns as a partner of the firm has no effect whatever on the trusteeship created by the title. Accordingly, although that party no longer remains a *partner*, he none the less remains a *trustee* unless and until the whole body of trustees dispose of the property to other disponees, or alternatively unless and until that particular party executes a minute of resignation as trustee expressly demitting the office of trusteeship conferred on him by the terms of the title.

In exactly the same way, where a new partner is taken into a firm, he does not automatically become a trustee on any of the heritable properties belonging to that firm and has no title to any such property simply by virtue of becoming a partner. If the intention is for that new partner to become a trustee, formal *trust* documentation is required to effect an alteration in the feudal title held by trustees for the firm.

It follows that, in this case, following on the deaths of Mr and Mrs A, the heritable property remains vested in the three surviving trustees to whom it was originally conveyed along with the two deceased partners. Even though in the meantime Mrs C and Mr B have resigned as *partners* of the firm, they remain trustees in terms of the title. The two agreements entered into between Mrs C and Mr B respectively and the firm, by virtue of which each of these two parties has resigned as a partner, are not sufficient to effect a resignation of the trusteeship conferred by the original disposition in their favour and are therefore not sufficient formally to divest Mrs C or Mr B of their trust title or to transfer the property directly to Mr D who, as 'sole partner', is now the sole beneficial owner of the subjects in question.

It follows from this summary of the general principles in this case that it is not competent simply to record a notice of title in name of Mr D as sole beneficial owner, because the dissolution agreements by Mrs C and Mr B do not, in either case, operate as effective links in title.

There are two alternative methods which can be adopted to divest Mrs C and Mr B as trustees:

(*a*) a formal minute of resignation by each of them, or a single minute by both of them, in terms of which they formally resign the office of trusteeship in terms of the Trusts (Scotland) Act 1921; or

(*b*) a formal disposition by all three parties jointly as surviving trustees, narrating the death of Mr and Mrs A and narrating the agreements by virtue of which Mrs C and Mr B ceased to be partners of the firm, as a result of which Mr D has become the sole proprietor in whose favour the conveyance would be granted.

On the recording of that disposition in the Register of Sasines, all three parties would be divested as trustees and Mr D would become the sole beneficial owner in his own right and not merely as a trustee.

I should perhaps add that, although Mrs C is apparently refusing to co-operate because of some dispute as to her entitlement to interest from the firm, her title to the property is as trustee and not for any beneficial interest, since the beneficial interest rests with the firm. She could therefore be compelled, by court action if necessary, either to grant a formal minute of resignation or to grant the joint conveyance, in one or other of the methods suggested. As a trustee expressly so designated in the title, she is bound to implement the directions of the beneficiary (here Mr D), whether or not she may have a personal claim against the partnership or individual partners thereof. But that individual claim against the partnership does not entitle her to any right of retention or lien on the heritable property pending settlement of that claim.

2   I suggested in my earlier letter that there might be a simpler method of rearranging the securities than the method proposed in the original letter of instructions. Having considered the whole circumstances and in particular the terms of the individual securities, I have come to the view, however, that it would probably be safer and more satisfactory to deal with the securities in the manner originally proposed, that is, by taking a discharge in favour of the firm and the individual partners thereof of the existing securities and by taking a fresh standard security from Mr D as individual beneficial owner in favour of the bank and B and C with appropriate ranking clauses as required.

3   I am still of the view, however, that, in the circumstances, the correct procedure is for the title to remain in the sole name of Mr D as beneficial owner; and, if it is not to become a partnership asset, it should *not* appear in the balance sheet. The fact that the firm is borrowing' does not make it necessary for the security itself to be granted by the firm. Accordingly, once Mr D has become infeft in his own name in one or other of the methods suggested above, I would prefer to see the firm and Mr D jointly grant standard securities in favour of the two creditors in terms of which the *firm* as such would acknowledge receipt of the loans in question and undertake all the *personal* obligations as a firm (possibly guaranteed by individual partners as required), but that the security therefor would be granted explicitly by Mr D as an individual and as the beneficial owner of the subjects in question. There is no reason whatever why the borrowing by a firm should not be secured upon the property belonging to an individual, whether he is a partner of the firm or not, and this is commonplace in practice. This then removes any problems in relation to the disposal of the property on death. If any other method is adopted, and in particular if the property appears in the balance sheet of the firm, there is a strong possibility that the property would be treated as a firm asset, in which case, as already pointed out, whatever the nature of Mr D's claim against the partnership might be *vis-à-vis* the property, the whole of the value of that claim is necessarily moveable and as such subject to claims to legal rights; and, for practical purposes, he would deny himself the ability to dispose of the property in *specie* as freely as he pleases. I cannot see any advantage in including the property in the balance sheet of the partnership, with a note, as suggested in your letter.

There are, however, taxation implications in relation to income tax and inheritance tax and possibly capital gains tax which I have not taken into account in giving this advice and on which I think the parties should first take separate advice before proceeding further. In particular, if the proposal is that the property remains in the exclusive ownership of Mr D, but is to be property owned by the partnership, that may involve a lease by him to the firm. This in turn introduces complications because such leases may not be valid; and the granting of leases also carries with it implications as to rent with consequential income tax implications. Likewise the granting of a lease may affect the inheritance tax allowances available. The tax implications *must* be examined carefully before the arrangements are concluded.

Manual, para. 3.5.

5   Sale of heritage

Feudal title – beneficial interest – Succession (Scotland) Act 1964, s 17 – Trusts (Scotland) Act 1961 – protection for purchaser – deduction of title

Date: November 1989

Memorial

A was in the course of concluding missives for the sale of a house. A was the widow of J.A. J.A. had been a beneficiary in B's Trust. The following questions arose:

1   Did A's title derive from her position as executrix of J.A.'s estate. Did s 17 of the Succession (Scotland) Act 1964 apply?

2   Was the disposition granted in favour of A onerous inasmuch as it was in implement of the trustees' obligations under the trust deed? If so, would protection be available under the Trusts (Scotland) Act 1961?

3   Were the proposed purchasers entitled to be informed of details of the intromissions of B's trustees to ascertain whether the disposition in favour of A had been granted 'in breach of trust'?

4   Did the repetition of the words 'as aforesaid' and/or the failure to repeat the recording date in a deduction of title clause render the deed defective?

5   Was A's title marketable?

Opinion

1   No. It is important to distinguish in this context between feudal title and beneficial interest. It may well be, and no doubt is, the case that A derived her beneficial interest in the property in question under the will of her husband and, to that extent, through the confirmation in her favour as his executor. But, when it comes to the question of feudal title, it has to be accepted that the property was last vested in the trustees of the late B under the 1969 disposition. The next writ in the progress of feudal titles is the 1989 disposition in favour of A, and that title derives directly from the trustees of the late B who conveyed the property, vested in them as trustees, to A on a narrative which clearly excludes *sale* as the cause or consideration for the granting of the disposition. Instead, the disposition is granted by these trustees, feudally vested in the property, in favour of A as an individual on a narrative which refers *inter alia* to the trust disposition and settlement and codicils by the late B, to the will of the late J.A., and to a deed of variation among A and others, which, I presume, varies the terms of the will of the late J.A., not the terms of the trust disposition

19

and settlement, but this is not made clear in the narrative of the 1989 disposition.

The Succession (Scotland) Act 1964, and in particular the protection provided by s 17 of that Act, applies only in cases where:

(*a*) heritable property has vested in an executor. But there is no evidence here that heritable property vested in A as executor and indeed, as the solicitors correctly point out, the confirmation in the estate of the late J.A. shows that he owned no heritable estate. So, on the face of it, the confirmation is *not* a title to the subjects in question; and

(*b*) it applies only for the benefit of a *bona fide* purchaser for value from that executor.

But the first of these conditions is certainly not satisfied here and the second does not really apply because there is no purchase from an executor. Accordingly, since the requirements of s 17 are not satisfied in this case, the purchaser would have no resulting protection.

2   The 1989 disposition by the trustees of B in favour of A may or may not be an onerous disposition in the sense referred to in the letter of instructions. For my part, however, I do not think that is relevant. The Trusts (Scotland) Act 1961, s 2, operates in its terms to protect against challenge a title granted by trustees in a transaction purportedly entered into in relation to the trust estate by virtue of those powers impliedly conferred on trustees in the Trusts (Scotland) Act 1921, s 4. If the transaction in question comes within any of the powers in that section, the title of the disponee from those trustees, whether in good faith or not, is put beyond challenge; but the transaction itself *must* be a transaction within one or other of the 1921 Act, s 4, categories. The powers in the 1921 Act, s 4, include power to sell the trust estate or any part thereof; and power to compromise claims connected with the trust estate which might conceivably be applicable here. But, on the face of it and without further competent corroborative evidence, I do not think a purchaser from A is obliged to accept the 1989 disposition as being immune from challenge under the protection afforded by the 1961 Act, s 2, since it is not evident on the face of the deed or from other information so far provided that the transaction (the 1989 conveyance by the trustees to A) was either a *sale* under the 1921 Act, s 4(1)(a) or a *compromise* under s 4(1)(i). There is no doubt whatever that the purchaser is entitled to be satisfied on this point and can therefore properly require production of appropriate evidence which, as I see it, is exactly what the solicitors are trying to do by the inquiries which they have raised.

3   For the reasons set out in answer to question 2, the short answer to this question is in the affirmative. Unless the seller's agents can demonstrate unequivocally that the 1989 disposition is a transaction within the meaning of the 1921 Act, s 4(1), ie, sale or compromise, they have to satisfy the purchaser that the disposition was properly granted in implement of the purposes of the trust.

The risk to the purchaser is that, in 1989, the trustees of the late B, as infeft proprietors of the subjects in question, either conveyed them to the wrong beneficiary or wrongly conveyed them to one of the beneficiaries to the disadvantage of another beneficiary or beneficiaries, and to that extent acted in breach of trust. Accordingly, I think the onus now lies on the seller's agents to satisfy the purchaser C, that there was no breach of trust and that the 1989 disposition was properly granted by the trustees of the late B in favour of A. No doubt it was so granted, in part satisfaction of her deceased husband's prospective share in the residue of the estate of the late B. But I think the purchaser's agents are undoubtedly entitled to be satisfied on that point because, at least on the information so far produced, the purchaser will not enjoy the protection afforded by the 1964 Act, s 17, or the 1961 Act, s 2, and so must satisfy himself that every transaction within the prescriptive progress (and the 1989 disposition is clearly within the progress) was intrinsically and *extrinsically* valid.

4   Yes, but with qualifications.

First, the standard feudal rule is that an uninfeft proprietor having an unrecorded title to, but not infeft in, heritable property cannot grant any deed relating thereto on which a disponee from him can take a valid infeftment by the direct recording of a conveyance in favour of that disponee. Under the Conveyancing (Scotland) Act 1924, s 3, the deduction of title facility was introduced to allow a disposition to be granted by an uninfeft proprietor, provided it complied with the requirements of that section. The section in turn requires that, if a disposition by an uninfeft proprietor is to operate of itself as a mandate for infeftment, the granter of that disposition must deduce title. The requirements for a clause of deduction of title are laid down in ss 2, 3 and 5 of the Act and in Sched A thereto. It is generally accepted that strict adherence to the statutory requirements is essential if the disposition is to have the benefit of the dispensation provided by the 1924 Act, s 3. Failure to observe the statutory requirements therefore disqualifies the deed as a mandate for infeftment but it does not, of course, render the deed totally invalid. It simply prevents the deed from operating as a mandate for infeftment by *de plano* recording.

The 1989 disposition is undoubtedly defective as a conveyance by an uninfeft proprietor under s 3 in that:

(*a*) the date of the last infeftment, which is a statutory requirement, is not stated in the clause of deduction of title, nor indeed does that date appear anywhere else in the disposition; and

(*b*) there is no reference in the clause of deduction of title to the Register of Sasines in which the last recorded deed was recorded.

These omissions are fatal to the validity of a clause of deduction of title which must adhere strictly to the statutory requirements and so, to that extent, the 1989 disposition is invalid but only as a mandate for infeftment. It remains valid as a general disposition (see Halliday, para 21–40).

The second qualification is that, notwithstanding these defects in the clause of deduction of title, arguably no clause of deduction of title was required at all. That is because the 1969 disposition was granted in favour of a number of persons as trustees, one of whom was M.G., the first of the joint disponers in the 1989 disposition. Accordingly, it is not strictly the case that the 1989 disposition was granted by uninfeft proprietors. One of the three grantors was infeft as trustee under the 1969 deed. That being the position, the narrative of the 1989 disposition should have taken a somewhat different form and, had it done so, no clause of deduction of title would have been necessary. Whether the disposition is none the less valid in the form in which it takes is an open question and, for my part, I am inclined to the view that it probably is valid. But, as the matter is easily cured, I do not think the point is worth pursuing.

As stated above, a disposition by an uninfeft proprietor (if that is what the 1989 disposition is, which is doubtful) is none the less valid as a general disposition although it may not operate as a mandate for infeftment by *de plano* recording. It is, in other words, a perfectly valid mid-couple or link in title and can be so used in any subsequent disposition. In other words, to cure the defect (if there is a defect) in the 1989 infeftment arising out of the defective deduction of title clause, all that is now required is for the disposition by A in favour of the purchaser to contain a clause of deduction of title in an alternative form, namely:

> 'which subjects are now vested in me, my title thereto being recorded in the said Division of the General Register of Sasines on ... September, 19.. or otherwise were last vested in (here name and design the parties last infeft as per the 1969 Disposition) whose title thereto was recorded in the said Division of the General Register of Sasines on .... and from whom we acquired right, following on the deaths of the said .... on .... and .... on .... as aforesaid, by Deed of Assumption and Conveyance the said Mrs .... and me, the said .... as Trustees foresaid in favour of us, the said .... and .... as Trustees foresaid dated and registered as aforesaid.'

This is the solution which Halliday suggests in such circumstances in para 21–40.

5   No. In my opinion, the inquiries put on foot by the solicitors are justified – though they perhaps go rather too far – and the title is not yet marketable until further evidence has been produced to satisfy them on the questions which they have raised. As to the questions I have the following comments.

(*a*) Solicitors and are entitled to see the death certificates of deceased trustees and the deed of assumption and conveyance.

(*b*) Under the trust disposition and settlement of the late B there is power to purchase heritage. In any event, that power apart, it is not clear from the 1969 disposition whether the trustees purchased heritage or whether it was made over to them gratuitously by J.A. It does not seem to me to matter which of the two assumptions (or any other assumption) is correct. There is no doubt whatever that, in 1969, by an *ex facie* valid and recorded disposition, the trustees acquired title to the property and all antecedent inquiry is now cut off by the positive prescription. Further, the property was conveyed to them as trustees under the trust disposition and settlement of the late B and the codicils thereto and, therefore, on the face of the 1969 disposition which is, in its terms, a probative deed fell to be held by these trustees, in the absence of any contradiction in the 1969 disposition, the inevitable presumption is that the disponees hold the property as an accretion to the trust estate and, therefore, in terms of, and for the purposes set out in, the trust disposition and settlement. It seems to me quite unnecessary for the solicitors to speculate as to the reasons why, or circumstances under which, the property may have been acquired by the trustees, given their powers and the terms of the 1969 deed; and I would resist any further inquiry.

(*c*) There is no necessity to register the will of the late J.A., because he owned no heritable estate. The will is registered in the Sheriff Court Books and that is invariably sufficient for all purposes, except where the will itself is to be used as a link in a heritable title, and that is not the case here.

(*d*) The solicitors are entitled to see the will of the late J.A. and the deed of variation, assuming it refers to J.A.'s will and not B's trust disposition and settlement, and that information should be provided to them.

Manual, para 3.8.

6   Curators and judicial factors
Pro indiviso shares of property – death – incapacity – *curator bonis* – confirmation – links in title – Trusts (Scotland) Act 1921, s 23 – procedure to cure defects.

Date: August 1990

Memorial
A property vested in two sisters (Miss AB and Miss CB) as to one-half *pro indiviso* share each. There was no survivorship destination. Miss CB died. Executors (Miss AB and Mr D) confirmed to her one-half *pro indiviso* share. Miss AB was also a beneficiary under the will. Miss AB became incapax before a disposition had been granted. Mr D was appointed *curator bonis*. The question was how a disposition of the property could be granted to the intending purchaser.

Opinion
I will deal with the problem in two parts, taking each one-half *pro indiviso* share separately.

1   *Miss AB's share*
Miss AB is infeft in a one-half *pro indiviso* share but, as you correctly state, there is no survivorship destination in the title and the other half of the property therefore passes to her, not by destination but under the late Miss CB's will and confirmation.

So far as Miss AB's one-half share is concerned, she is already infeft in that one-half by the recording of the original disposition in favour of herself and her sister and no further action in relation to her one half is necessary or competent. A *curator bonis* appointed to administer the estate of an incapax, as in this case, does not make up title to the estate of his ward, and the decree appointing the curator does not operate as a title. Instead, the *curator bonis* in effect acts as a judicial attorney subject to the approval of the Accountant of Court and, in that capacity, requires no title (see Halliday, para 4–15 and Burns (4th edn), p 309, last para). That being so, although I am not clear as to why her one-half *pro indiviso* share of the house was omitted from the original petition on which decree was granted, appointing Mr D as curator, the fact that he has since obtained from the court power of sale of the whole property, not merely a one-half *pro indiviso* share, is perfectly sufficient to provide a valid title to a purchaser from him *quoad* this one-half share.

2 *Miss CB, deceased*

Under her will, the late Miss CB appointed her sister and Mr D as executors. They have confirmed to her estate which includes, in terms of the confirmation, her one-half *pro indiviso* share of the whole property. Thus that one-half *pro indiviso* share has irrevocably vested in the two executors. In terms of the will, the beneficial interest in the property passed to Miss AB, but there is no docquet on the copy certificate of confirmation transferring the interest to Miss AB. I assume that there is no docquet on the confirmation itself and no separate conveyance thereof. On these assumptions, the one-half *pro indiviso* share of the property which belonged to the late Miss CB is still vested in her executors.

The first suggestion in your letter is that the curator acting on behalf of his ward, Miss AB, might resign office on her behalf as executor. I do not think this is competent. The function of a *curator bonis* is to manage and preserve the estate of the ward in the expectation that she will recover her capacities. His powers go no further than that except insofar as they are specially conferred by the court. So, according to J. C. Irons *The Law and Practice in Scotland relative to Judicial Factors* (1908), p 310, the curator has no power over the person of the incapax, nor is the status of the incapax affected. In particular, I can find no authority in Irons or in the reported cases to support the proposition that a *curator bonis* can affect the position of his ward in the office of executor or trustee to which the ward has been appointed by some other person. In other words, I do not think that it is competent for a *curator bonis* to resign on behalf of Miss AB as executor.

The second suggestion in your letter is based on a passage from *Currie on Confirmation* (7th edn), p 92, where the author says that if the incapax is also the universal legatory, the *curator bonis* can petition to be appointed as executor dative *qua curator bonis*. That may be possible where no confirmation has yet been issued and where the incapax is the sole executor as well as the universal legatory. But that is not the position here in two respects:

(*a*) confirmation has already been issued in favour of the incapax and Mr D; and
(*b*) in any event, although the incapax is the sole residuary legatee, she is not the sole executor.

In these circumstances the procedure suggested by Currie is not, in my view, competent. On this point there is direct authority in *Martin* v *Ferguson's Trustees* (1892) 19 R 474: 'The *curator bonis* stands in this position – he claims the appointment as Executor Dative and he does so upon the ground that his ward is appointed Executor Nominate ... but in order to make out his case he has to found upon the Act of Sederunt of 1730.' But the Act of Sederunt of 1730, while giving right to officers of court to be confirmed to an estate in which the ward has a beneficial interest, is careful to say: 'unless some other person having a title offers to confirm ...'. In this case, not only has someone having a title offered to confirm, two persons have been confirmed as executors nominate. I do not see how it could conceivably now be competent for the curator to apply to the court for a second appointment as executor dative. This suggestion, in my view, is likewise not viable. I therefore agree with the Commissary Office on this point.

The third suggestion is that the curator might sign on behalf of the ward as executor. Looking to the limited nature of the curator's appointment, and even though in this case the ward has a beneficial interest in the estate, I do not think that this is a competent procedure, and I agree that the curator could not sign in the capacity of executor in place of his ward.

Finally, it is suggested that a notice of title be recorded. I entirely agree that this does not advance matters. If it is competent to record a notice of title, it is equally competent to grant a disposition deducing title. But, in my view, neither of these is competent because, as you state, the links proposed by Messrs X in their suggested draft notice of title are not the appropriate links regarding the bequest in the will of the late Miss HA. What Messrs X are suggesting is that, instead of relying on the confirmation, title can be deduced, *quoad* the late Miss CB's share, directly through the will. This is, I assume, on the basis that Miss AB is the sole residuary beneficiary and, as such, is entitled to the beneficial interest in the *property*. I accept that it might have been possible, if the purchasers had been prepared to accept a title in this form, to deduce title through the will on the footing that the whole residue of the estate, which includes Miss CB's one-half *pro indiviso* share, is bequeathed to Miss AB. In my view, however, it is now too late to adopt this approach because the executors have already confirmed to Miss CB's estate which expressly includes the deceased's one-half *pro indiviso* share of the subjects; and, as a result, it has already vested in her executors. *Quoad* title, therefore, Miss AB, as direct residuary legatee under the will, is no longer in a position to use the will as a link in title because of the vesting in the executors. In any event, it is doubtful whether a beneficiary can competently deduce title through the will, after the 1964 Act (see (1965) 10 JLSS 153 and Gretton in (1987) 32 JLSS 111).

Having said all that, it has to be conceded that we are faced here with a pure technicality in relation to title. So far as beneficial interest is concerned, there is no conceivable difficulty because the *curator bonis* has been validly appointed; he has been given power to sell the whole property; and his ward is beneficially entitled to the whole property, *quoad* one-half in her own right and *quoad* the remaining one-half under her sister's will. The only possible impediment to the obtaining of a valid title to the whole might be if Miss CB's estate was insolvent which, clearly, is not the case.

The solution to the technical defect in this title is, in my view, a petition to the court under the Trusts (Scotland) Act 1921, s 23. In terms of that section, where a trustee becomes incapable of acting, she may, on application by a co-trustee or other interested party, be removed from office. Such application under a *mortis causa* trust, which is what we have here, may be made to the Court of Session or, much more helpfully, to the sheriff court from which the original confirmation of the trustees as executors was issued. Such an application is a mere but necessary formality; but it will, of course, take some time to obtain decree.

Since the defect in title is of a purely technical nature, which must be curable by the procedure suggested above, it seems to me that the purchaser could safely settle the transaction on 20th December as proposed if the sellers are prepared to deliver the keys against consignation of the price pending removal of Miss AB as trustee and executor under her sister's will. Once so removed, the *curator bonis* is *in titulo* to grant a disposition of the whole property to the purchaser. *Quoad* Miss AB's own one-half share of the property, no further title is required. The conveyance runs in the name of the *curator bonis* on her behalf, she being already infeft in that one-half *pro indiviso* share. *Quoad* the other half *pro indiviso* share vested in the deceased Miss CB, Mr D can convey in his capacity as sole remaining executor in Miss CB's estate by virtue of, and deducing title through, (i) the confirmation and (ii) the decree of removal of Miss AB as trustee and executor in her sister's estate.

I do not think there is any other competent procedure.

Manual, para 3.14.

DELIVERY

7   *The need for delivery*
Delivery of deed – revocation of gift *animus donandi* – *rei interventus*

Date: November 1990

Memorial

An opinion was sought on the following questions:

1 Was the memorialist legally entitled, prior to the recording of the deed or at any other time, to revoke the gift of a one-half share of the property to his daughter (Miss A), bearing in mind particularly that (*a*) he provided the full price and (*b*) there was no contractual arrangement between the disponees?

2 Did any *animus donandi* exist at any point, including (*a*) when the memorialist decided to put the title into the joint names of himself and his daughter or (*b*) when the feu disposition was sent to the Keeper for recording. (The memorialist argued that his decision to put the title in joint names was not a gift but merely a device to secure a successful visa application by his daughter's fiancé.)

3 Did the presumption against donation apply in the circumstances of this transaction?

4 In the light of the decision in *Forrest-Hamilton's Trustee* v *Forrest-Hamilton* 1979 SLT 338 (a case which did not relate to heritable property), could it be successfully argued on behalf of the memorialist that his motive as well as his intention would have to be considered in determining whether there was in fact any *animus donandi*?

5 Was the decision in *Brown's Trustee* v *Brown* 1943 SC 488 relevant in the circumstances of this transaction?

6 Did the application of the rule of *rei interventus* apply?

Opinion

1 I do not think that the questions posed here are strictly relevant. The true test to be applied in considering whether or not a gift has been perfected and has become irrevocable is not whether the deed has been recorded – although that has some bearing in a different context – nor who provided the price, nor whether there was a contractual arrangement – although again that may have a bearing if some contractual arrangement can be established – but whether there has been delivery by donor to donee.

    That being so, what we have to concentrate on is the date on which the feu disposition in favour of the memorialist and his daughter Miss A was deemed to have been delivered to her, *quoad* her one-half *pro indiviso* share.

I would point out that, although I am asked whether the memorialist is entitled, prior to recording or at any other time, to revoke the gift, the deed was presented for recording (apparently on the instructions of one disponee only) but has since been withdrawn from the Register and in that sense remains unrecorded.

The memorialist must take into account that what he is dealing with is a heritable title granted, albeit on his instructions, in favour of himself and his daughter and the survivor of them. There is no doubt that that deed was delivered by M, the disponers, to Messrs Z & Son as agents for the memorialist and for Miss A. Thereafter, the same agents signed a warrant of registration on behalf of both parties, the deed in the meantime having been stamped with the appropriate stamp duty. Having signed the warrant, which is in correct terms looking to the terms of the dispositive clause in the feu disposition, and having signed it presumably in their capacity as agents for the memorialist *and* for Miss A, Z & Son then sent the deed to the Keeper of the Registers to be recorded, in terms of the warrant, on behalf of both parties.

In McBryde *Contract*, chapter 7, there is a detailed and well-researched text on delivery of deeds. I would refer the memorialist in particular to the principles extracted from the reported cases by Professor McBryde.

The significant factors in determining whether or not the deed was delivered in the present case include the following.

(a) Delivery requires both intention to deliver and actual delivery. On the facts as stated in the memorial, it seems to me that Miss A would have no difficulty in establishing both intention and actual delivery even though there may have been an underlying motive in taking the title in these terms.

(b) In the case of gratuitous deeds, delivery to an *agent* for the donee is as good as delivery to the donee herself. In the present case, the agents who revised the feu disposition on behalf of the disponees clearly did so as agents both for the memorialist and for Miss A. The fact that they were acting for both parties is, in my view, proved beyond question by the fact that they signed the warrant on behalf of both parties. The deed was then presented, with that warrant of registration, for recording in Sasines.

I emphasise at this point that there is no suggestion that the deed was taken in these terms by mistake, or that the warrant of registration and the presentation of the deed for recording with that warrant was done by mistake. It was quite deliberately done on the instructions of the memorialist for a purpose which may or may not have been legitimate, but which had as its underlying motive a clear intention that Miss A should become the heritable proprietor of a one-half share of the dwellinghouse in order to achieve an intended result, namely the obtaining of a visa for Miss A's fiancé. This hinged on Miss A's ability to demonstrate that she was truly the beneficial owner of a share of a heritable property in Scotland, not merely nominally or as trustee, but as beneficial owner. Had she held title to one-half of the property in any other capacity, that would not have been sufficient to achieve the desired result.

Clearly, therefore, although the memorialist may have hoped or expected that his daughter would in due course return one-half of the property to him or deal with it on his instructions, he must have intended *at the time* that she should truly become the owner of a one-half share, given the terms of the deed and the factors which induced him to give these instructions to his solicitors.

Bearing these factors in mind, I am inclined to the view that the deed was delivered to Miss A, and therefore became irrevocable *quoad* the one-half *pro indiviso* share conveyed to her by the feu disposition, during March 1990, being the date when the deed was actually handed over by the seller's solicitors to Messrs Z & Son who, by their own admission, consider themselves to be, and indeed must have been, acting for Miss A when they accepted delivery of the deed in the terms in which they had revised it. That fact is more than sufficiently confirmed by their subsequent actings in signing a warrant of registration on behalf of both parties and sending the deed to the Keeper.

In so doing, they were acting perfectly properly and on the instructions of the memorialist. As I understand it, it was only some months after the deed had been so presented that the memorialist, for reasons disclosed in the memorial, had a change of heart. I quote: 'In these circumstances, the memorialist decided to revoke his gift of a one-half share in the property to his daughter.'

The critical question is whether at that date (presumably some time in July 1990) the memorialist had it in his power to revoke a gift of the one-half share.

In my view, he had no such power. The gift had become complete and irrevocable probably during March 1990, when the deed was delivered to the common agent, but certainly at the latest during May 1990, when the agents acting on behalf of both parties sent the deed to the Keeper for recording.

Section 142 of the Titles to Land Consolidation (Scotland) Act 1868, which authorises the direct recording of deeds in the Register of Sasines, and s 141, which requires that every such deed should carry a warrant of registration, taken together with the Conveyancing (Scotland) Act 1924, s 10, and Sched F thereto, require that every deed presented for registration must carry a warrant, that the warrant must specify the person or persons on whose behalf it is presented for recording and must be signed by that person or persons or by his or their agents. It is beyond doubt that the deed was presented for recording on behalf of Miss A, as beneficial owner of a one-half *pro indiviso* share, by her duly authorised agent and was delivered at latest on the date of such presentation. In this context I would quote from Halliday, para 9–11:

> [I]f, however, the donation was of property such as heritable property where the transfer to the donee was by deed of conveyance and the donee has a complete *ex facie* absolute title, an averment by the donor or his representative that donation was not intended and that the property is truly held on behalf of the donor or for purposes inconsistent with absolute ownership by the donee amount to a declarator of trust and can be proved only by the writ or oath of the donee.'

I accept that Miss A, as donee of a one-half *pro indiviso* share, did not in fact complete her infeftment because the deed was subsequently withdrawn from the Keeper, but it must be assumed that it was withdrawn without her authority and so I would not regard the fact that Miss A has so far failed to achieve an infeftment as significant in determining whether or not she has acquired an absolute and indefeasible right to her share of the property. The mere fact that the deed was presented for recording with a warrant of registration signed on her behalf as disponee of a one-half *pro indiviso* share and that the subsequent withdrawal of the deed was not made because the deed had been incorrectly presented in the first place but because of a change of mind on the part of the donor renders the withdrawal of the deed totally irrelevant, in my view, in determining a question of delivery. The facts of delivery are sufficiently proved by the presentation of the deed following on the preceding history of the transaction. By that delivery the donation of a one-half share to Miss A became absolute and irrevocable subject only to contradictory evidence of that apparent fact by writ or oath.

There is no suggestion that Miss A held the share as trustee or nominee; indeed that would have defeated the purpose of the exercise. I am not fully informed of the procedure for visa applications, but no doubt there are statements, possibly sworn statements, by her and her fiancé to the effect that she was the beneficial owner of the one-half share of this property. If she now comes forward and admits on oath that the arrangement was a sham, there may be serious repercussions in relation to the visa application.

The short answer to question 1 is that the memorialist is not legally entitled to revoke the gift at this stage.

2   I accept that there is a general presumption against donation, but that is only a presumption. Taking the whole transaction as it developed, my view is that there is evidence of a final and completed intention to donate at latest when the deed was sent for recording with the warrant of registration signed on behalf of the memorialist and his daughter. It is of course possible that the gift, although *ex facie* absolute in its terms, was subject to a secret condition that it would be given back if required, or that, notwithstanding the *ex facie* absolute quality of the conveyance in her favour, Miss A took one-half share of the property in trust for her father.

If the intention was a trust, that can only be proved by writ or oath. If that intention can be proved, her father could compel her to convey the share back to him. In that event, care would have to be taken to eliminate the survivorship destination. But it seems to me very unlikely that any claim that the conveyance was in trust would succeed.

In relation to a conditional gift, it would be up to the memorialist to prove that this was the case. If his daughter denies it, he is in very serious difficulty. We are dealing with heritable title and any such contractual condition would normally require probative writ. In any event, the condition in this case, even if established, might well be held invalid by the court on the footing that it was, if not illegal, at least contrary to public policy.

3   No. The presumption against donation applies only in circumstances where there is some doubt, arising out of the mechanics of making the gift, as to whether or not a gift was intended and was effectively made. In the present circumstances, there seems to me no ambiguity whatsoever because, on the express instructions of the donor, and with his knowledge

and approval, the title to the property was taken in joint names, albeit that he paid the whole price. I am not advised whether or not there was a loan and, if so, whether the daughter was a party to the heritable security on the property. If she was, that in itself would be absolutely conclusive. But in any event, the instructions to the solicitors, the form in which the deed was taken and then presented for recording, and the fact that the deed was allowed to lie in the hands of the Keeper until some totally extraneous event occurred which produced a change of circumstances, all seem to me to exclude the presumption against donation.

4　The decision in *Forrest-Hamilton's Trustee* is not relevant in the present situation because it related to donation *mortis causa* and to bank accounts in joint names, to both of which special rules apply which have no application in the case of an *inter vivos* gift of heritable property evidenced by a delivered writ, which is what we have here.

Motive and intention are factors to take into account in determining whether or not there was *animus donandi*; but, for the reasons stated above, unless the memorialist can establish by legal action that the conveyance to Miss A was truly in trust or that the gift was subject to a legitimate condition, my view is that motive and intention must give way to the overriding evidence of delivery of a probative deed in unambiguous terms.

5　No. The decision in *Brown's Trustee* applies exclusively to the question of revocability or otherwise of the survivorship destination in the title. It was not suggested in that case, and there is no other decision where this has been suggested, that the rights of the immediate disponees were anything other than full proprietary rights in their individual *pro indiviso* shares. The only question was whether or not donor or donee could revoke the destination in the title.

The decision is applicable in this case to the extent that the title contains a survivorship destination. *Brown's Trustee* would apply so as to prevent Miss A from revoking that destination *mortis causa*. But, notwithstanding that limitation, she is at the moment on the face of the title, and until some contradictory result has been achieved (which I think is unlikely) will remain, the *inter vivos* proprietor of a one-half *pro indiviso* share of the property and is free to dispose of it as she pleases. Indeed, even though the title is not recorded, she could now proceed by way of an action of division and sale and claim half the proceeds. Accordingly, the memorialist is in a position of some difficulty and exposed to that risk for which, in my view, there is no effective remedy without the co-operation of the daughter as ostensible donee.

6　No. There is nothing whatever in this situation which would allow any application of the rule of *rei interventus* to affect the rights of Miss A.

Further reading
Requirements of Writing (Scotland) Act 1995 – abolition of proof by writ or oath.

Manual, para 4.1.

STAMP DUTIES AND VAT

8   *Liability to duty*
Stamp duty – deed of trust – liability

Date: November 1991

Memorial

Outline planning permission was obtained for the development of a site. The title was to be obtained from a variety of disponers, and then shortly afterwards sold or leased on in parts. If the memorialists took title to all the various parts they would be involved in considerable stamp duty liabilities. It was suggested that at settlement of the purchase transactions they should not take a disposition in favour of themselves but a deed of trust by the sellers containing:

1   An acknowledgement of the price.

2   An undertaking to hold the title in trust and, when called on, grant a disposition in favour of the memorialists or nominees of the whole site or part of it.

What was the efficacy of such a suggestion and were there any drawbacks?

Opinion

I am afraid that the scheme suggested in the memorial to avoid stamp duty on a purchase and subsequent sale-on will not achieve the desired result. The reason is that, although in the ordinary case a deed of trust does not attract *ad valorem* stamp duty, there are exceptions to this rule. One of the exceptions is where the deed of trust operates to transfer the right of ownership, as it would do in this case on the terms suggested for the deed of trust. There is a fairly early English authority exactly in point, *Chesterfield Brewery Co* v *IRC* [1899] 2 QB 7, where it was held, correctly in my view in light of the provisions of the Stamp Act 1891, that a declaration of trust by a vendor in favour of a purchaser (which is in substance what is proposed here) is a conveyance or transfer on sale.

The only recognised way in which stamp duty can be avoided on a sale-on is by allowing the seller to retain the title to the property until the sub-sale is concluded and then for the purchaser to convey the property, with the consent of the original purchaser, to the sub-purchaser. There is no doubt that, in that situation, stamp duty is not payable twice. But the risk of course is that, in the interim, the seller will be sequestrated or go into liquidation, and, if the purchase price has been paid to the seller, as it probably would have been, the original purchaser would lose the price, as in

Gibson v *Hunter Homes Designs Ltd* 1976 SC 23. It may be in the special cir-cumstances of this case, where the seller of at least part of the area of ground is a district council, that this would be an acceptable risk, but I imagine that it would not be an acceptable risk in the case of limited companies and partnerships.

If such an arrangement is to be considered in the case of the district council, then, at the settlement of the transaction, instead of taking a deliv-ered disposition, the original purchasers would simply take a letter of obligation from the district council to deliver in due course a duly executed disposition, in terms already agreed, in favour of a sub-purchaser. That does not amount to a declaration of trust – a point established in *Gibson* v *Hunter Homes Designs Ltd*. Accordingly, no stamp duty would be payable at that point. On completion of the sub-sale, the district council would grant the Disposition in its agreed form directly to the sub-purchaser, with a nar-rative to include the consent of the original purchaser, and a saving of stamp duty would be achieved.

I cannot think of an alternative solution.

Manual, para 5.1.

CREATION OF THE NEW FEUDAL ESTATE

9 *Creation of the new feudal estate*
Creation of timeshare schemes in Scotland

Date: January 1990

Memorial
The last decade has seen an increase in the amount of leisure time that is available to individuals. One outcome has been an interest in timeshare schemes. When such schemes first arrived in Scotland, it was unclear as to whether it would be possible to feu shares in them, and how this would be justified in accordance with the feudal system of tenure.

An opinion was sought on this broad question.

Opinion
This is certainly a novel proposition for which, as you know, there is no direct precedent in point.

As I understand it, the proposal is that the developers are to grant feu dispositions of separate *pro indiviso* shares in a particular property to separate individual feuars, possibly over a period of time; but, in the end of the day, the whole of the property will be so feued and vest, in *pro indiviso* shares, in a number of individual feuars who will take infeftment by the recording of their individual titles on different dates. The Keeper has suggested that sub-feuing of *pro indiviso* shares is of doubtful competency, and, as a result, if and when such a transaction falls to be registered in the Land Register, he would exclude indemnity in respect of any loss arising from a defect in the proper constitution of the feudal relationship. Clearly, that is a serious threat to the viability of the proposals although, as the Keeper points out, this exclusion does not imply that the title as a whole is invalid. It relates strictly to the creation of the feudal relationship but not to the validity of the proprietary title of the individual owner. Put another way, ownership is guaranteed but tenure is not. That is, in any event, the present position under warrandice in the Sasines system (see *Brownlie* v *Miller* (1880) 7R(HL)66). None the less, if a feudal relationship is not duly constituted, then undoubtedly a question may arise as to the enforceability of feuing conditions, and on this the efficacy of the whole scheme may well depend.

First, on the question of competency, I disagree with the Keeper. Naturally, I appreciate his cause for concern but I think his misgivings are unfounded.

In the modern feudal system we no longer have wardholdings.

Accordingly, although clearly there might have been objections in principle to the granting of a feu to several proprietors on that form of tenure, the same objections in principle cannot be raised to a new grant in feu-farm where the sole consideration now, in addition to payment of the *grassum,* if any, is implementation of the conditions of tenure. Feudal casualties, carriages and services, and feuduty, have all now been abolished under the relevant Acts.

The granting of land on feu-farm tenure by a superior to two or more vassals in conjunct fee is of ancient origin. In particular, I refer to Stair II, 3,41 (p 368 of the 1981 edition). Book II is concerned with real rights, and Title 3 is concerned with infeftment in heritable property on sub-infeudation and the resulting rights of the vassal. In para 41, Stair, having dealt with various forms of tenure and the general principles of public and base infeftment, deals with what he calls 'another division of infeftments', namely those which are granted to one person and his heirs or 'to more persons and their heirs ... sometimes as conjunct infeftments ...'. He then goes on to describe conjunct infeftments as 'conjunct fees, whereby the fee is disponed jointly to more persons and their heirs, which may be to three or more persons, who by the infeftment become all fiars jointly and equally; whence there arises a communion by which they do possess the fee *pro indiviso,* until division thereof be made ...'. He distinguishes this form of *pro indiviso* holding from an infeftment to an incorporation, or to trustees for an incorporation, which, clearly, to Stair, involved something quite different. So, in the earliest of our institutional writers, sub-infeudation to two or more *pro indiviso* proprietors, and their subsequent infeftment, was clearly a familiar concept.

I have on my desk at the moment two writs granted more than 100 years before Stair wrote this passage. One is a charter by the Bishop of Dunkeld in favour of a lady and her son in fee; the other is a charter by the Abbot of Balmerino in favour of a husband and wife as proprietors in fee. Clearly, in each case, the resulting ownership is *pro indiviso.* There is no provision in either title for a survivorship, nor anything to indicate a joint right of property. The right conferred is clearly a right of property in common.

It seems to me, from this passage in Stair and from the illustrations cited above, that the concept of subinfeudation in *pro indiviso* shares was established many centuries ago, and nothing has happened since then to qualify or derogate from that general proposition. Instead, subsequent legislation has fortified the position, if fortification were required. The reason is that, until 1747, a superior having granted a feu charter, whether to one or several vassals *pro indiviso,* was not obliged to give entry (except in the case of apprisings) to any successor from the original vassal except strictly in terms of the destination in the original charter. If the superior agreed to give entry, the appropriate procedure was for the superior to grant a charter of resignation or a charter of confirmation in favour of the singular successor of the original vassal. Until 1747 this was entirely at the discretion of the superior, again subject to the qualification in relation to apprisings. However, by the Tenures Abolition Act 1746, s 12, the superior was required by statute to give public entry and grant a new infeftment to any heir or disponee who applied for entry on a retour or a procuratory of resignation. The Transference of Lands (Scotland) Act 1847, s 6, made a similar provision for entry by confirmation. Finally, under the Conveyancing (Scotland) Act 1874, s 4, any proprietor of land – which, of course, includes the proprietor of a *pro indiviso* share – on the recording of his title, is automatically entered with the true superior, and writs of resignation and of confirmation are abolished.

Taking public entry with the superior in either of these ways, by resignation or by confirmation, before 1874 involved the granting by the superior to the applicant of a charter (or writ) by progress, on the strength of which he renewed the investiture in the subjects passing to the applicant, either by succession on death or under a disposition or its equivalent. The charter or writ of resignation, and the charter or writ of confirmation, operated as a mandate for infeftment in the subjects to which the applicant had title, allowing him to procure himself infeft therein, and become publicly entered with the true superior. That then became automatic on the recording of the title to the interest in question under the 1874 Act, and the active participation of the superior was no longer required. The point of these observations on feudal procedures is that, long before 1874 and going back into the mists of antiquity, *pro indiviso* ownership of heritable property in Scotland has been a known and recognised feature of the feudal system, at least on feu-farm tenure.

Quite apart from cases where property was conveyed by disposition to two or more persons in *pro indiviso* shares, which the Keeper acknowledges to be competent, there were other situations where by the operation of law or by destination two or more persons might become *pro indiviso* proprietors of a single feu. So, failing a prior male heir, heirs portioners succeeded equally to heritable property on the death intestate of their ancestor, in *pro indiviso* shares. The principle of succession by heirs portioners to *pro indiviso* shares is established beyond argument. There is old authority for *pro indiviso* succession under destinations in *Carnegie* v *Clark* (1677) M 12, 840. The pursuer in that case concluded, successfully, for infeftment in one-half of the property, as heir of provision. I think it is also firmly established that a conveyance to two or more disponees is competent, in equal (or in unequal) *pro indiviso* shares *inter se*, on which together or separately, each of them can take an infeftment.

The consequence of these principles inevitably is, in my view, that, as a result of the legislation referred to between 1746 and 1874, a *pro indiviso* proprietor, whether as disponee or by succession, could require the superior to grant, to him alone and independently, a charter, whether of resignation or of confirmation, on which that person could then take a separate and distinct infeftment as vassal of the superior in the *pro indiviso* share. Since 1874 infeftment by one *pro indiviso* proprietor in a *pro indiviso* share passing to him, whether by disposition or on succession, automatically creates a separate and distinct infeftment in the person of that proprietor in his *pro indiviso* share, independently of and separately from the other proprietors holding other *pro indiviso* shares in the same unit of property. This in turn implies not only a separate infeftment but separate public entry by the *pro indiviso* proprietor with his superior on what can only be described as a separate and independent tenure or holding.

It may be argued that all the illustrations given above involve the subdivision of a single unit of heritable property among two or more *pro indiviso* proprietors who, *simultaneously*, derive their right from the same disponer, or, in the case of succession, on the same death. Initially, of course, this is usually so. But, once property has been subdivided into *pro indiviso* shares, the owner of the individual *pro indiviso* share is free to deal with that share in any way he pleases. Thus, an heir portioner succeeding along with her sisters to, say, a one-third *pro indiviso* share of her father's heritable property is then free to deal separately and independently with that *pro indiviso* share by any competent method. In particular, she can convey it *inter vivos*; she can bequeath it by her will; or she can grant heritable securities thereover. Likewise, the single infeft owner of a whole property may convey a one-half *pro indiviso* share to a disponee from him. The disponee takes a separate and independent infeftment by recording that disposition. He is then separately infeft in his one-half *pro indiviso* share.

That being so, I cannot see why in that situation the *pro indiviso* proprietor should not then be entitled to sub-feu. Admittedly, this will raise problems for the vassal in relation to occupation and use of the subject-matter of the grant; but that is a problem which confronts any *pro indiviso* proprietor *vis-à-vis* the other *pro indiviso* proprietor or proprietors of the property in question, and the law provides for this by the action of division and sale.

If it is competent for the owner of a *pro indiviso* share of property, already separately held on a separate infeftment, thereafter to sub-feu the same, again I cannot see any reason in principle why the owner of the whole property should not set about sub-feuing that whole property in *pro indiviso* shares *ab initio*. In other words, I cannot see why there should be any basic prohibition in principle against sub-feuing individual *pro indiviso* shares, when such shares can clearly be held separately from the other shares in a particular property and be dealt with separately from the other shares, once subdivision has taken place.

It is an accepted feudal principle that a single unit of heritable property can be subdivided laterally or vertically into any number of smaller subdivisions. So, a tenement of four flats can be subdivided so that each of the four flats passes into individual ownership, thus creating four separate owners of parts of the same building. There is no doubt that such subdivision can be effected by subinfeudation just as effectively as by a disposition of the individual flat (see, for example, *Duncan v Church of Scotland General Trustees* 1941 SC 145, where the validity of such a title was not questioned). That being so, on general principle and in the absence of any specific rule to the contrary which so far I have not come across, it would seem to be equally competent for the owner of the block of four flats to sub-feu it in one-fourth *pro indiviso* shares to each of four *pro indiviso* proprietors. In the ordinary way, of course, there would be no point in doing so, but, on the other hand, there seems to be no general principle to prevent him if he wished to do so.

The Keeper refers to a distinction drawn by the Joint Consultative Committee between (*a*) a conveyance of a heritable property as an exclusive right to the disponee together with an associated *pro indiviso* right in ancillary property as a pertinent of the main subject conveyed, such as a right in common to the solum of a tenement in which an individual flat is feued or conveyed, and (*b*) a feu purely of a *pro indiviso* share of the whole subjects. A clear distinction must be drawn between those cases, particularly tenement cases, where certain components of the subjects conveyed to the disponee of an individual flat are conveyed to him in common but are, for practical purposes, inseparable from the tenement itself. This applies, in particular, to a right in common to the roof, main walls and solum, etc.

In other cases, there may be a conveyance of an individual property coupled with a conveyance of a *pro indiviso* share of associated property ancillary to the main subjects conveyed but not integral to or inseparable from the main subjects themselves.

In the first case, it really would not be sensible to contemplate a separate sale of a *pro indiviso* share of a main wall – or the solum of a tenement – at least while the tenement was still standing. But in the second class of case, where a *pro indiviso* share of a separate and distinct property is conveyed along with and as a pertinent of the main subjects, subsequent separation of that pertinent from the main subjects is not impossible and indeed not unknown. To illustrate the implications of this second class of case, where the subjects conveyed in *pro indiviso* shares can be separated off from and held on a separate title from the original principal subjects, I refer to two cases which, in different ways, illustrate the working of what I consider to be the correct principles.

1   *Baird & Co v Feuars of Kilsyth* (1878) 6 R 116. In that case a superior granted feu charters to individual feuars of steadings of land. In each separate charter he also feued in feu-farm, in explicit terms, a proportional part of the lands of Barrwood to each vassal along with the other inhabitants of the burgh. Note particularly that in this case there was a *reddendo* payable for the steading and a separate *reddendo* payable for the proportional part of Barrwood. The precept in the charter specifically authorised the giving of sasine separately to the *pro indiviso* part of Barrwood, and infeftment followed accordingly.

The essence of the debate, so far as Barrwood was concerned, was not so much whether it was valid to sub-feu a *pro indiviso* share but whether the right conferred in each feu charter was in the nature of a *pro indiviso* right of property in common or something less than that – for example a mere servitude.

The case was heard in the Outer House by Lord Rutherford Clark and in the First Division by Lord President Inglis, Lord Shand, Lord Deas and Lord Mure. Lord Deas dissented on grounds that do not affect the point at issue here. The remaining judges, whose combined opinion must carry very considerable weight, were unanimous that the right conferred on each individual feuar was a *pro indiviso* right of property in Barrwood. The real point at issue involved the ownership of the minerals below the surface and, consistently with the decision as to the right conferred, the court came to the view that each individual feuar of each steading also had a *pro indiviso* right in the minerals under the common property. You will note that the right derived directly from a charter by which the *pro indiviso* part of

Barrwood was feued to each individual vassal along with his exclusive right of property in the steading. So, Lord President Inglis at p 140 states: 'I think these feu grants conveyed a right of property in Barrwood to the feuars – a right of common property – and that each of the feuars had a proportional *pro indiviso* right of property in the subject.'

Clearly, this is a case where the common property, although originally intended to operate as a pertinent for the benefit of the individual feuars of the individual steadings, was none the less susceptible of being dealt with, by conveyance or otherwise, by the whole body of *pro indiviso* proprietors if they so decided. It is not a pertinent of a type which is, of necessity and in perpetuity, inseparably associated with the individual right of property in each individual steading. None the less, the court held that this separate and independent area was susceptible of being feued in *pro indiviso* shares by individual charters granted no doubt at various dates on which infeftment was held to have been properly taken by each individual feuar. The whole point of this case was to determine who was the owner of the minerals under the common property. If counsel could have persuaded the court that the separate subinfeudation of *pro indiviso* shares in the common area was invalid and incompetent under feudal law, that would have achieved the objective of the pursuers in this case. The title does seem to have been attacked on this ground, because Lord Rutherford Clark says at p 122: 'The pursuers have criticised the terms of these titles and they maintain that no valid infeftment has been taken in Barrwood either as a *pro indiviso* or several right.' This was the first question which he disposed of. He seems to have come to the view, without difficulty, that the charters of *pro indiviso* shares of the common area were competent. 'It dispones and in feu-farm and heritage lets and demitts a proportional part of Barrwood. The conveyance seems consistent only with the disposition of property. The dispositive words are applicable to Barrwood only and as a separate subject. There is a separate *reddendo* for that subject.... What truly is material is that a proportional part of the lands is disponed and the right so conveyed cannot, it is thought, be short of a right of property'. And at p 123: '[P]ro indiviso rights of property were duly created by the original charters.' There was also some debate as to whether or not sasine had been properly taken, the common property being discontinuous from the individual steadings; but again Lord Rutherford Clark came to the view that the sasine was in order.

There does not seem to have been any serious argument before Lord Rutherford Clark or before the First Division that, on basic feudal principles, it was incompetent for a superior to sub-feu a *pro indiviso* share of a given area.

2   The same principle is illustrated in the decision in *Grant* v *Heriot's Trust* (1906) 8 F 647. Simplifying the facts, each house in a terrace of individual houses in Edinburgh was feued off by feu contract, each to individual absolute proprietors as an exclusive right of property. (I might perhaps say that the report is slightly confusing. The original developer obtained a feu contract from the superior of the whole area; he then sold and conveyed to individual purchasers. But, and this is the important point, each disponee

from the developer *then* obtained from the superior a charter, sub-feuing the dwellinghouse exclusively to each owner.) In the same feu contract, there was conveyed to each of these proprietors a *pro indiviso* share of a common area of garden ground, subject to certain conditions and under a prohibition (held to be invalid as a real burden) against the raising of an action of division and sale in relation to that *pro indiviso* right. Later, because of subsequent developments in the City of Edinburgh, the group of proprietors owning the garden ground in *pro indiviso* shares conveyed it to a body of improvement trustees, so that the garden ground then became separated from the individual dwellinghouses to which, originally, the *pro indiviso* shares were attached (as it were) as a pertinent but which came to be separated from the principal property as a separate and independent right of property vested in the improvement trustees for improvement purposes.

In my opinion, this is, again, a clear case where a superior feued off *ab initio* a *pro indiviso* share of an independent property, albeit that, in the same conveyance, he also feued an absolute right of property in an adjoining dwellinghouse. In the nature of things, the feu contracts would not be simultaneous but must have been granted over a period of time, and the individual titles would have been recorded at different dates. The court had no difficulty in holding that the right of property so feued was a proprietary right of common property, which vested a *pro indiviso* share of the common garden ground in each of the individual disponees. The court had no difficulty in holding that the prohibition in the titles against the action of division and sale was incompetent and invalid, and they had no difficulty in holding that the *pro indiviso* proprietors, even though *ab initio* it may have been intended that the property should be held in perpetuity as a pertinent in association with the dwellinghouses, had none the less acquired a separate and independent title to a *pro indiviso* share of the garden ground. They were therefore *in titulo*, as a group, to convey away the whole area separately from their dwellinghouses to a disponee from them.

On the strength of these decisions and of the authorities cited therein, and the arguments supporting them, I cannot see that, in feudal law, there can be any absolute bar in principle against the sub-feuing of a *pro indiviso* share to a series of individuals as is proposed in the present case. Of course, such *pro indiviso* shares may be subject to cross rights of common interest. But the same applies, in special situations, to individual properties separately owned – for example, flats in tenements. See Gordon, *Scottish Land Law*, para 15–05.

Finally, if there is a rule which effectively prevents and invalidates the subinfeudation of a *pro indiviso* share, it is surprising that this is nowhere stated by the institutional writers or by the writers on conveyancing such as Duff, Menzies, Bell, Craigie, Burns, Halliday, Rankine and Gordon. *Green's Encyclopaedia*, vol 3, para 1382, refers to 'A clause in a feu charter granting a *pro indiviso* share' without comment or qualification as to its validity. None of these authorities suggests that subinfeudation of a *pro indiviso* share is incompetent in feudal theory, although admittedly none of them suggests that it is; nor was there any such suggestion in the decisions quoted above.

On the other hand, there are a number of authorities, from the institutional writers onwards, who state quite clearly that *certain* heritable properties are indivisible or are divisible only on certain conditions. Thus, reverting to heirs portioners, although it is the case that any ordinary heritable property passes to heirs portioners in equal *pro indiviso* shares as *pro indiviso* proprietors, that rule is excluded in the case of the mansion house on an estate which goes to the eldest daughter. It is also excluded in the case of individual superiorities, *not* because a superiority is of its nature indivisible and cannot be held in *pro indiviso* shares as such, but because of the feudal rule that a vassal cannot be answerable (at least without his consent) to more than one superior in a single feu. These rules are quite clearly laid down in such special cases. But no equivalent rule is even hinted at in any of the authorities in relation to heritable property generally.

For this combination of reasons, it seems to me that the proposals, if I understand them correctly, are entirely unobjectionable and I see no reason why the Keeper should feel it necessary to exclude indemnity in respect of the tenurial element of the grant in such cases.

Manual, chapter 6.

10   Reddendo
Right to draw water – annual sum payable – Land Tenure Reform
(Scotland) Act 1974 – validity

Date: September 1986

Memorial
The memorialists reached agreement to purchase a plot of land with outline planning permission for the erection of a dwellinghouse. It was intended that the water supply should be obtained from a burn situated to the west and north of the plot. The sellers sought to obtain an annual sum for the right to draw the water, which was to be reviewable every five years. The memorialists had the following questions:

1   Was the annual sum struck at by the Land Tenure Reform (Scotland) Act 1974, s 2?
2   If such an obligation to pay was accepted and then entered the feu disposition, could it safely be ignored?
3   Were there any suitable clauses for incorporation into the missives which would protect the memorialists?
4   Was there anything further the memorialists should be aware of?

Opinion
1   The question raised is a novel one and there is no reported authority. For my part, however, I agree with the arguments put forward by the agents, that the proposed annual payment of £10 per annum, reviewable at five-yearly intervals, is struck at by the Land Tenure Reform (Scotland) Act 1974, s 2, on the grounds stated in the memorial.

The right to be conferred on the purchasers is a perpetual servitude right to draw water, attaching to the subjects of purchase as a pertinent of the dominant tenement. If an annual payment is to be made for the benefit of that pertinent, it can only be justified in terms of s 2 if it can be shown that the payment is a payment to defray, or a contribution towards, some continuing cost. But, according to my instructions, there is no cost to be incurred by the sellers of the servient tenement in installing or maintaining the water supply. Indeed, it would be inconsistent with a servitude right that the servient owner should be so burdened because, in the law of servitudes (with the sole exception of the servitude *tigni immittendi*), there is never any burden or liability on the servient owner to maintain. Admittedly, if the purchasers were to share a collecting tank or pipes or other apparatus with one or more other dominant proprietors sharing in the servitude of water supply, the annual payment might be described as a contribution towards some continuing cost related to the land. Unless, however, that cost was incurred by the owner of the servient tenement himself, as one of the users, there would be no obligation to make the payment to the servient owner. Instead, the payment would take the form, familiar in tenement titles, requiring the burdened proprietor to contribute a *proportion* of the total cost of maintenance or repairs. But this is not at all the form of the proposed payment in this case.

For these reasons, I am reasonably confident that, if the matter came to the courts, the payment would be held to fall within the 1974 Act, s 2, and, as such, would be held to be illegal and unenforceable.

2   On the assumptions reached in the foregoing answer, any such provision included in the title of the purchasers could safely be ignored and would be unenforceable without in any way imperilling their title. This is expressly provided for in the 1974 Act, s 2(2), in terms of which the inclusion of a provision in a deed purporting to impose an illegal annual payment does not render the deed itself void or unenforceable. Instead, it simply renders the provision unenforceable, leaving the deed to receive effect otherwise according to its terms. The answer to this question, accordingly, is in the affirmative.

3   Notwithstanding the preceding answer, I would regard it as unsatisfactory to agree in the missives to a payment which is intrinsically invalid and, *a fortiori*, to include such a provision in the formal title. In the context of a purchase for a capital sum of £5,000, a continuing payment of £10 per annum, albeit subject to five-yearly reviews, is a fairly pointless provision and I would have thought, if the implications of the 1974 Act, s 2, are drawn to the notice of the sellers' agents, it should be possible to negotiate for the exclusion of this proposed payment, possibly by a very small increase in the purchase price.

If, however, the sellers' agents insist on maintaining this provision, it ought to be linked in some way to the cost of living index or the increase in the level of inflation, so that the purchasers are not undertaking an open-ended commitment.

4   It is difficult to see what more one can suggest to assist the purchasers in this situation.

Provisions of this kind for a continuing annual payment are really not appropriate in the situation envisaged here, where the right is intended to be permanent and the payment is not in any way associated with a contribution towards continuing costs.

The typical situation where a payment of this kind is introduced into a title is where the right conferred is intended to be of a temporary nature. To avoid establishing a permanent heritable right, one proprietor may grant a concession to his neighbour for payment of an annual sum by way of wayleave, with a provision for termination of the right either on notice or on a given date or at the will of the neighbouring proprietor. The purpose, in that case, of introducing an annual payment is to avoid any possibility of the person enjoying the benefit of the right for the prescriptive period then seeking to assert a permanent title to that right by prescriptive possession.

In the present case, that is of course quite inappropriate in that the right conferred is intended to be permanent. An annual payment of this kind associated with a permanent right is something which is beyond my experience and should, I think, be resisted.

Alternatively, if the sellers seek to claim that the payment of £10 per annum is a contribution towards continuing costs, the provision should be recast so as to relate it directly to the costs involved, as a stated proportion thereof. In view of the fact that there seems to be no element of contribution towards common costs, this by itself would have the effect of rendering the provision unnecessary and demonstrating to the sellers that the provision was, almost certainly, unenforceable for the reason set out above.

Manual, para 6.18.

THE FEU CHARTER

11 Common property
Burden – validity – pre-emption right – contrary to public policy –
whether should be included in land certificate

Date: July 1989

Memorial
Questions arose regarding the enforceability of a burden in a disposition
which appeared to be discriminatory.

1   Was the burden contrary to public policy and therefore unenforceable?

2   If the burden was unenforceable, would its inclusion in the land certificate affect the marketability of the property?

3   If the burden was unenforceable, should it be deleted from the land
certificate?

4   If a minute of waiver was obtained, would the Keeper then delete the
burden from the land certificate?

5   Was there anything else of which the memorialists should be aware?

Opinion
1   Yes. In terms of the judgments in the *Tailors of Aberdeen* v *Coutts* (1834)
13 S 226, in order to constitute a real burden or condition effectual against
singular successors the burden must not be contrary to law, and must not
be contrary to public policy. In my opinion, the condition in the clause of
pre-emption in this case is unenforceable on both grounds.

Under the Race Relations Act 1976, s 21(1), it is unlawful for anyone,
in relation to premises of which he has power to dispose, to discriminate
against another person, *inter alia*, by refusing his application for those
premises. The terms of the pre-emption clause in this case clearly offend
against the definition of 'discrimination' in s 1 of the 1976 Act. Further,
although a simple right of pre-emption by itself is unobjectionable, the
right of pre-emption in this case is directed at prospective purchasers of
'coloured race' or non-British nationality, which is clearly discriminatory
within the meaning of the 1976 Act, and the discriminatory provision is so
intermingled with the pre-emption provision that the two cannot be segre-
gated. Therefore, the *whole* clause of pre-emption falls and cannot, in my
opinion, be insisted on by any proprietor of other flats in the block.

In any event, even if I am wrong in that view, the terms of the 1976 Act
are such that a clause of pre-emption in this form inevitably, in my view,

must be contrary to public policy, and on that separate ground the clause of pre-emption is not enforceable by any of the proprietors of the other flats.

2   No. The fact that the title and, in this case, the land certificate includes an unlawful or unenforceable burden or condition cannot affect the validity of the title as such and therefore cannot affect its marketability.

In any event, even if the condition were enforceable, I doubt if it would affect the marketability of the title. I appreciate that some solicitors regard a clause of pre-emption in a title as adversely affecting the rights of the proprietor for the time being but, in my experience, a clause of pre-emption very rarely works in that way. For one thing, prospective purchasers usually do not know that there is a right of pre-emption in the title. For another thing, even if they do know, in the vast majority of cases rights of pre-emption are not taken up and so very few purchasers are deterred from making an offer simply because there is such a right in the title.

In the present case, where the right of pre-emption is in my opinion plainly unenforceable on the grounds above stated, it could not conceivably have any effect on the marketability of this title, not even in the case of an offeror who was within the prohibited classes because, in my opinion, such an offerer could not be discriminated against by the exercise of the pre-emption.

So far as the present purchasers are concerned, and their building society, the existence of a right of pre-emption does not significantly affect their rights in that if the proprietors themselves or their heritable creditors on a repossession, sought to sell the subjects, I do not think they would suffer any prejudice by the presence of the right of pre-emption in the title, in that:

(a) prospective purchasers are very unlikely to be deterred;
(b) if a prospective purchaser makes an offer and the pre-emption is not taken up (which in any event in my view cannot be because it is unlawful), the sellers obtain the full market price from the then purchasers; or
(c) if the right of pre-emption is taken up (which in my view again it cannot be), the sellers still get the full market value but from one or other of the proprietors of other flats in the block rather than from the offerer. But the full purchase price is still paid.

For this combination of reasons, I regard the clause as not adversely affecting the title in this particular case.

3   This is a question of some difficulty which, since the matter is urgent, I have not thought it appropriate at this stage to explore further because I think some further research might be required. Generally speaking, the Keeper has a discretion to include or exclude burdens from a title as he chooses, leaving it to the parties to claim compensation if they think they are so entitled. On the other hand, once a burden has been included in the title sheet, its removal is more difficult. That being so, I think it unlikely that the Keeper will agree to delete the condition, although he might have been persuaded at an earlier stage not to incorporate it in the title sheet.

4   Yes. I am not advised whether the original writ containing the offensive clause of pre-emption was a feu charter or a disposition. If it was a feu charter, the consent of the superior is probably necessary although it is difficult to see what legitimate interest the superior has to enforce. If the original writ containing the condition was a mere disposition, the consent of the superior is unnecessary.

Undoubtedly, a minute of waiver by the proprietors of the other flats in the tenement would certainly be effective to discharge this condition once and for all – looking, particularly, to the provisions of the Land Registration (Scotland) Act 1979, s 18. When that minute of waiver was presented to the Keeper, he would then delete the clause of pre-emption from the title sheet and the land certificate.

5   As stated above, it is not clear from the titles whether, on the original subdivision, the titles of the individual purchasers took the form of feu charter or feu disposition or merely dispositions. The point of this observation is that, if the original break-off conveyances were in the form of feudal writs – for example, charters or feu dispositions, as is possible – the right of pre-emption has possibly already been extinguished under the Conveyancing Amendment (Scotland) Act 1938, s 9, as amended. If, on the other hand, the original break-off conveyance took the form of a disposition, the right of pre-emption will not have been extinguished under that section.

Further reading
Brookfield Developments Ltd v *Keeper of the Registers of Scotland* 1989 SLT (Lands Tr) 105, on the discretion of the Keeper to exclude burdens from the title sheet.

Manual, para 7.13.

DESCRIPTIONS

12 *Separate tenements*
Disposition of salmon fishings – whether restrictions valid – rod and line only

Date: March 1985

Memorial
The memorialists were in the course of negotiating for the purchase of salmon fishings. Various prohibitions were included in the draft disposition. These included a prohibition on fishing for salmon other than by rod and line (Clause septimo); and the fishing rights were to be enjoyed by angling associations in the locality (Clause octavo). Opinion was sought as to whether

1 The prohibitions were generally acceptable.

2 The clause seeking to restrict use to rod fishing should be deleted.

3 Alternative clauses could be recommended.

Opinion
1 Yes, provided the right which is purchased and thereafter conveyed to the memorialists in implement of the contract of sale and purchase is the full right of salmon fishings, which I assume to be the case. The imposing of restrictions on the method of exercising the right so conveyed does not in any way derogate from the right of property in the salmon fishings which will vest in the memorialists by conveyance thereof from the disponer.

By analogy, consider the case where ground is sold and conveyed to a purchaser subject to an absolute prohibition against erecting buildings of any kind thereon. The conveyance to the purchaser is a conveyance of the land, but the land is then subjected to a restriction on its use. That restriction does not in any way derogate from the complete legal title to and the *whole* interest in the land conveyed to the disponee; but it does impose a legitimate limitation on the way in which he uses his complete and undoubted right of property.

On the other hand, to prohibit the disponee from building on the land does not imply that the disponer reserves to himself the right to build thereon; nor, of course, does it imply that the disponer reserves the right to allow some third party to build on the land so conveyed. It is simply a restriction on what would otherwise be an unqualified and unfettered right of use and enjoyment.

The restrictions proposed on the method of fishing seem to me to be on all fours with the illustration given above.

The cases cited in my instructions – *Richmond* v *Seafield* (1870) 8 M 530 and other cases of that kind – relate not to an express grant of salmon fishings with restrictions as to the mode of exercise thereof, but rather as to whether or not, in the absence of an express grant, possession of salmon fishings by rod and line on a mere title 'with fishings' can set up by prescription an absolute title to salmon fishings in competition with an express grant thereof followed by possession.

As I understand it, that is not the position here. The memorialists will receive an express grant of the full and complete right of salmon fishings, carrying with it an entitlement to exercise that right by any legitimate means, whether by net and coble or by rod and line; but, for the reasons set out in the subsequent clauses of the proposed title, one of these legitimate modes of fishing – net and coble – is, by agreement, not to be exercised by the memorialists as disponees and owner of the fishings who, otherwise, would be entitled to exercise their salmon fishing rights by that means, as well as by rod and line.

The memorialists will note that the section in *Green's Encyclopaedia*, vol 7, para 300, where *Richmond* v *Seafield* is referred to, starts off with the proposition: 'The right to salmon fishings may *also* be established by a grant "cum piscationibus" followed by prescriptive possession of salmon fishings.'

The point of this is that a right to fish *cum piscationibus*, without any reference to salmon fishings, is not by itself a sufficient title to the salmon fishings. But, given possession of the salmon fishings, the title thereto can be established by prescriptive possession. The question then arises, but *only* then, as to whether rod and line is a sufficiently adequate method of exercising the right to set up a title by possession; and there is then a doubt as to whether possession by that mode, in competition with possession by net and coble, can create the full title to the fishings.

Assuming that, in this case, the *whole* right of salmon fishings is to be conveyed, the question of setting up a title by possession does not arise.

It would be a different matter if the disponer proposed to convey to the memorialists 'All and whole the salmon fishings in' a given stretch of water 'by rod and line only but excepting from the right of fishings hereby conveyed any right to fish in the said stretch of water by net and coble'.

A conveyance in that form, arguably, conveys to the memorialists a right of rod fishing only and reserves to the disponer the right to fish by net and coble which he might transmit to another disponee. See the form of conveyance of salmon fishing in the *Encyclopaedia of Legal Styles*, vol 4, Form 312 at p 261, where the whole and entire right of salmon fishings in a given stretch of water is conveyed, and, in contrast, the conveyance in Form 315 at p 265, where there is conveyed to a disponee the mere right to fish with one rod only in a given area of water. The second form of conveyance in Form 315 is not dissimilar to the conferring of a servitude right of way over a given access route which does not deprive the grantor from conferring a similar right of access to other grantees as well.

On the other hand (to take that analogy a step further), if a disposition conveys the solum of an access road to a disponee, so that he becomes the proprietor thereof, but prohibits the disponee from using that solum for any purpose other than as an access to an adjoining property, the whole right of property in the solum of the road passes to the disponee; and the disponer retains no remaining rights therein which he could pass on to anybody else. In particular, the disponer could not confer a right of access over that solum on any other disponee, because he has conveyed the full right of property in the solum of the access route under a restriction limiting the use to an access only.

As I understand the position here the disponer is proposing to convey the salmon fishings in the fullest sense but to limit their mode of user. There would therefore be no question here of the disponer reserving to himself any remaining right in the salmon fishings or any right to exercise these fishings by some other method which the memorialists are prohibited from exercising in their title.

For these reasons, I regard the limitations on the fishing right as unobjectionable, *provided* the memorialists are prepared to accept that a condition of this kind is consistent with the right which they are seeking to acquire.

2   In view of my answer to question 1, I do not think it necessary to delete the clause restricting the exercise of the right to rod and line only.

3   The suggested substituted Clause octavo may more acceptably express the limitation which the disponer is seeking to impose on the memorialists and, to that extent, I would regard it as an improvement on the clause proposed by the disponer. I would regard that as a matter for negotiation between the memorialists and the disponer; but I do not think that either clause imperils the title of the memorialists to the *whole* right of fishings, assuming that is what is conveyed to them under the dispositive clause of the proposed conveyance.

If the memorialists are still concerned as to the nature of the restriction in Clause septimo, a clause along the following lines might be accepted by the disponers as achieving the same result, without implying the same limitation on title which is causing anxiety to the memorialists, namely:

> 'Notwithstanding the absolute nature of the conveyance of the salmon fishings hereinbefore conveyed, and without in any way derogating from or limiting the title of our said disponees and their foresaids to the said salmon fishings, it is hereby expressly provided and declared that our said disponees and their foresaids shall not in all time coming exercise the right to fish for salmon and fish of the salmon kind by any method other than by rod and line, which restriction is hereby imposed with a view to securing the use and benefit of the salmon fishings hereinbefore conveyed in accordance with the purposes of Clause octavo hereof.'

I think that makes it perfectly clear that the whole of the salmon fishings are conveyed to the memorialists but that, in exercising their right to fish, the memorialists have agreed to deny themselves the right to fish by net and coble or any means other than rod and line. If the restriction is phrased in these terms, there cannot be any possible doubt as to the nature of the title which the memorialists are acquiring.

Manual, para 8.3.

13   *Special cases – tenements*
Tenement – definition of roof – allocation of costs for repair

Date: April 1986

Memorial
There was an outbreak of dry rot in a tenement building stemming from defective maintenance of the roof.

The proprietors agreed that the roof and liability for repairs thereto were mutual, but three questions arose:

1   What is the definition of 'roof'?

2   Should the cost of eradication of the dry rot within the top floor be treated as mutual?

3   Did the fact that the outbreak of dry rot was apparently attributable to lack of maintenance of the roof affect the liability for repairs?

Opinion
I am asked for my opinion on three questions relating to an outbreak of dry rot and liability for resulting repairs in a tenement building.

1   *What constitutes the roof?*
Surprisingly, there is no authoritative statement either in the institutional writers or in any of the cases on the exact delimitation of the 'roof' of a tenement. There are, however, two cases which are closely in point.

In *Taylor* v *Dunlop* (1872) 11 M 25 the proprietor of a dwellinghouse containing two square storeys and the unoccupied roof void above the upper floor sold the second or upper flat of the tenement, and imposed on the disponee a burden of maintaining and upholding the roof of the tenement without any right of relief from the lower proprietor. Some time later, the proprietor of the upper flat proposed to extend his property into the roof void, and the owner of the lower flat objected.

It is important to note, however, that, apart from the burden of maintaining the roof, the dispositions of the upper and lower flat were otherwise silent as to the ownership of the roof or roof void.

In that state of title, and in particular in the absence of any express provision in the titles as to the ownership of the roof, the court held by a majority that the owner of the upper flat also owned the right to the space between the ceiling of his flat and the sloping roof over the house; and accordingly was entitled to use the roof void for his own purposes. It is significant, however, that Lord President Inglis dissented, and took the view that, when the upper flat was conveyed, it was necessarily bounded on its upper surface by the mid-line of the joists separating the ceiling of the upper flat from the roof void.

In *Watt* v *Burgess's Trustees* (1891) 18 R 766 two dwellinghouses on the second floor of a tenement together with the attic storey of the tenement were conveyed to a disponee, under burden of a fourth part of the cost of maintaining the roof. The owner of the second floor and attic then proposed to convert his attic flat into a square storey and to build another storey on top.

The court held that he was not entitled so to do on the basis, *inter alia,* that the second floor and attic flats conveyed to the disponee were merely a stratum carved out of the larger estate of property which theoretically extends upwards indefinitely. On that view of what was conveyed, accordingly, the upper-floor proprietor had no right in the air space immediately above the slates and so could not encroach upwards into that air space.

In the present case, the 1979 disposition conveys to E Ltd a dwellinghouse on the third or top floor of the tenement. Taken by itself, and consistently with the construction of the conveyances of flats on lower floors in the tenement, this would imply that the disponee acquired a right of property only as far upwards as the mid-line of the joists forming the ceiling of his flat.

In addition, that same disposition then conveys a right in common with the other proprietors in the tenement to the outside walls, *roof,* etc.

I also observe from the timber specialists' reports that there are water pipes and water tanks in the roof void which, I assume, serve all the flats in the tenement.

Although the matter cannot be regarded as altogether free from doubt, my view in this and comparable cases is that, taking into account all these factors, the whole of the roof and the roof void, extending downwards to the mid-line of the joists which form the base of the triangle of the roof and sustain the ceiling of the top flat, is 'roof' in terms of the provision in the title, and therefore belongs, in common, to all the proprietors therein. For the same reason, the whole of that area including the whole roof structure and the beams above referred to down to the mid-line are subject to the common repairing obligation in the titles.

2   *Is the cost of eradication of dry rot within the top-floor flats to be treated as a mutual item?*
The position here is undoubtedly somewhat complicated.

(*a*) For the reasons given above, my view is that the beams sustaining the ceiling of the top-floor flat are owned exclusively by the top-floor proprietor up to the mid-line thereof and, above the mid-line, are the common property of all proprietors in the tenement as part of the roof. Accordingly, if the whole of a ceiling beam has to be replaced because the existing beam has rotted, half the cost would fall on the top-floor proprietor and the other half would fall on the proprietors of all the flats in the tenement.

(*b*) Dry rot in any of the beams forming the sloping timbers holding up the slates, the sarking if any, and any vertical supporting beams between the sloping roof timbers and the horizontal beams forming the base of the triangle of the roof are wholly the responsibility of all the proprietors of the tenement as a mutual repair to the roof.

(*c*) In terms of the title, the outside walls are mutual along with the roof and other items in the tenement. Insofar as the dry rot has attacked laths or timbers forming part of the main wall, these too are mutual repairs and the responsibility of all the proprietors.

(*d*) Any infestation in an internal wall will be the sole responsibility of the proprietor of that flat except where the internal wall divides one top-floor proprietor from another, in which case the responsibility would be mutual to those two top-floor proprietors.

(e) If the dry rot has spread down as far as the floor, the same position obtains as in relation to the beams sustaining the ceiling: the floor-boards and the joists supporting the floorboards down to the mid-line thereof are the exclusive property of the proprietor of the upper flat and must be replaced and repaired by him, whereas that part of the joists supporting the floorboards below the mid-line are the exclusive property of the proprietor below and must be repaired by the lower proprietor.

(f) Windows and window frames are not, in my view, part of the main walls; accordingly, if there is any infestation in windows or window frames, the cost of repair thereof falls on the owner of the flat exclusively.

3 *Does the fact that the outbreak of dry rot is apparently attributable to lack of maintenance of the roof in any way affect the liability for repairs?*

It is not suggested in the memorial that any of the proprietors in the tenement knew of the defective state of the roof and, in that knowledge, failed to take steps to put matters right. Assuming that to be the case, there seems to be no duty on any proprietor of a flat in a tenement to carry out regular inspections in order to ensure that repairing and other comparable obligations are implemented. Further, the duty of each proprietor to implement his common law obligation under the law of the tenement does not imply an *absolute* duty. If damage to the tenement results, there is therefore no liability on any individual proprietor unless negligence or *culpa* can be established.

That rule would apply here with equal force, and, since it seems unlikely that any individual proprietor in the tenement had reason to know of the defective state of the roof but ignored it, failure to maintain the roof would not in any way alter the ordinary liability to repair in terms of the titles or at common law.

For a general discussion on the nature of the liability of a proprietor in a tenement to implement his common law and conventional obligations as to maintenance, etc, see *Thomson* v *St Cuthbert's Co-operative Association* 1958 SC 380.

Manual, para 8.6.

14   Special cases – tenements – roof burdens – examination of individual titles
Law of the tenement – variations – Conveyancing (Scotland) Act 1874 – Land Registration (Scotland) Act 1979

Date: July 1991

Memorial
A purchaser wanted to buy a second-floor property in a tenement, the title to which contained a burden to maintain the roof, chimney heads, etc, on

the basis of feuduties payable. There were six flats in the tenement. The titles to four of the six made no reference to the roof.

Opinion was sought, first, as to whether the roof burdens were apportioned on an equitable basis, and, secondly, as to how many of the titles of the individual properties in a tenement should be examined prior to purchase.

Opinion

1   It is certainly the case that, in the absence of any express contrary provision in all the titles, or all the *relevant* titles, the law of the tenement applies. Insofar as the roof is concerned, the law of the tenement dictates that the proprietor of the top flat owns the roof and roof space immediately above the same. If there are two (or more) flats on the top floor, each owns that part of the roof immediately above him.

It is also the case that, in the absence of express contrary provision, the top-floor proprietor has an absolute obligation, based on common interest, to maintain the roof in wind- and watertight condition for the protection of the whole tenement, at his own sole expense. This obligation applies to the whole roof if he owns the whole of the top floor, or to that part of the roof which covers his particular flat, where there is more than one flat on the top floor.

It is also undoubtedly the case that, with older properties such as the tenement here, liability for roof maintenance is likely to be by far the costliest maintenance obligation, so that, if the whole burden lies with the top-floor proprietor, that is indeed a serious matter.

The law of the tenement can be varied by express provision in two ways.

(*a*)   In the conveyance of an individual flat, there may also be conveyed to the disponee a right in common with the other proprietors of flats in the same tenement to various components of the tenement including, for example, the solum, foundations, main walls and roof. The style of clause, and the inclusion or exclusion of individual items in the tenement, vary from one set of titles to another.

(*b*)   Whether or not there is any reference to a right of common property, it is also commonplace and competent to incorporate in a disposition an express repairing obligation requiring individual proprietors of individual flats in a particular tenement to contribute towards the cost of maintaining, say, the roof, which would otherwise be the exclusive liability of the top-floor proprietor in a specified proportion. Again, the method of determining the proportion varies. It may be equal, it may be by reference to rateable value, or it may be, as in this case, by reference to apportioned feuduty.

Commonly, individual titles of individual flats contain both these elements, ie, there is a conveyance of a right in common to the roof, etc, and, in addition, there is an explicit obligation to contribute towards the cost of maintenance thereof.

It is not sufficient, however, for a condition to appear in the title to the top flat in a tenement purportedly apportioning the cost of the repair of the roof in certain proportions as among all the proprietors of flats in the tenement. Such a provision will only effectively distribute the burden of maintenance if an equivalent provision appears in all the other titles of every flat in the tenement. Occasionally, such a provision appears in the title to the top flat only, and no others, in which case nothing is achieved and the whole liability for roof maintenance remains with the proprietor of the top-floor flat. Occasionally, a repairing obligation of this kind appears in some but not all the titles, in which case, depending in part on the wording of the clause, the top-floor proprietor may be entitled to recover some of the cost of maintaining the roof but is left with a larger overall share in that, in part, he is bound to contribute under his title and, in part, in relation to those flats which contain no maintenance provision, the law of the tenement continues to apply and the top-floor proprietor bears that share which might otherwise have been imposed on a lower-floor proprietor.

Where a right in common is conveyed to all proprietors in the tenement, but nothing is said about maintenance, the general view seems to be that they are under obligation to maintain the common items in equal shares.

The foregoing is simply by way of general background.

Turning now to the title in question, the disposition of the west half flat, second floor – the flat in which your client is interested – contains a conveyance of a right in common with the other proprietors to the solum and the back green but nothing else. So far as burdens are concerned, there is a reference to the original feu charter. The disposition then apportions feu duty, and purportedly imposes a burden of payment of a share along with the other proprietors in the tenement – pro rata according to apportioned feuduties – of the common expense of upholding and maintaining common passage and stair, back green and walls, *roof*, chimney head, rainwater conductors, soil and other pipes, and all others common or mutual to the said tenement.

Examining this particular title in isolation, there is a valid apportionment of the cost of maintaining the roof. But, as stated above, it is not sufficient for a burden to appear in one title. It must appear in the title for each flat in the tenement in order to spread the burden among all the proprietors.

The disposition of the west half flat on the first floor above the ground floor of the tenement also conveys a right in common with the other proprietors to the solum and to the back green but nothing else. When it comes to burdens, the feu charter is again referred to. It apportions the cumulo feuduty and imposes the burden of payment of a part or share, along with the other proprietors in the tenement, pro rata according to apportioned feuduty of 'the common expense of upholding and maintaining the whole of the said tenement'.

I am bound to admit that I have not come across this form of burden before and I am not sure as to how it falls to be construed.

That being so, there are I think several possible meanings to be put on this clause, which indicates that the court might hold that the purported burden of payment of a share of the common expense of upholding and maintaining the whole tenement is not sufficiently precise to impose a real burden.

Alternatively, since the burden takes the form of imposing a liability to pay a share 'of the common expense', the court might well hold that this was a provision of limited application and was intended to apportion only those expenses of maintenance which, in the law of the tenement, are common to all proprietors therein – for example, the cost of maintaining the common passage and stair, which is invariably a common liability. But the provision cannot be taken literally as imposing a liability to share in the cost of maintaining 'the *whole* tenement' because the whole tenement includes, in the main, the individual flats therein and the internal structure, fittings, etc, which are clearly the liability of the individual owners.

In the result, whatever the intention may have been, I think the burden fails in its purpose and would not be given effect to by the court. The resulting position therefore is that, notwithstanding a fairly clear repairing obligation in the title to the top-floor flat, that obligation is ineffective simply because it is not repeated in the titles of the other flats on the lower floors and therefore the law of the tenement continues to apply, leaving the two top-floor proprietors to shoulder the whole burden equally. If part of the roof covers the common stair, the liability for the maintenance of that small part of the roof would be a common liability on the users of the stair.

The original feu charter could have apportioned the cost of specified repairs on individual flats if and when sold to individual owners; but a general obligation imposed on the original vassal to erect and maintain the tenement, while binding on individual owners severally, does not in my view achieve that result.

The law of the tenement would apply to apportion the cost of such maintenance among individual owners, which produces the same result so far as your client is concerned (see *Duncan Smith & McLaren* v *Heatly* 1952 JC 61). Further, if the feu charter itself achieves this result, why impose a separate burden, purportedly to the same effect, in each disposition?

2   The second question is whether, in examining the title to a top flat in a tenement with particular reference to the maintenance of the roof, it is sufficient to examine, in addition, merely the title to the flat immediately below or whether the titles to all the flats should be examined.

There are a number of variables which may affect the position.

(*a*)   Where the title in question extends to the whole of the top flat, the law of the tenement implies at common law that the owner of that flat is liable for the maintenance of the whole roof in a wind- and watertight condition for the benefit of the proprietors below, on the basis of common interest.

Where there are two or more flats on the top floor:

(i) each proprietor is liable in the law of the tenement to maintain that part of the roof immediately above his flat but nothing more; and
(ii) where the common stair goes up to the top floor in such a way that part of the roof covers the common stair, as it normally does, all the proprietors in the tenement using the common stair (which may or may not include the proprietors of the ground-floor flats) are jointly liable in equal shares for the maintenance of that part of the roof covering the common stair.

(*b*) The proprietor of a flat on any floor other than the top floor will not be liable to contribute to any part of the cost of maintaining the roof (except the common stair as noted above) unless:

(i) there is a specific real burden in his own title imposing, in clear and unambiguous terms, an obligation to contribute towards the cost of the roof by reference to a fraction (eg, 1/8th), by reference to the rateable value, for which provision is made in the Abolition of Domestic Rates etc (Scotland) Act 1987, by reference to feuduty, which continues to apply even though feuduties are redeemed as they may or may not be, or on some other basis. Provided the method of determining the share is sufficiently precise, the lower-floor proprietor will be liable for that share of the cost of the roof. The shares need not be equal; or
(ii) the title of the lower-floor proprietor gives him a right in common to the roof.

Generally speaking, the same applies to any other items for which a specific repairing obligation is imposed in the individual title – for example, main walls, drying green, boundary walls, etc.

(*c*) Broadly speaking, conditions imposing obligations to maintain individual parts of a tenement can be constituted in three common ways.

(i) The original feu charter or disposition may occasionally contain a detailed code for the maintenance of the whole tenement including the roof and other common items. On the recording of the disposition, these burdens immediately become real upon the whole tenement and every individual flat therein. Accordingly they continue to apply in every subsequent disposition of every flat in which the original charter or disposition should be referred to for burdens. Even if not so referred to, since the burdens have been made real initially by the recording of the feu charter or disposition, they probably transmit against singular successors of individual flats. While it *may* be technically possible to confer a right in common to roof, solum, etc, in the original tenement title, I have never seen this done.
(ii) By deed of conditions. This is commonplace in the West of Scotland but, until comparatively recently, not so common elsewhere. The deed of conditions, like the original feu charter or disposition referred to above, will contain a code for the whole tenement prescribing the basis of repairing obligations for each flat. There are, however, two traps here.

—In the case of *any* deed of conditions recorded prior to 4th April 1979 it is essential, for the purposes of the Conveyancing (Scotland) Act 1874, s 32, that each break-off disposition of an individual flat in the tenement *must* refer to the deed of conditions for burdens. Unless it does so, the burdens are not imported into that particular title. In other words, where a deed of conditions is recorded prior to 4th April 1979, no real burdens are actually created by the recording of the deed.

It is only when the deed is referred to in a title that the conditions are imported into that particular title but not into any other title unless likewise referred to therein. Accordingly, it is perfectly possible that, where a deed of conditions is recorded before 4th April 1979, it may have been referred to in some of the titles of individual flats but not in others. In that case, the conditions apply only to those flats where the reference is included.

Where a deed of conditions is recorded on or after 4th April 1979 the Land Registration (Scotland) Act 1979, s 17, applies. Under that section, on the recording (or registration in operational areas) of a deed of conditions, all the burdens therein immediately become real burdens and there is therefore no need subsequently to refer to the deed of conditions in individual break-off dispositions, although this is, of course, good practice. *But* that only applies 'unless it is expressly stated in such deed that the provisions of' the 1979 Act, s 17, are not to apply. It is possible, under this section, to allow certain burdens to become real at once on the recording of the deed of conditions post 4th April 1979 but, by express provision, to exclude certain burdens unless they are specifically referred to in each subsequent disposition.

It is commonplace for a deed of conditions to be recorded which *expressly* disapplies the provisions of s 17 to the entire deed. In that event, the position is the same as for a deed of conditions recorded pre 4th April 1979, ie, the real burdens will only become real if the deed of conditions is subsequently referred to, and then only in those titles in which the reference appears. I have not, so far as I recall, seen a deed of conditions which disapplies the 1979 Act, s 17, to some only of the conditions but not the whole, although this is clearly competent under the terms of s 17.

—Frequently a deed of conditions relating to a tenement or a development estate generally will contain an elaborate definition of what are to be the common parts (eg, solum, roof, etc) in tenement titles. This is perfectly competent and is good practice, *but* merely to include such a definition of common parts does not automatically create rights in individual titles to individual flats on the recording of the deed of conditions. Instead, even though the deed may purportedly create common rights in a tenement, it is essential that each subsequent break-off disposition of each flat should specifically convey, as an addendum to the description in the disposition, a right in common to the common parts of the tenement as defined in the deed of conditions. Lacking such a conveyance, no right in common will vest in the disponee.

(iii) The third common way of constituting conditions is by express provision in the individual break-off disposition of each flat. This was the commonest situation until comparatively recently; now a deed of conditions has become much more generally used. Where this method is adopted the share of the cost of repairs of common items in the tenement, including the roof, etc, will become a real burden on the proprietor of an individual flat in the tenement *only* if his title contains that express provision but subject to the qualification dealt with below in cases where the individual title conveys a right in common – for example, to the roof. In this context, in my opinion:

—it is not sufficient to impose a detailed code of mutual contributions for individual items in the tenement in the first break-off disposition and then, in subsequent dispositions, simply to refer to that break-off disposition for burdens. The reason is that, under the reference provisions in the 1874 Act, s 32, real burdens need no longer be set out at full length in every transmission. Instead, a real burden 'may be validly and effectually imported into any deed ... relating *to such lands*' – ie, if the top flat is the *first* to be conveyed away, in any subsequent deed relating to that flat – 'by reference to a deed' (here, the first break-off disposition of the top flat) 'applicable to such lands'. Clearly, a reference to burdens contained in a top-flat disposition which is inserted in the disposition of a lower flat does not comply with the 1874 Act, s 32, requirements and is therefore inept; and

—the argument that the original feu charter bound the original vassal to maintain the tenement as a whole does not, in my view, effectively create an obligation on individual disponees of individual flats to contribute towards various items in the tenement under which, in the law of the tenement, individual proprietors are solely responsible for maintenance. This point was dealt with at some length in answering the first question in the memorial.

The individual break-off disposition of each flat may, in addition or alternatively, convey a right in common to certain common items in the tenement, typically the solum, main walls and roof. It is believed that, where a right in common is so conveyed, each proprietor having such right is equally liable for a share of the cost of maintaining the common items as being a common owner. See an article in (1983) 28 JLSS 472 where K. G. C. Reid explains the difficulties in seeking to recover a contribution to common repairs on the basis merely of common ownership.

I think it follows from the foregoing that, unless a detailed code for the apportionment of burdens has been imposed in the original title to the whole tenement, as in (i) above, or unless a deed of conditions has been recorded on or after 4th April 1979 in which the 1979 Act, s 17, is not disapplied, as in (ii) above, it is essential, to be sure of the position – particularly in relation to the top flat and maintenance of the roof – to examine the title to *every* flat in the tenement. I cannot see any purpose in examining only the title to the flat immediately below, and I am not aware of the source of that suggestion. It would be valid only in the case of a two-storey building but not for the normal three- or four-storey tenement. For a case in point, there is a short comment in (1968) 13 JLSS 90, referred to at [para 33.76 of the 6th] edition of the *Conveyancing Manual*, where the above views are summarised in condensed form.

If the procedure I have advocated is not followed, the situation which exists here would be overlooked. Apparently there was a detailed provision in the title to the top flat apportioning the cost of maintenance of the roof, etc, on an equitable basis but that condition had not, at least in my view, found its way into the titles of the lower flats and was therefore not effective as a real burden on those flats. This left the proprietor of the top floor with a misleading title in terms of which, apparently, he was only liable to pay a share, whereas, in fact, he would have been liable for the whole cost of maintaining the roof above his flat.

Surprisingly, Halliday, para 21–65, states that it is not usual in practice to examine the titles of flats other than the flat being purchased. He goes on '[B]ut if there are circumstances which indicate the possibility of conveyancing error, such as a history of disposal of various flats for the first time by different persons over a considerable period, it may be prudent to make enquiry. It is one of the advantages of a deed of conditions applicable to the whole tenement that it significantly diminished this risk.' The inference is that while he accepts in theory that examination of the title to every flat is necessary, he does not regard it as essential in practice, although admitting the risk.

For my part, I have no hesitation in advising that a solicitor who is examining a title to a flat, particularly a top flat, even where the individual title contains an apportionment of burdens on an equitable basis, is taking a risk if he does not examine all the other titles. If he fails to do so, I think that he would be liable in negligence. The basis for this view is that solicitors go to a lot of trouble, particularly when purchasing a top flat, to ensure that there is specific provision in the missives to the effect that the burden of maintenance of the roof, etc, is shared equitably; but, as with other aspects of missives, unless this is followed up in the examination of title stage to ensure that the apportionment of maintenance has been properly carried through and has been duly constituted as a real burden in the title of every individual flat, the solicitor has failed in his duty to the client. Having said that, however, I would be willing to bet that 95 per cent of solicitors in Scotland take the risk and do not insist on looking at every other title.

Take a tenement of six flats, three west and three east, ground, middle and top. Suppose that there is a positive obligation imposed on each of the three westmost flats to pay a one-sixth share of the cost of maintaining the roof of the tenement (ie, the whole roof, covering both west and east flats and the common stair) and that, in the titles of the three eastmost flats, nothing is said about maintenance of the roof. The position is as follows.

(a) In the law of the tenement, each proprietor on the top floor (ignoring the common stair and roof thereover) is responsible for maintaining the roof over his flat. Suppose that the proprietor of the westmost top-floor flat spends £600 on maintaining and repairing the roof above his own particular flat. He then looks to the titles to see what he can recover from the other proprietors in the tenement. He can clearly recover £100 from the ground-floor west and middle-floor west flats. But since the titles of the three eastmost flats are silent, he cannot recover anything from any of those proprietors. So he pays £400 and the two other westmost flat proprietors pay £100 each.

(b) If the proprietor of the eastmost top floor flat spends £600 on repairing the roof above his flat, he is in a slightly better position. He can recover £100 from each of the three westmost flats because, in this case, all three west flats have a common repairing obligation in the title. But he cannot recover anything from the ground and middle eastmost flats. Accordingly, the eastmost top-floor proprietor pays £300, and each of the three westmost flat proprietors pay £100 each.

(c) Carrying the illustration to its logical conclusion, if there is a repair of £600 to that part of the roof which covers the common stair, each of the three westmost flats must contribute £100 because their individual titles expressly so provide. The remaining £300 would then be payable in equal shares (ie, £50 each) by all six proprietors in the tenement as being responsible jointly for the common stair.

(d) Possibly, however, if the main door flats on the ground floor have no rights in the stair, only the middle- and top-floor proprietors would be jointly responsible at common law for maintaining the roof above the common stair, in which case the contributions would be £100 from each of the three westmost flat proprietors in terms of the specific obligation in each of their titles which relates to the whole roof, plus £75 each from the two middle- and the two top-floor flats under the law of the tenement.

The same general principles apply if a right in common to the solum, main walls, roof, etc, is conveyed to each individual owner but if there is no specific repairing obligation in the title. This is in fact not a common situation, although it can occur, and I have not thought it worthwhile to set out a detailed computation of the individual contributions.

Manual, para 8.6.

15   Special cases – water rights
Flow of water – possible diversion due to operations on neighbouring land – whether owner of land affected could prevent operations – rights of neighbouring proprietors

Date: February 1983

Memorial
The memorialist had taken a lease of a small property on an estate. A burn flowed through the middle of the land. The burn was subject to flash flooding throughout the winter. High concrete walls were constructed to ensure that the water stayed between defined parameters. Plans were made by the landlord to plant adjacent land with trees. The memorialist feared that extra water would be directed towards his land causing severe flooding and ruining any stock of young plants on his land. The memorialist wished to interdict the landlord from carrying out the proposed planting.

The memorialist sought an opinion on the following questions:

1   Could the landlord alter the drainage of the hill and expect the burdened

tenement to accept the added surge of water which must automatically follow in times of heavy rain?

2   What remedies did the memorialist have?

(*a*) Would interdict be likely to prove successful?

(*b*) What remedies would be available against the dominant tenement in respect of flood damage?

3   What course of action would maintain the interests of the memorialist?

Opinion

It is not easy to answer the questions asked by the memorialist with any precision for the reasons set out below.

Something may depend upon the nature of the operations proposed to be carried out on the adjoining property and in particular whether or not these operations are in the ordinary course of agriculture or forestry. Since I do not pretend to be an expert in these matters, I thought it appropriate to take some general advice from a company with whom I have regular dealings on forestry matters on the intentions of the new proprietor of the land in question in relation to these operations.

Subject only to qualifications regarding cross-drains, the operations to be carried out by the landlord are normal agricultural operations. That being so, I do not think it possible to argue that the landlord is creating a *novum opus* on the land in the objectionable sense. What he is doing, in my view, is simply exercising his prerogative as landowner to cultivate the land in whatever way appears to him most beneficial and appropriate.

In particular, the furrows which the landlord intends to open up on the upper property will be created solely for the purpose of the planting of trees and, as I understand it, this is the normal method of planting in such situations. The operation is therefore a perfectly natural forestry operation.

Admittedly, by opening up furrows, no doubt there will be an increase in the rate of flow of natural water from the upper property to the lower. However, that, as I see it, is merely incidental to the method of cultivation employed. There is no suggestion that the landlord is acting in any way out of spite or maliciously, and indeed he is not even carrying out artificial drainage. It just so happens that, because of the methods of cultivation employed, the flow of surface water towards the lower proprietor may be increased. Against that background I answer the questions posed in the memorial.

1   Yes, subject to the qualification that, as indicated in the case of *Campbell* v *Bryson* (1864) 3M 254, the court may think it appropriate to intervene and to regulate the rate of flow of surface water on to the inferior property. As the opinions in that case indicate, this is always a matter of facts and circumstances in individual cases. I am bound to say, however, that in my view, in a case of this kind, the court would be very slow to interfere with the normal and legitimate operations of the upper proprietor in the circumstances set out in the memorial even though, as a result, more

water may arrive on the inferior property. This is because the standard rule of law is that surface water can be expected to flow from the upper to the lower property and the inferior proprietor is bound to accept that flow of water even though, by operations on the upper proprietor's land, the rate and amount of flow may be altered.

I think it is pertinent to point out that, in *Campbell* v *Bryson*, the upper proprietor was introducing field drains into his property, the result of which inevitably would be to increase the natural flow of water on to the inferior property. In this case, in contrast, no drainage operation is involved, although the ploughing of furrows for the planting of trees may, to some extent, produce the same results. Lord Cowan, in *Campbell* v *Bryson*, summarises the position thus:

> 'Now, although to some extent there may be thereby imposed some greater burden on the inferior heritor, I do not think he has a legitimate interest to prevent the respondent draining his lands in the ordinary way in which such lands require to be drained in order to make them agriculturally useful and beneficial to the owner. The water is still to descend by the new operation from no other ground than it would have descended from naturally upon the inferior heritor. That is the important matter ... it is not contended that this natural servitude, which the inferior tenement is under, shall entitle the superior heritor to form a drain by which he shall convey to his ground water *which would not naturally descend on the inferior heritor* [emphasis added] ... but there is nothing of the kind contemplated here. All that is contemplated is simply this, that water that previously descended on the surface shall now ... the due cultivation of the land, be brought to the same point by means of drains which are to be covered. That is all that is intended, and I cannot see the least ground for holding such operation illegal, though it should cause a slight increase in the quantity of water.'

2(*a*) An action of interdict is certainly competent but I would be surprised if it succeeded without very compelling evidence on the part of the memorialist as to the resulting damage to his property from the proposed operations. Even in that event, I think the best that the memorialist could expect would be some regulation of the flow of water, possibly by insisting on certain cross-drainage, rather than an absolute bar on the upper proprietor from carrying out forestry operations of any kind.

In the passage in Erskine quoted with approval in *Campbell* v *Bryson*, Erskine qualifies the general principle with this rider:

> 'But, as this right' [the right to alter the natural drainage and so the natural flow of water from upper to lower properties] 'may be overstretched in the use of it, *without necessity*, [emphasis added] to the prejudice of the inferior ground, the question how far it may be extended in particular circumstances must be arbitrary.'

According to the judgment in *Campbell* v *Bryson*, that implies that the court may, in appropriate cases, regulate the operations of the upper proprietor. Whether or not they would intervene in a case of this kind is hard to say because there is no question here of the operations being carried out 'without necessity' since they are in the normal and natural course of forestry operations. Further, all we have so far is the opinion of the memorialist as to the result of the ploughing of these furrows, and no one has yet made any exact calculations of the increase in the natural flow of water. As mentioned above, evidence of substantial increase and inevitable resulting damage would, I think, be required before the court would intervene.

(*b*) Unless the court has been asked to intervene, and has intervened, to regulate the method of forestry operations on the upper property, and has laid down regulations which the upper proprietor has ignored, I do not think the memorialist has much chance of claiming damages arising out of what are normal and ordinary forestry operations.

3   In spite of the doubts expressed in answer to question 2, it seems to me that the only practicable method of proceeding is for the memorialist immediately to raise an action of interdict against the upper proprietor. The purpose of doing this would be not to prohibit operations altogether but to regulate the method of forestry operations in such a way as to minimise the impact on the memorialist of the increased surface flow of water. It is impossible to say whether the memorialist would be successful without more information on the location and geography of the properties. For instance, it might be possible for the memorialist to protect his property by introducing a cross-drain along his side of the boundary line to carry away the increased flow of water in a controlled fashion. If that can be done, I think it is the course of action which the memorialist would be told to adopt by the court. If it is impracticable, it is just conceivable that the courts might order the landlord, if he goes through with his operations, to put in a cross-drain to produce a similar result. Before any firm view could be formed on this aspect of the matter, the advice of a field-drainage expert would be necessary.

Manual, 8.9.

16   Methods of description – general description – marketable title
Description of flat – whether valid – plan – whether title marketable

Date: April 1991

Memorial
A written description of a flat did not identify the property clearly; it referred to a plan with no scale or indication of location. The question was whether it was a sufficient and valid description to render the title to the flat marketable.

Opinion
The classic definition of the requirements of a description of heritable property in a conveyance is given in Bell's *Lectures*, p 588, and quoted by Professor Halliday in *Conveyancing Law and Practice in Scotland*, para 18–05. According to Bell, the description must embrace everything

intended to be disponed; must not contain anything not intended to be disponed; and, most importantly, that the subjects disponed shall be capable of clear and absolute identification. Halliday comments that the description must identify the lands so as to distinguish them from all other lands; but that is all that the common law requires.

In the present case the written description in the deed makes no attempt to identify the subjects but instead refers to a plan which has no scale, no compass point, nor any indication of location and, as such, in the view of the purchasers' agents, fails to identify the subjects.

I have considerable sympathy with the criticisms made by the purchasers' agents but, in my opinion, the written description and the plan taken together do contain sufficient to identify the subjects conveyed in a manner which distinguishes the subjects from all others. That is Professor Halliday's requirement in the passage mentioned above and I think that it is met in this case. I base this opinion on the following factors.

1   In the written description, the subjects are described as an upper flatted dwellinghouse known as flat X in the estate shown within red boundaries on the plan annexed, together with the garden ground also shown within the same red boundaries and numbered X, and, in addition, the garage plot also shown within red boundaries and numbered X on the plan, and the garage (if any) erected thereon. There is no doubt that, if the plan had been prepared to the normal professional standards, that description would have been beyond challenge.

2   So far as the plans are concerned, the purchasers' criticisms are justified. I do not think it can be said, however, that the plan does not contain any form of location. We are not dealing here with the notorious 'floating rectangle'; instead there is detailed information which, taken together, leaves no doubt as to the general location of the flat in the context of the adjoining properties and services, including the road. So, for example, the flat in question is clearly one of six flats in a block on plots numbered seven to twelve. The written description tells us that these numbers relate to the estate, and presumably there is no duplication of plot numbers. The adjoining properties on either side are shown and the position of the road is clearly indicated. If that information is compared with the Ordnance Survey map (which I have not seen), I think there could be no doubt as to the *location* of this flat; and so, on that point, I think the misgivings of the purchasers are unfounded.

Given all the information on the plan, the lack of a compass point is not, by itself, sufficient to invalidate the description because, again, by matching the plan with the Ordnance Survey sheet, it would be possible to provide an exact compass point if that were thought to be necessary. In fact, however, a compass point serves no purpose if the property is otherwise adequately identified as, in my opinion, it is in this case. In fact, I am not sure that the purchasers' agents are correct in stating that there is no compass point. The somewhat blurred line and markings at the very left-hand edge of the plan may in fact be intended to indicate the north point, with north lying to the top of the plan; but I may be mistaken in this.

3   The lack of any scale on the plan is more serious and in many cases would undoubtedly be fatal. In the present case, however, I have come to the view, not without some difficulty, that the lack of any scaling is not sufficient to invalidate the description. What is described in the description is a flat in an existing building already constructed at the date when the disposition was delivered. The implication is that, at that date, there already existed on the ground an identifiable building comprising the six flats above referred to, with external boundary walls and steps leading thereto which are quite clearly shown, although on a very small scale on the plan in question. In addition, I suspect that the boundary features at the top and bottom ends of the red-encircled rectangle were already constructed at the date of delivery and are shown by black lines on the plan. In any event, even if they were not constructed at that date, it would be possible, by taking measurements of the building and then extrapolating them on the plan, to arrive at a fairly accurate identification of the red-enclosed area.

The same argument applies, generally speaking, to the garage and the garage forecourt, and to the common access paths.

4   I have no information on this point, but I think it almost certain that the titles to the other five houses in this block of six flats, and indeed the titles to the surrounding houses as well, will almost certainly contain a description based on the same plan. If so, that in itself materially assists in distinguishing this particular flat from all others and, at the same time, for practical purposes, it eliminates any possibility of challenge by a neighbouring proprietor whose title rests on an identical plan.

5   Finally, although no measurements are given, the area edged in red is stated to extend to 132 square metres, which is an additional and fairly important piece of information to complete the picture.

In the result, although the description in this case, and in particular the plan, hardly measure up to the standard which one might expect in a deed of this kind, the written description and the plan taken together do in my opinion satisfy the minimum requirements referred to by Professor Halliday in the passage quoted above.

I am fortified in that view by the fact that the deed has been accepted for registration by the Keeper. This is not, of course, a test of validity in itself; and, in a number of situations, deeds are recorded, albeit under protest from the Keeper, which are defective in a variety of ways. None the less, the Keeper has a duty to see to it that the Register of Sasines is so maintained as to secure its efficiency for the purpose for which it was created. That duty in turn obliges him to refuse to record any writ which does not contain the essentials to enable him to frame the statutory minute for the minute book. See *MacDonald* v *The Keeper* 1914 SC 854. In that case, the Keeper had refused to accept for registration a conveyance of 'my flat in the tenement 140 McDonald Road', which was not further described in the conveyance. In particular, the location of the flat within the tenement was not indicated in the deed. The court upheld the decision of the Keeper on the ground that the description was inadequate to identify the house in question so as to distinguish it from all the other flats in the same tenement. As the description was framed, it was equally apt to refer to any one of the several flats in the tenement building 140 McDonald Road. In the present case, the Keeper clearly felt that he had sufficient information in the description to satisfy the minimum requirements and so the deed was accepted for registration.

For this combination of reasons, although not without some difficulty, I conclude that the description is a sufficient and valid description and that the title to the flat in question is therefore marketable.

Further reading
Beneficial Bank plc v *McConnachie* 1996 SC 119, 1996 SLT 413 in relation to a specific description of a tenement.

Manual, para 8.12.

17   Methods of description – description by reference
Description in disposition by reference to description in contract of excambion – contract of excambion subsequently uplifted from register – whether description by reference rendered invalid – Conveyancing (Scotland) Act 1874 – accretion – procedure to cure defect

Date: September 1990

Memorial and opinion
I am asked to advise whether a conveyance by A Ltd in favour of the purchasers recorded in the General Register of Sasines in 1989 must be accepted by the purchasers as valid in terms of the antecedent contract for the purchase of these subjects entered into between them and A Ltd, in terms of which the sellers undertook to deliver a valid disposition.

The circumstances are unusual. A short time before the granting of the disposition in favour of the purchasers, the sellers had entered into a contract of excambion with their neighbour by virtue of which two areas of ground belonging to A Ltd were exchanged with two areas of ground belonging to the neighbour for the principal purpose of straightening marches. The contract of excambion is, in its terms, perfectly valid and effective and contains a detailed plan to which reference is made for the description of the subjects. It was duly recorded in September 1989 and the agents for the sellers assured the agents acting for the purchasers that it had been so recorded. They exhibited a copy and a copy of the plan so that the purchasers' solicitors could use it in a description by reference of the subjects conveyed to the purchasers under the disposition implementing the antecedent missives.

In view of the fact that the subjects in the contract of excambion were described primarily by reference to the plan, a description by reference was clearly the most convenient method of describing the excambed subjects in the conveyance in favour of the purchasers. In so doing, the agents acting for the purchasers naturally and justifiably relied on information provided by agents acting for the sellers as to the date of recording, and they used that date in the description by reference in their own disposition. In terms of the Conveyancing (Scotland) Act 1874, s 61, and Sched O thereto, as amended by the Conveyancing (Scotland) Act 1924, Sched D, the date of recording is one of the essential components for a valid statutory description by reference; and if the date is wrongly stated, at least by more than a matter of a few days, there is no doubt that such a description would not be valid under the statute. Whether or not such a description would be valid as a description by reference at common law is a different question, to which I will advert later.

After the disposition in favour of the purchasers had been recorded during September 1989, containing, *inter alia*, the statutory description by reference to the contract of excambion, the contract of excambion was withdrawn from Register House by agents acting for the sellers without consulting the agents for the purchasers or informing them that it had been uplifted. The deed was withdrawn so that the appropriate stamp could be affixed, since it had apparently been recorded unstamped.

It is neither necessary nor appropriate for me to comment on the propriety or otherwise of uplifting the contract of excambion in this way, without consulting the purchasers' agents. The purchasers' interests were materially affected because of the way in which the description in the disposition in their favour had been framed. In fact, it is probably the case that the point did not occur to the sellers' agents when uplifting the contract. As the result of being uplifted, and because of the delay which then occurred in the stamping of the document, the original recording date of X September 1989 was lost; and, although the contract of excambion has been or will be re-recorded in the Register of Sasines, it will bear a new recording date. As a result the sellers' agents, albeit inadvertently, have invalidated the statutory description by reference to the contract of excambion in the disposition in favour of the memorialists.

In terms of the missives, the sellers were bound to deliver a valid disposition. The professional practice, in such a contract of sale and purchase, is that the purchasers' agents frame the disposition, and in particular the purchasers' agents frame a description for insertion in that disposition in terms which they, in their discretion, consider to be appropriate to the circumstances in order to achieve a valid title for their client. It is not the function of the sellers' agents to revise the disposition, and in particular the description therein, except insofar as such revisals are necessary for the protection of the sellers. Admittedly, as a courtesy but not a necessity, the sellers' agents will in the ordinary way draw the attention of the purchasers' solicitors to inaccuracies in the draft disposition, so that these may be corrected, and that is part of the normal revisal process. For a further discussion on professional practice in revising, I refer to a series of articles by A. I. Phillips, commencing with 1 Conveyancing Review 229, although I really do not think there is any doubt as to professional practice on this point.

It follows from the foregoing that the sellers' agents, when revising a draft disposition, are not entitled to alter the terms of a statutory description by reference in such a way that what would be a valid description is rendered invalid because the sellers' solicitors have deleted, or propose to delete, one of the statutory essentials of the statutory description by reference. In substance, however, this is exactly what the sellers' solicitors have achieved by allowing a date of recording of September 1989 to be used in the description by reference in the draft disposition prepared by the purchasers' agents, and, after that disposition was recorded and without consultation, uplifting the contract of excambion from the record and in the process giving it a new recording date. As a matter of professional practice, the sellers' agents had no right to uplift the contract of excambion, at least without first consulting with and informing the purchasers' agents of the problem. There are, in any event, alternative solutions which might have allowed the original recording date to stand. That being so, the purchasers' agents are now entitled to insist that the matter be corrected so as to restore the validity of the statutory description by reference in the form in which they originally drafted it in the recorded title of the memorialists.

The sellers' agents maintain that no corrective action is required on two grounds.

1 *The description is a valid common law description.* I think it must be accepted that a description in a disposition cannot qualify as a valid statutory description by reference, and so cannot have the statutory advantages and statutory sanction provided by the 1874 Act, as amended, *unless* it complies with the statutory requirements. In this case, what was intended to be a valid statutory description by reference fails so to qualify, not through any fault of the purchasers' solicitors but by the unilateral actings of the sellers' agents in withdrawing the contract of excambion from the Keeper.

It must also be accepted that the conveyance in favour of the purchasers, although clearly not containing a statutory description by reference, *may* contain a valid description by reference at common law. For the reasons given here, I consider that fact to be quite irrelevant, but I would make two comments.

(*a*) There are undoubtedly indications in the authorities and in reported cases that a description by reference at common law is a valid way of describing heritable property. On the other hand, there is no decision directly in point which declares that such a description is a valid description for all purposes. Instead, the indications in the reported cases are all by way of *obiter dicta*. Further, none of these references declares that a common law description by reference, albeit valid, has the same statutory and conclusive effect as a statutory description by reference which complies with the statutory requirements. It is also legitimate to enquire why it was felt necessary in the Titles to Land (Scotland) Act 1858 to introduce a specific provision for the statutory description by reference, if that method of description was already recognised as valid at common law.

(*b*) In all the references to the common law description by reference, it seems to be envisaged that the description by reference at common law is by reference to an earlier recorded deed where the deed has already entered the Register of Sasines and the recording date is known and specified in the referring deed. In that situation, there cannot be any doubt as to the identity of the deed which is being referred to in the common law description. This occurs most commonly where, in a description by reference intended to comply with the statute, the necessary statutory reference to the county of registration is inadvertently omitted. Such a description by reference, containing all the other necessary statutory essentials, would certainly be valid as a common law description by reference. But that is not what we have here. Instead, the conveyance in favour of the purchasers refers to a contract of excambion ostensibly already recorded but which in fact was not duly recorded at that date and will not appear in the register or in the minute book as having been recorded on that date. This immediately raises some doubt as to the identity of the deed referred to for description; and of course if the deed referred to for description cannot be identified to the exclusion of all others, the description by reference may be invalid or at least may require proof. I refer here in particular to Burns's *Practice*, p 330, dealing with description by reference at common law and quoting from Lord McLaren's judgment in *Matheson* v *Gemmell* (1903) 5 F 448. Lord McLaren states that it is perfectly legitimate at common law to 'eke out' a generalised or incomplete description by reference to an earlier deed. In that case, the deed referred to had in fact been recorded and the date of recording was correctly stated. So, Lord McLaren also observes: '[I]n practice it was not infrequent to give a reference to *prior* deeds' [by which, I think, he must mean prior recorded deeds] 'for the purpose of enabling subjects to be more easily identified.'

The description in this case raises some doubt as to whether it is a valid description by reference at common law. That doubt would not have arisen if the description as framed by the purchasers' agents had been left undisturbed; and the doubt is created not by any fault on the part of the purchasers' agents but by subsequent actings unknown to them which, for the reasons given above, invalidated what had been a valid statutory description by reference. Accordingly, whether or not a valid description by common law was introduced into the disposition in lieu seems to me quite irrelevant.

In that state of matters, it seems to me that the purchasers' agents are perfectly entitled to insist that the sellers' agents put matters right.

2 *Accretion.* The sellers' agents argue that accretion will also operate to cure the defect in the title. This is correct but only up to a point, and it has absolutely no application to the defect in the description.

When A Ltd granted the conveyance in favour of the purchasers, the latters' agents thought that they were infeft in two of the areas to be conveyed (being areas in the contract of excambion) whereas, because of the withdrawal of the contract of excambion, the disponers were not in fact infeft therein. As a result, while the conveyance to the purchasers may be valid as a general disposition of these two areas, it is not a conveyance which, as it stands, can create an infeftment in these two areas for the benefit of the purchasers. So, although the disposition in favour of the purchasers is now on the record, there is no doubt that the purchasers are not infeft in these two areas because, at the date of the recording of the purchasers' title, the sellers were not infeft therein. The only way in which the purchasers could have obtained infeftment in these areas, given that the sellers were not infeft, was by the incorporation of an appropriate clause of deduction of title.

If the contract of excambion is recorded now, that will create an infeftment for the purchasers in the two areas in question, and accretion will operate to validate their infeftment therein from September 1989, being the date of the recording of the disposition in favour of the purchasers. To that extent, therefore, accretion will correct the lack of infeftment. I would emphasise two points, however.

(*a*) The recording of the contract of excambion now will validate by accretion the infeftment of the purchasers in the two areas in question if, but only if, no impediment has occurred in the meantime to prevent the operation of accretion. Such an impediment could have occurred, for example, if a receiver had been appointed to A Ltd in the interim, or if they had gone into liquidation. Accordingly, searches will be required down to the date of the recording of the contract of excambion in the Register of Sasines and in the Companies Register to make sure that A Ltd remained competent to convey the two areas up to the date of the recording of the contract of excambion.

(*b*) While the recording of the contract of excambion may, and almost certainly will, correct the lack of infeftment in the two areas concerned and, to that extent, will validate the purchasers' title beyond challenge, subject to clear searches, the operation of accretion in this way has absolutely no effect on the invalidity of the statutory description by reference which remains invalid as a statutory description regardless of accretion. Accordingly, while the recording of the contract of excambion is necessary to produce the accretion effect, it does not solve the problem of description.

In these circumstances, remedial action is required to put the purchasers' title beyond challenge in the form which the purchasers' agents intended the description in that title should take. They drafted the description to achieve that effect. That effect would indeed have been achieved on the information provided to them by the sellers' agents, but, by the subsequent withdrawal of the contract of excambion, the statutory description by reference which the purchasers' agents were careful to incorporate in their description has been invalidated. That is quite sufficient to justify the purchasers' agents insisting on rectification.

A short illustration underlines the point. Suppose that, at the examination-of-title stage, the purchasers' agents had submitted a draft disposition to the sellers' agents containing a statutory description by reference. Suppose that, for whatever reason, the sellers' agents had deleted the date of recording of the contract of excambion from the purchasers' agents' draft description and, when returning the draft, stated that they had deleted that date because it was unnecessary, and, without it, there would still be a valid description by reference at common law. If the sellers' agents had persisted in that attitude, the purchasers' agents could have raised an action of implement and the court would have insisted that the deleted date of recording be restored to the draft disposition. The uplifting of the contract of excambion has exactly the same effect and in my view the court would take the same attitude as a result.

That being so, in order to put the purchasers' title beyond challenge and restore it to the state in which it should have been, there are, I think, three alternative ways of proceeding.

(*a*) Obtain from A Ltd a conveyance of new in favour of the purchasers. This will also involve obtaining new searches brought down to the date of recording of the new disposition and assumes that there is no impediment in A Ltd's title or capacity to dispone which has occurred in the interim. In addition, it may also be necessary for the purchasers themselves to reconstitute any securities already granted over the property on the faith of the original description.

(*b*) As an alternative, it must be possible, although there is no direct precedent on this particular point, for the parties to petition the court for rectification of the disposition using the new facilities in the Law Reform (Miscellaneous Provisions) (Scotland) Act 1985, s 8. Under s 8(1)(a), where the document (the purchasers' disposition) fails to give effect to the agreement (the missives) and fails to express accurately the common intention of the parties to that agreement at the date when it was made, the court may order the document to be rectified in whatever way it thinks appropriate to give effect to the common intention. The common intention here was to produce a valid statutory description by reference for the reasons stated above, and that common intention has been frustrated by the actings of the sellers' agents. In these circumstances, I see no difficulty in the court ordering rectification. The only somewhat unusual result will be that the deed recorded during September 1989 will be rectified so as to contain a description which refers to a deed not recorded until some months later. In practice, that would be an impossibility, but, given the provisions of s 8, I see no reason why that should be an impediment to the granting of an appropriate order in this case. The only purpose of stating the date of recording is to give the description its statutory quality and provided the date of recording is stated, the deed must have that quality, even though the recording date is posterior to the date of recording of the deed itself.

Alternatively, under s 9(4), the court might order the purchasers' disposition to be rectified as from the later date of recording of the contract of excambion. In the circumstances, this might be a more logical step. It would be equally effective so far as rectification and the validity of the description in the purchasers' disposition are concerned; and it would also be perfectly effective so far as infeftment in the two areas is concerned as from the date of the recording of the contract of excambion. On balance, I am inclined to favour taking the later date for rectification because it avoids the anomaly of a description by reference in the purchasers' disposition which refers to a future (and at the date when that deed was prepared unknown) date of recording of the contract of excambion. But there may be other reasons why it would not be appropriate – for example, if there are any securities with an order of ranking.

Under s 8(4), a document so rectified shall have effect as if it always had been so rectified. That, however, refers purely to the technicalities of the description. It does not avoid the necessity of subsequent searches against A Ltd to make sure that they were still in a position to convey the two areas in question at the date of recording of the contract of excambion and these searches must be obtained. The same applies if a later date is fixed under s 9(4).

(c) If the sellers' agents decline to co-operate in either of these alternatives, it is open to the purchasers' agents to raise an action of declarator or of implement. The purpose of the action of declarator would be to obtain a decree from the court which categorically stated that the description in the purchasers' disposition was as valid and effectual a title in favour of the purchasers as it would have been if it had contained a correct statutory description by reference not subsequently invalidated by the actings of the sellers' agents. Whether or not the court would be prepared to grant such a declarator, I cannot say.

Alternatively, or if such an action of declarator were not obtained, then the purchasers are undoubtedly entitled to raise an action of implement against A Ltd for delivery of a disposition containing a valid statutory description by reference. Again, further searches would be required.

Whichever of these methods is adopted, the whole expenses must be paid by the sellers' agents since they are wholly, albeit inadvertently, responsible for the position and must take the consequences of having so acted.

Of all the foregoing methods available, the simplest and quickest would be an action for rectification under the 1985 Act if that is competent, which I think it must be. But, if a decree under that section cannot be obtained because the court thinks it inappropriate under the circumstances, the other alternative methods of correcting the title remain available.

Further reading
Conveyancing (Scotland) Act 1874, Sched O, replaced by Sched D to the Conveyancing (Scotland) Act 1924.

Manual, para 8.16.

RESERVATIONS

18   The implication of reservations
Dwellinghouse – standing timber – discrepancy in boundary – right of access – mine workings

Date: March 1988

Memorial

A number of questions arose in relation to a title.

1   It was not clear whether a right of pre-emption in respect of a dwelling-house and a reservation of standing timber had been drafted such that they would pass to the memorialists who wished to purchase the property and exercise the right of pre-emption over the dwellinghouse. Was Professor McDonald of the view that both had been validly created?

2   A discrepancy was noted in the boundary between a deed recorded in 1977 and one recorded in 1983. Was the proposal to provide a corrective disposition which narrated the position stemming from the 1977 deed sufficient to protect the memorialists?

3   Was a formal letter sufficient to grant a servitude right of access?

4   Looking to a mineral reservation clause, it appeared to the memorial-ists that payment for any damage caused by mine workings would only be in respect of damage done to the surface and buildings – for example, a lorry knocking down an outhouse – and not for any damage caused by the actual workings – for example, subsidence. Professor McDonald was asked for his interpretation of the clause.

Opinion

1   I have always had serious doubts as to whether or not a reservation of standing timber could be competently constituted as a real burden or real condition binding on a singular successor. Undoubtedly, such a reservation is binding as between the original contracting parties on the basis of contract, but whether or not it is real is a much more difficult question. The general rule is that a disponer can only reserve to himself such heritable rights as can completely be made the subject of a separate infeftment as a separate tenement. Thus, minerals and salmon fishings can competently be reserved. But it is possible to convey the minerals or the salmon fishings on a title which can be recorded to create an infeftment for the disponee. Whether that is feasible in the case of standing timber I very much doubt and, for that reason, I doubt the validity of the reservation as a real condition binding on singular successors.

73

The reservation of timber will certainly bind Mr and Mrs B, purchasers from Mr and Mrs A, the original disponers, and there would seem to be no reason why Mr and Mrs A should not assign their rights to that timber to a disponee from them or a subsequent proprietor. My advice would be for the memorialists to obtain an assignation directly from Mr and Mrs A.

In the case of the right of pre-emption, this is a recognised right which can be constituted as a real condition binding on singular successors in the affected property for the benefit of the original disponer and his successors. However, one of the requirements for a real condition of this kind is that the creditor area must be defined. The normal phraseology would therefore be to reserve a right of pre-emption in favour of the disponer and his or her successors in title as proprietors of the remainder of the subjects of which the 'pre-emption subjects' form part, but that has not been done in this case. Instead, the right of pre-emption is reserved to Mr and Mrs A 'and their foresaids', and, as the agents correctly point out, 'their foresaids' is not anywhere defined.

On this ground it can be argued that the right of pre-emption has not been properly constituted as a real condition and therefore would not be binding on a singular successor from Mr and Mrs B, although it may be personally binding on them as a contractual obligation. Again, it would certainly improve the position of the memorialists to take an assignation directly from Mr and Mrs A of their entitlement to the right of pre-emption reserved to them in the disposition in favour of Mr and Mrs B and I would so recommend. The assignation of both reserved rights can be included in the same deed.

2   I do not see any difficulty here. Granted that the two plans are not consistent *inter se*, there is no doubt that, in determining the matter of title, the 1977 plan rules; and that clearly excludes the area in question, circled in pencil on that plan. It also clearly defines the boundary on that side of the subjects conveyed by the 1977 disposition.

The fact that the 1983 feu disposition incorrectly shows the line of the south-east boundary cannot, of course, in any way affect the title or the extent of the property conveyed by the 1983 disposition. Being plainly an error in that respect, the necessary implication is, I think, that the boundary at that point will be mutually maintained on the original 1977 line, not on the 1983 line. In any event, mutual maintenance of the actual boundary, not the erroneous boundary on the 1983 plan, is implied at common law. I do not think that the 1983 disposition could possibly have the effect of imposing an obligation on the feuars to maintain a boundary wall in which they had no titular interest. To that extent, I consider the position acceptable and I think the method proposed by the sellers' agents will satisfactorily correct the error in the title.

3   There is no doubt that there is a discrepancy between the original access area coloured orange on the 1977 plan and the access area coloured green on the 1983 plan, in that the green access area extends significantly further north-eastwards than the 1977 access route, but for limited purposes.

What we are dealing with here is, of course, a servitude right, and it is well known that a servitude right can be created by mere agreement, provided the agreement is probative. Once so constituted, it persists in perpetuity until discharged or lost by the negative prescription. I therefore do not take the same view as the agents in this case. The right granted by Mr C to Mr and Mrs A was expressly granted not only to them but to their successors, and is referred to as a right of access for the specified purposes. This, in its terms, is sufficient in my view to set up a servitude right of access in perpetuity for the benefit of the proprietors of the subjects.

Having said that, I entirely agree that it is unsatisfactory for a right of such significance to the owner of the subjects to rest on this informal document. For one thing, a letter 'adopted as holograph' (which this is) is not probative. To be binding, it requires proof of the probative quality of the words 'Adopted as holograph – Mr C'. For another thing, in the case of servitudes, both dominant and servient tenements should be clearly identified, and that is not achieved by the document in this case. On the other hand, it is unnecessary for a formal document to enter the Register of Sasines, although that is probably advisable in all such cases.

My recommendation would be that the purchasers should insist on obtaining from Mr C a formal deed of servitude extending the access to the full length of the green line, defining the dominant tenement and imposing whatever restrictions are appropriate on the use of the access on this route. The deed should then be recorded in the Register of Sasines on behalf of the purchasers. I would not be happy to rely on the holograph letter from Mr C, although it may achieve its purpose.

4   I think that the memorialists are being pessimistic as to the provisions of the mineral reservation clause. The wording is fairly standard and, in my view, does not have the effect which the memorialists fear it might.

First, the right to compensation for damage done by underground workings is a natural right of property and, if the mineral owner is to escape liability for compensation, compensation must be specifically excluded in the title of the proprietor of the surface, which is not done here.

Secondly, the wording is such that, in my view, it does specifically cover compensation for underground workings which themselves cause damage to the surface of the land or to buildings erected or to be erected thereon. 'All damages which may be done to the surface of the said piece of ground or the buildings erected or to be erected thereon by any such workings or operations whether above or below ground as such damages shall ... be ascertained, etc.'

Under that clause, I think the superior is undoubtedly bound to pay for any damage caused by the actual workings, including subsidence damage, not only to existing buildings but to future buildings as well. I would be perfectly satisfied with a clause in this form.

Further reading
Requirements of Writing (Scotland) Act 1995.

Manual, para 9.1.

BURDENS

19   Real and personal conditions
Transmission to singular successors – proprietors with no right of
property – collection of common charges

Date: November 1990

Memorial
A housing association was in the habit of requiring purchasers to contribute
to the care of the common ground/open spaces that were part of the larger
area on which their houses were situated. No title to the common ground
was included in the dispositions. Owners questioned the right of the
housing association to make such a charge since the common pieces of
ground were not adjacent to their homes.

The following questions arose:

1(*a*) Was the obligation to keep in good repair, etc, and to contribute to
the care of the common areas contained in the deed of conditions a
real burden and transmitted to singular successors?

(*b*)   Was the right enforceable against a proprietor who had no right of
property in the common parts, but rather an interest in the amenity
of the neighbourhood?

2   If the answers to the above were in the affirmative:

(*a*)   Was the proprietor for the time being liable for any accounts for
common charges, including arrears dating before the current proprietor's date of entry? If so, was there likely to be prejudice resulting
from the delay in pursuing recovery?

(*b*)   Was settlement of the amounts due only a personal obligation, or
would it transmit against a successor?

(*c*)   Did the charges have to be apportioned on a transfer of ownership?

(*d*)   What were the implications of the decision in *David Watson Property
Management* v *Woolwich Equitable Building Society* for the collection of
common charges?

Opinion
1(*a*) In my opinion the obligation imposed on each feuar under the
specimen feu disposition to pay a defined share of the cost of maintaining, repairing and, where necessary, renewing roadways and all
other areas and open spaces within 'the feuing area' has been effectively
imposed as a real burden or real condition on the original vassal under
the individual feu disposition in his favour. As such, it will undoubtedly
transmit against each singular successor in the feu in perpetuity.

76

My only qualification is in relation to Clause ninth of the schedule of the deed of conditions which refers to all such areas as may be situated within 'the feuing area'. I have not seen a copy of the deed of conditions itself, only a copy of the schedule. The feu disposition does not in its terms define 'the feuing area', nor is it defined in the schedule to the deed of conditions, but I think I can safely assume that 'the feuing area' is explicitly defined in each individual deed of conditions for each feuing estate. The opinions expressed below are made on that assumption.

That qualification apart, I cannot see any way in which an original feuar or his successor could successfully maintain that the repairing obligations generally in the schedule to the deed of conditions, and particularly in Clause ninth dealing with roadways, open spaces, etc, had not been validly imposed as a real burden or a condition of tenure, because:

(i) The conditions in question, and in particular the conditions in Clause ninth, are contained in a deed of conditions duly registered or recorded in Sasines before the feu disposition was granted and delivered.

(ii) Although this may not be strictly necessary now in terms of the Land Registration (Scotland) Act 1979, s 17, the specimen feu disposition exhibited expressly declares that the feu is conveyed with and under the conditions, restrictions, real burdens and others specified in that deed of conditions.

(iii) I assume that in each case the feu disposition in question has been registered or recorded, which is essential to make the conditions real. But even if the original feu disposition was not recorded and the original or present proprietor has no infeftment, the conditions still bind him as uninfeft proprietor under a special feudal rule which I do not think it necessary here to amplify.

(iv) The conditions thus imposed on each vassal, and in particular the conditions in Clause ninth, in my opinion satisfy all the basic requirements as summarised in paras 10.9–10.14 of my *Conveyancing Manual* [6th edition]. The only possible argument which a feuar or singular successor might seek to raise is that the condition is not sufficiently precisely framed. As the memorialists are aware, in the case of real burdens and real conditions the courts apply very strict rules of construction and will examine closely the language in which any purported real condition is imposed. In this context, taking the provisions of Clause ninth in isolation, I do not see any prospect of the feuars generally escaping from the plain, clear and unambiguous obligation imposed on each of them to maintain, repair and, when necessary, renew roadways and open spaces, and, separately, to pay a share of the cost of such maintenance, repair and renewal in a defined ratio. There are, I think, only three possible grounds – all insubstantial – on which an individual feuar might seek to escape from the implication of the burdens imposed by Clause ninth:

—The deed of conditions declares that each feuar '*shall be respon-sible* for the maintenance ...'. It would be usual in practice to provide explicitly that each feuar shall maintain, repair and 'when necessary renew' rather than that each feuar shall be responsible. But, any feuar who seeks to argue that the language used here is not sufficient to impose a positive obligation to repair would certainly fail.

—The schedule to the deed of conditions declares that 'each feuar *shall be liable* for a share ...' whereas, in practice, it would be usual to say that each feuar *shall pay on demand*. Again, however, the intention seems clear and unambiguous and I do not think that a feuar has any prospect of success in evading liability to pay because of the wording used.

—The standard of repair required is to the reasonable satisfaction of the superiors. There is always a difficulty in a condition of this kind and it seems to me that 'the reasonable satisfaction of the superiors', in relation to a standard of maintenance or repair, is sufficiently precise to exclude any possibility that a feuar might escape from his obligation. Any feuar seeking to avoid the repairing obligation on this ground would found on such cases as *Murray's Trustees* v *St Margaret's Convent* 1907 SC(HL) 8, where the feuars were prohibited from erecting 'unseemly buildings'. The same question was considered more recently in *Mannofield Residents Property Co Limited* v *Thomson* 1983 SLT(Sh Ct) 71, where the question was considered in some depth by the sheriff with particular reference to the question of precision in relation to a prohibition on a disponee from placing any nuisance or obstructions on roads or streets or doing any other act which might injure the amenity. The Sheriff Principal on appeal, upholding the sheriff, concluded without difficulty that the notion of injury to residential amenity was sufficiently clear and capable of objective assessment to satisfy the 'need for precision' rule. Applying the reasoning of the sheriff in that case to the pro-visions of Clause ninth, I regard an obligation to repair 'to the reasonable satisfaction of the superiors' as falling within the same general principle as the clause in *Mannofield Residents* and I feel that this is therefore a perfectly valid real burden.

I can find no other possible grounds in the feu disposition or in the schedule to the deed of conditions on which any feuar could suc-cessfully claim that the conditions of Clause ninth (and, for that matter, other repairing and similar obligations in the deed of con-ditions) were not properly imposed as real burdens and would not transmit against a singular successor. Accordingly, in my view, the conditions in general and the provisions of Clause ninth in par-ticular were originally, and remain, enforceable in perpetuity.

1(*b*) My attention has been directed to the fact that, in each individual title, the roadways, etc, and in particular the open areas and other like spaces within 'the feuing area', were not conveyed to the individual feuars on the feuing estate as property in common. Provided the feuing area itself is defined, I regard this fact as wholly irrelevant, when, at the relevant date the whole feuing area has already been fully developed. I assume this applies in all these cases. It is perfectly common in feudal law to impose a repairing obligation on an individual vassal in respect to property or parts thereof associated with the individual feu but in which the individual feuar has no proprietary rights, though he will inevitably have a right of common interest. This regularly occurs in two typical situations:

(i) Roads. The practice as to roads varies. In some developments, the road is conveyed to the feuar up to the mid-line. In other cases, as in this case, the road is excluded from the feu altogether, and no right in common is conveyed. None the less, I think it is settled beyond argument that an obligation on each individual feuar to make up and to maintain the road (usually until taken over by the local authority although that is not strictly relevant) is enforceable.
(ii) Tenements. In the law of the tenement, the solum belongs to the ground-floor proprietor and the roof to the top-floor proprietor. Frequently, in tenement titles, this rule is varied to give each proprietor a right in common to the solum and the roof and, in addition, repairing obligations are imposed with particular reference to other common items. But it is common practice to impose pro rata obligations on individual owners of flats in a tenement to repair the roof, main walls, etc, without varying the law of the tenement so far as ownership is concerned. Accordingly, the owner of each individual flat may be taken bound to contribute to the cost of maintaining the roof without being given any proprietary share therein, although again, of course, the individual owner always has a common interest in the roof.

I entirely appreciate the point that individual owners of individual houses may resent having to pay a share of the cost of maintaining open areas at some distance from their properties. In practice, exactly the same situation regularly arises in relation to tenement blocks, particularly corner blocks, where, not infrequently, three tenement blocks, one in each of two streets at right angles and the third on the corner thereof, are treated as a single unit for repairing obligations in the roof, etc, although, for practical purposes, each of the three tenements could be treated as a separate unit. In the result, the proprietor of a flat in one tenement may find himself contributing a share of the cost of repairing the roof of the adjoining tenement, and this invariably causes considerable resentment. But there is no doubt as to his liability.

It is of course the case that, if the repairing obligations were restricted in scope (in the tenement illustration) to a share of the cost of maintaining the roof of one particular tenement, not all three, the share would be, say, one eighth as opposed to one twenty-fourth; and, overall, this evens out so far as all the feuars are concerned. But this is a very common cause of complaint from feuars not only in tenements but also in private developments and the explanation given above as to the varying ratio of the share of the cost of repairs seems to cut very little ice in practice. That, however, does not affect the rule nor does it in any way affect the liability of individual feuars.

Accordingly, the individual feuars here have no grounds for arguing that they should not be liable for the cost of common repairs to open spaces, etc, at some distance from their properties provided the open spaces lie within the defined 'feuing area'.

It follows that the obligations in Clause ninth are enforceable against each individual feuar in the feuing area, notwithstanding:

(i) that each individual feuar has no right of common property in the open space or other defined area on which expenditure by way of maintenance is incurred; and
(ii) the distance from the individual feu. The only question is whether or not the area in question lies within the 'feuing area'; if it does, the individual feuar is liable to contribute.

2(*a*) It is a standard feudal rule that the feuar for the time being is personally liable to the superior for only those feu duties which have become due during his own period of ownership. In this context, period of ownership implies, by virtue of the Conveyancing (Scotland) Act 1874, s 4(2), both the recording of the title of the individual owner and the giving of notice of change of ownership to the superior. Until both these events have occurred, and in particular until notice of change of ownership has been given, the disposing vassal remains personally liable to the superior for feuduty. The new proprietor only becomes personally liable for feuduty when both events have occurred.

It is likewise a standard feudal rule that the original vassal is liable not only to pay feuduty but also to implement all the other conditions of the feudal grant. In like manner, provided the conditions are duly constituted as real conditions or real burdens (which in this case they are, at least in relation to the repairing obligations in Clause ninth of the deed of conditions schedule), each successor to the original vassal is personally liable to the superior if he has a recorded title and notice of change of ownership has been given. In practice, however, because of the abolition of feuduty, the giving of notice of change of ownership has become erratic and is very often overlooked. This has the following consequences in relation to the question asked here:

(i) Adopting the accepted feudal role for feuduties, which I think must apply likewise to payment of the cost of common repairs in terms of the deed of conditions, the superiors are certainly entitled to require payment personally from any individual proprietor having a recorded title if, in addition, notice of change of ownership has been given. In that event, the superiors can sue the individual owner by way of personal action for payment of the amount outstanding. If, however, notice of change of ownership has not been given, then, strictly speaking, I do not think there is any *personal* liability on the individual owner, although there are other means of ensuring that the payment is duly made, as discussed below.

(ii) Whether or not notice of change of ownership has been given, the present proprietor is certainly not *personally* liable for arrears of maintenance payments which fell due during the ownership of some predecessor in title.

(iii) Notwithstanding the answer to question 2(*a*) above, however, the present proprietor is undoubtedly the feuar as defined in the deed of conditions, whether or not notice of change of ownership has been given. As such, he is liable under the obligation in Clause ninth which makes him responsible for maintenance and he is liable for payment of his share of the cost thereof. At first sight, this seems to be a contradiction of what is said in answer 2(*a*), but this is not strictly so. The reason is that, if notice of change of ownership has not been given, personal liability, enforceable by personal action, may not be available against the individual owner for the time being. None the less, the obligations in Clause ninth are real conditions or real burdens and transmit against and are enforceable against the proprietor for the time being, regardless of notice of change of ownership but, in that case, only by way of real remedies, ie, poinding of the ground, etc, which, for practical purposes, are wholly unsatisfactory and rarely used. As explained below, however, there is a much more effective method of securing payment, even though there may not be a direct personal liability in individual cases. The same applies to payment of arrears in respect of maintenance charges falling due before the date on which the present proprietor took his infeftment.

On the second point raised in question 2(*a*), my view is that the fact that the housing association have failed to issue notices, or to follow up notices already issued, requiring payment from the proprietor for the time being of a share of the cost of common repairs as against a previous proprietor does not prejudice the entitlement of the housing association to recover the amount due.

(i) There is no personal liability on the present proprietor to pay a share of the cost of common repairs which accrued prior to the date of his infeftment and the giving of notice of change of ownership. Undoubtedly, the previous proprietor remains personally liable for the payment of the outstanding accounts, whether rendered or not.
(ii) The entitlement of the housing association to recover outstanding accounts is, however, cut off by the short negative prescription, and any amount due and outstanding for more than five years is therefore lost and irrecoverable, at least by way of per-

sonal action, from the past or the present proprietor. Whether or not such an outstanding liability still constitutes a real burden is more difficult. In Sched 1 to the Prescription and Limitation (Scotland) Act 1973, a variety of obligations to pay sums of money, including liability for feuduty and other periodical payments under land obligations, are cut off by the short negative prescription. In contrast, except as provided in para 1(a) of that Schedule, any obligation relating to land is not cut off.

On balance, I am inclined to the view that the court would treat contributions to common repairs as a periodical payment. In that event, the obligation to pay is extinguished and must therefore, I think, cease, to remain as a real burden on the subjects. That being so, my inclination is to treat arrears which are more than five years overdue as being irrecoverable by any method whatsoever.

On the other hand, a mere administrative failure on the part of the housing association to record an intimation of a notice of change of ownership cannot relieve either the previous proprietor or the present proprietor of personal liability. But of course, for the reasons noted above, if notice of change of ownership has in fact been given but not recorded, that does cut off any continuing personal liability for subsequent contributions as against the previous proprietor who has intimated his change of ownership. It does not, however, in any way absolve the previous owner from personal liability for the cost of common repairs falling due before the date on which notice of change of ownership was actually received.

The resulting position can only be described, at best, as very unsatisfactory because:

(i) there is no way whatever in which the superior, even if he knows about it, can compel a departing vassal, whether original or a singular successor, to give notice of change of ownership in order to shift the personal liability on to the present proprietor; and
(ii) although in theory the outgoing vassal remains personally liable for future feudal obligations even after delivery of the disposition to his successor until notice of change of ownership is intimated, tracing the outgoing vassal, particularly after any substantial lapse of time, may be difficult if not impossible and recovery from him by personal action would almost certainly involve litigation and would be strenuously resisted.

That being so, my advice would be to adopt other methods of compelling payment, as indicated below, leaving it to the individual present proprietor in each case to recover what he could from the vassal from which he originally acquired the feu.

2(*b*) The exact date on which the personal liability of an individual vassal arises may cause problems in individual cases. In other words, given the obligation in Clause ninth which involves the imposing of liability for maintenance and repair and the imposing of liability to pay a share of the cost thereof – which, strictly speaking, are two different things

– at what date does an individual feuar become personally liable? Burns (4th edn), p 209, discusses a related problem in the context of sale and purchase and the apportionment between seller and purchaser with particular reference to a notice by public authorities requiring repairs to common properties. Six possible dates are suggested by Burns and no firm conclusion is reached.

For my part, I think I would be inclined to regard the date of the notice to the individual feuar requiring payment of his share of the common repairs as being the date at which the personal liability was constituted, but the point is clearly not beyond doubt.

If that is the correct view of the matter, then, applying the rule which applies in the case of feuduties, it is the case that the personal liability to pay a share of common repairs, taking the date of issue as the date when that liability arose, will determine which proprietor is personally liable for payment. There is no doubt that, at whatever date the personal liability arises, it will not transmit and cannot be enforced as a personal liability against the successor. But again, since we are dealing here with real conditions and real burdens, that does not mean that the sum is irrecoverable. It simply means that a personal action against the new proprietor is incompetent in relation to demands issued to the old proprietor before the change of ownership.

It is, however, an accepted feudal rule that payments due by a vassal to his superior, including in particular payment of feuduty and other payments falling due in terms of his feu charter – which would include payment of a share of common repairs – impose a personal liability on the vassal for the time being. As such, they are recoverable by personal action. But such payments are also real burdens on the feu and are therefore recoverable not only from the original vassal during whose period of ownership the liability arose but also as against singular successors by way of real actions, which include, in particular, real diligence such as poinding of the ground.

In practice, recovery by way of real action or real diligence is no longer considered practicable. There are only three types of real action available in such circumstances: the superior's hypothec; poinding of the ground; adjudication. None of these is satisfactory and they are rarely, if ever, used in modern practice.

Even though the real remedies for recovery are, for practical reasons, not normally resorted to, the feudal rule continues to apply – that any liability incurred by a vassal, while it may be recoverable by personal action as discussed above, is also automatically a real burden on the feu itself. As already mentioned, this makes available to the superior recovery of all sums due, whether by the present proprietor or a previous one by way of real action. Much more importantly, however, failure on the part of a previous or present vassal to discharge any such real burden renders the feu subject to irritancy at the instance of the superior by express provisions in his specimen feu disposition.

However, in the case of feuduty at any rate, the right to irritate only applies to arrears which have accrued during the ownership of the same superior. Thus, the housing association could not seek to irritate a feu in respect of liabilities personally incurred by a vassal prior to the transfer to the housing association. For practical purposes, I think that any such arrears would have to be written off, but, if this creates a serious problem, I can look at the possibility of recovery by real action or real diligence.

In respect of any areas which have accrued during the ownership of the housing association, there is no doubt that they have the right to irritate, which is available to them not only against the individual proprietor who owned the property at the time when the liability first arose but also as against the present proprietor of the feu, even though the liability first occurred prior to his taking over from his predecessor in title. So, Halliday, para 19–62, states: '[W]here a real burden or condition has been created in a feu grant, the superior may enforce it by the various remedies already discussed, including the drastic compulsitor of irritancy, and these remedies are available to successors of the Superior by reason of the continuing feudal contract by tenure.' They are also likewise available as against successors to the original vassal – see Halliday, paras 17–19 and 17–28.

There is no doubt that, in the present case, an action of irritancy is available to the superior in respect of failure on the part of each vassal to observe the conditions set out in the deed of conditions. In the specimen feu disposition the subjects are conveyed subject to the burdens in the deed of conditions; in addition, there is a specific declaration that in the event of any contravention of or failure to fulfil these burdens, the vassals shall forfeit their rights by way of irritancy and the feu then reverts to the superior.

Strictly speaking, irritancy, involving such forfeiture, is not a remedy for recovery of sums due because, on irritation of the feu, the subjects revert to the superior but he loses his right to recover arrears personally from the vassal against whom the irritancy was directed. In practice, however, that disadvantage is more apparent than real because, in any case where an irritancy or risk thereof has been incurred, the threat of irritancy, involving as it does forfeiture by the vassal (and the vassal's secured creditor) of his feu, freed and disencumbered of all heritable securities and other subordinate rights granted by him or his predecessor in title, is invariably sufficient to produce the desired result and to ensure discharge by the vassal of his feudal obligations, including payment of arrears of maintenance charges which have become real burdens by virtue of the provisions in the feu disposition and the deed of conditions to which it refers.

Accordingly, although, as stated above, *personal* liability will not transmit to a singular successor for arrears of common maintenance charges which accrued during a previous ownership, that restriction does not apply to the right to irritate; and so, for practical purposes, although in theory the present proprietor of an individual feu is not *personally* liable to pay arrears which accrued during the ownership of his predecessor in title, if he fails to pay (arguing that he is not personally liable), he renders himself liable to irritancy; and the threat of irritancy, in all bar the most extraordinary of circumstances, will almost certainly ensure prompt payment of outstanding arrears. Irritancy proceedings require a court action, and the raising of the action must be intimated not merely to the individual feuar for the time being but also to heritable creditors; and they will almost always see to it that the arrears are paid.

Taking into account the potential for irritancy which is available to the superiors, subject only to the restrictions referred to above, my inclination would therefore be, in all cases where arrears of contributions to common repairing obligations are outstanding, to write an explanatory letter to each of the vassals concerned, requiring payment; pointing out that these contributions constitute real burdens in terms of the titles; and that one of the consequences of failure to observe the obligations involves irritancy or forfeiture of the feu. If a letter in these terms does not produce the desired result and if an individual vassal still refuses to pay, I would advise the raising of an action of declarator of irritancy which, as mentioned above, must be served not only on the vassal but also on all others having an interest in the title, including in particular heritable creditors ascertained by a search. This, almost certainly, will produce the required payments.

2(*c*) No. There is no obligation whatsoever on the superiors to apportion common charges as between seller and purchaser. The deed of conditions, Clause ninth, imposes an obligation on each feuar which, in my view, means the proprietor for the time being at the date when the superiors seek implement of that obligation. Towards the end of Clause ninth, the method of levying the common repairing contribution is prescribed; and again, in terms of that clause, the superiors are to issue written notices to each of the feuars. In my view, that means the individual proprietor of each individual feu at the time when the superiors in their discretion decide to issue the relevant notice. It is entirely up to the agents for seller and purchaser to arrange for mutual apportionment of these notices as appropriate.

This has always been the position in relation to feuduty and still applies in those cases where it is not redeemable. I see no reason why any different rule should apply in relation to demands for payment of a contribution towards common repairs.

2(*d*) The decision in *David Watson Property Management* v *Woolwich Equitable Building Society* 1992 SLT 430 is limited exclusively to the relationship of a heritable creditor in possession and to debts due by the debtor. The decision in that case is based on the terms of the Conveyancing and Feudal Reform (Scotland) Act 1970, s 20(5), and the terms of that section have no general application which could in any circumstances be applied to the relationship between the superior and an individual vassal so as to modify the views expressed above.

The decision is relevant to a limited extent in the present situation in that, if a heritable creditor enters into possession, a question may then arise whether, and if so to what extent, that heritable creditor in possession is liable to the superiors for payment of the cost of common repairs as provided for in Clause ninth.

There is no doubt that, as a matter of general law, which is not affected by the provision of the 1970 Act, a heritable creditor who has entered into possession in the technical sense is personally liable for all the obligations of the individual heritable proprietor relating to the property as from the date when the creditor entered into possession. So, if a heritable creditor is in possession of an individual feu, and that fact is known to the superiors, they can recover from the heritable creditor by *personal* action all subsequent contributions to common repairs due in terms of Clause ninth.

The 1970 Act, s 20(5), goes no further than the common law as it applies between an original feuar and a singular successor. So, any purely personal obligation of an individual proprietor (in that case, a liability to pay the factor), not being a real burden, remained personal to the proprietor and did not transmit against the heritable creditor in possession.

The same will apply in any feu in which a creditor has entered into possession. If a liability has been incurred which is a real burden and if that liability has not been implemented by the vassal, including payment of a share of the cost of mutual repairs, I would regard that as transmitting as a real burden and recoverable from the heritable creditor but only by real action. Again, for practical purposes, that is not a satisfactory solution. But the threat of irritancy is equally applicable to a heritable creditor in possession as it is to an individual feuar; and so, by threatening irritancy proceedings, I think the superiors will succeed in recovering arrears of maintenance charges incurred during the period of ownership of the debtor/proprietor. As real burdens on the feu, the heritable creditor will almost certainly be willing to pay all such sums due in order to stave off the possibility of irritancy which, of course, would involve total forfeiture of his security.

No other points occur to me at this stage, but this opinion deals with complex matters and may raise special problems which I would be happy to deal with if required.

Manual, 10.3.

20 *Distinction between real conditions and real burdens – transmissibility*
'Beers tie clause' in disposition – whether would transmit to singular successors – whether enforceable – minute of waiver – alternatives

Date: March 1990

Memorial
The following questions arose with regard to a 'beers tie clause' in a disposition.

1   Was the clause transmissible, given that there was no reference to the disponee's successors in the clause?

2   Did the omission of a schedule of beers from the deed affect the validity of the burden and if so how?

3   Could the burden be enforced in view of the omission in 2 above?

4   If the burden was not transmissible, but the purchasers could not obtain a waiver, should an application be made to the Lands Tribunal, or was some other remedy available?

Opinion

1   I am asked to advise whether the 'beers tie clause' in the disposition in favour of the memorialists would transmit as a real burden against a singular successor as purchaser. I answer this question in the negative for five reasons.

(*a*)   First, as a matter of pure construction, the subjects are conveyed in the disposition to X Ltd and their successors and assignees whomsoever. There is no definition in the dispositive clause of the term 'the disponees'. When it comes to the beers tie clause, an additional burden is imposed: 'that the disponees undertake ...'; and that additional burden is declared to be a real burden affecting the subjects disponed. In the absence of any definition in the disposition of the term 'disponees', I think the burden is personal to X Ltd, and would not include singular successors. See, purely as illustration, *Peter Walker & Son (Edinburgh) Ltd* v *The Church of Scotland General Trustees* 1967 SLT 297. The court in that case decided that the intention of the parties in imposing the burden was irrelevant, and that singular successors were not bound by a clause which admitted of a doubt. There must obviously be a doubt here and, in the light of that decision, a very strong doubt indeed as to whether or not singular successors were intended to be covered by the clause. Accordingly, the ratio of that decision, in my view, is that the burden would not transmit against singular successors on this ground. It is true that the burden is declared real but that does not necessarily imply that it will transmit. It might have been made real for the better enforcement thereof.

(*b*)   The burden in this case is imposed in a disposition, not in a feudal writ. It is a standard principle in relation to burdens in a disposition that they must be praedial in their nature if they are to transmit against singular successors. In other words, the burden must be imposed by the disposition on the disponee and his successors as proprietors, for the protection of a *legitimate* neighbourhood interest on the part of the disponer. This means that the condition of its nature must be truly a 'neighbourhood' condition, designed to protect the amenity of an adjoining property retained by the disponer. I assume, on the facts stated in the memorial, that the brewery company do not retain any such property, in which case the condition is also unenforceable on this ground in a question with singular successors. See Gordon, *Scottish Land Law*, para 23–02, and the cases there cited.

(*c*) A purported real burden imposed by disposition will not be enforceable as against a singular successor in the subjects if the sole purpose for which the burden was imposed was to create a commercial monopoly or was in restraint of trade. See *Aberdeen Varieties Ltd v Jas F. Donald (Aberdeen Cinemas) Ltd* 1940 SC(HL) 52; *Phillips v Lavery* 1962 SLT (Sh Ct) 57; and *Giblin v Murdoch* 1979 SLT (Sh Ct) 5. The ratio of these decisions has recently been affirmed in the Outer House in *Donald Storrie (Estate Agency) Ltd, Petitioners*, 1987 GWD 20–774. It seems to me inevitable that the condition in this case was imposed purely in restraint of trade and on that footing cannot transmit against a singular successor.

(*d*) A real burden other than a pure money burden, if it is to transmit as such against singular successors, must be permanent. See *Corbett v Robertson* (1872) 10 M 329 and *Magistrates of Edinburgh v Begg* (1883) 11 R 352.

(*e*) Finally, on purely technical grounds, the real burden fails for lack of precision because (no doubt by inadvertence) the beers to which the beers tie clause relates are said to be those specified in the schedule annexed and subscribed as relative to the disposition, but no such schedule is annexed. In constituting a real burden, such an omission is fatal. There was, however, such a clause in the original missives and it may be that, given appropriate proof, the clause could be rectified under the Law Reform (Miscellaneous Provisions) (Scotland) Act 1985, s 8. But whether or not the court would rectify as against a singular successor, taking into account the provisions of s 9, must be open to doubt.

For this fairly formidable combination of reasons, my view is that there is no possibility whatsoever that the brewery company in this case could enforce the burden in the disposition as against a singular successor.

2   I have dealt with the omission of the schedule of beers in my previous answer. The immediate effect is to render the clause unenforceable but that does not affect the validity of the disposition as a title to the subjects.

3   The brewery company may be able to enforce the condition in the disposition as against the memorialists on a purely personal basis, relying either on the missives or on the clause in the disposition if amended by rectification under the 1985 Act. Since the matter is urgent, and since this aspect of the point does not affect the purchaser, I leave aside at this stage the question of personal enforceability on whatever ground because, for the reasons given in answer 1, that cannot conceivably affect a singular successor as purchaser.

4   If the brewery company refuse to grant a minute of waiver, there are, I think, four possible solutions.

(*a*) I understand that the title is at present with the Keeper for registration.

Representations could be made to him that the burden was unenforceable and so should be omitted from the burdens section of the title sheet. For a recent decision on this point, see *Brookfield Developments Ltd* v *Keeper of the Registers of Scotland* 1989 SLT (Lands Tr) 105. Although the decision of the Tribunal seems to be self-contradictory in parts, there is a clear statement in that decision at p 109 H–I that the Keeper has a positive and imperative duty not to include in the title sheet burdens which are unenforceable. If the condition does not appear in the title sheet, it will certainly not transmit against a singular successor.

(*b*) The validity and enforceability of the burden in the disposition as a real burden and its transmissibility against a singular successor could be tested by an action of declarator.

(*c*) As a real burden, the clause in the disposition may qualify as a land obligation, but, I think, fails so to do, because the brewery company cannot show that it was imposed as an obligation relating to land enforceable by a proprietor of an interest in land by virtue of their being such a proprietor. In other words, since they are not neighbouring proprietors, they do not have a praedial interest and so the burden in question is not a land obligation for the purposes of the 1970 Act. This in itself renders it unenforceable for the reasons stated above, but it also means that the Lands Tribunal would not discharge it.

(*d*) I would have thought that, in the circumstances, this was a transaction which might suitably settle on an indemnity, in that, in my view, there is no possibility of successful enforcement of the burden against a singular successor, and so the risk is negligible. In any event, failure to implement the burden in the disposition is not supported by an irritant and resolutive clause; and so failure to implement it would not incur an irritancy or otherwise imperil the title. At worst, failure to observe the clause would resolve itself into a question of damages and that is something which may suitably be covered by indemnity.

Manual, para 10.4.

21   The intention to burden
Schoolhouse to be used only for 'educational purposes' – condition breached – irritation of feu

Date: May 1990

Memorial
A feu charter in favour of an educational authority, granted in 1929, burdened the subjects conveyed with a provision that they should be used only for educational purposes. This burden was breached and the superiors wished to irritate the feu.

The memorialists queried whether an application to the Lands Tribunal might be successful, whether they should proceed with a compulsory purchase order, or whether there was an alternative.

Opinion

Two preliminary points fall to be disposed of.

1   I have not seen the whole file but, on the copy correspondence provided, there is a letter from X Estate, signed by the factor but not adopted as holograph and therefore not probative, dated July 1988, in terms of which the factor, on behalf of the superiors, agreed to accept a capital sum of £250 in payment of compensation for the minute of waiver previously requested by the council. In my view, by virtue of that acceptance, there was then an informal written agreement already in existence, as referred to by Lord McMillan in *Mitchell* v *Stornoway Trustees* 1936 SC(HL)56, where the facts are not dissimilar. On the strength of that letter, the council proceeded with their plans to erect two houses in the garden of the schoolhouse and, in the process, incurred substantial expense. This is clearly something which followed on naturally from the acceptance by the factor and is directly referable to that acceptance. Accordingly, the council having subsequently acted at considerable cost and to their substantial disadvantage on the faith of that purported but informal agreement and in a manner 'not unimportant', the agreement must be held to have been validated by *rei interventus*. To that extent, therefore, the superiors are committed to agreeing to the erection of the two dwellinghouses in the schoolhouse garden.

The solicitors for the superiors take the view that the council were in breach of the feuing conditions by permitting the house to be occupied other than as a schoolmaster's house. The tenant of the schoolhouse is, however, a schoolmaster in a teaching post, presumably employed by the memorialists, although this fact was not known to the solicitors when they wrote that letter. There is nothing in the feu charter which requires the schoolmaster's house to be occupied by a schoolmaster actually teaching in the school on the same feu. Under burdens clause (Second), the school building cannot be used for any other purpose; but mere non-use is not a breach of that prohibition. Under burdens clause (Third), the provision as to use applies uniformly to the entire feu, not merely to a part. The schoolhouse is, I think, still used for the purposes of the Education Acts. Accordingly, in my view, the council are not in breach of the feuing conditions. It therefore follows that, since clause (Third) has not been breached, the superiors are not entitled now to exercise the option of reversion provided for in that clause. I would make two further points about reversion.

(*a*) Clause (Third) purportedly imposes a real condition or real burden on the feuars but, in my view, that clause almost certainly fails to qualify as a real condition. The reason is that, in terms of clause (Third), if the feu ceases to be used 'for the purposes of the Education Acts' for the space of one year continuously, the reversion option comes into operation. It is settled beyond argument that a real condition, to be effective, must be expressed in clear and unambiguous terms, and, in particular, it must be evident on the face of the deed containing the burden or condition exactly what the feuar is required to do, or not to do, in order to comply with the provisions of the charter. If that is not self-evident from the terms of the charter itself or from the terms of some earlier recorded deed, the purported condition is ineffective and unenforceable as a real condition. In *Aberdeen Varieties Ltd v Donald* 1940 SC(HL)52 a purported real condition was imposed in a disposition by which the disponees were expressly prohibited from using the subjects for the performance of any stage play 'which required the approval of the Lord Chamberlain under the Theatres Act 1843'. The defenders maintained that, since the extent of the burden did not appear fully on the face of the title (it was necessary to refer to the Act to determine what was and what was not permitted), the condition failed to qualify as a real condition. The Lord Justice-Clerk took the view that there was substance in that objection, and Lord Jamieson considered it to be a fatal objection to the constitution of a real condition. The House of Lords did not require to express a view on that aspect of the condition because they found in favour of the defenders on a different ground. The fact that, in the *Aberdeen Varieties* case, the condition appeared in a disposition, whereas here it appears in a feu charter does not, in my opinion, make any difference in this context.

Whether or not the memorialists are to be considered as singular successors is not altogether clear but at least the point is arguable. If they fall to be treated as universal successors, they may be personally bound to give effect to the option.

(*b*) It is undoubtedly the case that a clause of return or of reversion operates automatically when the event provided for occurs, but in contrast to a clause of pre-emption or redemption each of which requires the vassal actually to convey the subjects to the superiors, none the less some formal evidence would be required to establish the facts. This would involve an action of declarator on the part of the superiors to establish that the right of reversion had come into operation (which in my view has not yet occurred) and that the superiors had exercised their option to enforce the right.

It follows from the foregoing that the superiors are not entitled to exercise their option under clause (Third) in the feu charter and to bring about a reversion of the feu; nor are the memorialists at present in breach of the feuing conditions. The question of irritancy has not yet arisen. That being so, it is still open to the memorialists to apply to the Lands Tribunal for a variation of the feuing conditions insofar as they obstruct their intentions and I would have thought that the chance of success is good. The proposal by the memorialists to use some of the surplus ground for housing seems to me to be a reasonable use which undoubtedly cannot be achieved without the consent of the superiors, given the present burdens in the title. If restrictions on building and use, as contained in clauses (Third) and (Fourth) of the feu charter, were the only obstacles to the proposals of the memorialists, I would have little hesitation in advising that an application to the Lands Tribunal would succeed.

However, clause (Third) of the feu charter contains not merely what is in effect a restriction on use but, also, purportedly creates an option for the superiors to recover the feu against payment of compensation in certain events. That condition may or may not be enforceable for reasons referred to above. No such condition has, so far as I am aware, been considered by the Lands Tribunal and there appears to be no case in point. But the recent decision of the Tribunal in *Banff and Buchan District Council* v *Earl of Seafield's Estate* 1988 SLT (Lands Tr) 21 gives some indication of the Tribunal's approach to conditions of this kind. In the *Banff and Buchan* case, the title contained a clause of pre-emption for the benefit of the superior. The council had already constructed local authority housing on the feu and applied to the Lands Tribunal for a variation of the feuing conditions to allow additional houses to be constructed. At the same time, the council asked the Tribunal to discharge the superior's right of pre-emption on the grounds that there was a conflict between the superior's right to pre-empt and the statutory right of council tenants to purchase their houses. The Tribunal refused to discharge the right of pre-emption *de plano* but proposed a modified pre-emption clause allowing the superior to exercise his pre-emption except in cases where the tenant of a dwellinghouse had a statutory right to acquire it. The logic of that decision would seem to indicate that, if the memorialists in this case sought to discharge the superiors' option to acquire (assuming it to be valid), the Tribunal might not agree, although I would hesitate to forecast what substituted provision they might suggest.

On the question of costs incurred by the memorialists in preparing plans, etc, I would have thought the chances of recovery were remote. The original application to the superiors was for permission to erect two houses and that was apparently agreed to. If I am right in thinking that the informal agreement permitting two houses to be erected has been validated by *rei interventus* and so is binding on the superiors, it is difficult to see what could be abortive expenditure. If, on the other hand, the court or the Lands Tribunal come to the view that there is no case for *rei interventus* and so no binding contract between the superiors and the memorialists as to the erection of the two houses, there are no grounds on which a claim for reimbursement could be based. Such a claim could only succeed if the abortive expenditure could be attributed to breach of contract on the part of the superiors. If there was no contract, there cannot have been any breach and there is no claim.

When it comes to the two further houses which the memorialists subsequently decided to erect on this area of ground, for which there was never any purported agreement, again, in the absence of any contractual arrangement between the parties and a subsequent breach of that contract by the Superiors, there cannot be any grounds for claiming recovery of any costs incurred on these two houses. It also seems to me unlikely that the memorialists would be awarded their costs in any application before the Lands Tribunal.

I am also asked whether the memorialists should proceed with a compulsory purchase order or if there is any other alternative procedure by which they could achieve the desired result.

So far as compulsory purchase is concerned, I do not think it is competent for a local authority to acquire by compulsory purchase land which is already in its own ownership, albeit subject to conditions which frustrate developments. On the other hand, under the Town and Country Planning (Scotland) Act 1972, Part VI, and in terms of the interpretation section, 275, the Secretary of State has power to authorise a local authority to acquire land compulsorily on certain conditions; and land includes any interest in land and any servitude or right in or over land. Clearly, therefore, it must be possible for a local authority to acquire the superiority rights in isolation as 'rights over land' affecting the schoolhouse and surrounding area or to acquire the superiority itself as an estate in land. Either of these acquisitions, if authorised and implemented, would achieve the objective of extinguishing or consolidating the *dominium directum* with the *dominium utile* and deny the superiors any right to interfere in the development. The superiors would be entitled to compensation but it would be fairly minimal. This seems a cumbersome procedure but it may be that, confronted with the threat of compulsory purchase, the superiors agree to negotiate on reasonable terms with the memorialists.

Further reading
Requirements of Writing (Scotland) Act 1995 for the effect on probativity.

Walker v *Strathclyde Regional Council* 1990 SLT (Lands Tr) 17.
Hamilton v *Grampian Regional Council* 1995 GWD 8–443.
Ross and Cromarty District Council v *Patience* 1995 SLT 1292.
Henderson v *City of Glasgow District Council* 1994 SLT 263.

Douglas J. Cusine, Pre-emption Clauses and the Right to Buy (1994) 39 JLSS 331.

Manual, para 10.14.

SERVITUDES

22   Servitudes and burdens compared
Drains from septic tank passing through neighbouring property –
procedure to create valid right

Date: May 1988

Memorial
A developer erected houses on a piece of ground. Drainage was by way of
septic tank and drains passing through a neighbouring property.

The following questions arose:

1   Had a valid, enforceable, servitude right been created?

2   If a servitude had not been created in the disposition, had such a right
been created by acquiescence over the previous seven to eight years?

3   If a valid servitude had been created, was it binding on successors of the
dominant tenement?

Opinion
1   Yes. As I understand it, two criticisms have been made as to the constitution of the servitude in the 1980 disposition by A in favour of B:

(*a*) That the disposition in favour of B, although it validly dispones the
ground with appropriate words of conveyance, contains no dispositive
clause so far as the servitude right is concerned. Undoubtedly this is so,
but I think it is now settled beyond argument that, in contrast to proprietary land rights generally, a servitude can be constituted by mere
agreement without requiring words of conveyance or disposition, and
that agreement need not enter the record nor qualify the infeftment.
See *Cowan* v *Stewart* (1872) 10 M 735 and in particular the Lord
President at p 739. '[I]t is quite true that, according to our law, a document of this kind is sufficient to constitute a servitude.' See also
Rankine, *Land Ownership* (4th edn) at p 427: 'Positive servitudes may
be acquired or imposed by express grant *or agreement*.' Accordingly, the
fact that, in the 1980 disposition, there are positive words of *de praesenti* conveyance in relation to servitude right does not seem to me to
be a valid objection. The question is whether or not there is evidence
of *agreement*, and in my view there clearly is.

(*b*) The second criticism is that the alleged servitude constituted by the
1980 disposition lacks specification. In relation to servitudes, it has
been judicially observed that in the constitution of a servitude less
precise language is required than for the proper constitution of a real

burden or real condition. The fundamental question is whether, from the language used, the intention can be adequately ascertained. Applying that test in this case, I have no doubt that a valid servitude has been constituted and that there is sufficient specification thereof in that:

(i) In the narrative of the disposition, the granter states that he has agreed to grant permission to the disponees to carry drainage from the houses to be erected on the subjects thereby disponed, although, admittedly, the grantor does not specify in the dispositive clause the extent of the servient tenement nor define the land through which the drain is to be taken. There is, however, a plan attached to the disposition which clearly defines the line of the drain with reference to the dominant tenement, being the subjects disposed by the 1980 disposition and coloured red on the plan, and, in my view, it sufficiently describes the servient tenement. There is a clear line of intermittent dots and dashes leading from the septic tank, through the subjects disponed and through adjoining land to the west, stated on the plan as belonging to the disponer. This is described on the plan as a wayleave for a six-inch tile drain from the septic tank outfall to the river. In all the circumstances, I would have thought that that was sufficient specification for this purpose.

(ii) In any event, even if sufficient specification is lacking, I understand that this agreement was then acted on to the extent that the septic tank was formed and the drain constructed along the line shown on the plan, and was so constructed to the knowledge and with the consent of the disponer of the 1980 disposition.

It is settled that if, following on a formal or an informal agreement, A, as proprietor of an area of land stands by looking on and without objection while his neighbour, B, at substantial expense and to A's knowledge, constructs a road or drain or water pipe on or through A's land, A is thereafter personally barred by acquiescence and by his actings (or rather by his inaction) from subsequently taking objection to the existence of the road, drain or pipe. For a case in point I would refer the memorialists to *Robson* v *Chalmers Property Investment Co Ltd* 1965 SLT 381. The facts in that case bear some striking similarities to the facts here. A cottage was conveyed together with a right to draw water from a spring or well some ninety-five yards to the north-east of the property. There was some doubt as to whether or not that right still subsisted. But in any event the owner of the cottage, to the knowledge and with the acquiescence of the owner of the surrounding land, carried out certain works on the water supply, including the improvement of the reservoir or collecting tank and the laying of pipes on and through surrounding subjects belonging to the servient proprietor. The servient owner, having originally acquiesced, later objected to the installation and sought its removal. Whatever formal rights may originally have been conferred on the dominant proprietor, he having acquiesced in the laying of the pipes and the installation of the dam, was held to be personally barred from subsequently requiring the removal of the water supply system. In my opinion, exactly the same principle would be applied in this case, even if the terms of the disposition were not sufficient to confer a valid and enforceable right, which, in my opinion, they were.

The servitude right (or purported servitude right if it was not validly created by the terms of the 1980 disposition) was none the less contained in a disposition which was recorded in the General Register of Sasines in 1980. Accordingly, any singular successor of the disponer must be held to have been aware of the existence of this right at the date when he acquired the servient tenement. I think it is now settled on authority that, where a servitude right enters the record (as it did here) *in gremio* of the 1980 disposition, that is sufficient by itself to constitute the right, whether or not it was followed by possession. For a discussion of this aspect of the matter, see *Balfour* v *Kinsey* 1987 SLT 144. But the point is barely relevant here because the right to lay the drain was in fact exercised and followed by possession, to the knowledge of the servient owner.

If the servitude was fully and validly constituted by the terms of the 1980 disposition, *proprio vigore*, as I think it was, that is sufficient to create a permanent right binding on singular successors. Similarly, if a servitude right is constituted by informal agreement followed by actings, the actings or the acquiescence on the part of the servient owner are sufficient to create a servitude right. Once so created, that right has all the characteristics of a servitude right duly created by express grant.

In either case, therefore, the servitude right so created, whether by formal or informal agreement followed by actings, has all the characteristics of a servitude so far as the owner of the servient tenement is concerned, and successive servient owners are bound thereby.

Even if a servitude right as such has not been duly constituted by express or informal agreement followed by actings, I have no doubt that the original disponer was personally barred from objecting to the installation of the drains.

In some cases, acquiescence is and remains purely personal to the original acquiescer. Thus, if the title to a house contains a restriction on the use of the property, limiting its use to dwellinghouse use only, and if, without any visible structural alteration or expenditure, the superior acquiesces in the use of the house for some other purpose, he may be personally barred from subsequently objecting to that use. But a singular successor from the superior would almost certainly not be personally barred in these particular circumstances.

It is a different matter entirely where the original potential objector acquiesced in the construction of a drain on his land at substantial expense and where the presence of the drain and the inevitable expense involved must necessarily be known (or be deemed to be known) to a singular successor of the original acquiescer, since the deed creating the right appears on the record. Thus, Rankine on *Personal Bar*, at p 62, states that a singular successor, with express, or *plainly implied* notice, is fixed with the consequences of his author's acquiescence, and he cites a number of cases in support of that proposition. The implication is that, given the terms of the 1980 disposition which have been made public by recording in the Register

of Sasines and the known presence of the drain through the servient property, the present proprietor, as singular successor of the original acquiescer,
is equally barred by acquiescence from objecting to the continued presence
of the drain on his property, even if no proper servitude had been constituted in the first place.

For this combination of reasons, I think the objections taken by the
purchaser to the title to the drain in this case are unfounded.

2   I have dealt with this point in my answer to question 1.

3   Again, I have dealt with this point in my answer to question 1.

Manual, para 11.1.

23   Implied grant or implied reservation
Neighbouring tenements – creation of servitude – reservation –
rectification – acquiescence

Date: May 1989

Memorial
The memorialists contracted to sell a cottage which they owned. The
purchasers objected to the title on the ground that the memorialists had no
right to discharge sewage into the septic tank which served the cottage and
adjoining property. The following specific questions were asked.

1   Did the proprietors of the cottage have a title to discharge sewage into
the tank?

2   If not, had a servitude right been constituted?

3   If not, could a reservation of necessity be made out?

4   Can a servitude right be created by acquiescence?

5   Was there any possibility of a claim for negligence against the purchasing solicitors?

Opinion
1   No. If the memorialists do have a right to discharge sewage, which in
my view is very doubtful, that right is certainly not constituted by virtue of
their title.

2   No. I do not think there can be any doubt about this. The reason is,
that, until 1972, the area of land containing the septic tank, which was then
conveyed to the adjoining proprietor, was vested in the owners of the
cottage. It is a standard rule that, for the constitution of a servitude right,
there must be two distinct tenements. In the present case, the separation of
the two tenements did not occur until 1972, and accordingly the possession
required to establish a servitude right without title could only start to run
as from 1972. The period required to create a servitude right without title
is twenty years, and so no servitude right has so far been created.

3   In the case of *Murray* v *Medley* 1973 SLT (Sh Ct) 75, referred to in the

memorial, the pursuer maintained that, having sold an area of ground through which, unknown to the parties, a main water pipe passed serving the disponer's own retained property, a servitude right to retain the pipe had been created by implied reservation in the disposition to the purchaser of the ground in question. In rejecting the pursuer's argument, the sheriff relied on a statement in an English case, *Union Lighterage Co v London Graving Dock* [1902] 2 Ch 557, where a servitude of necessity by reservation was defined as a servitude without which the retained property could not be used *at all*; not one merely necessary to the reasonable enjoyment of that property. This decision follows the earlier case of *Wheeldon v Burrowes* (1879) 12 Ch 31 which, *inter alia*, affirmed the general proposition that, if the grantor of a deed intends to reserve to himself any rights over the subjects disponed by him to a purchaser, he must reserve these rights expressly in the disposition. The necessary inference from that decision is that the creation of a servitude by reservation will never be implied unless it can be shown to be absolutely necessary for the occupation and use of the property retained. For practical purposes, this in effect limits servitudes by implied reservation to servitude rights of access to landlocked subjects and nothing more.

I am advised that the proprietors of both properties knew where the septic tank was situated and that it was used by both properties. This cuts two ways.

On the one hand, it can be argued that, if the parties to the 1972 disposition had that knowledge, the inference is that the disponee accepted that the disponer was to continue to use the septic tank.

Against that, however, it can be argued that, since both parties knew the position, the disponer, when granting the 1972 disposition without any reservation to himself of the continued use of the septic tank, cannot have acted in ignorance and so must have positively intended not to reserve to himself any rights in that septic tank.

The only solution on this point would be a reduction of the 1972 disposition or, under the Law Reform (Miscellaneous Provisions) (Scotland) Act 1985, s 8, rectification of the terms to give effect to what is suggested as having been the common intention of the parties to the 1972 deeds. It may be that such an action would have succeeded had it been raised as between the original parties to the 1972 disposition if the disponer could have proved that the disponee knew and accepted that the disponer was to continue to use the septic tank. But in *Anderson v Lambie* 1954 SC (HL) 43, where the question was raised directly as between original disponer and disponee, there are clear indications in the judgments that the disposition would not have been reduced if third parties, relying on the record, had acquired rights in the subjects conveyed by that disposition; and likewise, in the 1985 Act, s 9 (1), the court is *not* empowered to order rectification of a document where a third party (here the present proprietors), acting in reliance on the record, has acquired a title to the subjects.

Accordingly, it is now too late to contemplate the possibility of reduction or rectification in order to give effect to what might originally have been argued as having been the common intention of the parties in 1972.

4   There is no doubt that, in appropriate circumstances, the court will sustain a claim to a servitude right as having been constituted by acquiescence. The case of *More* v *Boyle* 1967 SLT (Sh Ct) 38 is referred to in the memorial, and certainly the question of acquiescence was debated in that case, but the court did not reach a conclusion one way or another. The sheriff observed that, to create a servitude by acquiescence, it would seem to be necessary that the thing acquiesced in should be visible and obvious, especially where it is of such a character or cost as to be inconsistent with its having been allowed merely during pleasure. *Robson* v *Chalmers Property Investment Co Ltd* 1965 SLT 381 is an illustration of such a case. The owner of the servient tenement, having acquiesced in the laying of pipes and the installation of a dam, was held to be personally barred from requiring the removal of the resulting water supply system.

In the present case, there are three difficulties confronting the memorialists.

(a) It cannot be said in this case that any costly operations were carried on under the eye of the owner of the servient tenement. In 1972, when the ground was conveyed to the adjoining proprietor, the septic tank had long since been installed. Thus the case does not fit easily into the general requirements for a servitude created by acquiescence as discussed in the two cases referred to above.

(b) It may be argued on behalf of the memorialists that, in accepting a conveyance of the ground in 1972 the disponee, knowing that there was a septic tank serving the disponer's property, must be held to have acquiesced in its continued use for that purpose. But that is not necessarily so. It could equally well be that the disponee, when taking the disposition, was under the impression that the disponer was to create his own sewerage system and, in the interim, refrained from objecting to the continued use of the tank (if he even knew about it) until the necessary works were carried out.

(c) However matters may have stood with the original disponee, an argument based on acquiescence seems almost unsustainable in a question with a singular successor from the original 1972 disponee unless it could be proved positively that the present proprietors knew that the tank was still being used by the memorialists (or their predecessors in title) and that, in that knowledge, they acquiesced in the continued use of the tank on an indefinite basis. Further, even if it can be shown that the present proprietors have thus far acquiesced, I am doubtful whether such acquiescence would bar them from now insisting on a discontinuance of the present use of the tank by the memorialists.

Accordingly, although there is the possibility of setting up a servitude right by acquiescence, I would not myself be optimistic of success, on the authorities referred to above.

5   Before I could answer this question, I would require more information as to the circumstances surrounding the acquisition of the property by the memorialists and the information available at that time to their solicitors. On the face of it, however, there is certainly the possibility of a claim for damages against the memorialists' solicitors on the footing that the

question of the sewerage system should have been more thoroughly investigated.

It is now generally accepted in the profession that a solicitor has a duty to ensure that, when purchasing a dwellinghouse for a client, the purchaser is guaranteed continued use of services such as water, drainage, electricity and the like. An offer to purchase a dwellinghouse regularly contains a standard clause designed to ensure that the purchaser is protected in this way. In the present case, I would have expected the offer to contain a clause on these lines. When the solicitors came to examine the title and observed the provisions relating to the septic tank in the 1954 disposition, I think they had a duty to enquire further as to the situation of the tank, looking to the 1972 disposition which conveyed away part of the property and with it the septic tank. If the memorialists' solicitors failed in what I consider to be their normal professional duty in these respects, then on the face of it they would be liable in damages.

On the other hand, much may depend on the terms of the survey report, if such a report was obtained, and on other information provided to the solicitors at the time of the purchase, particularly with reference to the location of the septic tank. It would, however, seem that, prima facie, there may be a case for a claim, and certainly that aspect of the matter should be explored further.

Manual, para 11.6.

SUBORDINATE CLAUSES

24   *Warrandice*
Errors in disposition – company name spelt incorrectly – errors in narrative – warrandice clause – whether rendered title unmarketable

Date: April 1983

Memorial
The memorialists, a limited company, concluded missives for the sale of part of an estate. The purchasers objected to the title on the following grounds.

1   The name of a consenter to two dispositions had been patently altered; the alteration was declared in the testing clause. The disposition was sealed with a seal containing a different spelling. Both spellings were erroneous.

2   The dispositions contained narratives which were incorrect – referring to an 'oral declaration of trust', whereas what was produced was an 'oath in respect of declaration of trust'.

3   The dispositions contained a warrandice clause in which the consenters were taken as bound in absolute warrandice. The purchasers argued that the clause was inept.

The memorialists asked whether, on any of the above grounds, the purchasers were entitled to reject the title as not being marketable.

Opinion
1   The defect is purely technical, but I think there is sufficient doubt as to the validity of the two dispositions to render the title unmarketable, since the deeds are both within the prescriptive period. I am fortified in that opinion by the view expressed by Professor Halliday (so far unpublished), which I take the liberty of quoting.

> 'Minor errors in the name of individual persons may not invalidate the deed ... on the principle of *falsa demonstratio*; but the separate legal *persona* created by incorporation of a company only exists in the company whose name is registered; and so a deed intended to be granted by or in favour of that company but which renders its name inaccurately is granted by or to a body which has no legal entity. In practice, a supplementary corroborative deed is necessary.'

In this case, the active consent and participation of A Ltd is essential to the validity of both dispositions on the facts there narrated, because B Ltd state explicitly in the narrative of each disposition that they have sold the subjects in *pro indiviso* shares to, *inter alia*, that company and, following on that sale, are acting as bare trustees. The narrative of each disposition further narrates that it is the consenters (including A Ltd), not B Ltd as trustee, who have sold their respective *pro indiviso* shares to C Ltd. It is therefore essential for all of the consenters validly to consent to the granting of the dispositions. Without proper evidence of consent the two dispositions, although *ex facie* validly divesting B Ltd and investing C Ltd, would remain open to challenge at the instance of a non-consenting purchaser on the rule in *Rodger (Builders) Ltd* v *Fawdry* 1950 SC 483. A Ltd are incorrectly designated in both deeds and cannot therefore be said to have validly consented.

I cannot find any Scottish case directly in point, but I would refer the memorialists to *Palmer's Company Law* (23rd edn) vol 1, p 79 and again at p 1134, for some related English authorities. Of the cases cited there, *Re Vidiofusion Ltd* [1974] 1 WLR 1548 confirms the view stated above. In advertising a winding-up petition, the name of the company was spelt 'Videofusion Limited'. It is clear from the judgment that, in the ordinary way, the courts in England will regard any inaccuracy in the spelling of a name as invalidating the necessary statutory advertisement. In this case, however, the court came to the view that the error in spelling was of such a minor nature that it could be disregarded, but McGarry LJ laid down four conditions, all of which must be satisfied before the courts will disregard even such a minor discrepancy in the spelling of a company's name. I regard it as significant that, notwithstanding that very minor error, the parties had to apply to the court for a dispensation from the statutory requirement and that the application was not simply dismissed as unnecessary.

In the present case, not only is the name of the company wrongly spelt in the two deeds, but a different and also erroneous spelling appears on the seal. In these circumstances, I do not regard the four conditions laid down in *Vidiofusion Ltd* as being satisfied. I therefore regard the objection to the title on this ground as being validly taken, and consider the title to be unmarketable on this ground.

The marketability of the title implies a title so regular in form and so correct in all particulars that no one late dealing with the purchaser will be able to take exception to it on any ground. As it stands, the title does not satisfy that requirement, although the defect is of a purely technical nature and is not such as to entitle the purchaser to resile. The memorialists must be given an opportunity to put the title right.

It may be appropriate to touch on the nature of the unmarketability in this case. Each of the dispositions is, *ex facie*, a valid and effective conveyance by the infeft proprietor to C Ltd, but in each case the narratives make it clear that the consents of all the nominated companies are required. On the assumption that the affidavit correctly states the position, all the requisite consents have been embodied *in gremio* of the two dispositions, except for the consent of A Ltd because of the error in the spelling of the name of that company in the deeds and on its seal. Each of the dispositions is therefore open to challenge, but only by A Ltd. Unless and until effectively challenged by that company, the two dispositions effectively convey the whole subjects to the disponees. All that is required to put the title right, therefore, is one deed by B Ltd and by A Ltd, using its correct name and a correct seal, narrating the error in the dispositions and expressly binding A Ltd as a consenter to the two dispositions and in the warrandice obligations granted therein. It is unnecessary, in my view, in order to validate the title, that the two dispositions should be reframed and re-executed by all the parties.

The fact that B Ltd is now in liquidation does not, in my view, bar it from granting the corrective deed because, by virtue of the expressed declarations of trust in the narrative of the two dispositions, it is undoubtedly holding the property as bare trustee for a number of companies, including one incorrectly designated in that narrative. Looking to the terms of the warrandice obligations in the dispositions, and to the fact that, as it now turns out, *quoad* the *pro indiviso* share of A Ltd, B Ltd has declared that it held that *pro indiviso* share in trust for a non-existent person, I think the liquidator of B Ltd is bound to grant the necessary corrective deed. The property was held in trust by B Ltd, and it is settled that property held in trust does not form part of the assets of a liquidated company. Therefore, so far as property held in trust by B Ltd is concerned, including this *pro indiviso* share, the liquidator is, I think, obliged to deal with it separately from the assets in liquidation and to implement the company's obligations as trustee *quoad* that *pro indiviso* share.

If A Ltd is in liquidation, that may pose problems, but there is no information on this point in the memorial.

I have also considered whether or not objection to the defect in the spelling of the name might be resisted, looking to the Trusts (Scotland) Act 1961, s 2 of which provides protection to a purchaser dealing with a trustee. Section 2 only covers cases where a trustee, in exercising one of the statutory powers, may be acting at variance with the terms or the purposes of his trust. But that is not the point in this case because, having narrated the sale to the purchasing companies, B Ltd declares itself to be a bare trustee for these companies as consenters; and it is the consenters, not B Ltd as trustee, who then sold to C Ltd. In my view, in these circumstances, the purchaser does not have the benefit of the protection afforded by s 2 to exclude any possible challenge by a non-consenting beneficiary.

2   Any writ within the prescriptive progress must be both intrinsically and extrinsically valid, which implies that a purchaser examining the title has a right to be satisfied on any material matter stated in the narrative.

In this case I do not consider that the mode of reference to the oral declaration in the narrative of the two dispositions is open to objection on the grounds stated by the present purchaser.

(*a*) I regard the description of the oral declaration as being substantially accurate. The affidavit cannot, in my view, be construed as a declaration of trust by B Ltd, because that would imply a deed granted in name of and by the company under seal, whereas the affidavit is simply sworn by two officers of the company who have been authorised by the company to make it. That authorisation by the company is not contained in any written document, but was simply granted at a meeting

103

of the company. In trust law, a trust may be created without a written document but the proof of the constitution of the trust requires the writ or oath of the granter. It is settled that the writ need not be a formal probative document, but some written document by the alleged trustee is a prerequisite to proof by writ as an alternative to oath. It may be that a minute of a company meeting, signed by the chairman as a correct minute, might come within the definition of writ for this purpose, but there is no indication in the affidavit that any such written minute exists. If so, I do not think that the affidavit, standing alone, would be accepted as a writ of the company for the purposes of the Blank Bonds and Trusts Act 1696.

(*b*) So far as title is concerned, the question as to whether or not a valid trust had been created prior to the granting of the dispositions is, in my view, irrelevant, and the reference in the dispositions to the earlier oral declaration of trust is technically unnecessary because, *in gremio* of the narrative in the two dispositions, B Ltd explicitly declares, in a probative deed executed under seal, that from a particular date it held the subjects in question in trust for the nominated companies. Each of the dispositions therefore operates effectively, by itself, as a declaration of trust for the purposes of the 1696 Act, superseding the earlier oral declaration, and so rendering irrelevant any question as to whether or not the earlier affidavit effectively evidenced the creation of the trust.

Since, in my view, the earlier affidavit is not by itself a declaration of trust, I think it follows that it is not liable to stamp duty.

The dispositions, however, contain an expressed declaration that B Ltd holds the subjects in trust for the nominated companies. That being so, this raises a question as to whether the dispositions themselves are sufficiently stamped, on the footing that a deed which performs two distinct and separate purposes is liable to stamp duty in respect of each such purpose, notwithstanding that there is only a single deed. See the Stamp Act 1891, s 4.

The appropriate remedy for insufficiency of stamp duty on one of the writs in the progress is adjudication. Taken by itself, insufficiency of stamp duty will not allow the purchaser to reject the title and resile, unless the seller declines to adjudicate or, on adjudication, fails to pay the duty.

For this reason, I take the view that the purchaser is entitled to require the memorialists to have the stamp duty on the dispositions adjudicated in order to remove any question as to whether or not they are sufficiently stamped. In the process of adjudication, it will be necessary to lodge the antecedent 'oaths in respect of declaration of trust', and that will resolve any doubts there may be as to the liability to stamp duty on that document.

3 Warrandice is not a feudal clause and the terms of the warrandice obligation cannot in any circumstances affect the validity of a title. I am not aware of any rule which entitles a purchaser as of right to a series of obligations of absolute warrandice from the foundation writ to the purchaser's own title. Indeed, it often happens that, for quite legitimate reasons, such a chain of warrandice is not available. If, for example, within the progress

of title, the infeft proprietor has made a gift of the property and granted simple warrandice only, I do not think that a subsequent purchaser can object to that limited obligation. Nor indeed could he object if the donor had expressly granted no warrandice whatsoever.

In any event, the warrandice obligations in the dispositions seem to me to reflect correctly the liabilities of the parties. In each of the dispositions, B Ltd grant warrandice. The only limitation on that absolute undertaking of warrandice is that the same is granted 'as if the subjects were conveyed to us as bare trustee foresaid.'

I do not regard this limitation on the initial warrandice obligation by B 'as a nonsense', as suggested in the memorial. If there is a defect in the title which would be covered by the warrandice obligation in the dispositions, B Ltd as heritably vest, and having granted warrandice subject only to the foregoing qualification, could not escape from liability under that obligation unless it could show that the defect was of a kind which would not or could not have occurred if the subjects had been conveyed by B Ltd as beneficial owner to B Ltd as bare trustee on behalf of the nominated companies. In other words, this obligation of warrandice by B Ltd covers everything other than a defect attributable to one or other of the nominated companies. On that interpretation of the warrandice obligation, I regard it as entirely satisfactory. Indeed, a restriction of this kind is not unusual in the case of sub-sales where the infeft proprietor as original seller grants warrandice but only to the same effect as if he had conveyed the subjects to the first purchaser, leaving it to the first purchaser to warrant the title to the second purchaser.

In this case, B Ltd as bare trustee then grants warrandice from its own facts and deeds and binds the consenters in absolute warrandice. This is in fact the standard warrandice obligation by a trustee, although it is admittedly doubtful to what extent, if at all, a trustee can bind a beneficiary in warrandice by the use of this form of words. In this case, however, it seems to me irrelevant to consider whether or not B Ltd as Trustee has power to bind the nominated companies in absolute warrandice because the nominated companies themselves then grant warrandice, each to the extent of their respective *pro indiviso* shares.

In the result, in my view, all the beneficial owners – B Ltd in the first instance and thereafter the individual nominated companies for their respective *pro indiviso* shares – have all granted absolute warrandice for their respective interests, and there is no break in the chain as the purchaser's agents maintain, even if that were material, which I doubt.

Accordingly, I do not think the purchaser has any valid objection to the title on this ground, except of course that A Ltd has not effectively granted warrandice, for the reasons set out in Answer 1 above.

Further reading
Requirements of Writing (Scotland) Act 1995, which abolishes the requirement of proof by writ or oath.

Manual, para 12.8.

REGISTRATION

25 Rectification of the Register

Burden in disposition restricting use of ground – discharge from Lands Tribunal – whether burden personally enforceable – land certificate issued by Keeper – burden omitted – rectification

Date: March 1988

Memorial

A commercial company, D (UK) Ltd (henceforth 'D'), owned a large area of ground from which it ran its commercial operations. When it closed the operations, it sought to sell the ground in defined areas. In the area of ground that was acquired by the memorialists, there was a burden which required that the subjects be used only for the purpose of storage of building materials or the parking of commercial vehicles for associated commercial use, and no other use was permitted without the prior written consent of D.

The memorialists wanted to sell the property on, but the presence of the burden in the title meant that it was difficult to find a purchaser. The memorialists approached D to see whether a waiver could be obtained. D agreed to do this but only on payment of a price that the memorialists considered excessive.

The memorialists asked the following questions.

1 Would it be appropriate to apply to the Lands Tribunal to have the burden discharged?
2 If compensation were requested, what would a reasonable level be?

Opinion

It is settled, by a series of decisions, that a building condition or restriction may be validly imposed on heritable property not only in a feudal grant but also by way of disposition, provided it satisfies certain familiar criteria: the condition must not be illegal, vexatious or inconsistent with the nature of the property conveyed; it must appear in the dispositive clause of the disposition and enter the record; and it must be clear and unambiguous in its terms.

On the face of it, the burden in this case satisfies these requirements and thus it might qualify as a real condition running with the land. In my opinion, however, the burden in the title of the memorialists is not enforceable by D, the original disponers, nor by any other adjoining proprietor for the following reasons.

The neighbourhood requirement

According to K.G.C. Reid in an article in (1984) 29 JLSS 9 at p 10, a disponer can only validly constitute a condition as a real condition on the land if he has some 'proprietorial connection' with the burdened land. In the case of a disponer, this necessarily means that he must be the owner of neighbouring land. Further, the right to enforce such a real burden cannot be separated from that proprietorial interest and necessarily passes with it. I agree with that general proposition, subject to certain qualifications in particular cases which have no application to the situation here.

In the present case, in 1985, D conveyed the remainder of the property which it previously owned to Z Properties, and the disposition imposed a real burden restricting the use of the subjects. Prior to the granting of the 1985 disposition, D had already sold off three adjoining properties, one to CD & Co and the remaining two to Z Properties. In each of the three earlier dispositions, no comparable burden was imposed. By the granting of the 1985 disposition, D was wholly divested of its proprietary interests in that area. There is no indication in the 1985 disposition that the burden imposed was for the benefit of properties previously disposed of by D; indeed the burden imposes restrictions which the disponee must comply with except with the prior consent of D.

Against that background, it seems clear that the burden was not imposed for any legitimate 'neighbourhood' reason; in particular, it cannot have been imposed for the benefit or protection of any property retained by D because it retained no such property.

It may be technically possible to impose a real burden, in circumstances such as this, for the benefit of adjoining properties previously owned by the disponer and enforceable by the disponees of those adjoining properties, but that would require an express provision in the deed creating the burden, which is not what we have here.

I assume that D did not undertake any obligation to impose this burden when granting the three previous dispositions of adjoining areas. Accordingly, since there is no evidence that the burden was imposed for legitimate 'neighbourhood' reasons, my view is that, on this ground alone, it is not enforceable in a question with a singular successor of the original disponee, although it may have been binding as between D and its immediate disponee under the 1985 deed, as a personal contractual obligation.

Restraint of trade

It is settled by the decision in *Aberdeen Varieties Ltd* v *Donald* 1939 SC 788; 1940 SC (HL) 52 that, if a restriction is imposed in a disposition limiting the use of the property not for the protection of a patrimonial interest in adjoining property belonging to the disponer but with a view to preserving a perpetual commercial monopoly or imposing a restriction in the nature of a restraint on trade, such a restriction will be unenforceable, certainly in a question with a singular successor. In that case, a theatre was conveyed by disposition containing a prohibition against its use for the production of stage plays. The intention was to protect the goodwill of another theatre then owned by the disponer. The property passed into the hands of a singular successor who challenged the validity of the prohibition as a real condition, and the challenge was upheld. According to Lord Wark at p 796, the prohibition was unenforceable because the evident purpose was unlawful to the extent that the objective was to create a commercial monopoly. See also Lord Justice-Clerk Aitchison at p 798 who referred to *Tailors of Aberdeen* v *Coutts* (1834) 13 S 226 and Rankine, *Land Ownership* (4th edn), p 369, and underlined that, according to these authorities (and several others) real conditions are enforceable only if they are imposed for the benefit of an individual, not as such but as the owner or occupier of adjacent premises. That decision has been considered in several later cases, the most recent of which is *Giblin* v *Murdoch* 1979 SLT (Sh Ct) 5. The general tenor of the decision in *Giblin* is that any condition in a disposition, whose principal purpose is to achieve restraint of trade, is unenforceable not only in a question with singular successors but also in a question with the original disponee, as being a contractual condition intended to achieve a purpose which the law does not recognise as legitimate. See also *Phillips* v *Lavery* 1962 SLT (Sh Ct) 57 and *Macintyre* v *Cleveland Petroleum Co Ltd* 1967 SLT 95.

The Lands Tribunal considered the decision in *Aberdeen Varieties* and *Phillips* v *Lavery*, with particular reference to the restraint of trade doctrine, in *CWS* v *Ushers Brewery* 1975 SLT (Lands Tr) 9. They quote with approval from the opinion of Lord Justice-Clerk Aitchison in *Aberdeen Varieties* to the effect that, if a restriction is not intended to protect the dominant property as such or its amenity or any of the requisites of its proper enjoyment, but is simply devised and intended to create a monopoly or to impose a restraint on trade in perpetuity for the benefit of a trading or commercial concern, it cannot receive effect, and in particular cannot be constituted as real burden or real condition. The circumstances in the *CWS* case were very special, as the report shows, and the Lands Tribunal held that a condition in restraint of trade was enforceable. The condition had been imposed expressly for the benefit of adjoining properties with a view to creating a viable small shopping precinct in circumstances where, without the restriction, the objective might have been difficult or imposs-ible to achieve. The Tribunal therefore took the view that the restrictive conditions in this particular case were wholly connected with adjacent heri-table properties which formed part of a distinct small neighbourhood and were imposed solely for the purpose of protecting the proprietary interests of an adjoining property. Accordingly, the adjoining property had a patri-monial interest in the enforcement of the conditions and on that basis the Lands Tribunal treated them as enforceable.

That element is not present here. In my opinion, therefore, on this second ground, the prohibition is altogether unenforceable both in a ques-tion with the original disponee on grounds of contract and, in a question with a singular successor, as a real condition.

Interest to enforce
It is a familiar rule of real conditions that not only must the proprietor seeking to enforce a condition have a title to enforce it, he must also have an interest to enforce. In addition, it is settled, on authority, that in the case

of co-feuars and disponees, where there is no element of continuing personal feudal relationship as between superior and vassal, the interest must be a patrimonial one. In the present case, it could be said that D has an interest to enforce the conditions in the 1985 disposition and that the interest is patrimonial in that it is now seeking to extract consideration for the granting of a minute of waiver. But 'interest to enforce' in this context means a legitimate interest, and that in turn implies that the conditions sought to be enforced were imposed originally for proper 'neighbourhood' reasons, and that, if the conditions are not observed, there will be a resulting monetary loss to the owner of an adjoining property arising directly out of the failure to enforce them.

By express provision in the 1985 disposition, D is the only person who has a title to enforce the burden, and I assume that title to enforce has not been communicated to any adjoining proprietor by subsequent disposition or assignation. Accordingly, in my opinion D is not in a position to instruct a legitimate interest to enforce the conditions, which is essential if they are to succeed. I refer again to the opinion of Lord Justice-Clerk Aitchison in *Aberdeen Varieties* at pp 798 *et seq*. The Lord Justice-Clerk points out, with particular reference to the conditions which were before the court in the case of *Tailors of Aberdeen*, that, on analysis, all the conditions are found to depend on some principle of the law of neighbourhood, apart from which they could not be regarded as lawful conditions, as being inconsistent with the full enjoyment of the owner's right of property. He then refers to the decision of Lord President Inglis in *Patrick* v *Napier* (1867) 5 M 683 and quotes a passage from his opinion to the effect that, in the case of praedial servitudes, the burden imposed on the servient tenement must be so imposed for the purpose of creating an advantage or benefit for another praedium. The Lord Justice-Clerk took the view in *Aberdeen Varieties* that exactly the same rule applied to real conditions, in that they are restraints on one tenement for the benefit of some other tenement which stand to each other in some relation of neighbourhood and are allowed by the law as legitimate, since they are conducive to the full use and enjoyment of the dominant property. He goes on to comment that, in considering whether a restraint on use satisfies this requirement of a real condition, it is essential to inquire as to the interest of the dominant owner to enforce it. As between disponer and singular successors of a disponee, an interest to enforce is not to be presumed, and it is therefore essential to establish whether or not the dominant owner, for whose benefit the restraint or prohibition was imposed, has a patrimonial interest sufficient in law to entitle him to enforce that restriction as a real condition against the owners of the burdened property.

When that test is applied in this case, it is immediately apparent that D cannot conceivably establish an interest to enforce.

Jus quaesitum tertio

The property conveyed by the 1985 disposition was so conveyed subject to the restriction referred to above. I understand that that property has since been subdivided. There is a general principle to the effect that, where property is subject to a valid real condition and is subsequently subdivided, then, in the absence of any special factors, the proprietor of each subdivided part has a title to enforce the restriction in the original common title as against proprietors of other parts of those subjects. In my opinion, however, that rule would not apply in this case for the benefit of the purchasers of other lots from the memorialists, for two reasons.

(*a*) A *jus quaesitum tertio* will not be created in circumstances where the disponer, when imposing a condition, reserves to himself the right to consent to a variation. That rule would apply equally, in my opinion, to the condition in this case where the subjects are not to be used for anything other than the permitted uses, except with the prior consent of D, who imposed the condition in the first place.

(*b*) In any event, if the condition was illegal and unenforceable when first imposed by D, as I think it was, it does not become enforceable simply because a third party has acquired part of the subjects. If the condition was unenforceable *ab initio*, it cannot become enforceable by a subsequent sequence of events. In the result, in my view, D is not in a position to enforce the condition in the 1985 disposition and has no prospect of success if it attempts to do so; and, for the reasons above stated, there is no other proprietor who could instruct a title to enforce that condition.

Against that background I can now answer the questions in the memorial.

1 An application to the Lands Tribunal for the variation or discharge of a land obligation is appropriate under the Conveyancing and Feudal Reform (Scotland) Act 1970, s 1. On the face of it, the condition imposed in the 1985 disposition is valid and effective as a real condition since its content is not patently unlawful and prima facie it otherwise satisfies the definition of a 'land obligation'.

As to the basis of the application, while it may be possible to make out a case under s 1(3)(a), and it could do no harm to found on that subsection, the case here would really rest in part on (b) and mainly on (c).

It is now settled that an application under s 1(3)(c) is competent where the burdened proprietor wishes to use the property for a particular use prohibited in the title, even though the parties opposing the application can show that, in terms of the title, the property can still be used beneficially for some permitted purpose not struck at by the prohibitions. See Halliday on the 1970 Act (2nd edn), p 28, and the cases there cited, and the case of *Leney* v *Craig* 1982 SLT (Lands Tr) 9 at p 11: 'Section 1(3)(c), in contrast, looks forward to the proposed new use.' This is how the Tribunal have in past cases interpreted the phrase 'impedes some reasonable use of land'. The opinion of the Tribunal in *Leney* v *Craig* goes on to quote from Lord Cameron in an unreported appeal in 1972, where he emphasises that it is the restrictive use to which the applicant seeks to put the land which is the subject-matter of s 1(3)(c). Accordingly, the fact that the land can be used for a variety of legitimate purposes which comply with the restrictions does not prevent an application to have those restrictions discharged or varied.

In my opinion, however, an application to the Lands Tribunal is not appropriate, for two reasons.

(*a*) Under the 1970 Act, s 1(2), a 'land obligation' is an obligation relating to land which is enforceable by a proprietor of an interest in land by virtue of his being such proprietor and which is binding on a proprietor of an interest in other land by virtue of his being such proprietor. For the reasons given above, in my view there is no benefited proprietor in this case, who has a title to enforce the restriction in question; accordingly the restriction is not a 'land obligation' and therefore the Tribunal have no jurisdiction.

(*b*) In any event, the Tribunal made it clear in *CWS* v *Ushers Brewery* that, although they had jurisdiction to determine who were benefited proprietors in relation to an enforceable land obligation, they took the view that an applicant must seek declarator in the courts if his argument was that a land obligation is totally unenforceable on the grounds that it is contrary to public policy. For these reasons, my view is that the Lands Tribunal would probably not be prepared to adjudicate on an application in this case. The appropriate remedy would therefore seem to be an application to the court for a declarator that the burden imposed by the 1985 disposition is unenforceable on the grounds above stated. This is probably a quicker and more effective method of forcing the hand of D in that it would be called as a defender in any such action of declarator as being the only party who, on the face of it, has a title to enforce the condition. Once the summons has been served, it may be that a reasonable consideration could be negotiated if this opinion, or an edited version, was produced to D when the summons was served, with a reminder that if the action were defended, expenses might be awarded against it.

2   The basis on which D is seeking to assess the consideration payable to it for discharging the burden underlines, in my view, that the burden cannot be justified as a 'neighbourhood' condition. If it were intended as a genuine and legitimate restriction on use for the benefit of adjoining properties (which in my view cannot possibly be established), the correct method of assessing compensation for a waiver is not by reference to the consideration obtainable by the memorialists but by reference to the diminution in value which the benefited property would suffer if the condition were relaxed. In this case, since there is no benefited property, there is no realistic method of calculating reasonable compensation for waiver, and this is underlined by the negotiations between the parties on the question of consideration.

When it comes to considering compensation or consideration for granting the waiver, all one is concerned with is nuisance value. I have no doubt that, for the reasons set out above, D would never succeed in enforcing the condition. But, of course, a purchaser may not be happy with the title as it stands, and therefore some action may have to be taken by the memorialists to clear the title. In that context, I would have thought that an offer of, say, £XX plus expenses would be an adequate inducement to D to grant a minute of waiver if it can be persuaded that, on the grounds given in this opinion, it has no hope of enforcing the condition in the title. My inclination would be to proceed on that basis, coupled with a fairly firm indication that, unless the offer is accepted and the minute of waiver quickly produced, an action of declarator will be raised and, if defended unsuccessfully, D would be liable in the expenses.

Supplementary memorial
A further question has been raised.

Given that there was a working arrangement between one of the directors of D (Mr Y) and the memorialists, the ultimate disponees of the subjects, is there any possibility that the restriction on use contained in the disposition by D in favour of that director might be personally enforceable as against the memorialists?

Supplementary opinion
In my opinion, there is no such possibility. It is perfectly true that, for certain purposes, a disposition operates as a contract between the disponer and the immediate disponee, with the result that any conditions, whether intended to operate as real burdens or not, are always enforceable (assuming that they are legitimate conditions) by the disponer against the immediate disponee, just as any contractual condition is enforceable as between the original parties to a contract.

The disposition of 1985 by D to Mr Y was granted for consideration and contained the restriction in question which, on the face of it, is not intrinsically illegal. Accordingly, if Mr Y still retains the subjects, there is a possibility that D might enforce that condition as against Mr Y, on the basis of contract, notwithstanding that the restriction might not validly transmit as a real condition or real burden against singular successors. But that right of enforcement could only apply as between the original contracting parties, D and Mr Y. In my view, there is no possibility that the condition might be enforced against the memorialists as singular successor because there is no direct contractual relationship between D and the memorialists, and without a direct contractual relationship between the parties, the condition cannot be enforced personally against the memorialists on the basis of contract.

Second supplementary memorial
A new circumstance arose. The Keeper issued a land certificate. The burden created in the disposition by D in favour of Mr Y, recorded in 1985, was omitted from the burdens section of the certificate. The memorialists asked the following questions.

1 Should they seek confirmation from the Keeper that the burden was omitted because it is not an enforceable obligation?
2 Was there a possibility that the burden was overlooked and omitted in error?
3 Would the agents for the memorialists be acting in good faith if they accepted the land certificate without inquiring from the Keeper as to why the burden was omitted?

4   Would a purchaser who had been made aware of the burden in the title be acting in good faith if he accepted the certificate without further inquiry being made to the Keeper?

5   If it was considered that the Keeper had validly omitted the reference to the burden, what action should be taken on behalf of the memorialists?

6   Section 9 of the Land Registration (Scotland) Act 1979 provides for rectification of a land certificate in certain circumstances. Who in this case would be entitled to apply for rectifications?

7   There was no exclusion of indemnity on the land certificate, but considering the circumstances of this case, is there any way in which the Keeper's indemnity could be affected?

Second supplementary opinion

The burden could have been omitted from the land certificate for one of two reasons:

(*a*) because the Keeper, having considered the terms of the burden, came to the conclusion that it was unenforceable and therefore, not being a real condition, not appropriate to insert it. If the Keeper took that view, then, as I see it, that is the end of the matter. Or;

(*b*) because the Keeper omitted it by mistake. It seems exceedingly unlikely that this is what happened, but I understand that this is believed to be the explanation.

The question now is whether the Keeper has power to rectify the title sheet and land certificate by introducing at this stage the burden in the 1985 disposition.

The 1985 disposition is part of the progress of titles which the Keeper must have examined to satisfy himself as to the validity of the title as a whole. The burden clearly appears in the 1985 disposition and on the record, and is subsequently referred to for burdens in subsequent transmissions of the property. Accordingly, not only was the burden obvious to the Keeper as being incorporated in a writ which formed part of the prescriptive progress, the 1985 disposition was specifically referred to for burdens in the two writs presented to the Keeper with Form 1 for first registration and Form 2 on the dealing.

In my opinion there is no statutory authority which would allow the Keeper to rectify the Register and introduce the 1985 burden into the title sheet at this stage. This is because the memorialists are proprietors in possession of the whole subjects in the land certificate. If the burden is now to be introduced, this necessarily involves rectification of the title sheet since the land certificate has now been issued. There is no doubt in my mind that, to a limited extent, rectification by introduction of the burden into the title sheet at this stage would prejudice the proprietor in possession, because it would materially affect the present (and future) negotiations of the memorialists for the sale of the property.

If the Keeper is to attempt to rectify the Register, he can only do so if authorised by the provisions of the Land Registration (Scotland) Act 1979, s 9, in terms of which he may exercise his power to rectify in four situations.

113

These are set out in s 9(3)(a). Section 9(3)(a)(i), (ii) and (iv) are patently inapplicable because it is not possible to bring this case within any of the three provisions. Accordingly, we are left with s 9(3)(a)(iii) which entitles the Keeper to rectify the title sheet and land certificate only if he can show that the inaccuracy (here, the omission of the 1985 burden) has been caused wholly or substantially by the fraud or carelessness of the proprietor in possession.

There is no other possible ground on which the title sheet and land certificate can now be changed. In particular, under s 9(3)(b), the court or the Lands Tribunal are similarly limited in their power to order rectification, as is the Keeper under s 9(3)(a). It is certainly the case that, in a question with C Ltd, the Keeper might possibly have had an argument that the omission of the 1985 burden was caused by its carelessness in that, in the Form 1 application which was presented on its behalf following the disposition in its favour by Mr Y, the schedule of burdens on Form 1 refers expressly to writ numbers 1, 2 and 3 of the inventory Form 4 as being the writs referred to for burdens. The 1985 disposition is not included in the writs listed – correctly in my view because the burden is invalid as a real burden: see below. But there is no doubt that the disposition was presented to the Keeper because it is listed in the inventory as one of the writs in the progress of titles and was sent to him with the application for registration. Although there may have been 'carelessness' in the preparation of the Form 1, I do not think the Keeper could argue that the omission of the burden was caused substantially by the carelessness of C Ltd.

The schedule of burdens in Form 4 attached to the application did not draw the Keeper's attention to the burden, but the disposition was referred to as a burden writ in the subsequent writ in favour of C Ltd which formed the basis of the application for registration. The burden appeared on the record; the disposition formed part of the progress of titles; burdens which occurred in two earlier dispositions, although not referred to in the burdens section, were incorporated in the land certificate; and the 1985 disposition did not, in my view, impose a valid real burden. Taking these facts into account, it seems to me impossible for the Keeper to claim that the omission of the 1985 burden was caused substantially by the carelessness of C Ltd in not drawing his attention specifically to it.

However that may be, the question does not lie between the Keeper and C Ltd. The land certificate has now been issued to the memorialists following on a transmission by C Ltd to the memorialists and an application for the registration of that dealing on a Form 2 lodged by the memorialists before the land certificate had been issued in name of the original applicant, C Ltd. That being so, if the land certificate is to be rectified, it will have to be rectified as against the memorialists as proprietors in possession.

In the case of the registration of the dealing represented by the disposition by C Ltd to the memorialists, there cannot be any question of fraud as the cause of the omission of the 1985 burden from the land certificate, and, although it may be possible for the Keeper to argue that the omission was caused substantially by the manner in which Form 1 and Form 4 were prepared by C Ltd on first registration, I cannot see that that argument is open to the Keeper in a question with the memorialists on the application for the registration of the dealing Form 2 and relevant inventory.

The memorialists acted in good faith. They cannot, in my view, be held responsible for the failure by C Ltd to complete Form 1 properly, if that was the case. So far as the memorialists are concerned, it seems to me that the Form 2 which they completed and lodged with the Keeper following the dealing, is beyond reproach.

In the result, my view is that, since the land certificate has now been issued, and since the memorialists are proprietors in possession within the meaning of s 9(3) of the 1979 Act, the Keeper has no power to rectify the land certificate as against the memorialists by incorporating in the title sheet and in the land certificate the 1985 burden. He cannot possibly argue, in my view, that the burden was so omitted, and the resulting inaccuracy so caused, substantially by the carelessness of the memorialists.

Accordingly, the title sheet must stand as it is and cannot be rectified because the Keeper has no power of rectification. The only consequence of the omission (if there is to be any consequence) is that D has a claim against the Keeper for wrongly omitting the burden from the title sheet. Whether or not D has such a claim, however, does not affect the title sheet and will not result in any amendment unless the memorialists consent to it, which, in the nature of things, they will not of course agree to do.

Although it is not strictly relevant to the position of the memorialists, I think it may be appropriate to comment on the burden in the 1985 disposition which was omitted from the title sheet. In my opinion, as stated above, it is not and has never been valid as a real burden on the land. It was never enforceable in the first instance as a real burden or real condition, and accordingly it is inappropriate that it should appear in the title sheet at all for this reason.

It is settled, by a series of decisions, that a building condition or restriction may be validly imposed on heritable property not only in a feudal grant but also by way of disposition, provided it satisfies certain familiar criteria, namely: the condition must not be illegal, vexatious or inconsistent with the nature of the property conveyed; it must appear in the dispositive clause of the disposition and enter the record; and it must be clear and unambiguous in its terms. On the face of it, the burden in this case satisfies these requirements and so might qualify as a real condition running with the land. In my opinion, however, in the particular circumstances of this case, the burden is not enforceable by D, the original disponer, nor by any other adjoining proprietor, for the reasons set out in my first opinion, namely the neighbourhood requirement and the doctrine of restraint of trade.

My view, therefore, is that the purported burden was wholly invalid *ab initio* as a real burden or real condition. It was also, almost certainly, unenforceable as a personal obligation on the disponee, but that is not relevant to the present question. The point is that whether or not the condition was initially a valid personal condition (which in my view it was not); it was invalid *ab initio* as a real burden and so should never have been inserted in the burdens section of the title sheet. If my view is correct, and it is backed by ample authority, it cannot be described as a subsisting real burden or condition affecting the registered interest in terms of the 1979 Act, s 6(1)(e). Admittedly, under s 12(3)(g), the Keeper, by introducing a real burden into the burdens section, does not guarantee that the real burden continues to be enforceable. But in my opinion, if a real burden was never effective from the outset, it does not come within s 6 (1)(e) and as such has no place in the burdens section of the title sheet. The fact that, if the burden were inserted, the Keeper would not be guaranteeing its continued enforceability is irrelevant. If the burden is to enter the title sheet at all it must first satisfy the provisions of s 6(1)(e), and in my opinion in this case it patently does not do so.

This has three consequences.

(*a*) If the Keeper now seeks to rectify the Register by introducing the burden into the title sheet and then to amend the land certificate accordingly, the memorialists are entitled to object and would be upheld on the grounds above stated.

(*b*) If, as I think, the burden should never have been inserted in the title sheet, as never having been validly constituted, its omission cannot be attributed to carelessness.

(*c*) If D makes a claim against the Keeper on the grounds that, by omitting the burden, he has caused the company loss, the claim in my opinion is bound to fail in that:

(i) the burden was never effective as a real burden in the first instance and so could not be enforced against the memorialists; and
(ii) in any event, D cannot now demonstrate any legitimate interest to enforce the burden and so cannot possibly demonstrate any patrimonial loss.

Further reading
Short's Trustee v *Keeper of the Registers of Scotland* 1996 SLT 166.
Brookfield Developments Ltd v *Keeper of the Registers of Scotland* 1989 SLT (Lands Tr) 105.

Manual, para 13.33.

THE EFFECTS OF POSSESSION: PRESCRIPTION

26 *Prescription*

Purchase of school house – *confusio* – prescription – prerequisites –
status of feuing conditions

Date: June 1989

Memorial

The memorialist wished to purchase a school house from the education
authority. Various questions arose with regard to the title:

1 Whether the superior/vassal relationship was extinguished *ex confusione*
by virtue of the identity of the superior and of the vassal becoming, for the
prescription period, one and the same through the local government legislation, thus extinguishing the feuing conditions.

2 Whether, when the regional council became the education authority
and therefore acquired the consolidated feu, the feuing conditions
remained extinguished or were revived on separation of the two estates.

3 In the event that the view was taken that the superior/vassal relationship
was revived, what was to be the position of the superiority by reference to
the local government order?

Opinion

1 No. I reach this view with reluctance but it seems to me the inevitable
consequence of the facts and circumstances in this case.

In *Bald* v *Buchanan* (1786) M 15,084 it was held that *confusio* did not
apply to merge two adjacent feudal estates which had come into the same
ownership. That long-standing decision has since been approved in a
number of cases and must be regarded as settled law.

In the case of *confusio*, unless there is some technical impediment, the
mere fact that there is *concursus* of debtor and creditor in the same obligation automatically extinguishes it. The question of intention is not
relevant. In the case of two adjacent feudal estates, however, *confusio* does
not apply. Some further act or actings on the part of the proprietor of the
two estates are required to produce a merger of the two. This takes the
form either of a disposition *ad rem*, or the equivalent statutory minute of
consolidation, or the running of prescription on a title to the *superiority*
estate. I would emphasise this point, particularly in the light of what
follows.

If consolidation is to operate, there must be possession on the superiority title into which, after the prescriptive period, the *dominium utile* is consolidated and merged. If, in contrast, the proprietor of the two estates deliberately possesses on the *dominium utile* title (see below for further amplification) there is no possibility that, by such possession, he can incorporate the superiority into the *dominium utile* title. Instead the inevitable result is that, if possession is unequivocally on the *dominium utile* title, the two estates are never consolidated and remain permanently as distinct and separate feudal estates.

Prescription inevitably involves both title and possession. There is no problem about title in this case. The question is whether possession satisfied the requirements, to allow prescription to operate. Possession necessarily involves some element of *animus* or intention, however notional that may be. Indeed, in certain cases, particularly consolidation cases, intention may be implied from the nature of the title. So, Halliday, para 17–114, states that where a person owns both the superiority and the property, one title being absolute and the other limited (eg by entail), the question of whether consolidation operates by prescription depends upon certain presumptions 'as affected by the *intention* of the person'. He then quotes as authority the latest of the cases in point, *Glasgow* v *Boyle* (1887) 14 R 419. The facts in that case are simply stated. An estate was entailed and the institute took infeftment. The entailed estate included, in part, a superiority. A subsequent heir of entail acquired the *dominium utile* of the superiority on a separate title. Infeftment was later taken therein. The next heir possessed for the prescriptive period. It was argued that, by such possession, the *dominium utile* had *necessarily* merged with, and was consolidated in, the superiority title. The court rejected that argument, on the footing that the heir of entail in possession was entitled to ascribe possession to whichever of the two titles suited his interest best, unless the nature of possession was not consistent with the title to which he sought to ascribe it.

So, one of the prerequisites here is that possession by the local authority must have been consistent with the title to which they seek to ascribe that possession, and is unequivocally referable to it. This is a general rule of prescriptive possession and is well illustrated in the case of *Houston* v *Barr* 1911 SC 134. In that case A feued a cottage to B on a landed estate. B was also A's tenant in an adjoining field. There was an access road leading to the field along the front of B's cottage. B occupied the cottage, and the access strip as an access thereto, for the prescriptive period and then claimed ownership of the strip by virtue of prescriptive possession. B's claim failed because, although he undoubtedly had possessed, his possession was at least as referable to his *tenancy* of the field as it was to the *ownership* of the cottage. In other words, his possession was not unequivocally referable to his ownership of the cottage nor adverse to the superior's title to the access strip.

In the present case, the subjects were originally feued by the lord provost, etc, in favour of the school board. At the time of granting the feu disposition, the lord provost, etc, were infeft in the *plenum dominium*. The school board recorded the feu charter, thus becoming infeft in the *dominium utile* which thus emerged as a separate feudal estate on the recording thereof.

Some time thereafter, the *dominium utile*, still then used by the school board for education purposes, vested in the lord provost, etc, in their capacity as education authority, the functions of the school board having been transferred to the local authority in 1929. The lord provost, etc, as successors to the school board, did not take any infeftment in their own person, but I do not think this is material. See *Glasgow* v *Boyle.*

In the result, until 1975, when there was a further change, the *dominium directum* was held by the lord provost, etc, as original superiors under the feu disposition of 1904. The lord provost, etc, were also proprietors of the *dominium utile* for the period from 1929 to 1975 in their separate capacity as education authority, although not infeft in that capacity in the *dominium utile.* Throughout that period, the subjects continued to be used for their original educational purpose, and although the title to the two separate interests of *dominium directum* and *dominium utile* came together in 1929 in the person of the lord provost, etc, there was still a separation of functions. Such possession must, I think, be ascribed to the original title to the *dominium utile* granted in 1904. This is because, when the subjects vested in the lord provost, etc, in 1929, they did so, by express statutory provision, for educational purposes and continued to be used for educational purposes until 1975.

In the cases where this problem has been considered, the usual situation is that either the superiority or the *dominium utile* is held by an individual on a limited title, and the other estate is held on an absolute title. Clearly, where an heir of entail in possession occupies a landed estate and is vested in both the superiority and the *dominium utile* title, the quality of his possession does not differ significantly, whether ascribed to the superiority or to the *dominium utile* title. The peculiar feature of this case is that the quality of the possession of the subjects from 1929 to 1975 by the lord provost is clearly referable to the original school board title. The use of the subjects for educational purposes was continued by the local authority in whom the functions of the school board vested in 1929. Accordingly, by continuing to possess and use the subjects as a school, there is at least a presumption (to put it no higher) that such possession must be referable to and be founded on the original school board title. In cases where the quality of possession is identical, whether the title be superiority or *dominium utile*, the proprietor owning both estates can base his possession on one or other of the titles as suits his case best. In the peculiar circumstances of this case, however, I think it would be difficult for the local authority to elect to ascribe their possession between 1929 and 1975 to the superiority title because, up to the moment when they became owners of the *dominium utile* in 1929, the subjects were occupied and used by the school board under the original 1904 feu disposition, and they continued to be so occupied and used thereafter by the local authority, exercising their function as education authority.

This distinction was maintained in the local authority's own accounts. Further, throughout the whole period, the original feuduty of one shilling was regularly transferred, year by year, from 1929 to 1975, from the education account to the general improvements account by the local authority.

Millar on Prescription at p 58, commenting on *Glasgow* v *Boyle*, points out that where one person has two equally habile titles to superiority and *dominium utile*, he may ascribe his possession to one or other as he pleases. 'If he has not hitherto given any clear and deliberate indication as to which title he chooses to possess on, there is a presumption that he possessed upon the more favourable one.' In the present case, it seems to me that the local authority have given a clear and deliberate indication as to which title they chose to possess on, by maintaining the superiority and the *dominium utile* in two separate accounts within their accounting system; by continuing to possess as education authority in succession to the school board, and so ostensibly as vassals under the 1904 feu disposition; and, by way of confirmation of that possession, by transferring the amount of feuduty payable from the education account to the improvements account.

The actings of the regional and district councils following on local government reorganisation simply confirm the position.

In the result, by their own actings, the local authority have given clear evidence to rebut the presumption that consolidation was intended, even by implication, and, by their actings, I think they have made it impossible for themselves to maintain that, during the period from 1929 to 1975, their possession of the school as a school was directly and unequivocally referable to the superiority title, not the *dominium utile* title. My view is that the local authority positively ascribed their possession of the subjects between 1929 and 1975 to the *dominium utile* title, not to the superiority title; and so, on the authority of *Glasgow* v *Boyle*, there had been no consolidation prior to 1975. Thereafter, the question does not arise because the two estates, superiority and *dominium utile*, were treated as vested in two separate authorities.

I am therefore satisfied that there has been no consolidation in this case. There is, however, another point which I have not explored but which confirms the conclusion I have reached. Under the Local Government (Scotland) Act 1929, s 3, education functions were transferred to the local authority from the school board, and provision was made for the transfer of property under s 6 of the same Act. I assume that that section applies to the present case. If not, then I assume that there would be other comparable statutory provisions. The point is that, under the 1929 Act, s 6, property transferred as part of the transfer of functions *must* be held by the transferee authority for the *same* purposes as it was held by the transferor. Accordingly, when the school was transferred to the local authority in 1929, it was expressly transferred for specified statutory purposes under the Education Acts. I assume that it would have been improper for a local authority, in whom a school had vested in this way, at its own hand unilaterally and without consent from the Scottish Education Department gratuitously to transfer the school to a different local authority account. In other words, if and so long as the school was used for educational purposes, I think it would have to remain in the education account, under statutory regulation. In the present case, the use continued up to and beyond 1975 when the two accounts, and the relevant properties in each account, vested separately in the regional and district authorities respectively. But consolidation by prescription involves *animus* or intention, actual or implied.

There is no evidence of actual intention here. Is it possible to say that, by implication, the local authority, between 1929 and 1975, positively resolved to treat their possession of the school as possession of a property held on improvement account, not on education account? This would carry the inevitable consequence that, when consolidation had run its course, the property would automatically be transferred from one account to the other. If that was the local authority's intention, it was unlawful in that the local authority were clearly acting *ultra vires* with the intention of benefiting the improvement account at the expense of the education account. I would find it difficult to conclude that such a deliberate intention could be imputed to the local authority. That, however, is a question of administrative law, not of conveyancing, and it would require a good deal more research before coming to a firm conclusion. In the view which I take of the matter, such further investigation is unnecessary and I have not therefore pursued the point any further.

There is a further question as to vesting in 1975. It was assumed then, and it seems still to be assumed, that the school vested in the region as education authority from 1975 onwards. This may be correct, but if the local authority argument is correct and if consolidation had taken place, the property should have been transferred out of the education account and into the improvement account in 1949 when the twenty-year prescription had run its course on the superiority title. In 1975 the improvement account properties generally seem to have been transferred to the district, and on a strict view of the matter, the transfer should have included the consolidated title to the school.

2   When the regional council became the education authority they acquired the *dominium utile* only and not the consolidated fee. The rule which applies in consolidation cases is that unless and until the two separate feudal estates of superiority and *dominium utile* are effectively merged by consolidation, they remain two distinct and separate estates. Admittedly, so long as both estates are vested in one person, the obligations of vassal to superior are meantime suspended, but none the less the two estates remain distinct and separate. Accordingly, if one individual acquires the superiority and the *dominium utile* of the same subjects but does not consolidate, then, until prescription has run on the two titles, he is free to convey the superiority retaining *dominium utile*, or to convey *dominium utile* retaining superiority, to a disponee from him. No positive act of reviving the two distinct feudal estates is required. On the view which I take of the position, there were still two distinct and separate feudal estates of superiority and *dominium utile* in 1975, and it was only the *dominium utile* which passed to the region as education authority under the order in question. In that sense, but in that sense only, the effect of the vesting order was to revive the superior/vassal relationship.

3   According to a letter from the regional solicitor, it seems fairly clear that, contrary to my original assumption, the superiority in question is not part of the common good. From the date of its reacquisition in 1881, the property was specifically allocated by the town council to the general improvements account. It apparently so remained in the books of the local

authority until 1975. That being so, I would have thought that the superiority did come within article 4(a)(i) of the relevant order as being property to which a statutory use, or at least a statutory purpose, had been assigned on 15th May 1975. Somewhat surprisingly, the wording of 4(a)(i) differs from the wording in 4(a)(iii) in that in (i) the expression used is 'to which a statutory use had been assigned' whereas (iii) deals with cases 'where no statutory purpose or use has been assigned'. This seems to indicate that 4(a)(i) covers both use and purpose; and I would have thought the *purpose* in this case was fairly clear.

If I am wrong in that view, the superiority would certainly pass under article 7 and, by virtue of that article, would vest in the district council. That being so, it does not seem to matter very much whether the vesting occurred under article 4 or under article 7, because the result is the same.

It follows that the feuing conditions in the 1904 disposition have never been extinguished or discharged and therefore, at least in theory, remain enforceable according to their terms.

Manual, para 14.4.

27   Practical consequences of positive prescription

Boundary of river shifted – title – ownership – *a non domino* disposition

Date: July 1987

Memorial
A disposition was granted in 1985 which included a river. Over the course of time the line of the river moved, and the question arose as to what was encompassed in the title. The following specific questions were asked:

1   Did the memorialists' title include the particular area of ground from where the river had moved?

2   If the title did not include that area of ground, who were the owners?

3   If nobody owned it, could the memorialists acquire title by recording a disposition in their favour and possessing for the prescriptive period?

Opinion
On the evidence of the copy title deeds and other information so far provided, I am afraid it is not possible to answer the questions definitively, but I think that there may be sufficient in this opinion to point the memorialists in the right direction. Bearing that in mind, I answer the questions asked as follows.

1   There is not much doubt that the memorialists cannot at the moment claim a valid title to the area of ground between their present boundary and the bank of the River Z on its altered line. This is the area enclosed by the red line on Plan A.

I have come to this conclusion because the conveyance by AB in favour of the building society recorded in 1954 describes the subjects conveyed in terms which, in my view, are clearly bounding. In particular, every boundary of the two plots is described with stated measurements and by reference to the plan which appear to agree *inter se*. Admittedly, the south-east boundary of the southern portion of the subjects conveyed is described as being the River Z, and that would normally carry with it an implication that the subjects extended to the mid-line of the river, but I am not entirely clear as to the significance of the dotted line on the copy plan attached to the 1954 disposition as an extension north-eastwards and south-westwards of the south-east boundary. It is just possible that it was intended to indicate the *medium filum* of the river, although I think that unlikely. But even if that were so, the area disponed is so clearly defined, with stated measurements, area and by reference to the plan, that the terms of the description must be taken as bounding.

The normal rule therefore applies – that where subjects are conveyed in bounding terms, the disponee acquires only what was conveyed to him within the boundaries and nothing more. Further, even though he may possess land beyond those defined and stated boundaries, he cannot acquire a title by prescriptive possession because his possession is in contra-diction of and not supported by his title.

Accordingly, whether or not the south-east boundary was, in 1954, intended to be the mid-line of the River Z as it then ran, the shifting of the river southwards since that date would not have the effect of extending the subjects conveyed in a south-easterly direction up to the new line of the river bank.

2   This question raises problems. The copy plans attached to the copy disposition of 1960 are exceedingly difficult to interpret, partly because the colourings do not show up on the copy and partly because the scale of the relative plan is so small that identification of what is conveyed is extremely difficult.

I am inclined to the view, but only with hesitation, that the 1960 disposition very probably *did* convey the *solum* of the River Z along the whole of the south boundary of the memorialists' property; but I am only guessing at what the black lines on the copy of the relative plan imply. If that assumption is correct, the fact that the river has moved southwards since that date does not deprive the disponee under the 1960 disposition of his title to the *solum* of the river. Title to the *solum* of a river is not dependent on the *solum* being covered by water. Accordingly, if a title to the *solum* of the river has once been acquired by express conveyance (as I think probably happened under the 1960 disposition), the fact that the river later dries up or moves has no effect on that title, which remains vested in the original disponee. There are cases where a river shifts its line, and where the owner whose land is bounded by the river can then claim a title to the additional land between the old river bank and the new river bank. But this would not apply where the title is bounding; and the title seems to be bounding both in the case of the memorialists and in the case of the disponee under the 1960 disposition, although the latter point is not so clear.

Accordingly, with considerable hesitation, I come to the view that the disponee under the 1960 disposition probably does have a title to what was originally the *solum* of the River Z and which now embraces, or at least includes in part, the area marked on the plan accompanying my instructions.

3   The fact that the disponee under the 1960 disposition may have a title *per expressum* to the *solum* of the River Z on the line which it then followed, does not prevent the memorialists from acquiring a title now, by prescriptive possession to the area of ground enclosed within the red line on the memorial plan. Thus, if the memorialists were to convey that area to themselves by disposition which they recorded in the Register of Sasines and if they then positively possess that area for the next ten years without lawful interruption they will, by such possession, undoubtedly acquire a valid and unchallengeable title to the area enclosed within the red line, even though the same area may be included in the 1960 disposition. For an illustration of this exact point, see *Magistrates of Perth* v *Earl of Wemyss* (1829) 8 S 82. In that case, the magistrates of Perth were infeft, by express conveyance, in the Island of Sleepless in the River Tay. The Earl of Wemyss held on a barony title with a very general description containing no reference to the island but comprising land *ex adverso* thereof on the bank of the river. In addition, he possessed the island for the prescriptive period. In a subsequent competition between the magistrates of Perth and the Earl of Wemyss, the Earl was preferred on the footing that habile title followed by prescriptive possession overrode the express infeftment of the magistrates. Accordingly, the Earl was held to have acquired a title to the island by possession to the exclusion of the infeft proprietor.

Exactly the same principle would apply here if the memorialists proceed as suggested above and possess, uninterrupted, for the prescriptive period.

Further reading
Stirling v *Bartlett* 1993 SLT 763.
D. L. Carey Miller, *Alluvio, Avulsio* and Fluvial Boundaries 1994 SLT (News) 75.

Manual, para 14.7.

28   *Practical consequences of positive prescription*

Ownership of solum – interpretation of titles – requirements for
prescription – possession

Date: May 1989

Memorial
A property developer sought to purchase a large property comprising

basement, ground, first, second and third floors. The property was served by a common stair, access to which was enjoyed by an adjoining property, but which had been blocked off. The titles to the adjoining shop included the solum of the common stair. The developer wished to alter the common stair, and the question arose whether the title, plus prescription was sufficient to establish ownership.

Opinion

It is not possible on the information provided to give an opinion with any confidence but, since the matter is clearly urgent, I thought it appropriate to reply with certain points which may assist in resolving the problem; and at least will put you on your guard, because there are, on the face of it, some potential risks in the developer's proposals.

First, the title of the adjoining property, recorded during 1984, refers to an earlier deed for description and that deed would have to be examined. In particular, the 1984 disposition makes no reference whatsoever to the ownership of the solum of the common stair. The title to the adjoining premises, however, presumably in the earlier writs in the progress, includes either the solum of the common stair, or a right of common property therein, as opposed to a mere right of access by that common stair. In other words, the adjoining shop seems to have a proprietary right, not a mere servitude right of access.

The mere fact that the adjoining premises are not made liable for a share of the cost of maintaining the roof is totally inconclusive, and has no significance in determining right in the common stair and solum thereof.

The difficulty is that, if the title to the adjoining shop carries with it (as would appear to be the case) either the solum of the common stair or a right in common to that solum, it will be exceedingly difficult for the developer to establish that the adjoining proprietors have lost their right of property therein. That being so, I would find it very difficult to advise with confidence that the developer has acquired by prescriptive possession a valid and unchallengeable right to the common stair and solum thereof to the entire exclusion of the adjoining proprietors.

In the copy disposition of 1959 there is, again, a reference back to an earlier deed for description and a reference to rights, individual and common, effeiring to the subjects thereby disponed. However, there seems to be no reference whatsoever in the 1959 disposition to the ownership of the common stair or solum thereof; nor indeed is there any indication in the 1959 disposition as to who is entitled to the use of the common stair.

In order to establish a right of property by prescriptive possession in situations of this kind there are, in effect, three requirements:

(i) first, there must be a recorded title which, in its terms, would support the claim to exclusive ownership by possession following thereon,

(ii) second, there must be not less than ten years' possession (which must be peaceable, continuous, etc), following on that recorded title,

(iii) third, not only must that possession be referable to the prior recorded titles and consistent therewith, but in addition the possession must be adverse to any competing right.

It is on this last point that the developer runs into difficulty if, as it appears, the title to the adjoining shop carries with it either the solum or a right in common to the solum of the common stair.

The point can be stated simply thus: The proprietors of the subjects of purchase undoubtedly have a right of access by way of the common stair either because they have a right of property in common to the common stair and solum thereof or because they have an express or implied right of access thereby. There is nothing whatever the adjoining proprietors can do to object to or prevent the proprietors of the subjects of purchase from taking access to their respective properties by that common stair. So, in considering the nature of the possession enjoyed by the proprietors of the subjects of purchase, it is not enough simply to say that, without objection, they have continued to take access by that common stair for the prescriptive period because, by so doing, they are only exercising what is their entitlement and they are not contravening or overriding the rights of the adjoining proprietor to take access concurrently by the same stair.

This point is best illustrated by the case of *Meacher* v *Blair Oliphant* 1913 SC 417, which involved fishing in a loch. The common law rule is that the proprietors of all properties abutting on a loch have, by implication, a right to fish over the whole surface thereof: that right may be varied by express provision in the title. In *Meacher*, one proprietor did obtain a title to exclusive fishing over the whole loch and exercised those rights accordingly. But that proprietor, even although he had a title to exclusive fishing over the whole loch and exercised his right of fishing, could not have been prevented from so doing by any other proprietor since, in the nature of the right, all proprietors, including the one with the exclusive title, had the right to fish over the whole loch concurrently. Accordingly, the Court held that, although evidence of possession had been established, it was insufficient in the circumstances to establish exclusive possession.

The same would apply in this case although it is helpful that access from the adjoining shop onto the common stair has apparently been blocked off. If it could be shown that this was done more than ten years ago and that the adjoining proprietors have been positively deterred or prevented from using the common stair ever since, that may be sufficient evidence of exclusive possession to allow the positive prescription to run. The position, however, is by no means clear.

Alternatively, if the adjoining proprietor has merely a right of access over the common stair but no right of property, that mere servitude right of access can be extinguished by the negative prescription. In other words, if it can be shown that the adjoining proprietor has not used the common stair for twenty years, then any servitude right of access would be extinguished. That would not, however, be sufficient to extinguish a proprietary right. In the case of proprietary rights, failure to exercise the right for however long a time cannot extinguish that right, since it is *res merae facultatis*.

In the result, if the adjoining proprietor has a right or a right in common to the common stair and/or solum thereof, the developer's position is precarious because of the difficulty of proving possession to the exclusion of the adjoining proprietor, in the sense in which that term 'exclusive' was described in the case of *Meacher* above.

It is, of course, undoubtedly the case that, as soon as a developer commences operations on the common stair, the neighbouring proprietors, if they sense the possibility of turning the situation to their own financial advantage, will be closely examining their titles to see whether or not there is any possibility of such a claim – that is a risk the developer runs by commencing operations and so putting the adjoining proprietor on his enquiry.

Further reading
Hamilton v *McIntosh Donald Ltd* 1994 SLT 212.

Manual, para 14.7.

THE ESTATE OF THE SUPERIORITY

29 Infeudation and subinfeudation

Superiority – method of conveyance – assignation of rent – warrandice –
Orr v *Mitchell* (1893) 20 R (HL) 27

Date: February 1988

Memorial
A feu disposition was granted which conveyed the *dominium utile* of the
subjects. Subsequently, a larger piece of ground was conveyed, which
included the *plenum dominium* of those parts unfeued, and the *dominium
directum* of those parts already feued. On the sale of the first piece of
ground, the purchasers were offered both the *dominium utile* and the superiority. The question was asked whether the wording used in the
disposition was sufficient to exclude the ground itself from the conveyance.
The description used only identified the location and the extent of the
ground.

Opinion
It is a fundamental feudal principle that, when the superior, infeft in the
plenum dominium of his estate, conveys part on subinfeudation to a vassal
by feu charter, the land is conveyed absolutely to the vassal, but, notwithstanding that apparent absolute conveyance, the superior is not divested.
Instead, in feudal law, the superior remains infeft in the whole original
estate and his title remains entire; but, *quoad* the subjects feued, his title is
thereafter *burdened* with the subordinate rights of the vassal on the
recording of that charter. Following on the recording of that charter, the
superior's title to the subjects contained in the feu charter is none the less
a title to land, not merely a title to the superiority, although in substance
his rights are restricted to collecting feuduty and enforcing the feuing
conditions. It follows from this general principle that the appropriate feudal
method of transferring a superiority is by a conveyance of the land itself,
not merely of the *dominium directum* thereof.

The normal practice in a conveyance of what is in substance a superiority, is to dispone the land without any reference in the dispositive clause
to the subordinate rights of the vassal in the *dominium utile*. It is therefore
not possible to detect, simply by reading the dispositive clause alone,
whether *dominium directum* or *plenum dominium* is passing to the disponee.
On this aspect of title, the disponee must satisfy himself by examining
the prior titles and the search in order to discover whether any part of
the subjects to be conveyed to him have previously been sub-feued by the
disponer. If this is the case, although the land has been conveyed to the

purchaser, his rights will in effect be restricted to *dominium directum* only in those parts of the whole subjects so conveyed which had previously been sub-feued.

Admittedly, in a conveyance of *dominium directum*, the conveyancing practice is to incorporate what the memorialists refer to as 'the badges' of a disposition of superiority. These 'badges' have no feudal significance and no effect on the title of the disponee; they do not in any way restrict or qualify what is conveyed to the disponee in the dispositive clause.

The two standard 'badges' in this context are:

(i) an assignation not only of the rents but also the feuduties in favour of the disponee in general terms. Such an assignation is unnecessary to give a title to the disponee to collect the feuduties because, in feudal law, where the *dominium directum* transmits, the infeftment of the disponee on a conveyance of the land automatically entitles him to collect feuduties from vassals of his predecessor in title;

(ii) an exception in the warrandice clause, again in general terms, of feu rights previously granted by the superior or his predecessors in title. Again, however, the purpose of this is not to confer rights on the disponee, but to protect the position of the disponer against a potential subsequent claim by the disponee under warrandice.

It follows that:

(*a*) if these 'badges' are properly included in a disposition, ie where *dominium directum* only and the *plenum dominium* is passing, it is still not normally possible to determine from the wording used in these 'badges' whether the whole, or part only, of the subjects has been feued; and, if part only, which part;

(*b*) if the 'badges' are included in a conveyance in error, this has no effect on the validity of the conveyance to the disponee who, by that conveyance, acquires a title to the *plenum dominium* even although, by reference to the 'badges', it may appear that what is conveyed to him is, in part or in whole, *dominium directum* only;

(*c*) in a conveyance of 'mixed' estate, ie where a landed estate is conveyed and where parts thereof have previously been feued so that what passes to the disponee under that conveyance is in part *dominium utile* and in part *dominium directum* only, that conveyance, although containing the 'badges', will none the less carry to the disponee, if he is acting in good faith, the *plenum dominium* not merely the *dominium directum*, of parts of that landed estate which have previously been feued but where, for whatever reason, the feu charter has not been recorded prior to the recording of the title of the disponee of the mixed estate. See *Ceres School Board* v *McFarlane* (1895) 23 R 279 where exactly this situation occurred. In particular, the inclusion in the conveyance of the mixed estate of the 'badges' did not in any way limit or exclude the disponees' title to the *dominium utile* of a feu previously given off but where the charter had not been recorded.

These general principles are discussed in *Orr* v *Mitchell* (1893) 20 R (HL) 27. In that case, a superior had previously granted feus, reserving to himself the *dominium utile* in the minerals under the surface. He then sold the superiority, intending to retain the minerals for his own benefit. The subsequent conveyance to the purchaser of the superiority, following normal feudal practice, conveyed the land, albeit that the conveyance included the badges referred to above. As a conveyance of land, the deed was, of course, appropriate to carry the superiority but, in the absence of any further reservation of minerals therein, it could also be construed as carrying the minerals as well. This had not been the original intention but the disponee later claimed the *dominium utile* to the sub-adjacent minerals.

Two points emerge from the decision of the House of Lords in *Orr* which are relevant to the situation before us:

(i) in the ordinary way, the dispositive clause of a disposition is the governing clause and, if its terms are express and unambiguous, they cannot be cut down or qualified by contrary evidence gathered elsewhere in the deed;

(ii) on the other hand, if the words in the dispositive clause are ambiguous, it is legitimate to take into account other expressions elsewhere in the deed, outside the dispositive clause, in order to determine what the words in the dispositive clause were intended to mean.

In the context of the decision in *Orr* v *Mitchell*, this was crucial in that the narrative of the disposition quite clearly and expressly provided that the subject-matter of the conveyance was the superiority only and nothing else; and that the disposition was executed for the sole purpose of giving the disponee a feudal title to the *dominium directum*. Further, when the lands were described in the dispositive clause, they were described as 'the lands of Hillfoot ... belonging in property to John McArthur Moir'. There were thus two clear indications on the face of this disposition that the sub-adjacent minerals were not included, ie, (a) the reference in the narrative to superiority only and (b) the reference, in the dispositive clause, to the property of John McArthur Moir. His property included the surface only, but not the reserved minerals which were the property of the disponing superior.

This ambiguity in the dispositive clause, taken together with the clear reference in the narrative, allowed the House of Lords to interpret the dispositive clause as conveying superiority only, not the minerals as well. It seems fairly clear, however, that, had it not been for that special feature in the description in the dispositive clause, it would not have been permissible to refer to the narrative and so the deed would have carried minerals to the disponee.

In the present case, what we have is a conveyance of a landed estate extending to nearly 160 acres or thereby, plus the sub-adjacent minerals. Following on the description of the landed estate under four separate particular descriptions, each referring to a plan as delineating the subjects conveyed, there are a number of subjects excepted.

In the case of the subjects first conveyed by that disposition, nine areas are excepted. Eight of these had previously been sub-feued, but the ninth area had been disponed. Accordingly, whatever the original intention may have been in relation to the eight areas previously feued, the ninth area was clearly intended to be wholly excluded from the subjects conveyed, since the granter of this disposition was not in titulo to convey any interest therein. That being the position, it is significant that no differentiation or distinction whatsoever is made in the formula or language used when excepting the eight feus, as compared with the exception of the ninth disponed area.

The disposition proceeds on a similar pattern to except certain further feus and a further disponed area, again with no apparent distinction or differentiation between feus previously given off and subjects previously conveyed away by disposition.

It is fairly clear that only a relatively small part of the total area of 160 acres or thereby was thus excepted or excluded by these various exceptions and, in the main, what was passing to the disponee was the *dominium utile* of a landed estate.

In determining what effect these exceptions have in the context of the disposition which is the subject of this opinion, the following factors are relevant.

(i) In ordinary conveyancing practice, where the intention is to transfer *dominium directum* only and not *dominium utile*, it is not correct to except the *dominium utile* of feus previously given off from the subjects conveyed. See *Green's Encyclopaedia* vol 5, paras 618 and 619 and Burns *Conveyancing Practice* at p 347:

'There is not, and has never been, any difference between the form of a disposition of a superiority and the form of a disposition of property with three exceptions...'

The three exceptions are (a) a reference in the narrative clause to a sale of the superiority only – not present in this case; (b) assignation of feudu-ties – the effect of which is dealt with above; and (c) the exception from warrandice – again, dealt with above.

(ii) In the present case, exactly the same formula and exactly the same style of words is used when excepting subjects which have been previously feued and subjects which have been previously disponed. The sellers' argument is that, in the case of the subjects which have previously been feued, there is, by implication, a qualification to the exception in each such case restricting the exception to *dominium utile* only; but of course that does not apply to subjects which have been previously disponed. I find it exceedingly difficult to give any weight to that argument when exactly the same wording is used to except *dominium utile* only but not *dominium directum* in the case of feued subjects; and altogether to exclude *plenum dominium* in the case of the subjects disponed. If the two exceptions, of feus and of subjects previously disponed, were intended to have different implications, one would have expected different wording to be used but this has not been done.

Reading the dispositive clause entire but in isolation, I am driven inescapably to the conclusion that, as a result of the form which the exceptions take, the *dominium directum* of the various individual feus has effectively been excluded from the subjects conveyed and did not therefore pass to the disponee. The fact that this disposition contains the 'badges' of a superiority disposition is not, in my view, sufficient to alter that conclusion.

The only speciality in this case which might be relied on to modify that view is the inclusion, in the assignation of rents clause, of a reference to a schedule of feuduties which is attached to the disposition. So far as I can see, the feuduties assigned by reference to this schedule do coincide exactly with the various exceptions of feued subjects from the subjects conveyed in the first, second, third and fourth places. No explanation is given for this schedule in the assignation of rents clause but one reasonable assumption is that the purpose of the schedule is to identify feuduties payable by the vassals of the several excepted areas for the benefit of the disponees, which (if *dominium directum* only was intended to be conveyed) would facilitate collection of these feuduties by the disponees, standing in place of the disponers.

As noted above, however, an assignation of feuduties, although normally included in a disposition of *dominium directum*, serves only a very limited purpose, namely to give the disponee of the *dominium directum* a title to collect the feuduties from individual vassals in the short period between completion of the transaction and the taking of infeftment by the disponee. Once so infeft, the title of the disponee to collect feuduties rests on his infeftment, not on the assignation of the feuduties.

Further, although this is rare, it is a recognised feudal rule that feuduties can be assigned to an assignee without a conveyance of the *dominium directum* itself and this gives the assignee at least a personal title to collect the feuduties in place of the infeft superior granting that assignation.

Accordingly, in determining whether or not the *dominium directum* was intended to be conveyed in this case, I think it is fair to treat the assignation of feuduties and its incorporated schedule as neutral, giving no clear or conclusive indication one way or the other as to the intended effect of the exceptions in the dispositive clause.

In the case of *Orr* v *Mitchell* referred to above, the decision of the Court of Session was overturned in the House of Lords. The case was therefore clearly narrowly decided. In contrast to the disposition in this case, in *Orr* v *Mitchell*, there was a clear ambiguity within the dispositive clause itself, in that what was conveyed was 'ALL and WHOLE the town and lands of Hillfoot as at present possessed by John M. Moir'. In the narrative of that disposition, there is a clear reference to the superiority and feuduty of the lands of Hillfoot, and no more. Further, since the minerals under the lands of Hillfoot could not have been possessed by John M. Moir since he had no title thereto, that phrase in the dispositive clause was clearly to that extent ambiguous. There is no such ambiguity in this case. Further, the terms of the narrative clause in the disposition in *Orr* v *Mitchell* leave absolutely no doubt whatever that the intention was to convey simply *dominium directum* and no more. There is no such indicator in this case, and indeed, looking at the way in which the dispositive clause is framed, the apparent intention is to exclude *dominium directum*.

On that basis, I think it is very difficult to say that the dispositive clause in this disposition is not, in its terms, express and unambiguous. But, unless one can say that the dispositive clause is ambiguous, there is no room for qualifying or modifying the plain terms of the dispositive clause by reference to other provisions in the deed, which, in this case, do not really give a clear indication one way or the other. In particular, it is undoubtedly contrary to good conveyancing practice to except even the *dominium utile* of subjects previously feued in a conveyance of the superiority thereof; *a fortiori*, to except the land itself in unqualified terms.

In these circumstances, while the court might be disposed to reach the same conclusion as in *Orr* v *Mitchell*, the indicators in this case are very much weaker than the indicators in the disposition in *Orr* v *Mitchell*. For my part, I think the court would feel obliged to give effect to the plain terms of the dispositive clause as necessarily implying that the *dominium directum* and *dominium utile* of the excepted areas were totally excluded from the subjects conveyed. The disponees would therefore have no title to the superiority of the excepted areas.

Certainly, there is no clear precedent to which the sellers can point as supporting their view that an exception in these terms in the dispositive clause implies an exception merely of dominium utile, which allows a passing of the *dominium directum*. If anything, the authorities are quite clearly in the opposite sense. Against that, the case of *Orr* v *Mitchell* has special features which are not here present.

According to the memorialists, the sellers have offered a title both to *dominium utile* and *dominium directum*. While their title to the *dominium utile* is no doubt valid, I do not think they are in a position to offer a title to the *dominium directum* or at least they are not in a position to offer a marketable title, which is perhaps more important. Since the title to the *dominium directum* is not, in my view, marketable on the deeds produced, this is not a title which the purchasers are obliged to accept.

Manual, para 15.1.

FEUDUTY

30   Irritation of the feu

Pre-emption clause in disposition – whether right had been exercised –
whether right would prescribe

Date: June 1990

Memorial

A disposition contained a right of pre-emption and an irritancy clause. A
question arose as to whether the property had been offered to the superior
at the time of sale. There was no evidence of a Minute of Waiver. The
following issues were raised:

1   What was the present position with regard to the right of pre-emption
in the disposition?

2   Whether the superior was entitled to irritate without compensation, or
whether the superior was entitled to purchase the subjects at the price for
which the property was sold at the time when the clause of pre-emption
could have been exercised.

3   Whether any further steps should be taken with regard to the clause of
pre-emption, and whether it would prescribe.

Opinion

1   In terms of the 1972 disposition in this case, it is not lawful nor in the
power of the feuars (which includes expressly the original disponees and
their successors and assignees whomsoever) to sell the subjects or any part
thereof until the same shall first have been offered to the superiors (which,
again, includes their successors) at the same price (but without any reference to 'the same conditions' as is normal in such a clause) which may be
offered by any other person. All sales or dispositions made or granted
without such an offer having first been made are *ipso facto* declared to be
null and void in terms of this clause.

The clause appears *in gremio* of the dispositive clause of a feudal title
which has entered the record and has thus qualified the infeftment. It is, in
addition, declared to be a real burden. There is a further declaration to the
effect that, if any of the real burdens in the feu disposition are contravened,
all acts of contravention are void; and there is a consequent forfeiture
clause.

My view is that, taken by itself, the clause of pre-emption in this case is
clear and unambiguous according to its terms. It is settled law that a
clause of pre-emption in itself is not invalid and so remains effective and

enforceable, subject only to the time limits and certain other restrictions imposed on the operation of such clauses by the Conveyancing Amendment (Scotland) Act 1938, s 9. These restrictions are not in point in this case.

Under the 1986 disposition, the subjects were disponed by A to B. In the narrative clause of that disposition it is stated explicitly that the conveyance is granted in consideration of the sum of £X paid by B in consideration whereof the disponers 'Have Sold and Do Hereby Dispone...'

On the face of it, that disposition offends against the terms of the pre-emption clause, unless the subjects were first offered to the superiors at the price of £X, which seems not to have been done. As a result, the disposition is open to challenge on that ground. Admittedly, the conveyance was probably *not* in fact granted on sale in the accepted arm's-length sense, because A and B (both companies) were obviously associated in that (a) they have the same registered office and (b) the disposition, although granted for £X, was adjudged not chargeable with stamp duty. This raises a fairly strong presumption that the conveyance represented an internal company reorganisation but that is not what the terms of the narrative clause narrate. The disposition was duly recorded in the Register of Sasines and so ostensibly created an infeftment for the disponees.

Likewise, the 1988 disposition was granted by B, infeft under the 1986 disposition, in favour of C, again for a stated consideration of £XY. Again, in exchange therefor, the conveyance narrates that the disponers 'Have Sold and Do Hereby Dispone...' to the disponees. So, again, on the face of it this second disposition offends against the terms of the pre-emption clause as it represents a sale for a stated price. However, on closer examination, it seems fairly obvious that the companies B and C were associated, in that they have the same registered office and, notwithstanding the stated consideration, the disposition was adjudicated as exempt from stamp duty. In this case, although the deed was executed and presumably delivered (it was presented for stamping, which is normally effected by the disponee), this second disposition was not recorded. At best, therefore, it represents an effective personal title to the disponees.

In the case of *Hay's Tr* v *Hay's Trs* 1951 SC 329, the court was prepared to accept an agreed concession by both parties that the narrative in a disposition stated the facts incorrectly and, for the purpose of determining the rights of the parties under the destination therein, these erroneous statements could be disregarded and extrinsic evidence admitted to prove the true facts. In the more recent case of *Smith* v *Mackintosh* 1989 SLT 148, however, Lord Sutherland (correctly) disapproved of the decision in *Hay's Trustee* only to the extent to which the court in that case were prepared to accept extrinsic evidence as contradicting the plain terms of a probative deed. Accordingly, unless and until set aside or rectified under the appropriate procedures, the narratives in the two dispositions referred to above must be accepted at their face value as correctly stating the facts. (It is not legitimate to question the narrative in these two dispositions as that is contrary to the rule recently reaffirmed in *Winston* v *Patrick* 1980 SC 246 and the cases on which that decision proceeded.) On that basis I think it is clear beyond argument that there was a sale on each occasion within the meaning of the clause of pre-emption in the feu disposition because the narrative of each deed expressly so states; and so, *ex facie* of the titles, each disposition was granted contrary to the terms of the clause of pre-emption in the feu disposition. As a result, each disposition, if not void, is at least voidable at the instance of the superior by virtue of the express provision in the pre-emption clause. In addition, and alternatively, each of the two dispositions contravene the terms of a real condition or real burden in the feu disposition and as such an irritancy has been incurred on each occasion. I do not see any escape from this initial conclusion.

That view is, however, subject to the qualification that, at least in the case of an irritancy clause, the court have always taken the view that, notwithstanding the stringent terms in which such clauses are normally phrased, any breach of a feuing condition, whether for payment of feuduty or some other monetary sum or *ad factum praestandum*, does not in itself automatically avoid the feu disposition which was breached. Instead, to complete an irritation of a feu resulting from a breach of a feuing condition, it is essential in every case that the superior should raise an action of irritancy *ob non solutum canonem* and obtain and record a decree, in order to extinguish the rights of the feuar under the original feudal writ – see Halliday *Conveyancing Law and Practice* para 17–30 and the cases there cited. In my view, exactly the same rule would be applied by the courts to the statement in each of the two dispositions within the pre-emption clause, to the effect that any disposition granted in contravention of the terms of the pre-emption clause shall be *ipso facto* null and void. As is the case with an irritancy clause, I think the courts would take the view that nullity was *not* an automatic consequence of a breach of this condition and that, instead, a decree of irritancy or an equivalent decree of declarator would first be required to extinguish the right of the vassal under the original feu disposition. However, subject to the qualifications in my succeeding answers, I think there is no doubt that, on the face of it, an action of irritancy or its equivalent is bound to succeed.

Accordingly, in my view, the 1986 disposition conferred a valid but challengeable real right in the person of the disponee thereunder on the recording thereof; and that the 1988 disposition conferred a valid but challengeable personal title on the disponee thereunder. Both dispositions are, however, in my opinion, subject to challenge at the instance of the superior on the grounds that the clause of pre-emption in the original feu disposition has not been observed and so an irritancy has been incurred. Subject to the following qualifications, the superior can, in my opinion, set aside and reduce both the 1986 and the 1988 dispositions and resume possession of the subjects by the obtaining of an appropriate decree of irritancy.

2   I think there is no doubt that the feuars are in breach of the terms of the clause of pre-emption in the feu disposition. That being so, an action of irritancy is competent. I think it is also settled beyond argument that, if the superior succeeds in irritating the feu, there cannot be any question of his being required to pay compensation to the vassal. This point has, I think, been decided beyond challenge by two decisions, namely, *Cassels* v *Lamb*

(1885) 12 R 722 where, by a majority of the whole court, it was held that the vassal and sub-vassal in such circumstances are not entitled to any compensation on the superior's obtaining a decree of irritancy and in *Sandeman* v *Scottish Property Investment Co Limited* (1885) 12 R (HL) 67, although not directly on this point, followed *Cassels*. On the basis of these two decisions, any claim by the vassal for compensation, if the feu is irritated, seems bound to fail.

In addition, and in the option of the superior (and in his option alone), the superior could elect, if he preferred, to insist on implement of the clause of pre-emption in the feu disposition rather than proceeding by way of irritancy. I do not think there could be any reason in this case why the superior should elect to proceed by this route in the first instance but, if an action of irritancy failed (for which see below) then, as a fall-back, the superior might seek to adopt this alternative remedy. In the present circumstances, however, this seems to me a somewhat unrealistic proposition in that, to succeed, the superior would first have to set aside the 1986 and 1988 dispositions in order to reinvest A. He could then insist that, as a preliminary to any disposition by A to B at the price of £X, A should first offer the subjects to him at that same price. If the original sale had been an arm's-length sale, following on a negotiated bargain and if the purchaser thereunder was anxious to maintain his part of the bargain and to retain the subjects at the contract price, the superior might stand some chance of success on this alternative basis. But there is nothing in the clause of pre-emption in this case which would allow the superior, having set aside the 1986 and 1988 dispositions, then to require A actually to make an offer to the superiors at the stated price of £X. As the clause of pre-emption is framed, it is prohibitory in the sense that the vassal may not sell without first offering the subjects to the superior at the same price, but that does not place a positive obligation on the vassal to make an offer to the superior to sell at that price if he elects not to do so. Accordingly, while in theory, in certain situations, the superior may have the alternative of enforcing the pre-emption at the stated price, it does not seem to me that this is a practical possibility in the present situation.

3   The long negative prescription operates to extinguish rights and obligations which have been neglected and where no attempt has been made to enforce them for the full period of twenty years. Clearly, therefore, there may be an argument that the long negative prescription would apply in this case to extinguish whatever rights the superior may presently have, when twenty years have expired from the first sale in 1986. However, since the subjects were not offered to the superior on that occasion, and have since been sold in 1988, a new pre-emptive right was created for the superior by the 1988 disposition and so the period of the long negative prescription would probably continue at least until the year 2008. Further, if the subjects are subsequently sold, then that in turn would trigger off the running of a further period of twenty years from the occasion of the subsequent sale.

Apart from statutory limitation, a right of pre-emption is a real burden which subsists and affects the property in the hands of the vassal for the time being in perpetuity. Admittedly, by statutory provision, it is now generally accepted that, where the vassal has made one offer to the superior under the right of pre-emption and that offer is not accepted, then the right falls permanently and absolutely. But that only applies where an offer has been made. In the present case, no offer has been made and the statutory provision therefore cannot apply unless and until an offer is actually made to the superior. That being so, I cannot see any case to support the view that the right of pre-emption will be extinguished in the year 2006 unless some further steps are taken.

In any event, it may be that the right to exercise a right of pre-emption is *res merae facultatis*, in which case the negative prescription has no application at all by virtue of the Prescription and Limitation (Scotland) Act 1973, s 7 and Sched 3(c). It is therefore not safe to assume that the title will be free from challenge altogether after the year 2006.

4   As to the action which should now be taken, there are, I think, various possibilities which are to some extent affected by the following factors:

(*a*) As the clause of pre-emption is drafted, it imposes an obligation *ad factum praestandum* on the vassal which, so far, has not been implemented. But, in the case of conditions of tenure in a feudal grant, the settled rule is that an irritancy, whether legal or conventional, may be purged at any time before the decree of declarator of irritancy has been granted and recorded – see *Precision Relays Limited* v *Beaton* 1980 SLT 206 and the Conveyancing (Scotland) Acts (1874 and 1879) Amendment Act 1887, s 4. Further, in the case of obligations *ad factum praestandum*, the court will normally give time to the vassal to purge the irritancy on cause shown.

(*b*) A clause of pre-emption in a title is a land obligation. It is therefore, in theory at least, subject to variation or discharge by the Lands Tribunal. The difficulty is in establishing grounds for a variation or discharge – see *Banff and Buchan District Council* v *Earl of Seafield's Estate* 1988 SLT (Lands Tr) 21. The memorialists may wish, none the less, to consider the possibility of an application to the Tribunal. There is then a further difficulty in that the condition has already been breached and, as a result, an irritancy has already been incurred. This point was discussed in *James Miller & Partners Limited* v *Hunt* 1974 SLT (Lands Tr) 9 and is commented on by Halliday in *The Conveyancing and Feudal Reform (Scotland) Act 1970* (2nd edn), p 36. While it may be that, in certain situations, a discharge or variation by the Lands Tribunal may remove the risk of irritancy, I doubt whether that would apply in circumstances such as we have here.

(*c*) The most hopeful alternative seems to me to be rectification of the 1986 and 1988 dispositions, to reflect the actual circumstances of the transfer, because, although on the face of it there was a 'sale' at a stated price, it seems to me not unlikely that the 'sale' and the 'price' were purely artificially created for internal accounting purposes and that there was not in fact any true sale. Under the rule as to the conclusive quality of a probative writ, recently reaffirmed in *Smith* v *Mackintosh*

1989 SLT 148 and referred to above, I do not think it would be competent simply to lead extrinsic evidence to show that the narrative in the two dispositions in question is defective. The alternative of reduction or, more probably, rectification under the Law Reform (Miscellaneous Provisions) (Scotland) Act 1985 would, I think, be available to allow the memorialists to amend the terms of the 1986 and 1988 narratives so as to show that there was no true sale in the sense in which that term is used in the feu disposition, thus avoiding altogether a breach of the pre-emption. Clearly, this would require further investigation of the facts to see whether or not such a rectification was feasible in the circumstances but it does seem to me that this is worth exploring.

If the narrative in the two dispositions could be rectified – ie to show that there was no true sale – the superior would not be able to irritate on the basis that the right of pre-emption had not been offered. If it can be established that rectification is possible the memorialists could then approach the superior asking if he would be willing to waive his rights to pre-emption in terms of the deeds. If the superior was willing, the memorialists could agree to insert a right of pre-emption into a deed to take effect at the time of a future sale. If he refused, the memorialists could have the deeds rectified so that there was in any event no breach of the pre-emption right. In terms of the 1985 Act, any such rectification is normally retrospective and so the superior would be denied any entitlement either to pre-empt or to irritate in relation to the 1986 or 1988 dispositions. That would not, of course, remove his right of pre-emption on any future genuine sale by the memorialists, but presumably that is not a significant factor in relation to the present defect in the title.

I do not think there is any point in not taking action at this stage, because I cannot see that the problem will resolve itself by mere lapse of time and inaction on the part of the memorialists. Sooner or later, the question will have to be dealt with and the sooner the nettle is grasped the better it would be.

In this context, no doubt the memorialists will bear in mind that, if I am right in supposing that there was in fact no true sale and if, as a result, the narrative of the 1986 and 1988 dispositions could have been framed differently so as to escape from the effect of the pre-emption, then the memorialists may care to consider whether there may be a claim for professional negligence on the part of the solicitors who prepared the 1986 and 1988 dispositions which have created the problem for the memorialists and which might have been avoided by appropriate drafting.

Manual, para 16.3.

ENFORCEMENT OF BURDENS

31   Title to enforce

Title to enforce – interest to enforce – *jus quaesitum tertio* – acquiescence
in breach of real burden

Date: September 1989

Memorial

An offer was made to purchase a large commercial property in The Place
which the memorialists wished to develop. The title was derived from
several larger areas of ground. One of the writs contained several general
restrictions including a burden prohibiting the erection of buildings with
the exception of a greenhouse or vinery 'which burden shall operate as a
servitude ... in favour of the neighbouring feuars'.

The memorialists were concerned about the following matters:

1   Whether the burden operated to give a right to co-feuars on the basis
that it created a valid *jus quaesitum tertio*.

2   Whether the negative servitude against building would only have prescribed to the extent that it had already been violated, and thus be a
restriction on further building and extending buildings over the areas which
had not been built on.

3   Whether the construction of a car park would be restricted by the condition in question.

4   Whether application should be made to the Lands Tribunal in Scotland
for discharge of the condition.

Opinion

The subjects in question comprise the whole of the subjects described in a
disposition by the Trustees of the late Z in favour of WS. The description
in this disposition coincides more or less exactly with the site as delineated
on the site plan prepared by the architects. This area has a frontage to X
Street of 144 feet and extends northwards for a distance of 200 feet on the
west and east sides with the exception of an excluded portion at the south-
west corner which forms part of a tenement in South Street. This area
includes part, but not the whole, of two building stances feued separately
in 1853 in favour of A B and C D respectively. The relatively feu contract
in each case was followed by the recording of an Instrument of Sasine on
behalf of each disponee. The two feu contracts, and the two Instruments
of Sasine following thereon, are in substantially the same terms.

Each of these two building stances comprised an area of ground fronting

The Place on which a tenement has since been erected with back ground pertaining thereto and, in each case, to the north of the building stance and separated from it by a five-foot lane, two additional rear areas of ground delineated in a heavy black line on the site plan referred to above and marked thereon A and B. I emphasise at this point, because it is important, that areas A and B respectively comprised part only, but *not* the whole, of the subjects originally feued in 1853 to which the relevant Instruments of Sasine respectively relate. I will revert to this point later.

A furniture warehouse has subsequently been erected on part of area B, possibly encroaching also onto area A. The site of the warehouse is shown hatched on the site plan. The present proposal is to change the use of the warehouse to offices, to increase the height of the building by one storey, and to use the unbuilt ground as a car park. The memorialists are concerned in particular with the conditions imposed on the respective feuars in the 1853 contracts of areas A and B and have asked to be advised whether the development proposals offend against the conditions in the two recorded Instruments of Sasine.

The Instrument of Sasine relating to area A contains two potentially dangerous prohibitions so far as the developers are concerned, namely:

(1) On page fifth of the copy Instrument, there is a prohibition against carrying on, on the whole subjects of which area A forms part, any business, trade or employment or doing anything which might legally be deemed to be a nuisance or which should be harmful or disagreeable to . . . the neighbouring feuars and tenants of the subjects of which this particular area forms part, in whose favour it was declared that the prohibition should operate as a servitude on the area conveyed by that feu contract.

(2) More seriously for the developers, on page eighth of the copy Instrument, there is a further declaration to the effect that the feuar should not be entitled to erect any buildings whatever on area A except a greenhouse or vinery; and again this declaration in the relevant feu contract is to operate as a servitude on area A in favour of, in this case, 'the neighbouring feuars'. In this second prohibition, 'neighbouring feuars' are not more precisely defined.

Both these prohibitions seem to me to be framed in sufficiently clear and unambiguous terms to be enforceable as real burdens by anyone having a title to enforce. In each case, the prohibitions are imposed on the original vassal and his heirs and assignees; and, within the dispositive clause of the feu contract in each case, it is expressly declared that each piece of ground is disponed with and under, *inter alia*, these particular prohibitions. In these circumstances, in my opinion, both prohibitions have effectively been imposed as real burdens. The first one applies to the whole of the area contained in each feu contract; the second applies only to the northmost areas represented by areas A and B. In each case, the prohibition is declared to be a servitude although I doubt if it qualifies as such; but that does not, in my opinion, prevent the prohibition in each case from being effectively imposed as a real burden. See *Braid Hills Hotel Co* v *Manuels* 1909 SC 120 where a not dissimilar prohibition against erecting anything other than a greenhouse etc was declared to be a servitude but was held, none the less, enforceable as a real burden. In my opinion, the courts would apply the same criteria in this case and it would not be safe to proceed on any other assumption.

As far as area B is concerned and, to some extent, possibly a small part of area A, both prohibitions have been breached, for very many years (the exact period is irrelevant) by the construction of the warehouse on these areas which, of course, offends against both prohibitions as being used for business or commercial purposes, and as being a building on an area where no buildings are permitted other than a vinery or greenhouse. Although these terms ('vinery' and 'greenhouse') may be indefinite to some extent, they are I think sufficiently definite to be enforceable; and there is no possibility, in my opinion, that the present building on the site can be said to fall within one or other of these two classifications. Accordingly, the construction of the building and its subsequent use both offend against the prohibitions referred to above.

Two questions arise:

(1)   Who has a title to enforce the prohibitions in the two Instruments of Sasine above referred to?

Here, I think there are three distinct categories:
  (*a*) The present superior clearly has a title to enforce the prohibitions, although it is doubtful whether the superior could demonstrate the necessary interest.
  (*b*) The tenements in The Place were constructed on parts of the two areas conveyed by the two original feu contracts. At some subsequent date, areas A and B were separated from the title to the tenements in The Place and passed into different ownership. In my view, however, applying the 'subdivision rule', the proprietors of the flats in each tenement have, by virtue of that subdivision, acquired a *jus quaesitum tertio* to enforce respectively the prohibitions which apply both to the *whole* original area, on part of which each tenement is erected, and on area A and on area B respectively. I think this point must now be regarded as settled by the decision in *Lees* v *North-East Fife District Council* 1987 SLT 769. In that case, a single area of ground was conveyed under real burdens restricting the use of one part thereof for residences, and restricting the use of the other part for the construction of a swimming pool and ancillary offices. Residences were duly erected on the appropriate part and, thereafter, the swimming pool part passed into different ownership. The new proprietor proposed to use the swimming pool part for a different purpose, which was prohibited under the original title. The owner of one of the dwellinghouses objected, relying on a *jus quaesitum tertio* created by virtue of the subdivision. The Inner House held that the whole conditions in each disposition, of each dwellinghouse and of the swimming pool part, were mutually enforceable, and that the dwellinghouse proprietor had a title and an interest to prevent the use of the swimming pool part for a different purpose. Interdict was granted accordingly.

If anything, the conditions and the circumstances in this case are somewhat stronger than in *Lees*; and accordingly, in my opinion, the courts would apply exactly the same principle to both the prohibitions referred to above. The result is that, in the case of area B, on which the warehouse undoubtedly has been constructed, the proprietor of each flat in the tenement fronting area B has a title to enforce both the restriction against building on area B and the general restriction against using the whole area (both the tenement stance and the rear area B) for business or commercial purposes, but only *quoad* that whole area. Likewise, each proprietor of each flat in the tenement fronting area A has a title to enforce both prohibitions *quoad* area A, but not *quoad* area B, since originally the two feu contracts were independent and did not create cross-rights of *jus quaesitum inter se.*

In the case of area A, however, the title to enforce is only significant to the present proposals: (i) insofar as the intention is to use that part of area A as a car park, to which, I think, the proprietors of the flats in The Place fronting area A could object under the prohibition against business use; and (ii) if, but *only* if, the present depository is erected in part (no matter how small a part) on area A, then each proprietor of each flat in The Place tenement fronting area A has a title to enforce the prohibition against further building.

It would seem from the plans provided that part only but not the whole area A passed under the 1903 disposition. I am not advised as to who are now the proprietors of the remaining part of area A; but, if that has passed into different ownership from the proprietors of the tenement of flats in The Place fronting area A, the proprietors of that remaining part of area A will likewise have a *jus quaesitum tertio* to enforce the prohibitions in the title to area A, on a further application of the subdivision rule.

(c) In addition, a very much wider class of proprietors potentially has a title to enforce both prohibitions, which are expressly declared, in each title, to be imposed as servitudes. In the case of the prohibition against commercial use the servitude is declared to be for the benefit of neighbouring feuars and tenants of 'the said lands of which the said stance forms a part', which would seem to refer back to the larger area of nine acres described in the part and portion clause. In the case of the prohibition against building the servitude is declared to be for the benefit of 'the neighbouring feuars'. Given that the neighbouring feuars have already been referred to and more precisely defined in the earlier prohibition, there is certainly an argument to support the view that the same group of neighbouring feuars is intended to have the benefit of this prohibition. If that construction is considered too indefinite, there are none the less undoubtedly 'neighbouring feuars' in the sense that there are feus which actually adjoin the areas in question on the west, north and east sides and they would clearly be 'neighbouring feuars' in the sense that their properties actually adjoin the property in question. Accordingly, while it may be argued that this third potential group of enforcers is not sufficiently defined, I think there is a very real risk that the court might hold otherwise, at least for the benefit of any feuar whose property actually abutted on the areas in question.

(2) Who has an interest to enforce?

It is, of course, also necessary for any potential enforcer to demonstrate not merely a title to enforce but also an interest to enforce. In the case of the superior, it must be doubtful whether he can demonstrate any interest. In the case of proprietors in categories (*b*) or (*c*) above, however, their interest is immediately apparent, particularly so in the case of category (*b*) (proprietors of flats in The Place), especially those in the tenement fronting area B. They clearly have a title, and they clearly have the most significant interest in the present proposals, which may indeed adversely affect their amenity.

In the case of all potential enforcers, however, there is an argument that they *may* have lost their interest to enforce by acquiescence, in that, for at least 50 years and probably a good deal longer, the depository has existed on area B without apparent objection. The question then is whether, by acquiescence, the proprietors in some or all of the various categories have lost all interest to object to the present proposals.

There is no doubt whatever that all potential enforcers have lost their interest to enforce the prohibitions in the respective titles as regards the existing building and its use as a depository. It is settled beyond argument that, where a person having a title to object has knowingly allowed, without objection, substantial breaches of feuing conditions which involved the vassal in considerable expense (as is the position in this case) then he must in such circumstances be taken to have acquiesced. See *Ben Challum Ltd* v *Buchanan* 1955 SC 348. There is therefore no possibility of any potential enforcer now succeeding in an objection to the existing warehouse or its existing use. Further, acquiescence by an earlier proprietor transmits against and binds his singular successors where the breach acquiesced in is visible and obvious, as it must be in this case. Acquiescence involving loss of interest in such cases is, however, relative and is always a matter of degree. I think this proposition is best illustrated by the decision in *Millar* v *Christie* 1961 SC 1. In that case, there was an express grant of servitude right of access by a cart road for the benefit of a neighbouring property. The road was used for many years, for carts and other similar traffic, by the owner of the dominant tenement. Subsequently, the owner of the servient tenement put up a building which encroached onto the access area, reducing the width of it from 15 feet to 5 feet 9 inches; and so rendered it inadequate for the passage of carts. The First Division held that, while the access undoubtedly had been curtailed by the servient owner's encroachment, acquiescence in that encroachment had restricted, but had not wholly extinguished, the servitude right. Lord President Clyde refers with approval to the *dictum* of Lord Gifford in the earlier case of *Stewart* v *Bunten* (1878) 5 R 1108. Lord Gifford states: 'I am unable to hold, as a proposition applicable to such cases, that the concession of a part is the same as the concession of the whole. I think acquiescence, in its nature, goes no further than the thing acquiesced in. It does not in general infer consent to anything different and especially to anything which may be far

more objectionable.' In *Millar* v *Christie*, the court applied the same principle. Similarly in *Mactaggart & Co* v *Roemmele* 1907 SC 1318 (the leading
case on the effect of acquiescence on the title of a co-feuar having a *jus
quaesitum tertio* and to that extent relevant here) the court held that a
particular feuar who had failed to object to the erection of tenements
contrary to a prohibition in the title, was *not* barred by acquiescence from
later objecting to the erection of other tenements which he considered to
be more injurious to the amenity of his particular property.

If the present proposals did not involve any additional structural work,
but merely the internal conversion of the existing building to another use
and if there were no associated car parking proposals, I think it might be
difficult for even the tenement proprietors in the tenement fronting area B
to instruct an interest to object to a limited proposal of that kind, since it
is difficult to see how the amenity of the adjoining tenement could be
affected. But what is proposed here is to construct an additional storey on
top of the existing building which clearly may be offensive in terms of light
and prospect particularly to ground floor flats; and, in addition, to construct a car park on the surrounding vacant area which is always potentially
objectionable on the grounds of noise, air pollution, and visual amenity, etc
and which is clearly in breach of the prohibitions against commercial use.

In the light of the foregoing observations, I answer the specific questions
put to me in my letter of instructions thus:

1   I confirm that, in my opinion, there are a number of the proprietors,
certainly proprietors of all the flats in the tenements fronting area B, possibly the proprietors of the flats in the tenement fronting area A, and, almost
certainly, an indeterminate number of other 'neighbouring feuars' who can
competently instruct both a title and an interest to object to the present
proposals to convert the warehouse into an office with the addition of one
extra storey and the provision of car parking. Because of the number of
proprietors potentially involved, I agree that it is quite impracticable to
consider obtaining the consent of all potentially interested parties.

2   I agree that the servitude or burden prohibiting building on areas A and
B and the prohibition against commercial use imply acquiescence to the
continued use of the existing building for its existing use *but nothing more*.
In particular, by that acquiescence, proprietors having a title to enforce can
instruct an interest to enforce the prohibition so as to prevent the addition
of a further storey on the existing building, the extension of buildings onto
areas presently not built on, and the use of unbuilt areas as car parking.

3   The creation of a car park is not struck at by the prohibition which
restricts buildings on areas A and B to greenhouse or vinery; but, in my
opinion, is struck at by the general prohibition against use of the *whole* of
each stance for commercial purposes.

4   In my opinion, the only practicable solution in this case is to apply to
the Lands Tribunal in Scotland for a discharge or variation of the prohibitions in question. There is undoubtedly, in my view, a *jus quaesitum tertio*
vested in a number of proprietors, if only the proprietors of the flats in the
tenement area fronting area B. They also have the strongest interest. In

fact, I think the *jus quaesitum* goes much wider than that but certainly those proprietors do have *jus quaesitum tertio*. It is unlikely that all of them would consent and in any event the class of potential enforcers may extend to anything up to the whole original nine acres so that even obtaining the consent of proprietors of the flats in the tenement fronting area B would not be sufficient.

I would not consider indemnity insurance appropriate or indeed feasible. Given the views expressed in this opinion, I think it unlikely that any insurance company would be prepared to provide an indemnity because of the probability that there will be objections and that these objections are enforceable.

Without a discharge from the Lands Tribunal, there is no other practicable way in which the development could proceed.

Manual, para 17.2.

32   Loss of interest to enforce

Construction of burden – whether enforceable – whether Lands Tribunal
would waive – compensation

Date: October 1988

Memorial
At issue was the construction of burdens in a feu disposition, in respect of which the memorialists asked the following:

1   Whether a clause in the feu charter of 1896 entitled the superior to terminate the proprietor's right to sell liquor.

2   Whether an application to the Lands Tribunal might be successful, and if so, whether the Tribunal might be likely to award compensation.

3   Whether the use of the premises could constitute a nuisance.

4   Whether the superior could object to the use of part of the subjects as a car park.

5   Whether it was necessary to approach the superior for a minute of waiver in respect of the liquor prohibition.

Opinion
1   A prohibition against the sale of wines and spirits contained in a feu charter by superior to vassal is undoubtedly a valid and enforceable condition at the instance of the superiors, provided it otherwise satisfies the requirements of a real burden or real condition, namely:

(*a*) that it is inserted in the dispositive clause, which this condition is;

(*b*) that it enters the record as a qualification of the vassal's infeftment, which this condition has done; and

146

(*c*) that it is in its terms clear and unambiguous, which, in my opinion, the condition in this case is.

Further, the superior is deemed to have an interest in enforcing such conditions even although that interest may not be patrimonial – see *Earl of Zetland* v *Hislop* (1882) 9 R(HL) 40. The decision in that case has frequently been quoted in this context and has never been questioned. It also involved the prohibition against sale of liquor, in a public house in Grangemouth where the superior almost certainly had no patrimonial interest to enforce but was held none the less entitled so to do.

The superior's right to enforce a feuing condition in a charter is also *res merae facultatis* and is therefore not extinguished by the long negative prescription. Accordingly, the fact that the condition in this case first appeared in a feu charter of 1896 and has not since been insisted upon does not now prevent the superior from requiring the vassal to adhere to the condition.

It is the case that the superior's interest to enforce a feuing condition may be lost by acquiescence. This will certainly occur in cases where the charter contains a specific prohibition against certain acts by the vassal, and where the vassal contravenes the prohibition to the knowledge of the superior and expends substantial sums in the process. By failing to object to such expenditure, the superior may find himself barred from later insisting that the condition, originally enforceable, should now be adhered to.

That principle does not apply to mere prohibitions against particular uses. Thus, if a feu charter restricts the use of heritable subjects to a dwellinghouse only, that condition is enforceable in the first instance. If, subsequently, the vassal starts to use part of the dwellinghouse as an office or consulting room, and the superior does not object, and if such use does not involve any significant expenditure in adapting the premises for that purpose, the superior would not be barred from requiring the vassal at a later date to cease using the premises for purposes other than a dwellinghouse. Admittedly, by his acquiescence, the superior has certainly prevented himself from irritating the feu as a result of the past breach of that condition; but he is still entitled to insist upon observance of that condition in future years.

In the present case, the superior is in an even stronger position than in the illustration given above. This is because, when the charter was granted, the subjects were already being used for the sale of liquor as is evident from the terms of the feu charter. Notwithstanding that use, and the superior's express permission, as narrated in clause eighth, the power so to use the premises is then explicitly declared to be valid during the superior's pleasure and the superior is declared to be entitled at any time to withdraw that permission, whereupon the vassal is then obliged to observe the restriction on use. By virtue of that declaration, in my view, the vassal is personally barred from pleading acquiescence on the part of the superior in the use of the premises for the sale of liquor. Accordingly, at any time, the superior can require the vassal to cease the sale of liquor on the premises and to observe the prohibitions in clause eighth.

2   There is no doubt that the prohibition on use in clause eighth is a land

obligation and, as such, it would be competent to apply to the Lands Tribunal for a variation or discharge thereof. I am not aware of the local circumstances, but it seems to me that, unless there has been some dramatic recent change in the locality, the fact that the subjects have been used as a public house or licensed hotel since at least before 1896 makes it almost certain that the Tribunal would be prepared to waive or discharge the prohibition against the sale of liquor in clause eighth.

I do not think there is any prospect whatsoever of the superior's succeeding in a claim for compensation because of the very restricted circumstances in which compensation can be awarded in terms of the 1970 Act.

3   The reference in clause eighth to 'public house' occurs in the narrative of past use by the vassal, prior to the granting of the charter. When we come to the positive prohibition in that clause, however, the term 'public house' is not used. Instead, the charter declares that, without the permission of the superior, the feuar is not entitled to use the said houses or offices (which refers back to clause first in which a dwellinghouse and outhouse are referred to) or any part thereof, for selling any ale, beer, port or wine, whisky or other spirituous liquors. Accordingly, the fact that the premises are used as a licensed hotel is irrelevant in construing the prohibition, which applies with equal force to the sale of liquor from the premises, whether they be a public house or a licensed hotel.

Clause eighth also prohibits the vassal from using the feu, including buildings, for any trade or business that may be a nuisance or occasion annoyance to inhabitants in the neighbourhood. 'Nuisance' in this context must mean, I think, a nuisance actionable in law. It seems to me inconceivable that, after the lapse of nearly 100 years, any neighbour could now complain that this particular trade, which has continued throughout the whole of that period, is a nuisance or annoyance in terms of the charter. There is, however, a very remote possibility that the superior might challenge the vassal's use on this basis. Looking to the power of the superior to withdraw consent at any time, this is not really material; but it may be that, if the superior did receive complaints from neighbouring proprietors, this might induce the superior to withdraw the consent which, in my view, he may competently do at any time. To a very limited extent, therefore, this provision as to nuisance does marginally increase the risk to the vassal of some adverse action by the superior.

4   The prohibition in the charter of 1896 is repeated more or less verbatim in the feu charter of 1914. As I understand it, however, no buildings are erected on the 1914 subjects, which are used exclusively as a car park.

Clause seventh of the 1914 feu charter prohibits the vassal from using buildings on that piece of ground for the sale of spirituous liquors without consent. Accordingly, if there are no buildings on the ground, that prohibition does not meantime apply. In addition, however, there is also the same prohibition against use of the ground itself, not merely the buildings thereon, for any trade or business that may be a nuisance or occasion annoyance. The same considerations apply in relation to this prohibition as apply in relation to the same prohibition in the 1896 feu charter; and, after this lapse of time, I would have thought this now to be unenforceable. In any event, car parking is not struck at by the prohibition and so the superior has no entitlement to object to the use of the ground for that purpose.

5   Finally, I am also asked whether or not it is necessary to approach the superior for a minute of waiver in respect of the liquor prohibition.

No minute of waiver is necessary in the sense that, in terms of the 1896 feu charter, the feuar for the time being, and any purchaser from him, is entitled to continue to use the subjects as at present by express provision in clause eighth. Accordingly, if the subjects are now sold, the purchaser would not require to approach the superior in order to continue using the subjects as a licensed hotel. But, unless and until the superior waives or discharges his right to withdraw the permission to use the subjects for the sale of liquor as expressly provided for in clause eighth, there is a risk, for the reasons given above, that the superior might withdraw his consent at any time. In that sense, therefore, a minute of waiver is necessary to remove the superior's power of withdrawing consent; or, alternatively, an order of the Lands Tribunal.

I would certainly expect that, if the vassal approaches the superior for a minute of waiver in these terms, the superior would ask for a capital sum and, at a guess, he would probably suggest a figure in the order of £1,000 to £3,000. In asking for a capital sum, the superior would undoubtedly have in mind the vassal's right to apply to the Lands Tribunal for a waiver of this prohibition and such an application, as stated above, would almost certainly succeed.

In the ordinary way, and bearing in mind the probability of a Tribunal Order discharging the prohibition, the superior would take into account the probable costs of an application to the Tribunal (especially if objections are lodged) and, in addition, the cost to the vassal of the intervening delay in obtaining the necessary order. In this case, that delay might entitle the superior to withdraw his consent to the use of the premises as a licensed hotel which, in my view, he is quite entitled to do at any time; and, having withdrawn consent, he would then be entitled to enforce that withdrawal of consent by interdict. If, in the meantime, the vassal had already applied to the Lands Tribunal for a discharge of the prohibition, the court might well be prepared to sist an application for interdict pending the outcome of the Tribunal proceedings; and there is precedent for this in past cases. But that cannot be guaranteed, and, if the superior first obtains interdict before an application to the Tribunal is lodged, I am not at all sure that the vassal would succeed in having the interdict lifted. In the result, there might be a serious and costly hiatus in the use of the premises as a licensed hotel and undoubtedly this is a factor which the superior would take into account in calculating what capital sum to demand.

Bearing these factors in mind, I would have thought the safest course for the vassal to adopt in this case is first to apply to the Lands Tribunal for a variation or discharge of the provision of clause eighth in the 1896 charter thereby, as it were, putting his foot in the door before the superior takes action. If the superior then withdraws his consent and seeks to interdict the vassal, I would have thought it likely, but by no means certain, that the court would refuse to grant interdict pending the outcome of the Tribunal application – looking to the very long period over which the subjects have been used for their present purpose – unless there has been some recent and very significant local development which might make it appropriate for the superior to require the subjects no longer to be used as a licensed hotel. There is no indication of that in my instructions and I assume that this is not so.

Further, it may well be that this particular superior does not seek capital payments in such circumstances. That is no doubt a matter of local knowledge and is certainly something on which I personally could not advise.

If I were acting for a purchaser, however, I would not accept the title as it stands. I would insist that, before proceeding, the seller obtained either a minute of waiver discharging the superior's right to withdraw permission; or, alternatively, an order from the Lands Tribunal varying or discharging the prohibition in clause eighth.

Manual, para 17.8.

THE ESTATE OF THE VASSAL

33   Barony privileges

Sea-greens – foreshore – ownership – rights of navigation and fishing –
negotiation to purchase – sale to third party – possible redress

Date: November 1990

Memorial

The memorialists proposed to acquire property with a view to constructing
a marina. A number of questions arose with regard to the titles:

1   Who owned the saltings; and whether there was anything the memorialists should be aware of before carrying out excavation works.

2   The memorialists had been in negotiation with the local district council
with a view to purchasing an adjacent piece of land belonging to the
council. While the memorialists were compiling information the council
had requested, the council sold the ground to a third party without any
advertisement. Had the council acted *ultra vires*?

Opinion

1   As I understand it, saltings or, as they are commonly termed, sea-
greens, comprise areas of land, sometimes quite substantial areas, which
are not strictly speaking below the high-water mark of ordinary spring tides
but which are none the less occasionally or even regularly overrun on
exceptional occasions when the tide is particularly high. Because the inun-
dation of these areas is only occasional and not regular, they can in certain
situations be used as grazings. I assume that part or possibly the whole of
the area shaded red on the relevant plan may come within this definition.

The legal status of saltings as above described has not, I think, been
definitively determined but the position seems to be fairly clear. So, in
Rankine, *Land Ownership* (4th edn) at p 278, after dealing with the foreshore and rights therein, the author deals with sea-greens which, in his
opinion, are not part of the foreshore; and accordingly, since they are not
foreshore, they must be susceptible of private ownership on normal feudal
tenure, freed altogether from the restraints on ownership which apply in
the case of the foreshore, if ownership thereof has been established.

Rankine's view is based on a general statement in Erskine II, 6, 17 and
the case there cited by Erskine, *Bruce v Rashiehill and Others* (1714) M
9342. In that case, there was in fact an express conveyance of the sea-
greens in a barony charter; but it seems to me immaterial whether there is
an express conveyance of sea-greens as such or merely a conveyance of the
relevant area of land comprising or including sea-greens. The court held in

Bruce that the sea-greens were not *inter regalia*; that they were not a separate tenement; but that they are susceptible of being conveyed, or, if not conveyed, may be acquired by prescriptive possession as a pertinent of adjoining land.

In the present case, the ownership of the whole area has already been established by possession, whether it be partly or wholly foreshore, strictly speaking, or sea-greens. Accordingly, so far as ownership is concerned, there does not seem to be any problem here.

There are, however, certain points which may affect the memorialists in their proposals, the details of which I do not have:

(*a*) If and to the extent to which excavation is carried out on land which in fact forms part of the foreshore as such, and not sea-greens as above defined, such operations are legitimate only to the extent to which they do not interfere with the public right of navigation and fishing, to which every area of foreshore is invariably subject, no matter how the ownership thereof was acquired.

(*b*) Possibly more importantly, there are statutory restraints on operations of this kind which may limit the freedom of action of the memorialists under the Coast Protection Act 1949, as amended, which is dealt with in detail in Gordon, *Scottish Land Law*, paras 7–90 *et seq*, to which I would refer the memorialists for the detail of, and a comment on, these statutory provisions.

(*c*) Quite apart from the general public statutory control imposed by the Coast Protection Act, there may also, of course, be limitations on the freedom of action of the memorialists imposed by the Town and Country Planning Acts; and by the relevant Private Act.

2 On the facts as narrated in this question, I have no doubt that the memorialists are entitled to feel aggrieved at the way in which they have been treated by the local authority. Without having further and fairly detailed information on the sale to the third party, however, I could not attempt to advise as to whether or not the council had, in fact, acted *ultra vires*.

Local authorities have statutory powers of disposal both under the Local Government (Scotland) Act 1973 and, in the case of district councils as planning authorities, under the Town and Country Planning (Scotland) Act 1972. I am not specifically advised on this point but I would assume that the disposal by the district council in this case would be a disposal under the Town and Country Planning (Scotland) Act 1972, s 113, ie, a disposal of land held for planning purposes. That section has subsequently been amended in minor respects and in particular subsection (4) thereof has been repealed; but, these amendments apart, the section apparently still applies. As the memorialists will see, the powers of a local authority under that section to dispose of land are very wide. The council may so dispose to any person, in any manner and subject to any conditions which the council think expedient in the circumstances; but subject to the limitation that, in so acting, the council have a duty to secure that the best use is made of the land and, under s 113(3), with qualifications, to ensure that the land is disposed of at the best price and on the best terms that can be reasonably obtained. The fact that the memorialists had discussions with the local authority and their planning officials before disposal to a third party would not in itself imply any breach of duty under these provisions. However, under s 113(5), there is power to make representations to the Secretary of State and it may be that the memorialists might consider it worthwhile to make such representations because, as I understand it, although the land has been disposed of, there is no prospect of immediate development on the area in which the memorialists were interested and it is possible that the Secretary of State might intervene to assist the memorialists in an acquisition of whatever land they had in view to acquire. Whether or not this is a practical possibility I really could not say although, to be frank, I would rather doubt it.

Subject to the foregoing comments, my answer to this question therefore, is that, so far as I am informed, I could not say that the council have acted *ultra vires*.

Manual, para 18.2.

RESTRICTIONS ON THE USE OF LAND

34   Building control

Construction of 1981 and 1986 building regulations – application of ss 6, 10 and 11 of Building (Scotland) Act 1959, as amended

Date: December 1989

Memorial
The memorialists constructed an extension to their attic. Certain steps were then taken by the local authority. The following questions arose:

1   Whether the local authority had power to serve a notice on the memorialists or their successors in title under s 11 of the Building (Scotland) Act 1959, as amended.

2   Whether the local authority had power to serve a notice under s 10 of the abovementioned Act.

3   Whether the memorialists or their successors in the title were at risk under s 6 of the abovementioned Act in that there had been or it was proposed that there would be a change of use of any building in respect of which a building warrant was required.

Opinion
1   It seems quite clear from the letter from the local authority that the only grounds of objection to the use of the attic room as a bedroom would be under reg Q5(2) of the Building Standards (Scotland) Regulations 1981 (SI 1981 No1596) (the '1981 regulations'), which prescribes certain space requirements for an apartment. But, under reg Q1, there is an express provision to the effect that the regulations in Q5 are not to be subject to specification in a notice served under the 1959 Act, s 11.

According to the letter from the local authority, the original 1983 building warrant was granted for 'attic accommodation ancillary to the house'. In fact, that is not so. The original application for building warrant specified the proposed works as 'conversion of loft to play area' and the proposed use as 'play area'. The expression 'play area' does not appear in the 1981 regulations or in the Building Standards (Scotland) Regulations 1981–1986 (SI 1986 No 1278) (the '1986 regulations') as having a separate meaning of specification. As I read the plans for which warrant was granted in the light of the 1981 regulations, it seems to be quite clear that, whatever the proposed use may have been as stated in the application, by permitting the work to be carried out in accordance with that plan the local authority permitted the applicant to create an apartment in the house as defined in A5 of the 1981 regulations. That definition in turn looks to A7 which deals with 'rooms in houses' and defines an apartment as any habitable room not being a kitchen.

Under A5 of the 1981 regulations, room means any enclosed part of a storey of a building intended for human occupation, excluding bathroom, washroom, water closet, stairway or passage. According to the memorial, the room in question is enclosed and is not used for any of the excluded purposes. It is therefore, in my view, clearly a habitable room and, as such, an apartment for the purpose of reg A7.

By permitting an apartment to be formed within the house, I think the local authority have to accept the consequences. There was nothing in the 1981 regulations which prescribed whether an apartment should be used as a bedroom or as a study or as a play room. Accordingly, a new apartment having been authorised by the building warrant, the local authority had no jurisdiction, in my view, to dictate thereafter whether that room be used for one or other of these purposes. In particular, the height restrictions prescribed in the 1981 regulations applied not only to bedrooms. They applied generally to every apartment within the house.

I think it follows that, if the room was used from the outset or at any time before the 1986 regulations came into operation as a bedroom, that could not have been a change of use for the purposes of s 29 of the 1959 Act when the change was made, because the same provisions under the building regulations applied to any apartment within the house, whether used as a study, play room or bedroom.

Unfortunately, in the 1986 regulations, a clear distinction is made between a bedroom and other rooms in the house in that, by the 1986 provision Q5(1), bedroom is specifically defined; and under Q5(3), there is an additional special requirement for a bedroom.

The 1986 regulations also altered the height and space requirements but not specifically for bedrooms. The alterations in these respects applied generally to any apartment within the house.

That being the position, it seems to me that, under the 1986 regulations, the change of the use of the room in question to use as a bedroom would bring that room (as being part of a building) within a class of building to which additional provisions of the regulations apply, namely the provisions of Q5(3). That would not have applied before the 1986 regulations came into operation, because there was no distinction between a bedroom and any other room in this respect.

In the result, in my opinion:

(a) If the use of the room was changed to use as a bedroom before the 1986 regulations came into operation, that would not represent a change of use under s 29 of the 1959 Act because there is no additional, or more onerous, provision which applied to a bedroom under the 1981 regulations than applied to an apartment generally. Therefore, no further building warrant was required.

(b) If the change of use to a bedroom occurred (or is to occur) after 1986, then that would involve a change of use under s 29 of the 1959 Act in respect that, under the new regulations Q5(3), there are additional requirements which apply to a bedroom but which do not apply to any other class of room. Therefore, a further building warrant was (or is) required.

2   The powers of the local authority under s 10 of the 1959 Act are limited to cases where a building (or part thereof) has been constructed without warrant or in contravention of the warrant. That cannot apply here because there has been no further construction, and there is a completion certificate for the original work. That being so, there is no possibility of the service of a notice under s 10 on any proprietor.

3   I am bound to say I find this question exceedingly difficult to answer.

Although the matter is not free from argument, I have come to the view that change of use as defined in s 29(1) envisages a single act involving a change in the use of the room. I do not think it could be construed as implying the continuing subsequent use of the room for the new use. See, especially, s 29 – 'such change in the use ... as will bring it ...' and s 2 – 'No person shall – (a) ... conduct operations, or (b) change the use'.

The framework and syntax apply equally to (a) and (b). But a purchaser could never be prosecuted if he purchased a building after authorised construction has been completed. The same must, I think, apply to change of use. This could quite easily have been legislated for by saying, in (b), 'or use or continue to use'.

The appropriate remedy for failing to comply with the regulations is under s 11(5), after service of a s 11 notice. But such a notice cannot be served here – see 1986 regulation Q1(2); so, to continue the unauthorised use after the change has been made is not, in itself, an offence. The offence is the change of use itself.

If it can be firmly established that the use of the room had changed from play room to bedroom before the 1986 regulations came into operation, there is no risk of proceedings under s 6 of the 1959 Act because that change of use would not then have been a change of use within the meaning of s 29(1).

If the use of the room changed, or is to be changed, from play room to bedroom after the 1986 regulations came into operation, then I think it is arguable that the room (being part of a building within a particular class) is part of a building to which additional provisions of the regulations apply. Accordingly, changing its use to a bedroom technically involves a change of use and, for that, a building warrant authorising the change of use would have been, or would now be, required.

As to who is liable to prosecution, I am in some doubt. If the change of use occurred after the 1986 regulations came into operation but has already occurred, then there is no doubt that the present proprietors are liable to prosecution under s 6. But, on my view of s 29(1), a purchaser would not be liable to prosecution under s 6 because to continue an offending use after the use has changed does not seem to be an offence. So, if the purchaser himself makes the change, he would be liable. He would not be liable if the room is already in use as a bedroom before the date of entry.

Manual, para 19.42.

35   Repairs to houses

Sale by heritable creditor – whether district council charging order could be recorded after sale – effect of charging order

Date: June 1988

Memorial

A building society granted a mortgage to a borrower which was secured by a standard security. Subsequently, the district council issued a notice in terms of s 24(1) of the Housing (Scotland) Act 1969 requiring works to be carried out at the tenement. The district council carried out the work, and rendered a bill to the borrower.

The memorialists subsequently sold the property as heritable creditors. The proceeds were insufficient to repay the memorialists.

The following questions arose:

1   Could the district council record a charging order after the sale of premises by a heritable creditor?

2   If the district council recorded a charging order before the sale of the premises by the memorialists, would the property be disburdened of the charging order by virtue of the sale by the heritable creditor?

3   Would the position have been different if the security in favour of the memorialists had been dated prior to the repairs notice and, if so, did the memorialists have a right of recourse against the agents who acted for them when the security was granted?

4   Given that the decision in *Purves* v *City of Edinburgh District Council* 1987 SLT 366 states that the owner at the time the local authority seek to recover the expenses is the only party liable, was it still competent for the district council to record a charging order?

5   Was there anything else of which the memorialists should be aware?

Opinion

1   Yes. I do not think it makes any material difference whether the matter is dealt with under Sched 2 to the Housing (Scotland) Act 1969 or Sched 9 to the Housing (Scotland) Act 1987 because the provisions are, for practical purposes, the same. As I read the transitional provisions in Sched 22 to the 1987 Act a charging order, if made, will be made under s 109 of the 1987 Act, not under the 1969 Act, even although the work in this case was completed before the 1987 Act came into operation.

Section 109 of the 1987 Act provides, briefly, that expense incurred by a local authority under s 108 (or, previously, under s 24 of the 1969 Act) may be recovered by the authority from the person having control of the house. In terms of the decision in *Purves* v *City of Edinburgh DC* 1987 SLT 366 this means the person who had control of the house at the date when the local authority was finally in a position to make a claim. This may or may not be the person on whom the original notice was served, and who would, originally, have been personally liable for the cost. The reason is explained in the judgment in that case. Admittedly, the decision in *Purves* proceeds under the Civic Government (Scotland) Act 1982, but I do not think it is possible to distinguish in principle between the provisions of that Act and the provisions of the Housing (Scotland) Act 1987 in this respect.

The power to recover from the person having control under s 109(1) of the 1987 Act involves personal liability on that person.

By a further distinct provision in s 109(5), the local authority are empowered to charge the costs on the property itself as a real burden thereon which is, of course, quite separate from the question of personal liability. Personal liability implies the power to recover the amount due from time to time by personal action. The creation of a real burden by charging order gives the local authority power to recover by real action, using real remedies, which are quite a different matter although, for practical purposes, they fall personally on the proprietor for the time being of the burdened subjects. The imposing of the charging order and recovery of expenses thereby is dealt with in Sched 9 to the 1987 Act which also deals with the matter of ranking.

The procedure in Sched 9 involves the making of an order in favour of the local authority which provides that the property is charged with an annuity for repayment of the costs involved. The charging order must be recorded in the Register of Sasines but, unlike the ordinary heritable security, the date of recording in the Register of Sasines does not determine the priority of ranking of a charging order. Instead, in terms of Sched 9, para 4 the charging order takes priority over: (a) all *future* burdens; and (b) all *existing* burdens except: (i) feuduties etc and (ii) charges created for the benefit of a public authority.

Under Sched 9, para 6, every annuity so charged on any premises can be recovered in the same way as if it were feuduty which implies both personal liability and real remedies.

Finally, any owner of the premises (which, in my view, means any owner *for the time being*) may redeem by payment of an appropriate capital sum.

This effect of a charging order under the Housing (Scotland) Act 1987 (and the similar effect of a charging order under the Civic Government (Scotland) Act 1982) is in contrast to that of the type of charging order dealt with in the recent case of *Sowman v City of Glasgow DC* 1985 SLT 65, simply because of a significant difference in the language used in the more recent public statutes compared with the language used in the Glasgow Corporation Private Act. In particular, as the Lord President points out in *Sowman*, if a security of this kind is to have priority over rights already duly created by prior infeftment, that cannot occur at common law but must be achieved by statutory provision. In the Glasgow Corporation case, in his view, there was no general statutory provision to which the district council could appeal. The best that the district council could make of the Glasgow Corporation Act was to rely on the words in the relevant section imposing a liability on the proprietor to pay costs incurred by the Corporation as a 'real and *preferable* lien and burden on the land'. But, as the Lord President points out (at p 66), the use of the word 'preferable' does not necessarily imply that this burden is to be preferred to all others. 'If the statutory real right in security in favour of the (Corporation) is to have the priority of ranking for which they contend, this must be seen to have been conferred by (the statute).' He then goes on to contrast the wording used in the Glasgow Streets Sewers and Buildings Consolidation Order Confirmation Act 1937 (the 'Glasgow Corporation Act') (at p 67) with the wording used in the Building (Scotland) Act 1959, ss 13, 16 and Sched 6. Under the latter Act, a charging order is to be recorded and, on being so recorded, it becomes a charge on the land, with priority over all *future* burdens and incumbrances and all *existing* burdens and incumbrances *except* (again) feuduties etc and sums charged to public authorities.

The wording of the Building (Scotland) Act 1959 is almost identical with the wording used in the Local Government (Scotland) Act 1973. It seems quite clear to me that, in the Lord President's view, the wording used in the Building (Scotland) Act quoted above does have the effect of *expressly* conferring a special priority of ranking for the benefit of the local authority, in contrast to the wording of the Glasgow Corporation Act. I think his view is equally applicable to the wording used under the Housing (Scotland) Act 1987, Sched 9.

It follows from my view of the legislation that the district council can record a charging order at any time, whether before or after the sale of the premises; and this is quite clearly envisaged in the Lord President's judgment in *Purves* at p 368, col 2.

2   No. As the memorial correctly points out, on a sale by a heritable creditor, the subjects are disburdened automatically of all *heritable securities* and diligences ranking *pari passu* with or postponed to that of the security of the selling creditor. If, however, a charging order has already been recorded by the local authority before the building society proceed to sale, then that charging order automatically ranks in priority to the standard security in favour of the building society, even although recorded later, because priority of infeftment is *not* the test to be applied in determining the ranking as between the two, for the reasons given in answer 1 above.

That being so, the security created for the benefit of the local authority by the recording of the charging order, being neither *pari passu* nor postponed to the standard security in favour of the building society, will subsist and transmit against a purchaser.

In any event, according to the Lord President in *Sowman* at p 68, a charging order is not a 'heritable security'; and so, even if it were postponed to the building society's security, it would not be discharged on a sale by them and would transmit against the purchaser.

3   So far as the security is concerned, the position would have been no different whether the repairs notice had been dated prior to or after the recording of the standard security in favour of the memorialists. It was not in the power of the building society to prevent the notice from being served and, subject to possible objections to the content of the notice, there is very little which the building society could have done to mitigate its effect.

In practical terms, whether the notice was served before or after the recording of the standard security, it would have been possible for the building society to have taken control of repairs rather than to allow these to be carried out by the local authority in which case, of course, the question of a charging order would never have arisen; but, had the building society so acted, they would have incurred a liability on their own account in paying for the necessary repairs. It therefore does not seem to me that there was very much which the building society could have done to improve their position in relation to the serving of the repairs notice or to minimise the impact thereof.

As to the liability of the agents acting for the society, that is quite a different matter. The notice in this case was served in 1979; and the standard security was not granted until 1984. The agents acting for the building society, in my view, had a duty to enquire as to whether or not there were any outstanding notices and to warn their clients that, in this case, a notice had been issued and was apparently then still unimplemented. This would have allowed the building society to take into account the effect the repairs notice and, possibly, to undertake the funding of the repairs and so avoid the resulting charging order.

The state of the property, and the unimplemented notice were also, of course, matters to be taken into account and reported on in the building society survey; and the state of repair is something which should have been reflected in the valuation. The blame for the resulting loss does not therefore necessarily lie wholly with the law agents, if indeed they are liable at all; and I really do not have sufficient information to advise whether or not in this case there would be any liability.

4   Yes. The making and recording of a charging order is something quite separate and distinct from the making of a demand for payment under s 109(1) and is dealt with separately under s 109(5) of the 1987 Act. Once the demand for payment has been made under s 109(1), the local authority are free at any time thereafter to make and record the charging order. Accordingly, the district council in this case are still perfectly free to record a charging order as and when they please with the resulting priority of ranking which is referred to in my previous answers.

5   I understand that the subjects have been sold and I presume the missives will contain normal conditions to the effect that there are no outstanding unimplemented notices, orders or other matters. If so, and if this provision in the missives has not been qualified so as to require the purchaser to accept the possibility of a charging order, the building society as sellers are in breach of contract and would, in my view, require to free and relieve the purchaser of the expenses demanded and on the strength of which the charging order will be made. If the matter is not raised by the purchaser before settlement; if thereafter a charging order is recorded; and if the disposition by the building society as selling creditors grants warrandice from fact and deed only, it may be that the building society would not be liable in damages under warrandice.

It is open to the owner or any other interested party to redeem the amount imposed by way of charging order on the subjects and, subject to whatever the missives may provide, this is probably what the building society will have to do in order to satisfy the purchaser.

Manual, para 19.49.

(NB There are no opinions relating to Chapter 20 of the Manual.)

HERITABLE SECURITIES BEFORE 1970

36   Contract of ground annual

Contract of ground annual – recovery of arrears due – personal action –
diligence – irritancy – *jus quaesitum tertio* – waiver – discharge

Date: June 1991

Memorial
Various questions arose with regard to a contract of ground annual:

1   Could real burdens and conditions be imposed under the contract?

2   Had the creditor in a contract of ground annual both title and interest
to enforce the conditions?

3   What were the methods available to the creditor to recover arrears?

4   How could title to enforce the conditions in the contract be extinguished?

5   Might a third party have the title to enforce the conditions in the
contract?

6   How could the risk that third parties may succeed in enforcing a
prohibition in the contract be dealt with?

Opinion
1   The contract of ground annual is a peculiar deed in the sense that,
while it is intended primarily to secure payment to the creditor of the
ground annual sums, it also operates initially as the original title to the
debtor in the ground annual as disponee of the subjects burdened therewith. In that context, it was always perfectly legitimate for the creditor of
the ground annual to impose real burdens and conditions running with the
lands, in exactly the same way, and basically for the same reasons, as a
superior imposed real burdens and conditions on the vassal in a feu charter.
Accordingly, the title of the creditor to enforce the burdens in this title is
not merely personal to the original creditor. As real burdens, they remain
enforceable by the original creditor and his successors against the original
debtor/disponee and his successors as proprietors in perpetuity.

2   If the ground annual has not been redeemed, the creditor therein
certainly has a *title*, and probably also has an *interest*, to enforce all the
conditions in the title which are real, in order to secure payment of the
ground annual. If the ground annual has been redeemed but not
discharged, whether by deed of discharge or under the statutory procedures

introduced in the Land Tenure Reform (Scotland) Act 1974, then technically the superior may still have a *title* to enforce; but I think it would be
impossible for him to instruct any *interest* to enforce against the present
proprietor or his successors.

3   The methods available to the creditor to recover arrears are:

(*a*) a *personal* action against the original disponee or his universal successors; but for practical purposes that can be ignored. There is *no* right
of *personal* action against singular successors;

(*b*) real diligence, such as poinding of the ground; or

(*c*) a declarator of irritancy which, although strictly speaking not technically a remedy for recovery of arrears, is sufficient to ensure that the
arrears are in fact paid up. The procedure is statutory, under the
Conveyancing (Scotland) Act 1924, s 23(5) which produces an effect
equivalent to irritation of the feu. But the right to each ground annual
payment as it falls due is personal to the creditor therein and, as such,
is cut off by the short negative prescription. Accordingly, the risk is
limited to five years' arrears; and arrears of ground annual can always
be purged to avoid the effects of the statutory irritancy. In addition, if
the whole subjects were sold since 1974 but before the occasion of the
present sale, the ground annual should have been redeemed at the
statutory rate on the occasion of that sale. If there has been no intervening sale since 1974, and if the *whole* subjects are now being sold,
then the ground annual should now be redeemed. This means that the
total potential pecuniary liability is the redemption price of the ground
annual at the statutory rate plus five years' arrears.
Notwithstanding the foregoing, however, the ground annual is not
redeemable on sale if the subjects of sale form part only, but not the
whole, subjects affected by the original ground annual, which seems to
be the case here. In that situation, on a sale of part only but not the
whole, there is no compulsory redemption; the proportion of ground
annual continues to be payable; and the pecuniary risk is therefore
limited to five years' arrears of ground annual only and nothing more.

4   In order to extinguish the *title* to enforce, a formal discharge or completion of the statutory procedure on compulsory redemption would be
necessary technically to disentitle the creditor in the ground annual from
enforcing any of the conditions therein. But, since the conditions contained
in the original contract of ground annual were all designed to ensure
payment thereof and nothing more, the creditor in the ground annual,
when redeemed, cannot possibly instruct any *interest* to enforce and so, for
practical purposes, the conditions become unenforceable at the instance of
the creditor whether on voluntary redemption or on compulsory redemption under the 1974 Act.

5   In the ordinary case, as with a feu charter between superior and vassal,
so with conditions in a contract of ground annual, these conditions are a
private matter between the original creditor and his successors on the one
hand and the original debtor and his successors on the other; and, in the

ordinary way, third parties have no right to enforce. There is, however, a well-established feudal rule, which applies in the case of feus, that if the subjects feued are subdivided, then in the ordinary way, subject to certain exceptions and qualifications, each subsequent individual owner of *part* of the original whole has by implication a *jus quaesitum tertio* to enforce the real conditions in the charter as against each other proprietor of parts of the original whole. The same rule applies to real burdens in dispositions and contracts of ground annual.

In the present case, therefore, that rule must apply unless the subdivision of the subjects did not take place until only after the ground annual had been redeemed and discharged, which seems very unlikely.

In the result, in my view, the probability is that there are neighbouring proprietors, owners of parts of the subjects originally conveyed by the contract of ground annual of 1882 who, at least in theory, have a title to enforce all the conditions therein as being proprietors of parts of the original whole subjects. For a recent application of this rule, see *Lees* v *North-East Fife District Council* 1987 SLT 769. The fact that a superior may have waived or discharged a feudal restriction or prohibition in a question with his vassal, whether by formal waiver or by acquiescence, does not automatically extinguish the title of a neighbouring proprietor based on *jus quaesitum tertio* or, in the case of subdivision, of the proprietor of part to insist on the charter conditions in a question with a co-feuar. The rights of the superior to enforce and the rights of a co-feuar based on *jus quaesitum tertio* to enforce are separate and independent rights; and the co-feuar's rights continue to subsist even although the superior's right may be extinguished. Exactly the same rule applies to rights acquired by the *jus quaesitum tertio* on the subdivision of a larger whole.

In the present case, the subjects have been used as a public house since 1952. I think it necessarily follows that all present adjoining proprietors owning parts of the original whole who, as a result, by *jus quaesitum tertio*, have a title to enforce the prohibition against the sale of liquor, are personally barred now from insisting on that condition by their past acquiescence. But, in the case of restrictions on use, a singular successor to any of these adjoining proprietors would not necessarily be personally barred from insisting on enforcing that prohibition. Acquiescence by the creditor in a burden in a past breach thereof, where the breach consists of building or structural alterations on the subjects in question which are obvious and involve substantial expenditure, will almost certainly bar singular successors because the breach is obvious and involved expense. The same rule does *not* apply, however, or at least does not *necessarily* apply, to a breach of a prohibition against a particular use as in this case.

Accordingly, if there are neighbouring proprietors who own properties forming part of the subjects originally conveyed by the 1882 contract of ground annual, there is indeed a possibility that any purchaser from any of these proprietors *might* succeed in enforcing the prohibition in question.

6   Having explained the risk, there are really only two effective ways of excluding it, namely:

(*a*) To obtain a formal waiver from each of the 'benefited' proprietors, ie each proprietor of every part of the original whole, and to record that waiver in the Register of Sasines. Under the Land Registration (Scotland) Act 1979, s 18, that waiver would effectively bind singular successors in perpetuity and so remove the risk of challenge.

(*b*) Since it is usually impracticable either to trace all the owners of parts of the original whole who have a title to enforce or, if they can be traced, to obtain a minute of waiver from each of them, the alternative is an application to the Lands Tribunal for Scotland to discharge the condition in question which, in the present circumstances, would almost certainly be successful. Such an order by the Lands Tribunal removes the risk of challenge permanently so far as all potential objectors are concerned.

In the result, the question resolves itself into one of a commercial decision on the practical risks. These risks are, in my view, minimal but none the less the prohibition in question is, in theory, potentially enforceable. The safe advice therefore is, in all such cases, to insist on the obtaining of an order from the Lands Tribunal before proceeding with the contract.

There is really no other way in which an absolute guarantee can be given to the client that one of the adjoining proprietors or a successor in title may not at some stage seek to enforce the prohibition in question by interdict. Of course, should that occur, an application to the Lands Tribunal can still be made; but that implies at least a potential risk, and possibly an interruption, for a period, in trading on the premises.

Manual, para 21.23.

STANDARD SECURITIES

37   Deduction of title

Sale by heritable creditor – whether granter of standard security had been infeft – procedure to cure defect by surviving spouse

Date: August 1987

Memorial

The memorialists were seeking to purchase a property from a building society under their power of sale. The disposition, which was granted in favour of Mr and Mrs A, the sellers, had been dated August 1985, but had not been recorded until July of the following year. The warrant of registration was in the name of Mrs A only because Mr A had died in June 1986. The standard security had been granted by Mr and Mrs A and dated and recorded on the same dates as the disposition.

The memorialists were doubtful as to the validity of the standard security, and asked the following questions:

1   Did the certificate of confirmation in favour of Mrs A as *executrix dative qua relict* of her husband vest the one-half *pro indiviso* share, to which Mr A had a personal right, in her?

2   Did the standard security recorded in July 1986 provide an effective security?

3   Was it competent for the building society to grant a disposition in favour of the memorialists which would give them a valid unchallengeable title?

Opinion

1   Yes. There is no doubt that, although the disposition in favour of Mr and Mrs A was recorded, after the death of Mr A, on behalf of Mrs A only, it none the less operated effectively as a personal title to a one-half *pro indiviso* share of the subjects for the benefit of the late Mr A.

Following Mr A's death, Mrs A confirmed to that one-half *pro indiviso* share which was disponed to her husband under the disposition and, by virtue of that confirmation, his original one-half *pro indiviso* share of the subjects has undoubtedly vested in Mrs A as his executor.

2   Yes. But only to the extent of the one-half *pro indiviso* share of the subjects originally conveyed to Mrs A under the 1985 disposition.

The reason for this is fundamental. At common law, the granter of any formal deed affecting heritable property must be infeft. An exception to this rule was introduced by s 3 of the 1924 Act, which provided for deduction of

166

title in certain circumstances, but the section had no application to the granting of heritable securities. Under the Conveyancing and Feudal Reform (Scotland) Act 1970, s 12, a standard security may be granted by a person uninfeft if, in the standard security, the granter thereof deduces title.

In the present case, the only infeftment is the infeftment of Mrs A. Looking to the terms of the destination in the 1985 disposition which was subsequently recorded after Mr A's death and which contains no survivorship destination, the effect of the recording of that disposition with a warrant registration on behalf of Mrs A alone is to create an infeftment in her person in a one-half *pro indiviso* share only and no more. The standard security by Mr and Mrs A is granted on the footing that they are both infeft and contains no clause of deduction of title. Accordingly, insofar as the standard security is granted by Mrs A and to the extent of her one-half *pro indiviso* share, on the recording of that standard security in the Register of Sasines, a one-half *pro indiviso* share of the subjects (being Mrs A's one-half *pro indiviso* share) vested in the building society under s 11(1) of the 1970 Act.

In the result, although the 1985 disposition in favour of Mr and Mrs A has been recorded and the standard security has been recorded, there is no resulting infeftment in the one-half *pro indiviso* share of the subjects which passed to Mr A under the 1985 disposition; and the fact that Mrs A subsequently confirmed to that one-half *pro indiviso* share in her capacity as executor dative does not in any way alter the position. As a result, the building society can claim an infeftment in security in her original one-half *pro indiviso* share only and has no effective security on the one-half *pro indiviso* share of the subjects which belonged to the late Mr A because (a) he was at his death uninfeft; and (b) the standard security in favour of the building society contains no deduction of title in respect of Mr A's one-half *pro indiviso* share in which he had no infeftment.

I have no hesitation in giving an opinion in these terms on the title as it stands at present. A more difficult question would arise, however, if Mrs A were now to complete her title to the one-half *pro indiviso* share of the subjects originally belonging to Mr A to which she has confirmed under the confirmation of 1986. This could be achieved in one of two ways:

(*a*) it would be competent for Mrs A to complete title by recording a notice of title in her own favour as executrix and to become infeft as such; or

(*b*) if she is *beneficially* entitled to the property (as she almost certainly is, by way of prior rights), then she could transfer the beneficial interest in this one-half *pro indiviso* share to herself either by a docquet on the confirmation or by formal disposition in her own favour; and, in either case, could complete title to Mr A's one-half *pro indiviso* share of the subjects as his beneficial successor.

If she did so complete title, and became infeft in Mr A's one-half *pro indiviso* share, a question then arises whether by that infeftment, the standard security would be validated, *quoad* Mr A's original one-half *pro indiviso* share, by accretion. With some hesitation, I have come to the view that accretion would *not* operate to validate the standard security in this case. The reason is that accretion operates to validate a title which was granted by a person who, at the time of granting, either had no title whatsoever to the subjects conveyed or had a title but no infeftment therein and who subsequently becomes infeft in those subjects in his own person. Thus A uninfeft, grants a feu charter in favour of B which B records. Since a valid feu charter can only be granted by an infeft proprietor, B's title as vassal is initially invalid because his superior was not infeft when granting it. If A subsequently completes title, eg by the recording of a notice of title in his own favour, the mere recording of that notice of title validates the feu charter by A to B retrospectively as from the date of its recording. In this illustration, however, A has completed title in his own name to the *same* subjects which he had previously conveyed to B in the feu charter.

In the present case, Mr and Mrs A granted a standard security in favour of the building society jointly. It is immediately clear, from an examination of the conveyance in their favour, that each of them was entitled to a one-half *pro indiviso* share only, without survivorship.

Accordingly, by referring to the prior disposition, it is immediately apparent that the standard security in favour of the building society, although ostensibly granted jointly by Mr and Mrs A, was in fact a standard security by each of them over a one-half *pro indiviso* share to which each was entitled under the 1985 disposition. Mrs A subsequently took infeftment in her one-half *pro indiviso* share by the recording of the disposition and at the same time the standard security was recorded, thereby undoubtedly giving the building society a valid security over Mrs A's one-half *pro indiviso* share.

If Mrs A now completes title in her own person to the one-half *pro indiviso* share originally conveyed to Mr A, she is completing title not to the one-half *pro indiviso* share which she originally conveyed to the building society but to the one-half *pro indiviso* share which Mr A conveyed to the building society. In other words, she is not here completing title in her own name to the same subjects which she originally conveyed to the society when granting the standard security. In these circumstances, I do not think that the principle of accretion would apply because title is being completed to totally different subjects from the subjects which Mrs A originally conveyed.

The authorities seem to be agreed that, when infeftment is taken not by the original disponer but by someone representing him following on his death, accretion will not operate. Admittedly, the authority for this proposition seems to rest on a single case, *Keith* v *Grant* (1797) M 7767. But there are other comparable later cases where the same principle was applied. Accordingly, although the law of representation in heritage has altered substantially since 1797, my view is that the same principle would still apply and that completion of title by Mrs A, either as executor or as beneficial successor to her deceased husband, would *not* operate to validate the standard security on the basis of accretion in respect of Mr A's one-half *pro indiviso* share of the subjects.

3   No, certainly on one ground and possibly on two.
    (*a*) First, as a matter of title, the building society are only in a position

to deal with Mrs A's original one-half *pro indiviso* share of the subjects because their security extends to that one-half *pro indiviso* share only and no more. For the reasons given above, I do not think the position of the building society will improve even if Mrs A were now to complete title to the one-half *pro indiviso* share of the subjects which passed to her husband under the 1985 disposition.

(b) Further, although I have not seen the steps in procedure leading up to the exercise of the power of sale, I think that procedure might well be open to challenge in that the building society, when giving the statutory notice etc have no doubt assumed that they had a security over the whole subjects, not merely a one-half *pro indiviso* share thereof; and this may well have invalidated the notices and the subsequent procedure. I do not think it necessary further to explore this procedural aspect, because, for the reasons given above, I do not think the building society have a title to convey the whole subjects to the purchaser.

4   I assume that both sides wish to proceed with the transaction if that is possible. But, on the title in its present form, I really do not think the building society are in a position to realise their security without the co-operation of Mrs A. I am not sure whether or not that co-operation will be forthcoming.

If Mrs A will co-operate, it really would be better for the purchasers to take a disposition by Mrs A for her own interest as infeft proprietor of the one-half *pro indiviso* share originally conveyed to her under the 1985 disposition and as executor of her late husband in respect of his one-half *pro indiviso* share, possibly narrating the purported sale by the building society and, with their consent, conveying the subjects to the purchasers. She can competently do so in respect of her own one-half *pro indiviso* share in which she is already infeft; and, in respect of her husband's one-half *pro indiviso* share, she can convey as executor, deducing title through the disposition and the confirmation as the two links in title.

If Mrs A will not co-operate, then the building society cannot give the purchasers a good title and indeed are in serious difficulty themselves in the realising of their security. I do not propose to explore these difficulties further unless specifically asked to do so.

Manual, para 22.8.

38   Calling-up notice – standard condition 9(1)(a)

Calling-up notice in standard security – whether procedure followed valid

Date: January 1989

Memorial
The memorialist was owed certain sums which were secured by way of a standard security over the debtor's property in favour of the memorialists.

The debtor failed to make payments due. The memorialists personally served a calling-up notice on the debtor in accordance with Form D of Sched 6 to the Conveyancing and Feudal Reform (Scotland) Act 1970. Two months passed without action being taken. The memorialists took possession and advertised the property for sale.

The purchaser's agents took exception to the calling-up notice, arguing that there was insufficient evidence to show it had been properly served on the debtor in terms of s 19(6) of the 1970 Act which envisages delivery to the debtor or posting by recorded delivery or registered post. The purchasers were of the view that the absence of a court decree authorising the memorialists to exercise their remedies as heritable creditors or of a copy of the calling-up notice endorsed with acknowledgement of receipt by the debtor rendered the title unmarketable. Opinion was sought on this point.

Opinion

I am sorry to say that, in my opinion, the purchaser's agents in this case are justified in their objection to the title.

I take the point made by the memorialists that the note embodied in Form D to Sched 6 to the 1970 Act envisages service by some method other than by post. The implication of that wording is that Form D can be used as evidence of the serving of a default notice (as in this case) if signed by the creditor or by his agent; and that the notice can be delivered rather than posted. Against that, however, s 19(6) is quite specific. In a situation of this kind there are, in the Act itself, *not* in the schedule, only two alternatives, namely: (*a*) Form C signed by the debtor; or (*b*) Form D accompanied by the postal receipt.

Either of these Forms is 'sufficient evidence of service of that notice'; and it is this specific statement in the Act which, in my view, renders the present notice unacceptable as *evidence* of service, although arguably validly served. In other words, there is nothing whatever in the Act which states that such a notice (served by hand and docquetted as in this case) is of *itself* sufficient evidence of service, if it carries a docquet only but no postal receipt.

On the other hand, service of the notice of default is an essential preliminary to the default procedure as prescribed in ss 21 to 23. Under s 21(2), service of the notice is subject to the like requirements as service of the calling-up notice; and, under s 23, the creditor can sell the subjects only *after* due service of the notice of default. In the absence of competent evidence of service, the sale is necessarily invalid.

For my part, I would not accept that an inference to be drawn from a note to Form D in the schedule overrides what seems to me a perfectly clear-cut and unambiguous requirement in s 19(6) of the Act.

If the debtor is available, the simple solution is to obtain his signature now in Form C, Sched 6. There is no requirement in the 1970 Act or in the schedules that the acknowledgement of receipt of the notice must be given within a specific time limit or that it must antedate the sale. Accordingly, if the debtor is able and willing now to sign an acknowledgement, the problem is resolved.

If not, the only possible solution which I can think of is an action of declarator to the effect that the notice was duly and validly served; and I think the memorialists might have some difficulty in obtaining such a declarator because of the basic Scottish rule that two witnesses are required in any proof. Accordingly, unless the director who delivered the notice by hand was accompanied by somebody who can corroborate that fact, I doubt if the court would be prepared to accept his evidence alone and would not therefore give the required declarator.

In any event, there is a further difficulty. In the nature of things, the decree will almost certainly be a decree in absence. The probability is that the summons cannot be served personally on the debtor because, if that could be achieved, then the debtor would probably be willing to sign an acknowledgement of receipt. But, unless personally served, a decree of absence is open to challenge for twenty years. Accordingly, a purchaser may still be unwilling to accept as conclusive a decree in absence where there has not been personal service. This is the reason behind the provisions for decrees in absence in cases of irritation of the feu in the Conveyancing Amendment (Scotland) Act 1938, s 6(4). Accordingly, a decree of declarator is not necessarily the solution.

Failing an acknowledgement or a valid declarator, I can think of no other way in which the matter can be put right. In other words, the creditor will have to start again and serve the notice in the proper fashion. This in turn means that he is in breach of contract in relation to the bargain which he has concluded with the present purchaser because, on my view of the statutory provisions in the 1970 Act, if the first sale is invalid, as it is in this case, the whole procedure must start again of new and in particular the property must be advertised again of new under s 25 with a view to obtaining the best price obtainable. I think s 23 is mandatory on this point.

The alternative is indemnity, but of course no purchaser is obliged to accept an indemnity in lieu of a marketable title. Naturally, it may be possible to negotiate this with the purchaser in this case but the outcome cannot be guaranteed.

Manual, para 22.23.

FLOATING CHARGES

39   Creation of the charge

Floating charge – company incorporated in England – whether heritable
and moveable property in Scotland secured – ranking

Date: October 1990

Memorial
A limited company, incorporated in England, and owning moveable assets
and heritable property in Scotland, granted the memorialists, a limited
company also incorporated in England, a mortgage debenture incorporating fixed and floating charges. The debenture was dated 15th March
and registered with companies office in Cardiff on 4th April of the same
year. A number of fixed securities were granted by the company in favour
of Scottish lenders without permission of the memorialists.

The memorialists asked the following questions:

1   Did a debenture, registered in England, give any form of charge or
security over heritage in Scotland, and if so in what circumstances?

2   What would be the ranking of securities should a receiver be appointed?

3   If the grantor went into receivership or liquidation, would the debenture be an effective security over moveable property owned by the granter
in Scotland?

Opinion
1   Does the debenture create a charge over heritage in Scotland?

Although the debenture deed is, naturally, drafted entirely in English
terms it does contain, in my opinion, more than sufficient to create a valid
floating charge for the benefit of the memorialists over the whole of the
assets of the debtor company insofar as situate in Scotland.

I should first state that, as a matter of private international law, it is
I think settled that the creation of a security on any asset for the
benefit of a creditor must be valid and enforceable according to the *lex
situs*. It follows that, whatever the terms of the debenture may be, it
cannot create a security on any asset in Scotland except to the extent
to which it complies with Scottish rules. Accordingly, and in particular,
although the debenture deed, in clause 2(c), declares that it shall form
a fixed first charge over all the assets listed in that clause, including
freehold and leasehold property, book debts etc, that provision is totally
ineffective to create any *fixed* security on any asset in Scotland, even
although the clause may create a fixed security for the benefit of the

memorialists on assets situate in England under the comparable English rules.

None the less, although the debenture deed cannot create any *fixed* security on Scottish assets, it does, in my opinion, operate effectively as a *floating* charge because:

(*a*) In clause 1 of the debenture deed, the debtor company effectively creates what we would term in Scotland a personal obligation to pay on demand to the memorialists all monies which shall for the time being be due and owing or incurred to them by the debtor company, with interest as therein provided for.

(*b*) In the preamble to clause 2, the debtor company as beneficial owner then *expressly* charges all its undertaking and its property whatsoever and wheresoever, both present and future, as a continuing security for payment of the sums payable by the debtor company to the memorialists under the personal obligation created in clause 1. The wording of clause 2 really leaves no room for doubt, in that the debtor company '*hereby charges* all its undertaking and its property', which is a *de praesenti* charge.

(*c*) Having so charged its property, the remainder of clause 2 then applies that charge to various types of asset owned by the debtor company with various effects, depending on the nature of the asset. In particular, as regards the company's undertaking and other assets, present and future, not *effectively* subjected to a fixed charge, including explicitly any real or heritable property and any assets of the descriptions in subclause (c)(ii)(iv) and (vi) situate in Scotland, the charge created in the preamble to clause 2 is expressly stated to be a first floating charge.

(*d*) In that same clause 2(d), the debtor company then expressly undertakes not to create any mortgage or charge over any such asset ranking prior to or *pari passu* with the floating charge effectively created in subclause (d).

When floating charges were first introduced into Scotland by the Companies (Floating Charges) (Scotland) Act 1961, a form of instrument of charge was prescribed for use in Scotland in the first schedule to the Act. In my opinion, although the wording in the debenture deed differs from the wording in that schedule, the content of the debenture deed is quite clearly more than sufficient to create a floating charge over all the Scottish assets of the debtor company. Admittedly, if the 1961 Act had still been in operation, there could have been an argument that, since the statutory form was not adopted *verbatim*, no effective charge had been created; but by the Companies (Floating Charges and Receivers) (Scotland) Act 1972, the 1961 Act was repealed and no statutory form of instrument of charge was introduced in place of the form provided by the 1961 Act. That position still applies following on the Companies Acts 1985 and 1989.

Under the Companies Act 1985, s 462, it is expressly declared to be competent under the law of Scotland for an incorporated company, for the purpose of securing debt incurred or to be incurred by the debtor company, to create in favour of the creditor a charge (referred to in the Act as a floating charge) over all or any part of the property which may from time to time be comprised in its property and undertaking. In my opinion, the debenture deed in this case satisfies the basic requirements of s 462(1). In s 462(2) and (3) certain special provisions are made for the mode of execution of the instrument of charge but only as regards a floating charge created by a company registered in Scotland. In any event, the debenture deed in this case satisfies that statutory requirement and is, I assume, also validly executed under English law. On that assumption, I have no hesitation in advising that the debenture deed has created a valid floating charge over all the Scottish assets of the debtor company which continues to be enforceable according to its terms.

The debenture deed was duly registered with the Registrar of Companies in England, the debtor company being a company registered there, and the required particulars were delivered to the Registrar of Companies in England within the statutory 21-day time limit. Under Part XII of the 1985 Act it is now no longer necessary, as it used to be, to register the floating charge both in Scotland and in England; and, in the case of a company registered in England as this one is, registration of the charge in the English register alone suffices to validate the charge both on English and on Scottish assets and satisfies all the registration requirements.

2   If a receiver is appointed by the memorialists which I imagine they are now entitled to do, or if the company goes into liquidation, the floating charge immediately crystallises and becomes a fixed security on all the assets embraced therein. In particular, this would imply that the floating charge would become an effective fixed security on all heritable property in Scotland, on all incorporeal moveable property in Scotland, and all corporeal moveables. That fixed security would rank, for the benefit of the memorialists, in priority to all other creditors except:

(*a*)   creditors holding pre-existing *fixed* securities on individual assets in Scotland if validly constituted (I will revert to this point below);
(*b*)   any person who has effectually executed diligence on any Scottish asset (I have no information as to whether or not any such diligence has been executed);
(*c*)   the expenses generally of the receivership;
(*d*)   preferential creditors, being those creditors who have a preferential ranking in bankruptcy or sequestration under the Insolvency Act 1986, s 386.

In contrast, by virtue of the two standard securities granted in favour of the memorialists over two particular heritable properties in Scotland, the memorialists have an absolute priority under these securities not subject to any such prior ranking under (*c*) and (*d*) above. I assume that (*a*) and (*b*) above do not apply to these heritable securities.

3   It follows from my previous answers that, if a receiver is appointed or the debtor company goes into liquidation, the debenture deed will *immediately* then create a fixed security for the benefit of the memorialists and will

create a fixed security over all moveables then owned by the company situated in Scotland just as effectively as it would create a fixed security over Scottish heritable property.

So far as book debts of the debtor company are concerned, I think there has been some confusion of thought in the past few years, both in articles and in the decided cases as to the nature and effect of floating charges in relation to book debts.

First, a book debt is undoubtedly an asset of the company and part of its property and undertaking. It is an asset over which a creditor can obtain an effective fixed security. To do so, he requires to obtain an assignation from the creditor company of the book debt in question and then intimate that assignation to the book debtor. Having done so, however, he effectively creates a fixed security over that book debt which would take priority over other creditors in a subsequent receivership or liquidation. Because of the nature of the asset, fixed securities over book debts are uncommon but none the less they are perfectly competent; and, if created, they are one of the securities which, by statute, must be registered in the register of charges within the statutory time limit under s 410(4)(c)(i) of the Companies Act 1985.

In my opinion it follows inevitably that, on the appointment of the receiver or on liquidation, all book debts due to the company at that date are *immediately* attached by a fixed security for the benefit of the creditor in a floating charge just as heritable property is so attached but, again, subject to the preferential claims above referred to, namely:

(*a*) any prior fixed security thereon, which is unusual but possible;

(*b*) any effectually executed diligence, eg by way of arrestment followed by a decree of furthcoming;

(*c*) expenses and preferential debts which invariably rank before the notional fixed security created on the appointment of a receiver or on liquidation for the benefit of the holder of a floating charge.

I reach this conclusion from the decision in *Forth & Clyde Construction Co Ltd* v *Trinity Timber & Plywood Co Ltd* 1984 SLT 94. See the opinion of Lord President Emslie at p 96 where he states that the attachment of the debt by the notional fixed security created for the benefit of the holder of a floating charge on receivership or liquidation has effect as if the floating charge were a fixed security over that book debt. This view is confirmed by Greene and Fletcher, *The Law and Practice of Receivership in Scotland*, para 4.78. Admittedly, the same authors in chapter 8 make what appears to be a contradictory statement in relation to an English registered company which has granted in favour of the holder of a floating charge a first *fixed* charge over book debts, which is in fact the position in this case. According to Greene and Fletcher, such a charge over book debts would not be valid in relation to a Scottish book debt without assignation and intimation, which is of course perfectly true unless and until a receiver is appointed or the company goes into liquidation whereupon the floating charge immediately crystallises as a fixed security for the benefit of the creditor thereunder. For confirmation of this view, see St Clair and Drummond Young, *The Law of Corporate Insolvency in Scotland*, para 12.9.

Floating charges

In the meantime, of course, until either a receiver is appointed or the company goes into liquidation, the purported creation of a fixed security over book debts in clause 2(c)(vi) of the debenture deed as a fixed first charge is ineffective to create any form of security on any book debt due by a Scottish debtor. But that applies to every type of asset generally; and it applies only so long as the company is not in receivership or liquidation. Immediately a receiver is appointed or the company goes into liquidation, the memorialists automatically acquire a fixed security on all Scottish book debts, subject to the preferential claims referred to above.

Further reading

Re Anchor Line (1937) 1 Ch 1 for a view that a security created under English law may create a fixed security over moveables situated in Scotland.
AIB Finance Ltd v *Bank of Scotland* 1993 SCLR 851 for an interpretation of s 464(1)(a) of the Companies Act 1985.
Sharp v *Thomson* 1995 SLT 837 for a discussion of floating charges over heritage.
Companies Act 1989 (Commencement No 15 and Transitional and Savings Provisions) Order 1995 (SI 1995 No 1352) for amendments to s 464 of the Companies Act 1985.

Manual, para 23.2.

40   Ranking

Floating charge – inhibition – effect – Insolvency Act 1986 – effectually executed diligence

Date: February 1988

Memorial
A sequence of events took place as follows:

1   A Ltd ('the company') granted a floating charge in favour of a creditor dated 2nd and registered in the register of charges on 14th February 1986.
2   Notice of letters of inhibition was registered against the company on 24th September, followed by letters of inhibition registered on 9th October 1986.
3   On 23rd September 1987, a receiver was appointed.

The following question was asked:

The title exhibited by the receiver disclosed the inhibition referred to above which was still outstanding. Was the title good and marketable?

Opinion
There is a strong argument in support of the view that the receiver can

grant a valid and effective disposition which is immune from challenge at the instance of the inhibiting creditor. This argument is based on two grounds:

1 *The general principle*

An inhibition strikes only at future voluntary deeds of the inhibited debtor. In this case, the inhibition was registered against the debtor after the floating charge had been duly created, although admittedly before the receiver was appointed. None the less, I take the view that the subsequent appointment of the receiver is not a future voluntary act of the inhibited debtor because the receiver was appointed, under statutory sanction, in terms of a floating charge which had already been validly created before the inhibition was laid on.

2 *The special statutory provisions*

The matter does not, however, rest simply on general principle because, under s 55 of and Sched 2 to the Insolvency Act 1986 certain powers are conferred on the receiver, including power of sale, but these powers are expressly subject to the rights of any person who has 'effectually executed diligence on ... the property of the company prior to the appointment of the receiver ...'.

Further, under s 60(1)(b) of the 1986 Act the receiver is directed to pay over monies received by him to the creditor in the charge subject to, *inter alia*, the rights of any person who has effectually executed diligence.

Finally, under s 61(1) of the 1986 Act, when the receiver sells property subject to the charge and where that property is affected or attached by effectual diligence executed by any person, then, if the receiver cannot obtain the consent of that person, he may apply to the court for authority to sell.

These new statutory provisions under the Insolvency Act 1986 are in identical terms with the earlier legislation and so cases prior to the Act are still relevant. Further, as the memorialists point out in their letter, some of these cases caused considerable comment and criticism arising, mainly, out of the terms of the legislation, but Parliament did not take the opportunity of amending the legislation when enacting the 1986 Act.

The interaction of these statutory provisions with a sequence of events exactly similar to the sequence in this case was considered in *Armour and Mycroft, Petitioners* 1983 SLT 453.

The receivers in that case argued that the inhibition was not effectually executed diligence on the property of the company because the inhibition fell into the same category as, and had the same validity and effect as, an arrestment not followed by an action of furthcoming, founding on the decision in *Lord Advocate* v *Royal Bank of Scotland Ltd* 1977 SC 155. In that case, creditors who had arrested funds belonging to a company in the hands of the bank but had not proceeded with an action of furthcoming before a receiver was appointed to the debtor company, claimed to have 'effectually executed diligence on' the sum in the bank. The Lord Ordinary and the Inner House took the view that a mere arrestment, not followed by furthcoming, was not a completed diligence but merely the first step in completing the execution thereof. Accordingly, arrestment conferred on the creditor only certain rights *in personam* which entitled him to a preference in a competition but gave the arrestor no rights *in rem* over the subject-matter of the arrestment. In particular, Lord Emslie emphasises at p 169 that an arrestment is at best a step in diligence in *personam* and cannot properly be regarded as a 'diligence effectually executed on the subjects arrested'. The litigiosity established by arrestment does not confer on the arresting creditor any protection against those who have subsequently executed another more perfect diligence nor indeed against those who have completed security rights in the subjects, untainted by any voluntary act of the debtor in their creation.

The terms in which Lord Emslie, in this passage, describes the effect of an arrestment seem to me equally applicable to an inhibition, in that, in each case, the effect is merely to create litigiosity. In neither case is any nexus created on any specific asset nor any right *in rem*.

In *Armour and Mycroft*, the receivers argued that an inhibition could not be described as 'effectually executed diligence on the property' of the company. That argument was conceded by counsel for the inhibitor and accepted by Lord Kincraig. The necessary implication seems to be that if, as in this case, the inhibition postdates the registration of the charge, a receiver subsequently appointed can competently sell and can grant a valid and unchallengeable disposition to a purchaser relying both on the general principle and on the relevant statutory provisions as interpreted in the cases above cited. So, in his book *The Law of Inhibition and Adjudication*, George Gretton takes the view that the receiver can grant a valid disposition in these circumstances. He states categorically (at pp 126–127) that, on either of the approaches summarised in 1 or 2 above, an inhibition registered after the creation of a charge does not strike at the charge; that a floating charge is therefore not struck at by a subsequent inhibition; and at p 147 he states that, on the question of title, the law appears to be that if the floating charge was created (as in this case) before the inhibition, then the charge prevails and a purchaser is protected.

Unfortunately, although on the face of it that view is soundly based, the receivers in *Armour and Mycroft*, having succeeded in their argument as to the meaning of 'effectually executed diligence', then conceded that, although the charge was apparently, on that argument, not affected by the inhibition under (now) s 55 of the 1986 Act, none the less the receivers could not sell without the consent of the inhibiting creditor, under s 61(1). That concession was accepted by Lord Kincraig and his decision proceeded on that footing. In the result, although as a matter of general law and on the judicial construction of the statutory term 'effectually executed diligence', an inhibition which postdates the charge does not prevent the granting of a valid title by the receiver, the provisions of s 61(1) of the Insolvency Act 1986 apparently require the consent of an inhibiting creditor in such circumstances. Lord Kincraig was clearly acutely aware of this serious anomaly in the legislation, which he refers to on p 455 of the report. Admittedly, counsel for the receivers did not argue the point. Had they done so, Lord Kincraig might have come to a different conclusion; but, as the decision stands, he apparently accepted that the inhibitor was entitled to withhold consent to the sale and so to compel the receivers to apply to the court in terms of what is now s 61(1) of the 1986 Act. It is not clear what the remedy of the inhibitor might be if the receivers, in disregard of the inhibition, had proceeded with a sale; but there must be at least a risk that the inhibitors might be entitled to have the sale set aside, which, of course, puts the title of a purchaser at risk.

In these circumstances, I do not think it is safe to proceed except on the footing that the title in this case may not be valid without the consent of the inhibiting creditor.

On the question of marketability, the position is somewhat clearer. According to Lord Kincraig in *Armour and Mycroft*, standing the inhibition, the receivers cannot exhibit a clear search; and so, in the absence of an express provision to the contrary in the missives, the title would not be marketable. In his article in 1983 SLT 177, [David Hope, QC (now Lord Hope of Craighead)] states categorically that the search would not be clear in these circumstances.

I can therefore summarise my views thus:

(i) a disposition by the receiver to a purchaser in the present case would almost certainly be valid but, standing the decision in *Armour and Mycroft*, the purchaser should be advised of the risks involved in accepting a title from the receiver if the inhibition is not discharged or the inhibiting creditor does not consent and if a suitable indemnity is not obtained;

(ii) standing the inhibition, the search is not clear and therefore, in the absence of special provisions in the missives, the title is not marketable.

I am fortified in my opinion by the comment in Halliday, *Conveyancing Law and Practice*, para 21–80. 'Since doubt remains, however, the receiver should stipulate in the contract of sale that the inhibition will not be a ground of objection to the title.' Similarly George Gretton in an article in (1985) 30 JLSS 392 at p 394 reiterates his view that, where there is an inhibition which postdates the charge, the receiver can validly sell without regard to the inhibition. But he then adds: 'In doing so, the agent for the receiver should ensure, as in the case of liquidation, that the missives and letter of obligation do not promise a search clear of inhibitions against the company. The purpose of this ... is to ensure that the title, though a good one, cannot be objected to on the ground that the personal search is not technically clear.'

If the memorialists have a concluded bargain, without special provision therein, I think they are in a fairly strong position to require the receiver either to obtain the consent or a discharge from the inhibiting creditor or to apply to the court under s 61 of the 1986 Act.

If there is no concluded bargain, and if the memorialists are to proceed I think they have to take two factors into account:

(i) that their *own* title may be challenged by the inhibitor. If so, I consider that challenge could be successfully resisted;

(ii) that, on a resale of part or the whole of the subjects to a purchaser from the memorialists, objection may be taken to the title on this ground. Such an objection can, of course, be excluded by appropriate provisions in the missives of sale; and the memorialists would therefore have to consider whether or not, as a matter of commercial practicality, they are prepared to go ahead with the purchase on the footing that, when it comes to resale, they will introduce a provision into each contract of sale requiring the purchaser to take the title as it stands in this respect, with or without indemnity.

I understand that, in this case, the receiver was appointed at the request of the debtor. The question is then raised as to whether or not this would affect the quality of the actings of the receiver with particular reference to whether or not such actings involved or proceeded on a future voluntary act on the part of the debtor. My view is that the fact that a receiver was appointed at the request of the debtor does not in any way alter or affect the position.

Manual, para 23.6.

LEASES

41   The creation of a lease

Dispositions in favour of non-existent and nominee disponees – effect – liability of solicitors – service of calling-up notices – whether tenancy created – licence to occupy – implications for building society

Date: January 1988

Memorial
Certain mortgage frauds were perpetrated involving a building society. In some cases, a fictitious character took title to a property, and the same fictitious person granted a standard security. In other cases, title was taken, and security granted by a nominee. A number of the properties were let to tenants.

The memorialist asked a number of questions including:

1   What was the position of the building society in the case of the fictitious non-existent disponee?

2   What was the position of the building society in the case of the nominee purchasers, and was there any form of tenancy created in favour of the tenants?

Opinion
I have now had an opportunity of considering the problems raised; and I am writing to you now with some interim views.

The scenarios which you mention in your letter fall into two distinct categories:

1   *The fictitious non-existent disponee*
If, as you suspect, in at least one case the original purchaser/disponee who granted the standard security in favour of the building society was genuinely a fictitious non-existent person, then the position, in my view, is straightforward.

The original disposition in favour of the fictitious purchaser/disponee is void *ab initio* as was the antecedent contract of sale and purchase (if any); and, as a necessary consequence, the standard security granted in favour of the building society is also void.

Admittedly, the building society has an *ex facie* valid recorded standard security following on an *ex facie* validly recorded title. If the society was unaware of the fatal defect in their security, it could of course proceed innocently to exercise its power of sale and put the property on the market. Any purchaser from the society in these circumstances would obtain an apparently valid title; but in fact that title would itself be affected by the fatal defect in the antecedent disposition in favour of the fictitious disponee and the invalid standard security; and the conveyance in favour of the purchaser from the society could only be validated by prescriptive possession thereon. If, in the meantime, any interested party raised an action of reduction to set aside the void disposition in favour of the fictitious purchaser and the subsequent standard security in favour of the society, that action would, I think, inevitably succeed (given proof of the facts) and would bring down with it not only the original disposition in favour of the fictitious purchaser and the security in the society's favour but also the subsequent disposition by the society to the *bona fide* purchaser from it. This in turn would lead to a claim against the society under warrandice.

Given the knowledge, or at least the strong suspicion, that in this particular case the original disponee was a non-existent and fictitious person, and accordingly that his title and the security granted by that fictitious person in favour of the society were both void, I really do not think that the society can take any action under their apparent security, notwithstanding that it is *ex facie* valid until set aside, because, given knowledge, they would be making themselves a party to the original fraud.

I am therefore of the view that, in the case of the non-existent and fictitious disponee, there is no effective action which the society can take except an action for damages against the offending solicitor who, presumably, was a party to the fraud.

While it may be that, in the other cases, fraud on the part of the solicitor acting for the society may be difficult to prove, I would have thought that, in the case of the non-existent and fictitious disponee, evidence of fraud might not be too difficult to establish. After all, the solicitor acting for the non-existent fictitious purchaser, has got to show that he genuinely thought that he was acting on behalf of an existing and *bona fide* purchaser and, on his instructions, completed a contract for the sale and purchase, completed the disposition in favour of that person, recorded it on his behalf, applied for a loan on behalf of the non-existent person in the genuine belief that he was a *bona fide* purchaser, and completed the society's security in that belief. Obviously, however, this is a matter for further investigation once more information is available.

This may not, however, prove a very fruitful line of action for the society because, in the circumstances, it seems unlikely that a claim for damages, even if established, would in fact be met by the solicitor in question. If subsequent proceedings result in the solicitor being struck off the roll, the chances of recovery are fairly remote; and I understand that, while the Solicitors' Guarantee Fund would reimburse an individual client who had suffered pecuniary loss (as the society will have done in this case), the Guarantee Fund will not disburse to banks, building societies or other lending institutions where the claim is based on fraud on the part of the solicitor concerned.

I am afraid this is cold comfort to your clients but that seems to me inevitably to be the position.

It follows from the views here expressed that, in this particular case, where the owner/borrower is a fictitious person, there is no effective action which the society could or should take in relation to their security.

The only other line of action which occurs to me as possibly meriting consideration is an action directed against the original seller of the property if, as you surmise in your letter, he is the intermediary and the originator of the scheme. If that could be established, then it might possibly be worth considering raising an action of damages against that original seller coupled with an action of reduction to reduce the disposition by him in favour of the non-existent buyer and to inhibit on the dependence of that action so that, when the disposition was reduced and the property reverted to the original seller, the society would at least have an inhibition on it. Whether or not it is worth pursuing this course of action would depend mainly on two factors:

(i) whether it would be possible to prove a relationship between the original seller and the fictitious purchaser; and

(ii) the financial standing of the original seller who, in all probability, may become bankrupt as a result of these investigations in which case the inhibition would be of small advantage to the society.

It follows also from the views here expressed that there is no purpose in the society contemplating taking action against the occupiers of the property because, even if these occupiers are removed, there is no effective action which the society can take against the property itself under their security.

Having said that, however, there is an argument which has been advanced to me in other cases where a reputed fictitious purchaser was involved. The argument is that, since the rule in Scotland is undoubtedly that a person can call himself whatever name he pleases, anyone who instructs the title to a property to be taken in a fictitious name is in fact acting on his own behalf; and the fictitious name is perfectly validly and properly used as a genuine alias for whatever reason.

There may be some force in that argument; and of course it is the case that individuals do regularly trade under other names in a perfectly legitimate fashion. But, if that argument is to succeed, I think the onus would lie with the user of the fictitious name to show that it had been used honestly and in *bona fide* as a genuine alias under which the individual intended to trade. If the name and address are simply invented for the purpose of cloaking a fraudulent transaction, as seems to be the case here, then I do not think the courts would ever accept the alias argument and would, instead, treat the disponee as non-existent. I am inclined to the view that that is the position in the case of your supposed fictitious purchaser in one of the cases involved; and, for the reasons given above, I regard that as inevitably rendering the whole transaction, including the fictitious purchaser's title and the society's security, void *ab initio*.

2 *Nominee purchasers*

In certain of the cases, the title was taken in name of a nominee who, although not a genuine purchaser acquiring the property for his own occupation, was none the less a real and existing person albeit acting as nominee for the intermediary.

In such cases, I have no doubt whatever that a nominee who allows his name to be used in this way, who authorises a disposition to be taken in his name and who applies for a building society loan and signs the standard security must accept the consequences of so acting in a question between himself and the society. In other words, even although as between him and the intermediary he may claim to be a nominee, as between him and the society he is the borrower and is personally liable for all the consequences of having granted the security.

In these cases, therefore, although the nominee is acting purely as nominee for the intermediary, there is none the less a valid title and a valid security on the property which the society is entitled to enforce according to its terms.

One point causes me some concern. According to your letter, notices calling up the standard securities were served by recorded delivery post in all five cases; but all were returned. In the knowledge which the society has, I am not sure (although the point may well be covered by the terms of the security and by the society's rules) that the notice has been properly served if it were served on the nominee proprietor at the address of the property itself. In other words, if the society has reason to suspect that the property stands in the name of a nominee whose previous (and probably permanent and genuine) address they know from his mortgage application, then it may well be that the notice should be served on the nominee proprietor at the previous address given in the application form if that address is there given. On the other hand, if there is no other address for the nominee other than the address of the property being purchased (which is unlikely) then service at that address would suffice for the purpose of the calling-up notice.

Subject to that technicality, there is no doubt that the society, in these cases where there is a genuine but nominee proprietor, is entitled to serve either a notice calling up the loan or a default notice, or both; and, failing compliance with these notices, the society is then entitled to take whatever further steps may be required to enforce its security. The only problem which I perceive here is whether the notice was properly served, given the suspicion that the nominee proprietor may still be living at his old address; but that can easily be put right by serving a notice of default on the previous address.

When it comes to the subsequent procedure, however, there are a number of difficulties.

(*a*) Is there a tenancy?

The Rent (Scotland) Act 1984 (which consolidates and supersedes earlier legislation on rent restriction and protected tenancies) does not deal with this point explicitly. Under s 1 of the Act, a tenancy under which a dwellinghouse is let is a protected tenancy for the purpose of the Act unless certain conditions are satisfied; and these conditions do not apply here.

On the face of it, at least in those cases where there is an existing, albeit nominee, proprietor who has nominally permitted the premises to be occupied by third parties, the property has been let. On the other hand, each such property is subject to a valid standard security; and standard condition 6 of Sched 3 to the Conveyancing and Feudal Reform (Scotland) Act 1970 expressly prohibits the debtor/proprietor from letting the security subjects or any part thereof.

According to Paton and Cameron, *Landlord and Tenant,* p 519, the occupier must establish that his occupancy is *lawful* and is derived or flows from a tenancy or lease. In other words, the words 'tenancy' and 'let' when used in s 1 of the 1984 Act mean *lawful* tenancy, and *lawful* let. Paton and Cameron, however, do not cite any authority for that proposition; and it certainly is in contrast to the explicit terms of s 19(2) of the 1984 Act, dealing with sub-leases, where, in contrast to the wording in s 1, the wording used in s 19(2) refers explicitly to the premises being lawfully sub-let. The purpose of this explicit reference to 'lawfully' is to exclude from the statutory protection any sub-tenancies granted by a tenant protected under the Acts whose lease expressly excludes any power to assign or sub-let which is, of course, commonplace. Given that express exclusion, a sub-tenant would not be protected if the principal tenancy is terminated.

If it was thought necessary to emphasise the lawfulness of the sub-let in s 19(2), then it may be argued that the same terms, when used in s 1, do *not* require that the tenancy or the let should be 'lawful'. However, I think that it is simply an accident of drafting; and in my view, at least in those cases where the tenant has notice of the prohibition against letting, a purported lease granted by the heritable proprietor who is subject to a prohibition against leasing does not qualify for the protection of the 1984 Act.

There is support for that view in *Rodger (Builders) Ltd v Fawdry* 1950 SC 483, on the general principle that, where someone dealing with and taking a title from the infeft proprietor in the knowledge of a prior and adverse contractual obligation undertaken by the proprietor, cannot maintain the right which he then acquires in a question with that adverse interest.

Admittedly, in the case of these tenants, the principle is a little unrealistic in that it is very unlikely indeed that they have considered whether or not the proprietor has a title to grant a lease to them; but, none the less, the principle must I think still apply. The implication is that, although the nominee proprietor is an infeft proprietor and so *prima facie* has power to grant a lease, there is, on record, a contractual prohibition effectively preventing him from granting leases of which the tenants would be deemed to have notice at the date when their lease or right of occupancy was granted. Arguably, therefore, the lease was not *lawfully* granted, and the tenants were aware of this at the time when they took occupation. On that ground, they are therefore barred from obtaining the protection of the 1984 Act.

There is further support for this view in the English cases based on earlier legislation; and in particular, in the case of the *Dudley and District Building Society v Emerson* [1949] Ch 707 where the court held, based on an earlier common law decision and not on any technicality of statute, that the debtor–proprietor left in possession who grants a lease without the concurrence of a mortgagee can only give the lessee a precarious title inasmuch as, although the lease is good as between the tenant and the debtor–proprietor who granted the lease, the paramount title of the mortgagee may be asserted against both of them. This rule was held to apply in a question between a debtor–proprietor and a tenant under the Rent and Mortgage Interest Restrictions Act 1923. But of course this decision is based on technicalities of English law and on a different statute; and it may be that the Scottish courts would be reluctant to apply an English precedent in these circumstances.

None the less, the general principle still seems to me sound; and, on that ground, I think it is open to the building society to argue that no tenancy has been created and therefore the occupants are not protected by the 1984 Act.

The counter-argument is that the debtor–proprietor is undoubtedly infeft in the property and so, *prima facie*, has power to grant leases or rights of occupancy; and that the prohibition against letting is a matter personal to the debtor–proprietor and to the heritable creditor, with which third party tenants either have no concern, or they are entitled to assume that consent had been obtained from the heritable creditor; and that, in any event, a prohibition against letting in a heritable security cannot override or exclude statutory rights obtained by the tenant from the admittedly infeft proprietor. Further, the tenants may point to the decision in *Edinburgh Entertainments Ltd* v *Stevenson* 1926 SC 363. The general import of that case is that, where the debtor–proprietor is left in control of the property as is the case here, he has an implied mandate from the heritable creditor (in the case of *Edinburgh Entertainments*, an *ex facie* disponee) to grant leases. I think that argument would be difficult to sustain in the light of the specific prohibition in standard condition 6, but, none the less, it is a possible argument in support of a protected tenancy.

If a protected tenancy has been created, then, in my view, there is really very little the building society can do about it.

I had at first thought that there might be some remedy under Sched 2, Case 11(c)(vi) of the 1984 Act. The general effect of this provision is that, where property has been let on a regulated tenancy and where the dwellinghouse is subject to a heritable security granted before the tenancy (which is the case here) and where the debtor defaults, the creditor is entitled to sell and, for that purpose, can eject a tenant and obtain vacant possession. Unfortunately, however, Case 11 *only* applies to the debtor–proprietor 'who occupied the dwellinghouse as his residence' and who, following on such occupation, granted the tenancy agreement. I am assuming in these cases that the debtor–proprietor never took occupation; and so Case 11 does not apply at all.

There is no other provision in the Act which allows a heritable creditor to override the rights of a protected tenant in this way.

(*b*) Have the occupiers got a licence to occupy?

The distinction between a lease and a licence has not been significantly developed in the law of Scotland; but it is a distinction which is fairly clearly made in the English cases.

The point of the distinction is that, if the occupants can be shown to be mere licensees and not lessees, they are not protected under the Rent Acts and so can be evicted by, eg, a heritable creditor calling up his security.

Looking at the nature of the tenancies in these cases, and in particular the shifting tenant population, I think there may be a case to be made out for a licence rather than a lease, which would improve the position of the society to the extent that they would not then be concerned with security of tenure.

Alternatively, the tenants may argue that, even if they do not have a protected tenancy on the technicalities referred to above, they are none the less licensees and so lawfully entitled to remain on the premises until legally evicted. In this context, I draw your attention particularly to the provisions of Part III of the 1984 Act dealing with harassment and eviction without due process of law. Section 22 of the 1984 Act refers to 'the residential occupier'. This is necessarily wider than the terms of s 1 which, by implication, may require a *lawful* lease in order to create the statutory protection. Not so under s 22 where 'residential occupier' means a person occupying the premises as a residence under a contract giving him the *right to remain* in occupation. I think it is much more difficult to argue that a contract by the debtor–proprietor allowing a third party to occupy premises infringes on the prohibition against leasing. At least, there is certainly a serious risk that the courts might take that view, in which case the occupiers of the various flats come within the protection afforded to residential occupiers under Part III. This effectively means that, in order to evict them, the building society would have to observe the provisions of s 23 of the 1984 Act.

(*c*) Notice to tenants.

If the occupiers of the flats are not legally entitled to occupy, then they are no more than squatters; and there certainly is English authority for the obtaining of a court order to eject 'any person or persons in occupation' of premises, in the context of the earlier Protection from Eviction Acts. See *Ex parte Governors of Charing Cross Hospital* 1969 Current Law 2052. This case involved 'hippies' who were squatting on premises and who refused to give their names, which is rather more extreme than the facts in your case; but there would seem to be no reason why the court should not grant an order generally for the removal of unnamed persons in unlawful occupation.

On the other hand, in the only case which we have had of a comparable nature, we were required by the sheriff to obtain the name of, and serve notice on, at least one of the reputed tenants although, having done so, we then got an order for his ejection along with other unnamed persons occupying the premises.

The practice probably varies from court to court and it would certainly be prudent, in this case, to make enquiries of practitioners in your sheriffdom as to what view the sheriffs there take on the eviction of squatters unlawfully in possession.

If the sheriff is prepared to grant a warrant to evict either persons in occupation generally or one or more named persons along with others named in occupation, the sheriff officer implementing that decree is entitled to clear the house of anyone whom he finds there, whether named or not.

Once the calling-up notice has expired, I think there is no doubt that the society is then entitled to proceed at once to apply to the sheriff for a decree of ejection against the nominal owner and all others in occupation of the premises on the authority of that nominal owner; and if the procedure in your sheriff court is as you outline it, then I see no reason why the society should not take advantage of that procedure and apply accordingly. Provided a decree is obtained, I do not think that the society could be said to be infringing the provisions of Part III of the 1984 Act in relation to harassment. Further, given the prohibition in the standard security against letting, the nominal proprietor or any of the occupants has no real chance of succeeding in establishing a right to remain in possession although I accept that, if notice has to be given to the tenants (albeit short notice) there is a possibility of interdict.

It would not be desirable for the society to seek to obtain possession except by way of court decree, looking to the criminal implications of Part III of the 1984 Act.

The fact that the borrower or the intermediary is not aware of the proceedings does not seem to me in any way to invalidate them, subject only to the possible precaution of serving notice on the nominal borrower at his previous address.

The fact that the occupiers of the individual flats are unaware of the proceedings seems to be likewise immaterial if the sheriff is prepared to grant decree in these open terms. If not, then no doubt the sheriff will direct the society as to how they should proceed, which covers them against any unfortunate consequences arising out of such proceedings.

I am afraid I cannot make any further suggestions as to how the society might proceed in relation to clearing the premises and enforcing their security.

(*d*) Personal liability.

It is, of course, the case that, at least where there is a known and existing debtor–proprietor, that debtor–proprietor is *personally* liable for all the obligations in the standard security, including payment of the principal sum. The society may therefore think it worthwhile pursuing enquiries, probably through a private investigator, to establish the whereabouts of these debtor–proprietors if they are not to be found at the addresses on the loan application forms; and, having traced them, there may be merit in raising personal actions against them, coupled with inhibitions if that is appropriate.

The possibility of an action for damages against the solicitor has already been mentioned.

There seems to be no prospect whatever of success in an action for damages against the intermediary unless fraud can be established; and from your letter, that seems to be unlikely. But an investigation of the antecedent title in each case with a view to establishing the common identity of the previous proprietor might yield some benefit.

Further, it might be thought appropriate, at the same time when actions are raised for the ejection of existing occupants, to raise an action of interdict against the intermediary and the nominee proprietors, either jointly or severally, with a view to prohibiting them from granting any further leases or rights of occupancy to any new tenants. There is a possibility that letting may continue notwithstanding the raising of the action for ejection and that might prejudice the position of the society.

Further reading
Trade Development Bank v *Wariner and Mason (Scotland) Ltd* 1980 SC 74 says that where a lease is granted in breach of a clause in a standard security, the tenant's title is voidable.

Housing (Scotland) Act 1987.

Manual, para 24.1.

42   The creation of a lease

Lease – option to purchase – tacit relocation

Date: December 1987

Memorial
The memorialists entered into missives and took on the lease of commercial premises. The period of the lease ended, but continued for a further period of one year by tacit relocation. The landlords served a notice to quit on the memorialists. The memorialists maintained that they had an enforceable option to purchase the premises constituted in the missives drawn up three years earlier. An opinion was sought on this point.

Opinion
I am asked to advise whether an option to purchase the subjects of lease continues to be exercisable after the date of termination of the original lease during a period of tacit relocation.

In terms of an offer of 1983, the memorialists offered to take on lease the subjects known as A. The lease was to endure for a period of three years from and after 1984; and the offer provided, *inter alia*, that the tenants would have the option, exercisable by them 'at any time during the period of the lease' to purchase the premises at a fixed price and on certain other stipulated terms and conditions. The phrase 'the period of the lease' is not elsewhere defined either in the offer or in the qualified acceptance. The qualified acceptance added a provision modifying the option condition to the effect that, after an initial nine-month period, the landlords would be entitled to sell the subjects to a third party and thereupon to give notice to quit, with a provision for an option to purchase in that event.

No notice of termination was given by either party to the other to bring the lease to an end in 1987 which, in terms of the lease, was the formal termination date, nor at the third anniversary of the date of the final acceptance. It is not clear from the documents which of the two dates is the correct termination date but the latter date was adopted by the landlords' agents in a letter. Whichever of the two dates be the correct one, no notice having been given forty days prior to either date, the lease undoubtedly continued for a further year from one or other date under the ordinary common law rule of tacit relocation.

In September 1987, the landlords gave notice to the tenants requiring them to remove in April 1988 'on the conclusion of the current year's tenancy'; and, in that same notice, expressly declared that the notice was given without prejudice to the landlords' right in terms of the lease to offer the subjects for sale and called upon the tenants to exercise their option to purchase. Accordingly, by the letter of September 1987, the landlords' agents certainly made it clear that, in their view, the option to purchase in the original offer, as modified by their qualified acceptance, was still operative.

The tenants' agents responded in December 1987 with a letter formally intimating their intention to exercise the option to purchase to which they claim to be entitled under the original offer as modified by the qualified acceptance.

The landlords' agents take the view that, since the option to purchase was not exercised before the expiry of the original term of the lease it has ceased to be exercisable and they found on the decision in *Commercial Union Assurance Co* v *Watt & Cumine* 1964 SC 84. That view is rejected by the tenants' agents.

Where a lease is continued by tacit relocation, the weight of authority favours the view that, while there may be a new agreement to extend the term of the lease, no new lease is created. Instead, the original period of endurance stipulated for in the lease is extended for one further year. Tacit relocation therefore implies the prolongation of an existing lease by tacit consent, not the creation of a new lease. The legal effect is that all the stipulations and conditions in the original contract remain in force insofar as these are not inconsistent with any implied term of the original contract as so extended. The only necessary variation in every case is that a lease, if continued by tacit relocation, is so continued for the term of one year only. All other conditions, except insofar as inconsistent, continue to apply.

In the case of *Commercial Union Assurance Co*, there was a lease for original periods of twenty years and lesser periods which was not terminated by notice and therefore continued by tacit relocation after the stipulated ish. The lease itself contained an option to the tenant to renew the lease on the same terms which the tenant failed to exercise before the original term expired. The court held that the tenant was not entitled to exercise the option to renew after the expiry of the original term but while still in occupation under tacit relocation, on the footing that, since under tacit relocation either party was entitled to terminate the lease at the end of each successive year, an option to renew for a further period of years was inconsistent with that right.

In arriving at this decision, Lord President Clyde refers to and relies on the judgment of Lord Watson in the House of Lords in *Neilson* v *Mossend Iron Co* (1886) 13R (HL) 50. Having quoted Lord Watson's *dictum* to the effect that the conditions in the original contract remain in force insofar as these are not inconsistent with any implied term of the renewed contract, Lord President Clyde comments:

> '[O]ne of these implied terms is that, during tacit relocation, either party may terminate the lease by the requisite notice at the end of a year. It necessarily follows, in my view, from this that an option to the tenant to demand a further twenty years' lease is quite inconsistent with the landlord's rights under a lease from year to year ... a right in a tenant to renew the lease for twenty years is quite inconsistent, in my view with the right of the landlord in a yearly lease to bring it to an end at the end of the year.'

Lord Guthrie expressly takes the same view, and Lord Carmont concurs.

Had it not been for the decision in the *Commercial Union* case, I would have advised without hesitation that, in the present case, the tenants were perfectly entitled to exercise their option to purchase during a period of tacit relocation simply by reference to the wording used in the original lease, in terms of which the option is exercisable at any time 'during the period of the lease'. Applying the normal rule of tacit relocation, there is no doubt, in my view, that the 'period of the lease' has not yet come to an end because notice was not given to terminate the same at the original ish and so, by express provision in terms of the lease, the tenants are still entitled to exercise their option, because the lease still endures. It would be possible to argue, on the terms of this contract, that the expression 'the period of the lease' means the original three-year term and not a prolongation of that term by tacit relocation; and certainly it would have been possible so to provide by stating explicitly the period during which the option to purchase was to be exercisable. In my view, however, as the phrase is used in this contract, it applies not only to the original term of three years but to any extension of that term by tacit relocation.

In light of the decision in the *Commercial Union* case, however, I do not think that view can now be successfully maintained. If an option to renew for a further twenty years is inconsistent with the right of the landlord to bring a relocated lease to an end at the end of the year, then it is impossible to hold that an option to purchase does not have the same effect. I cannot figure any grounds for distinguishing in principle between an option to renew for a period of years and an option to purchase in this context. Standing that decision, therefore, my view is that the tenants' option to purchase has been lost by not having been exercised prior to, at latest, April 1987.

I am bound to say I reach that conclusion with considerable regret. While it may be that the decision in the *Commercial Union* case was correct, I think the grounds on which Lord President Clyde and Lord Guthrie arrived at their decision are undoubtedly open to criticism. Lord President Clyde, in particular, relies on and applies the judgment in the earlier case of *Neilson*. In so doing, in my view, he is not comparing like with like and draws unjustified conclusions from the *dictum* of Lord Watson. But these criticisms of the decision in the *Commercial Union* case are of little consolation to the tenants because, standing that decision, I really cannot see how they could succeed except by having the judgment in the *Commercial Union* case overturned, which would require certainly a seven-judge decision of the Court of Session; and, possibly, if the Court of Session took the same view of the decision in the House of Lords in *Neilson* as Lord President Clyde took in *Commercial Union,* then the tenants would have to appeal to the House of Lords in order to distinguish this lease from the lease in the *Commercial Union* case.

The only remaining question is whether the landlords' agents have altered the position by their letter of September 1987. In terms of that letter, the landlords give notice to the tenants to remove, but without prejudice to their rights to call upon the tenants to exercise a right of pre-emption which is part and parcel of the option to purchase clause in the contract. The question is whether, by referring to the option clause in their letter, the landlords' agents have either homologated or adopted that provision, thereby making the option exercisable in circumstances where it would otherwise not have been. In my view, however, the letter, while it may be embarrassing to the landlords' solicitors, does not have that effect.

Homologation implies that one party to an imperfect contract has, by his actings, agreed to be bound by it. Adoption implies that a person, by his actings, has agreed to implement an obligation which would not otherwise have been binding on him.

Homologation does not apply because, in this case, the original agreement was not informal or defective but was properly constituted by the original missives and remains properly constituted during the period of tacit relocation.

I do not think that adoption would apply either. The option to purchase undoubtedly was validly constituted and was exercisable during the original period of the lease. The fact that the option ceased to be exercisable on the expiry of the original term of the lease, as seems to be the case, is not something which, in my view, could properly be cured by adoption. Rather, if the option was to revive for the benefit of the tenants after the expiry of the original lease that would require a new contract or a modification of the existing contract; and in my view the letter from the landlords' agents does not have that effect.

In the result, in my view, as the law stands at present, the option to purchase has undoubtedly expired and can no longer be exercised by the tenants under the lease.

Further reading
Requirements of Writing (Scotland) Act 1995 on the abolition of homologation.

Manual, para 24.1.

43   Lease as a real right

Shooting lease – whether personal or real – Leases Act 1449

Date: May 1986

Memorial
Missives were concluded by the memorialist to sell an estate to a purchaser.

A shooting lease had been granted by the seller for a period of fifty years, with an option to renew for a further period of fifty years. The lessee under the shooting lease had never exercised the rights, but the purchaser wanted reassurance that he would not do so in the future. The memorialist argued that a lease of shootings was not binding on a singular successor. The purchaser wanted a renunciation of the lease.

The memorialist asked the following questions:

1 Was the lessee under the shooting lease entitled to enforce the lease against singular successors of the memorialist?

2 Was the title to the ground completely unencumbered?

3 What was the best solution for the purchaser if any doubt existed?

4 If the purchaser wanted to sell part or all of the land in the future, how should he protect his interests at that time?

Opinion
1 No, for the following reasons.

(a) At common law, a lease is purely a personal contract between the landlord and his tenant; and, as such, cannot bind a singular successor of the landlord. The common law rule has, however, been substantially modified by the Leases Act 1449 in the case of all those leases which comply with the provisions of the Act. In the case of such a lease, a tenant, by taking possession, secures for himself a quasi-real right which renders his lease enforceable in a question with subsequent singular successors of the landlord as proprietors of the subjects for the whole duration of the lease.

The 1449 Act does not, however, apply universally to every lease of every description. To come within the terms of the Act, the lease must satisfy certain requirements. So far as we are here concerned, these requirements include the following.

(i) The subject-matter of the lease must be land. This requirement has been liberally interpreted by the courts but, as the law at present stands, the position is that a mere lease of shootings, which is what we have here, does not come within this requirement of the 1449 Act; and accordingly a shooting tenant under such a shooting lease has no protection and no quasi-real right in a question with a singular successor of the landlord. This is the settled rule following on the decision in *Pollock, Gilmour & Co v Harvey* (1828) 6 S 913. But some reservations have been expressed on that decision in later cases; and in Paton and Cameron, *Landlord and Tenant* at p 106 Mr J. G. S. Cameron expresses the view that it would not be surprising if the decision in *Pollock* were reversed, should the matter again be raised in the court. My own view is that, should the matter be litigated again, the decision in *Pollock* would be upheld but, obviously, the question is not beyond argument.

(ii) A further requirement of the 1449 Act is that the lease must provide for a rent and the rent must not be 'illusory'. There is no reported case to give guidance on what is and what is not an illusory rent in this sense; but, in my view, in the present case, the yearly rent of one shilling if asked only would be so regarded. Accordingly even if a lease of shootings qualifies as a lease for the purposes of the 1449 Act, this particular lease is disqualified from the benefits of that Act because the rent is illusory.

(iii) A further requirement of the 1449 Act is that the tenant shall have taken possession of the subjects of let. According to my instructions, since this lease was first granted in 1959, the tenant has never exercised his shooting rights and cannot, therefore, be said to have entered into possession up to this date.

As I understand it, since the lease was granted, the property has twice transmitted to a singular successor, once in 1963 on the disposition by Mrs O to the memorialist although, in his title, the lease is specifically excepted from warrandice; and again on the conveyance by the memorialist to the purchaser where the warrandice obligation was absolute. It might be argued that the memorialist himself is personally barred from founding on the rule as to taking possession, and so could not defeat the rights of the tenant if he subsequently took possession, looking to the terms of the warrandice obligation in the 1963 disposition referred to above. But that certainly does not apply to the title of the present infeft proprietors, and the mere fact that the present infeft proprietors were aware of the existence of the lease when taking infeftment does not bar them from challenging the purported rights of the tenant. See *Millar* v *McRobbie* 1949 SC 1 where this particular point is explicitly decided.

Accordingly, if the tenant under the shooting lease now sought to take possession and to enforce the provisions of his lease, I think this could be successfully resisted by the present infeft proprietors on this ground.

(b) Even if I am wrong in my view that the lease in this case is unenforceable because it fails to satisfy the requirements of the 1449 Act in various respects, there is a further point relating to possession which favours the present proprietors and fortifies their title. The lease was granted in 1959 but possession was not taken following thereon. It is just possible to argue that the existence of the lease was 'relevantly acknowledged' for the purposes of s 7 of the Prescription and Limitation (Scotland) Act 1973 by the express provisions of the warrandice clause in the 1963 disposition, but, even if that argument is good, which I very much doubt, more than twenty years have passed since that 'acknowledgement' was made.

For the reasons given above, the lease, when granted, created only a personal right for the benefit of the tenant, whether or not that personal right could have been converted into a real right by taking possession or by the recording of the lease in the General Register of Sasines (see below). In fact, the tenant did not take possession and the lease was not recorded, and this position has continued for more than twenty years. In the result, in my view, the rights conferred on the tenant under the lease when it was first granted have now inevitably been lost by the running of the long negative prescription. Section 7 of the Prescription and Limitation (Scotland) Act 1973 is quite specific on this point. The only rights which remain enforceable, although not exercised for more than twenty years, are those rights listed as imprescriptible in Sched 3 to the Act. In terms of Sched 3(b), the right in land of the lessee under a recorded lease is an imprescriptible right; but that, I think, carries with it the necessary and inevitable implication that the right in land of the lessee under an unrecorded lease, if not exercised for twenty years, is then finally and irretrievably lost by the running of the long prescription. Accordingly, any claim by the tenant to be entitled to the shootings under this lease could, in my view, be successfully resisted on this ground, if on no other.

(*c*) There is, however, a further aspect of this lease which has to be considered. The lease was granted for a period of fifty years from 1958. *Prima facie*, therefore, the lease is recordable in the General Register of Sasines under s 1 of the Registration of Leases (Scotland) Act 1857 in terms of which any probative lease for a period exceeding twenty years may be so recorded. The 1857 Act does not require that the lease should satisfy the requirements of the 1449 Act. Accordingly, so long as the document is a lease (and that term is not further defined in the 1857 Act) it does not require to be a lease of land, nor does it require to have a definite ish, nor a rent which is not illusory.

Such a lease, when recorded, is effectual against any singular successor whose infeftment is posterior to the date of such registration under s 2. On the face of it, this provision is ambiguous in the sense that, if the tenant under the present lease were to record it today, he could not insist on his rights as tenant in a question with the present infeft proprietors whose infeftment antedates the recording of the lease; but, taking the terms of s 2 alone, it would seem that he might insist on those rights in a question with a singular successor of the present proprietors whose infeftment would, of necessity, be posterior to the recording of the lease. But in my view, s 2 has to be read along with s 16(1) of the same Act which equates the recording of a lease to the taking of actual possession by the tenant of the subjects leased. It is now too late for the tenant to take possession because (i) he has failed to take possession before the infeftment of a singular successor; and (ii) in any event, he has lost all his rights under the lease by prescription. Therefore, it is too late for the tenant now to record his lease in order to achieve the effect given to recording under the 1857 Act, s 16. Even if recorded, the lease would be of no effect in a question with both the present infeft proprietors and all subsequent successors.

(*d*) Finally, for completeness, I think it appropriate to mention the equivalent provisions in the Land Registration (Scotland) Act 1979, although of course these do not yet apply because the relevant county is not yet an operational area. In the fullness of time, however, when registration of title has extended to embrace the county, the pro-

195

visions of ss 2(1) and 3(3) of the 1979 Act might apply to the present lease. In terms of these two sections, a long lease is registrable; and the only way in which the tenant can acquire a real right enforceable against singular successors as proprietors is by the registration of the lease in the Land Register.

At first sight, there might appear to be some risk that, when the county becomes an operational area, the tenant could register his lease and thereafter enforce it against the then proprietor. I do not think that view would hold, however, looking to the provisions of s 3(1)(a) of the 1979 Act, in terms of which registration has the effect of vesting in the person entitled to the registered interest a real right in and to that interest. Although undoubtedly the tenant under this lease was originally entitled to an interest as tenant, he has forfeited that interest for the various reasons set out above. Accordingly, that interest is no longer capable, under any enactment or rule of law, of being vested as a real right in the tenant. The Keeper would therefore be entitled to reject an application for registration of this lease; and, even if he did accept it for registration, I think he would be bound to register the tenant's interest with an exclusion of indemnity. This would allow the then proprietor to apply for rectification of the Register so as to remove the lease therefrom.

As an alternative, if the tenant sought to establish his right as tenant in a question with some future proprietor of the subjects holding on a registered title (after the county had become an operational area under the 1979 Act) as being a lessee with an overriding interest under s 28(1), his claim would be bound to fail, in my view, because in the definition of 'overriding interest' paragraph (*a*) does not apply because the lease is a long lease; and, under (*b*), the tenant could not claim to have acquired a real right to the subjects by virtue of possession. Accordingly, any claim that the lease is an overriding interest will inevitably fail.

2   No. Admittedly, for the reasons set out in answer to question 1, my view is that, on a variety of grounds, the lease is unenforceable and does not bind the present infeft proprietors. On the other hand, the lease is a probative document which, prima facie, confers certain rights on the tenant; and the purchaser has necessarily been made aware of it from the exclusion from warrandice in the prior title.

Standing that lease, I think the purchaser is quite entitled to take the view that the seller has not demonstrated to the purchaser's satisfaction that he can fully implement his obligation in paragraph 1 of Sched 2 attached to the offer in terms of which entry with vacant possession is to be given on the date of entry.

My answer to question 1 is, in part, based on an *ex parte* statement as to the failure on the part of the tenant to take possession, which may or may not be correct. Beyond that, the views expressed above are merely expressions of opinion.

In these circumstances, and looking to the importance of the matter to the purchaser, I think the purchaser is entitled to require some further evidence that the tenant's apparent rights under the lease cannot be enforced and do not bind the purchasers. Certainly, this would be achieved if the tenant could be persuaded to renounce the lease; but, failing that, I think the purchaser is entitled to a decree to the effect that the lease is unenforceable. Counsel would be better able to advise on the appropriate form of action in these circumstances; but I would have thought that the choice lay between an action of reduction of the lease; a declarator that the lease was not enforceable as against the present proprietors; or an action of interdict against the tenant to bar him from seeking to exercise his purported rights thereunder.

I think such a decree would remove any remaining doubts which the purchaser may have and would be sufficient to render the title marketable. Anything short of that involves the purchaser in taking at least some risk, if only the risk of litigation as between him and the tenant seeking to enforce his purported rights. In any such action, my view is that the tenant is bound to fail. But that is only my personal opinion, and in any event might involve the purchaser in trouble and expense.

3   This question is already answered in my answer to question 2.

4   If the purchaser is prepared to settle the transaction on the footing that the tenant's rights are unenforceable but without insisting on either a discharge from the tenant, or appropriate decree, then the risk is that, when the purchaser in turn comes to sell, the same questions will be raised by a purchaser from him, with this added further disadvantage that the tenant has now been put on the alert as to the possibility of his rights under the lease which, probably, he had altogether forgotten about in the intervening thirty-five years.

I think the only way the purchaser could protect himself against a possible frustrated sale or claim for damages on breach of contract would be to disclose the existence of the lease at the missives stage and before a bargain was concluded, requiring any purchaser to take the lease as they find it but, no doubt, expressing the view here expressed that the tenant's rights under the lease are wholly unenforceable. There would certainly be no come-back on a seller who disclosed the position at the missives stage in this way although, just possibly, the existence of the lease might deter an otherwise willing purchaser; or it might have a depreciating effect on the price offered because of the potential risk of challenge by the tenant.

The alternative way of protecting the purchaser's position is to insist at this stage on obtaining a renunciation or an appropriate decree, either of which, if obtained, would entirely clear the title and remove all possible risk.

Further reading
Palmer v *Brown* 1989 SLT 128.

Manual, para 24.2.

44   *Procedure and effect of recording*

Date: April 1989

Memorial
The memorialists sought a wide-ranging opinion on the doctrine of *confusio* as applied to commercial leases:

1   There was some inconsistency in the textbooks as to the application and effect of the doctrine of *confusio* as far as it related to commercial leases. The memorialists had sought the opinion of counsel whose views had differed to those of Professor McDonald in an earlier opinion. Given the views of counsel, did Professor McDonald have anything further to add?

2   A granted a lease to B who in turn granted a sub-lease to C. D purchased the heritable interest of A and took an assignation of the leasehold interest of B.
(*a*)   Had the lease been extinguished by the operation of *confusio*?
(*b*)   If not, did the lease remain in existence, but the *jus crediti* was extinguished?
(*c*)   Did the fact that the lease had been recorded in the Register of Sasines, registered in the Land Register or in the Books of Council and Session make any difference?
(*d*)   What was the position with the sub-lease?
(*e*)   What were the liabilities of A, B, C and D *inter se*?
(*f*)   If the sub-tenant had lost his tenure, could the tenancy agreement under the sub-lease be preserved by conclusion of an agreement between D and C whereby the operation of *confusio* would be acknowledged, but the parties undertake to treat the lease as a binding lease, and if so what would be the terms of the binding lease?
(*g*)   If D accepted rent from C, are D and C bound to a lease, and if so on what terms?

3   If A grants a lease to B who in turn grants a sub-lease to C, and B assigns his interest to A or A sells his interest to B:
(*a*)   Would the lease be extinguished by the operation of *confusio*?
(*b*)   If not, would the lease remain in existence, but the *jus crediti* be extinguished?
(*c*)   If the lease and sub-lease were recorded in the Register of Sasines or registered in the Land Register or Books of Council and Session would that make any difference?
(*d*)   What would be the position of the sub-lease? Was it terminated with the sub-tenant losing his tenure?
(*e*)   What would be the liabilities of A, B and C *inter se*?
(*f*)   If the sub-tenant has lost his tenure, could the tenancy under the sub-lease be preserved by conclusion of an agreement between A or B and C whereby the operation of *confusio* would be acknowledged, but the parties undertake to treat the sub-lease as a binding lease, and if so what would be the terms of the sub-lease?

(*g*) If A or B accepts rent from C, are A or B and C bound to a lease, and, if so, on what terms?

Opinion

1 I think it is fair to say that the textbooks and, to some extent, reported cases, do disclose some degree of uncertainty in the application of the doctrine of *confusio* to the relationship of landlord and tenant.

Counsel examines the question in some depth in his opinion and concludes, not unreasonably, that the doctrine of *confusio* does not operate to extinguish the lease itself. He reaches that conclusion, as I understand it, on the decisions in *Healy & Young's Trustee* v *Mair's Trustees* 1914 SC 893, and in *Lord Blantyre* v *Dunn* (1858) 20 D 1188. With respect, however, these do not seem to me to be satisfactory authorities on which to base the proposition that the lease in such circumstances is not extinguished.

In *Blantyre*, the question of total extinction was not directly at issue. However, the Lord Ordinary states at p 1193 that: 'Surely, when there is no express provision to the contrary, the subordinate right of *tenancy must merge* in the higher right of *property*.' On appeal, the Lord President to some extent side-stepped the issue. Lord Ivory states categorically at p 1197 that, in the circumstances, he was unable to hold that there was any subsisting lease; Lord Curriehill, at p 1198, held that the leases themselves became extinct when the tenant acquired the right of property; and Lord Deas, again, side-stepped the issue. Accordingly, in my view, *Blantyre* v *Dunn* in fact supports the view that acquisition of the property by the tenant having a lease thereof extinguishes the lease.

Counsel quotes a passage from Rankine, *Leases* (3rd edn), p 525, which, in categoric terms, quite clearly supports the view that the lease is totally extinguished. Finally counsel quotes passages from Stair and Erskine to support the view that the concurrence of ownership and tenancy may produce a temporary suspension of the lease but not an absolute extinction thereof. Undoubtedly, these two passages from Stair and Erskine do support that view. But these are passages dealing with the general principle of *confusio* as it applies in contractual obligations; they do not refer directly to leases. Significantly, counsel omits from his quotation from Rankine a passage referring to the Tobermory leases case, *Campbell* v *McKinnon* (1867) 5 M 636 which, although appealed on other matters, was not appealed on this point.

In *Campbell* v *McKinnon*, the question was whether the vassal under a feu charter who had previously occupied the subjects under a lease, was entitled to continue to found on the lease following on delivery of the charter in his favour. In other words, given that the tenant had acquired the right of property in the subjects of lease, did the lease continue to subsist? Lord Curriehill, again, argues the point at some considerable length but, at the end of his opinion, and under reference to passages from Craig, Stair and Erskine, concludes that, when a person possessing as a lessee of lands acquires a title to the property previously leased, there is an implied renunciation of the lease. The passages in Stair and Erskine to which Lord Curriehill refers, are Stair II, 9, 37 and Erskine, II, 6, 44, both of which are passages dealing specifically with leases, and Erskine, in the latter passage, refers to Craig, to the same effect. These three authorities, when dealing specifically with the question of leases as opposed to the application of the rule to contractual obligations generally, are agreed that, when the proprietor acquires a tenancy or vice versa, the lease is (in the ordinary case) extinguished absolutely and not merely suspended. Lord Curriehill did not feel himself at liberty to decide contrary to these authorities; and for my part I take the view as Lord Curriehill, reinforced by the judgments in the Tobermory leases case in the Inner House. This is the view expressed also in *Green's Encyclopaedia*, Vol 3, para 890. The authors of that article were C. D. Murray KC and R. P. Morrison, both no mean authorities. The statement is made categorically in para 890 that, where a tenant has acquired the subjects of let as proprietor, the lease is extinguished; and, if the land is then again let, that represents a new lease, not a restored contract.

It is, of course, possible to construct a contrary argument; and there are undoubtedly two comparable, but different, situations where *confusio* will not operate:

(*a*) Where the superior acquires the *dominium utile* or vice versa. Originally, it was thought that, in this situation, *confusio* operated automatically. In *Bald* v *Buchanan* (1787) 2 RLC 210, however, it was decided beyond argument, on a decision which has never since been challenged, that the mere acquisition of two adjacent feudal estates by the same proprietor does not automatically imply merger; but that, in addition, the formal feudal procedure of consolidation is required to merge the two estates.

(*b*) In the case of a contract of ground annual. This situation is referred to in counsel's opinion, with particular reference to *Healy & Young's Trustee* v *Mair's Trustees*. But, as the judges are at pains to point out, that case involved a ground annual which is a permanent and irredeemable real right in land, completed by infeftment. It was that factor, in my view, which brought the case of *Healy & Young's Trustee* within the same *ratio* as *Bald* v *Buchanan*. See, in particular, Lord Johnston at p 901 and the Lord President at p 903: 'Lord Kinnear's opinion is quite unassailable – that a ground annual, being an *ex facie irredeemable* right, cannot be extinguished *confusione*. It is an irredeemable right in land completed by infeftment and ... there is no authority in principle for holding that it can be extinguished *confusione*.' See also the Lord President at p 902: 'Where the doctrine applies, it absolutely extinguishes the obligation...'. Admittedly, in that case, Lord Johnston does deliver himself of the view that in the case of leases, as in *Blantyre* v *Dunn*, confusion proper does not take place; but he does not explain how he arrives at that conclusion, which is, of course, *obiter* and seems to run contrary to previous authority.

I think it is also pertinent to point out in this context that, although a tenant may acquire what is frequently termed a 'real' right by virtue of possession, under the Leases Act 1449, or by registration of the lease under the Registration of Leases (Scotland) Act 1857, a lease remains essentially a personal contract between the original landlord and his tenant. Further, in order to create the real right under the 1449 Act for the benefit of the tenant, the lease must contain an ish, however far distant, and can therefore never be a permanent right. Notwithstanding the provisions for registration of the lease in Sasines, there is no feudal procedure by which a tenant as such can procure himself infeft. Instead, the effect of registration of a lease is, not to create an infeftment for the tenant, but to equate the position of the tenant under a registered lease with the position of a tenant under an unregistered lease who has entered into possession. See the 1857 Act, s 16.

Accordingly, while accepting that the matter may not be conclusively settled, I am of the opinion that, on the authorities above cited, the better view is that *confusio* does operate absolutely to extinguish the lease itself, rather than merely to suspend it, in the simple case where the tenant under the lease also becomes the proprietor of the subjects of let.

In the result, I adhere to the view originally expressed in my previous opinion and I beg to differ from counsel for the reasons set out above.

2 Before dealing with the answers to the further questions asked in paragraph 2 of the letter of instructions, I think it appropriate to make certain general comments on the operation of *confusio* which affect the position.

First, to quote from Gloag and Henderson, *Introduction to the Law of Scotland* (9th edn), para 15.20, *confusio* does not operate where there is any separation of interests but only where the full and absolute right of the creditor and the full and absolute right of the debtor merge in one person. Similarly, *Green's Encyclopaedia*, vol 4, para 390, in the article referred to above, states that, if there are adverse interests in the person of the creditor, these may prevent the application of the principle and keep the debt alive as a separate estate. That general rule applies, in my view, in the case of leases as it applies in the case of debts.

Secondly, I am assuming that, in the hypothetical situation envisaged in this question, the sub-lease by B to C was validly granted either because sub-letting was not prohibited by express provision or by implication, or alternatively that the landlord assented to the granting of the sub-lease; and that C has made his right real, either by entering into possession or by registration.

With these points in mind, I answer the questions asked in paragraph 2 thus.

(*a*) No. In my opinion, the granting of a valid sub-lease by B to C creates an adverse interest sufficient to prevent the operation of the ordinary rule of *confusio* when D subsequently purchased the subjects themselves from the original landlord A.

(*b*) It follows from my answer to (*a*) that the lease by A to B continues to subsist although, since D has acquired the subjects from A, the obligations contained in the principal lease by A to B cease to be enforceable as between D as landlord and D in his capacity as assignee of the original tenant B. To that extent, the obligations are suspended but not extinguished.

(*c*) In the circumstances outlined in paragraph 2, the recording of the lease and sub-lease, or the registration thereof, in the Register of Sasines, in the Land Register or in the Books of Council and Session, does not affect the position one way or another, unless C has not taken possession – see paragraph (*d*) below.

(*d*) On the view which I take, *confusio* will operate to extinguish a lease absolutely where the landlord and the tenant come to be the same person in the same capacity and as such both owner and tenant of the same subjects unless there is some impediment to such extinguishment.

In my original opinion, I took the view that creation of a real security over a registered lease which was recorded prior to the acquisition by the tenant of the subjects of lease was a sufficient impediment to prevent the operation of *confusio* and the resultant extinguishment of that security. I am still of the same view.

The granting of a sub-lease under which a sub-tenant has acquired a real right probably also represents such an impediment, suspending the operation of *confusio* during the subsistence of the sub-lease. If that view is correct, there is no problem so far as the sub-lease is concerned. The lease continues to operate as before, although, as between landlord and principal tenant, the mutual obligations *inter se* are not enforceable since the same person is both debtor and creditor in these obligations. It necessarily follows that, if the lease continues to subsist because of the impediment to the operation of *confusio*, the sub-lease continues to subsist as before and is totally unaffected by the coincidence that the landlord and the principal tenant are the same person.

If, however, the granting of a sub-lease is not a sufficient impediment to prevent the operation of *confusio*, the position of the sub-tenant is, none the less, in my view, very much the same. *Confusio*, in its application to leases, has been equated to an implied renunciation by the tenant in favour of the landlord – see the opinion of Lord Curriehill, quoted above, in *Campbell* v *McKinnon*. In such circumstances, where the tenant prior to such renunciation has granted sub-leases, it would seem, from the decision in the *Earl of Morton* v *His Tenants* (1625) M 15,228, that, notwithstanding such renunciation, the rights of the sub-tenants, if duly made real prior to the renunciation taking effect, remain enforceable in a question with the principal landlord by virtue of the Leases Act 1449. Accordingly, in general, whether *confusio* operates or not in these circumstances, the sub-tenant is entitled to remain in occupation on his sub-lease in a question with the infeft proprietor of the subjects.

I would emphasise, however, that if C is to enjoy the protection of the Leases Act 1449, he must have made his right as sub-tenant real, by possession or registration, *before* D (in good faith and without notice) perfected his real right as proprietor.

(*e*) So far as A is concerned, having sold the property to D, subject to the subsisting lease by A to B, A has no remaining rights or liabilities whatsoever. If, however, in the sale by A to D and in the subsequent disposition, A undertook to give vacant possession to D; and if the lease by A to B had not been recorded and if, in addition, D was unaware of the existence of that lease and so was a *bona fide* purchaser for value without notice, then D almost certainly would have a claim against A under warrandice.

Similarly, B having assigned his lease to D would have no remaining rights or liabilities in a question with C, his sub-tenant, or in a question with D, his assignee. Again, however, if B had warranted to D that D would get vacant possession and if D was unaware of the existence of the sub-lease which had not been recorded, D would again, almost certainly, have a claim against B for breach of B's warranty.

Accordingly, these qualifications apart, so far as rights and liabilities are concerned, these are restricted to rights and liabilities as between D as the heritable proprietor and as the assignee from B of the principal lease on the one hand, and C, the original sub-tenant, on the other.

Technically, there is this distinction depending on whether or not *confusio* has operated that, if *confusio* has not operated, C will continue in occupation of the subjects as sub-tenant of D, in his capacity as tenant under the original lease by A to B. If *confusio* has operated, the principal lease by A to B is extinguished immediately on its assignation to D; but, on the rule in the *Earl of Morton* case referred to above, C can maintain himself in possession in a question with D as proprietor in terms of what was originally the sub-lease but which, by *confusio*, has become the principal lease in the sense that C as tenant will hold directly of and under D as proprietor, the intervening principal lease by A to B having been extinguished in the process.

Either way, for practical purposes, C remains as tenant of D as his landlord; and the rights and obligations originally created by the sub-lease by B to C continue to apply as between D as landlord and C as tenant until the termination of the original sub-lease. There is no change in the rights and liabilities of C as sub-tenant resulting from the change in title to the property itself, whether or not the principal lease still subsists.

(*f*) For the reasons explained above, this situation can only arise, in my opinion, in the unlikely case where D as a *bona fide* purchaser for value without notice has acquired both the property and the tenant's right under the principal lease and has become infeft before the sub-tenant C has made his right real by possession or registration. In this unlikely situation, however, I have no doubt that D would not be bound by the terms of the sub-lease. See *Ceres School Board* v *McFarlane* (1895) 23R 279.

The creation of a lease is very simply achieved. Assuming that the original sub-lease by B to C contained all the essentials for a proper lease, then it would be quite sufficient for D as the proprietor and C as the original sub-tenant to enter into a very short agreement in effect homologating the sub-lease and equating it to a lease by D to C directly, without the interposed principal lease originally granted by A to B. If such an agreement were entered into, it really would not matter, in my view, whether the parties agreed to acknowledge that *confusio* had taken place or not. The essence of the matter would then be whether D and C had agreed that C was to become a tenant and if so on what terms. If, however, the matter proceeds as suggested in this question, then there is no doubt that the sub-lease would continue to operate strictly according to its terms as between D and C; and, if the sub-lease referred to the principal lease for terms and conditions, those terms and conditions would continue to operate as between D and C as conditions of the sub-lease, notwithstanding that the principal lease itself had been extinguished by *confusio*. In considering what are the terms of the agreement between D and C, the reference to a lease, which had been extinguished, as prescribing certain terms would be perfectly competent and, to that extent but to that extent only, the terms of the original lease by A to B would continue in operation for the purposes of defining the relationship between D and C.

(*g*) Again, this question only applies in the unlikely situation referred to in answer (*f*). But, if that situation occurred, and if there were no agreement but merely acceptance of rent, this in turn introduces a very wide range of possibilities because, in the ordinary way:

(i) a lease for a period of more than a year can only be constituted by probative writ or by informal writings followed by *rei interventus*; and

(ii) payment of rent, taken by itself, would certainly not be sufficient in my opinion to set up the sub-lease in the absence of other material factors.

To answer this general question more fully would require an exposition on the rules for the constitution and proof of the contract of lease which are dealt with in detail in Paton and Cameron, *Landlord and Tenant*, chapter 2. I do not think it is appropriate at this stage to answer this question at any greater length unless there is a specific problem on which further advice is required.

3   The same preliminary comments on the operation of *confusio* apply here as apply in answer to question 2. On that basis I answer the remaining questions in paragraph 3 as follows.

(*a*)   No.

(*b*)   The position is the same as in answer 2(*b*).

(*c*)   The same applies and the position is the same as in answer 2(*c*) but with this difference that B, the original tenant in this illustration, having acquired the property itself from A, must have been aware of the granting of the original lease since he was a party to it; and, further, B must give effect to the sub-lease which he granted to C, on the grounds of personal contract since, again, B was a party to that sub-lease. In this case, accordingly, the question of recording or registration is totally irrelevant to the question as posed on these particular facts, unless B in turn disposed of the subjects to a *bona fide* purchaser for value without notice. For the reasons referred to above, C could not maintain himself in possession in a question with such a purchaser unless he first made his own right real.

(*d*)–(*g*)   The answers to the remaining questions are the same as in answer to question 2 but again with this difference that, in my view, whatever the legal position may be in question 2, on the facts as stated in question 3, B, having granted the sub-lease in favour of C, is bound thereby on a personal contractual basis, without reference to the Leases Act 1449 or the Registration of Leases (Scotland) Act 1857 and, on that footing alone, would therefore be bound to give effect to the original sub-lease by B to C on a purely personal basis.

Further reading

Requirements of Writing (Scotland) Act 1995.

Kildrummy (Jersey) Ltd v *Inland Revenue Commissioners* 1992 SLT 787.

Manual, para 24.17.

COMMERCIAL LEASES

45   Tenant's repairing obligation

Lease – *rei interitus* – obligation on tenant

Date: October 1990

Memorial
The memorialists obtained a lease of a property. *Rei interitus* was not specifically excluded. However, one clause placed an obligation on the tenant to insure against specific risks, in particular 'in the event that any part or item of the subjects of let being destroyed or so damaged so as to render the same in whole or in part unfit for use by the tenants, the tenants shall still in so far as it is practicable to do so be liable for their whole obligations under this lease including payment of rent and other outgoings'. In addition, the tenant's repairing obligation was a full obligation extending to insured and uninsured risks.

It appeared to the memorialists that the intention was that notwithstanding damage, the lease would continue. They sought an opinion as to the construction of the lease on this point.

Opinion
The definitive decision in *Cantors Properties (Scotland) Ltd* v *Swears & Wells Ltd* 1980 SLT 165 dealt with exactly the problem involved in this lease; discussed the principles involved at some length; and concluded, in the circumstances and on the wording of that particular lease, that:

(1) it is perfectly competent for landlord and tenant expressly to contract out of the *rei interitus* rule if they so wish;

(2) if, however, the lease is *silent* on the matter, then such contracting out will not be easily inferred; and

(3) unless one or other party can point to a provision or provisions in the contract of lease which would elide the operation of this general principle, then the argument that *rei interitus* is excluded is bound to fail.

At first sight, accordingly, it would appear that the parties in this case might find it difficult to satisfy the court that, in the event of damage or destruction by fire, the lease should not be held to have come to an end under the general principle referred to above, because there is no specific provision which, in terms, excludes the rule explicitly.

In my view, however, that argument would fail in this particular case because of the distinguishing features between the lease here and the lease in *Cantors Properties (Scotland) Ltd*. Admittedly, there is no clause in the present lease or the continuation thereof which specifically excludes the operation of the *rei interitus* principle. To that extent, therefore, the parties here cannot point to a specific and express stipulation which in its terms excludes the operation of the rule. But I think it is clear from the comments of Lord Cameron in *Cantors* (at p 171, second column, second paragraph) that, although there are no *express* provisions in this lease in this case which would put the matter beyond doubt, there are undoubtedly provisions in the lease which, by necessary implication, exclude the rule.

I refer in particular to clause X of the lease in terms of which the tenants are required to insure and keep insured the buildings (which are the subject-matter of the lease) against loss or damage by a fairly exhaustive list of risks, including in particular fire. On page third, in the same clause, the lease then expressly provides that in the event of the buildings or any part thereof during the currency of the lease being destroyed or damaged, then and *as often as the same shall happen,* all monies received under the insurance policy must be applied by the tenants on rebuilding, repairing or otherwise reinstating within three years of the destruction. The provision underlined in the preceding sentence can only sensibly be read as necessarily implying continuation of the lease after each destruction and so, by implication, excluding termination *rei interitu.* Further, if the insurance monies prove insufficient for that purpose, the tenants are bound to make good any shortfall out of their own funds. That would be a remarkable obligation if the tenants were not to benefit therefrom because the lease came to an end. Finally, there is a declaration in this clause that if any part or item of the subjects of let is destroyed or so damaged as to render the same in whole or in part unfit for use the tenants still remain liable, so far as is practicable, for their whole obligations under the lease including payment of rent.

Taking these provisions as a whole, my view is that they provide clear evidence of an intention by both parties that the lease should not terminate *rei interitu,* quite sufficient to exclude by implication the operation of that rule.

There are only two points in clause X which, in my view, *might* cause problems:

(1) The tenants are taken bound to insure against a series of designated risks which seems to be fairly exhaustive; but, conceivably, the building might be destroyed by some other event. For example, it is possible to argue that the insurable risks do not in fact cover destruction of the hotel by a meteorite which is, arguably, not a thunderbolt. Subsidence, or the collapse of an adjoining building resulting in a loss of support and collapse of the hotel, would also not seem to be covered by the list of insurable risks. But that argument seems to me irrelevant in relation to *rei interitus* because the rebuilding provision is not tied to destruction or damage by any of the insurable risks but is limited in its scope, so that, even if destruction by meteorite or whatever was *not* covered under the designated risks, the tenants would still none the less be obliged to rebuild the hotel, using their own funds. Although this does not, in my view, affect the *rei interitus* exclusion, it may have adverse implications for the tenants and their funders – see below.

(2) In my view, clause X, had it stopped at that point, would have excluded the *rei interitus* rule by necessary implication. Instead, however,

the clause goes on ostensibly to exclude the rule by express provision, by way of the declaration that in the event of any part or item of the subjects of let being destroyed or so damaged as to render the same in whole or in part unfit, the tenants are still bound by the lease. It is just possible that one or other of the parties might argue that this clause applied so as to exclude the *rei interitus* rule only where part but not the whole of the subjects was destroyed. But I think that argument must fail.

There is a positive obligation on the tenants to keep the subjects in repair throughout the period of the lease and, where necessary, to replace or rebuild, the landlords being expressly excluded from any liability for maintenance and repair.

In contrast, in the lease in *Cantors Properties (Scotland) Ltd*, the tenants were admittedly under a positive obligation in clause three to repair and where necessary renew and replace the premises, damage by fire excepted, but there was no obligation 'to rebuild'. Lord Cameron (p 171, col 2) does not consider 'renew and replace' to be synonymous with 'rebuild'. The subjects in that case were in fact damaged by fire and so were not within the repairing obligations. In clause fourteen, the tenants were under obligation to insure against loss or damage by fire (which presumably explains the wording in clause three of the lease). The insurance policy was to be taken out in name of the landlords; and the tenants were bound to pay the premiums. But nothing more was said in the *Cantors* lease as to what was to happen in the event of damage or destruction.

Lord Cameron examines these clauses in some detail at p 171 of the report. In his view, looking to the wording of clause three of the *Cantors* lease, there was no positive obligation placed on the tenants to rebuild the subjects if destroyed by any cause other than fire. That is in direct contrast to the provisions of this lease quoted above which, in my view, undoubtedly impose a positive obligation on the tenants to rebuild the subjects, however destroyed or damaged, using the insurance monies or, if insufficient, their own monies for that purpose.

In the *Cantors* lease, the obligation on the tenants to replace was imposed in the case of damage or destruction other than damage by fire. But the insurance clause, although requiring insurance against damage by fire, did not then impose on either party an obligation to rebuild, so that, since the policy was taken out in the name of the landlords alone, if the subjects were destroyed by fire, the landlords were free either to take the insurance monies and, in their sole option, use them to rebuild or not as they thought fit. Lord Cameron states at p 172: 'I do not think that in this case the obligation in clause fourteen of the lease which requires the tenant to insure the premises let to the full insured value in the name of the landlord ... by itself ... implies an obligation on the landlord to rebuild...'.

This is in direct contrast to the lease in this case where there is a positive obligation imposed on the tenant to rebuild linked to the insurance provisions.

Accordingly, my view is that, by necessary implication from the clauses above quoted, the *rei interitus* rule has effectively been excluded from this lease. In the result, if the building is destroyed, whether by one of the insured risks or in any other manner, the tenants are bound to rebuild it and both parties continue bound in terms of the lease for the remainder of the term. It follows that additional insurance on the part of the tenants against the risk of termination of the lease *rei interitu* is not required.

I would, however, add one qualification. The obligation on the tenants obliges them to rebuild the premises however destroyed and whether *or not* that destruction comes within the insured risks in the existing insurance policy. This is a point on which I think the funding institution in this case are entitled to be satisfied, but no doubt this can easily be achieved within the terms of the existing policy modified as may be necessary to cover all conceivable risks.

Manual, para 25.49.

46   Alienation

Franchise – interaction between sub-lease and franchise agreement – Law Reform (Miscellaneous Provisions) (Scotland) Act 1985, s 5 – licence – whether consent of landlord required

Date: May 1990

Memorial
A Ltd were tenants of several retail shop units. They operated a franchise and wanted proposed franchisees to enter into a franchise agreement and a sub-lease of their shop units.

Opinion was requested on the following points:

1   It was of primary importance to A Ltd that if a franchisee was in breach of the terms of the franchise agreement, A Ltd could terminate the sub-lease. Were the clauses in the draft agreements (repeated briefly below) sufficient to ensure this and in particular that the situation would not arise where the franchise agreement had been terminated but the sub-lease continues?

2   Would the provisions of the Law Reform (Miscellaneous Provisions) (Scotland) Act 1985 protect a franchisee in the event of the franchise agreement being breached?

3   If there was a danger of the sub-lease not being terminated, were there any other provisions which Professor McDonald could suggest could be incorporated to help secure A Ltd's position?

4   Where a lease provided that landlord's consent to an assignation or sub-lease was required but no specific reference was made to sharing possession or granting an assignation or sub-lease of part only of the subjects, would A Ltd be in breach of its head lease if it were to grant, without the landlord's consent, a concession or a licence of an unspecified part of a shop premises or a sub-lease to a franchisee of part only of the shop premises?

5   Did Professor McDonald have any further comments to add?

Opinion

1, 2 & 3   These three questions are so closely interlinked that it would be easier to deal with them together in one answer.

The draft documents take the form of a franchise agreement which is the principal agreement between the parties and, in association therewith but in my view ancillary thereto, a document termed a sub-lease. The sub-lease creates the relationship of landlord and tenant independently of the franchise agreement although, admittedly, it is in its terms closely linked to the franchise agreement by various provisions. In particular, there is a provision in clause 4(1) to the effect that, if the franchisee contravenes the terms of that agreement (as to which the franchisor is to be sole judge) the sub-lease will terminate. Further, there is a restriction on user which prohibits the tenant from using the premises for any purpose other than to implement the obligation in the franchise agreement.

I think there is no doubt whatever that the relationship created between franchisor and franchisee under the sub-lease is that of landlord and tenant to which, in my view, the provisions of the Law Reform (Miscellaneous Provisions) Scotland Act 1985, ss 4–7 will necessarily apply. The consequence is that, with particular reference to the comment in question 1 in my memorial, I can envisage two situations, and there may be others, where the lease might well continue beyond the date of termination of the franchise agreement, namely:

(*a*) Where the franchise agreement is validly brought to an end because of some breach of its provisions but where, notwithstanding the provisions of clause 4(1) of the sub-lease, the tenant seeks to maintain himself in possession founding on the protective provisions in the 1985 Act, s 5. The term 'lease' is not positively defined in the 1985 Act although it is defined negatively by the exclusion of certain agreements from the operation of these sections. The definition is, I think, sufficiently wide to include the present sub-lease. It follows that the terms of s 5, in particular, would apply. Clause 4(1) of the sub-lease contains a provision purporting to terminate, or enabling the landlord to terminate, the sub-lease within the terms of, and struck at by, s 5(1)(a) of the 1985 Act. Accordingly, if the tenant founds on that section with a view to remaining in possession, then the franchisors would have to satisfy the court that it was fair and reasonable for the lease to be terminated. In practice, I do not envisage any particular difficulty in satisfying the court on this point but inevitably there may be a delay, possibly a substantial delay, between the termination of the franchise and the recovery of possession from the tenant if he resists giving up possession on the basis of this statutory provision. In the circumstances, there may well be no solution to this problem but I make certain suggestions below which might improve the position of the franchisors.

(*b*) Secondly, tacit relocation would not apply to the franchise agreement, but it will undoubtedly apply to the lease, as drafted, as a matter of general principle. But tacit relocation applies only by implication and can be expressly excluded. I would so recommend in this case. Otherwise, there is a risk that the franchise agreement might be brought to an end but that, because of want of the appropriate notice, the lease might continue for at least another year. Looking to the user clause in the lease, there would seem to be little point in the tenant seeking to maintain this but, given an awkward tenant or, possibly, insolvency or some other supervening event, the tacit relocation rule might create problems.

The principal arrangement between the parties is the granting of the franchise. The lease is a necessary, but subordinate, element in the agreement. A lease, by itself, is merely a contract between landlord and tenant in a conventional form but is, none the less, merely a contract. There is, therefore, no reason whatever why a lease should be framed as a separate document standing on its own with the usual conventional clauses. It would be equally competent to incorporate the agreement to sub-lease as an integral part of the franchise agreement. In this case, looking to the close relationship between the franchise and the occupancy of the premises, I would have thought it quite appropriate to combine the two documents rather than having two separate contracts. This has the advantage that it underlines the close connection between the franchise and the occupancy of the premises and would make it easier for the landlord to show that a provision in the composite agreement which terminates both the franchise and the lease in certain events (eg under an amended clause 8 in the franchise agreement taking account not only of failure by the franchisee to observe the terms of the franchise but also to observe the terms appropriate to the lease) was a provision which was fair and reasonable and on which the franchisor could therefore properly rely in seeking to bring the franchisee's right of occupation to an end.

At the same time, I would suggest some modification of language so as to make it right of the tenant in relation to the subjects a mere licence or right of occupancy rather than a formal lease or sub-lease, the occupation being purely for the purpose of implementing the terms of the franchise agreement. This, again, strengthens the position of the landlord *vis-à-vis* the terms of s 5 of the 1985 Act.

This composite agreement would be particularly suitable in cases where, as seems to be envisaged, the franchisee is sharing the premises with another trader, whether the franchisor itself or some other franchisee. There is a further point here. The provisions of ss 4–7 of the 1985 Act are directed at what are termed in the head notes 'irritancy clauses'. These are described, in each of the two sections, as provisions in the lease which purport to terminate it or to enable the landlord to terminate it in the event of some act or omission on the part of the tenant, whether by way of non-payment or non-observance of the terms of lease. These provisions are, of course, consistent with the conventional view that an irritancy clause in a lease is inserted purely in the interest of the landlord and gives him the option to bring the lease to an end prematurely in the event of certain acts or omissions by the tenant. If the licence to occupy is clearly subordinate to the franchise, and if its sole express purpose is to facilitate the operation thereof then arguably (*a*) there is no lease, as such; or (*b*) the right to occupy depends on continuation of the franchise. If the franchise itself is terminated or forfeit because of breach of the franchise provisions, the right to occupy is automatically forfeit; but the lease (if there is one) would not terminate by breach of the lease.

Further, a provision in a lease to the effect that it will endure until the ish and will then terminate, without tacit relocation, is not, in my view, in the nature of an irritancy clause because every lease must have a term; and, when the term arrives, barring tacit relocation, the lease is automatically terminated, whether at the instance of the landlord or the tenant; and in some cases is so terminated without notice. The point of this observation is that, in the draft sub-lease, there is a definite term which, I presume, coincides with the term of the franchise. It occurred to me that the memorialists might, with advantage, adapt the provision as to the ish so that the lease would endure (or rather the licence or right of occupancy would subsist) until (*a*) the stipulated date for termination; or (*b*) until the date on which the franchise was terminated by whatever means but in particular in terms of clause 8 of the present draft franchise agreement; whichever date first occurred.

In addition, the composite agreement would include an express provision excluding tacit relocation in any circumstances so that, whenever such termination date arrived, all the rights of the parties, both as to franchise and as to occupancy, would automatically cease and determine without any possibility of continuation by tacit relocation or otherwise.

Possibly the courts would not accept this arrangement as excluding the provisions of ss 4 and 5 of the 1985 Act, but at least it does give the memorialists an additional argument to exclude the effect of those provisions which otherwise will apply to the occupancy by the franchisee under the proposed sub-lease.

I appreciate that there may be reasons why these suggestions should not be adopted; but these are the only useful suggestions which I can make to improve the framework of the franchise agreement and sub-lease, with a view to protecting the memorialists against the risks envisaged in questions 1 to 3. I have not otherwise sought to revise the drafts.

4   The answer to this question must, I think, depend to some extent on the wording of the clause in the principal lease. If, however, the clause in the principal lease simply prohibits assignation or sub-letting without any further amplification, and in particular without any reference to parting with possession of part or the whole of the subjects, I think the courts would take the view that a formal assignation of an identifiable part, or a formal sub-let of an identifiable part, of the leasehold clearly infringed against a general prohibition in these terms.

So, where the provision takes the standard and conventional form of a let to the memorialists as tenants but excluding assignees and sub-tenants in general terms, that must, I think, prohibit an assignation both of whole or of part, and a sub-let both of whole or of part. On the other hand, if that provision is omitted and if, instead, there is a provision in the lease which prohibits the tenants from assigning this lease or sub-letting the subjects there is a stronger argument for the view that what is struck at here is assignation of the whole or sub-letting of the whole.

Whatever form the prohibition takes, I would have thought that, if the franchise agreement were drafted in such a form that the franchisee was entitled to trade along with the memorialists or some other occupant from an unspecified part of the subjects, it would be difficult if not impossible, on the ordinary clause, for the landlords to maintain that there had been any assignation or sub-lease because no specific premises are defined in the franchise agreement. In contrast, a sub-lease to a franchisee of a defined part of shop premises would certainly be struck at by certain sub-letting prohibitions, although not necessarily by all, as in the illustration given above. I think the distinction lies in relation to the identification of the subjects of let and the exclusive right of possession which a sub-lease of a defined part of the subjects would imply. Any such agreement relating to an identified part of the subjects and giving exclusive rights therein would, in my view, necessarily be a sub-lease and would therefore certainly be struck at, if the prohibition was wide enough to exclude sub-leasing of part.

Against that, if there were an agreement with a franchisee for a shop-within-a-shop, in some unidentified part of the subjects, the location of which was left entirely at the discretion of the landlord to determine, and where the location of that part of the subjects could be altered from time to time in the sole discretion of the landlord, I do not think that such arrangement would qualify as a lease in the technical sense nor would it create enforceable rights as against an overlandlord or a purchaser from him; and in these circumstances I would not have thought that such an arrangement would be excluded, at least on the ordinary exclusion of assignees and sub-tenants in conventional form.

5 I have answered the questions in general terms but, particularly in relation to question 4, each case would have to be treated on its merits and the language of the head lease carefully examined in the context of what was proposed before any firm conclusion could be reached.

Likewise, in the answer to questions 1 to 3, something may turn on the proposed relationship between the memorialists and the franchisee, and in particular, as to whether exclusive possession of the whole or of a defined part of the subjects is on offer to the franchisee or whether it is more in the nature of a shop-within-a-shop arrangement. Again, each particular case would have to be considered strictly on its merits in the context of the terms of the head lease, and with particular reference to the rights of the tenant in the context of the 1985 Act. Since the matter is said to be relatively urgent, however, I thought it best to deal with it on this general basis. If the memorialists wish to submit individual cases, I shall be happy to deal with these on an individual basis.

Manual, para 25.67.

AGRICULTURAL LEASES

47 Irritancy

Irritation of sub-lease – formal renunciation - warrandice

Date: November 1989

Memorial
A golf course was leased under a sub-lease to the memorialists. The memorialists agreed to purchase the course. The head lease contained a prohibition on granting of sub-leases without the prior written consent of the landlord. The landlord's agents claimed to have irritated the head lease. This was disputed by the tenants. The memorialists were concerned that, if the purchase proceeded, and the head lease had not been effectively irritated, they would remain liable to pay rent to the tenants even after purchase of the course.

The following questions were asked:

1   Could the memorialists rely on the grant of absolute warrandice from the seller, and would they have any further obligation to the tenants after purchase?

2   How could the memorialists obtain an unchallengeable title to the course with no possible claim by the tenants?

Opinion
1   As I understand it, a formal offer has been made on terms verbally agreed at least as to price but the offer has not yet been accepted. Accordingly, there is no binding contract of sale and purchase between the parties.

In that situation, I think it might be prudent to re-examine the terms of the offer in the light of the information now available, and possibly to amend the offer to make it perfectly clear that the memorialists, on purchasing the subjects, would be entitled to entry and actual occupation of the subjects as heritable proprietors, not merely as sub-tenants under the sub-lease. That point may have already been made plain in the missives in which case no amendment would be required; otherwise, I think amendment on that point would be prudent.

Provided the missives do so provide, I do not see any further difficulties so far as the memorialists are concerned in relation to title. If the missives stipulate for vacant possession as heritable proprietors, then the existence of a lease of the subjects would inevitably, in my opinion, render the title unmarketable on the terms of this particular contract. I accept that in general the existence of a lease may or may not constitute a breach of

213

warrandice and may or may not entitle a purchaser to resile, in the absence of any special provision in the title or in the contract. But, given a provision in the contract which stipulates for vacant possession as proprietors, that point is put beyond argument.

The point of this comment is that, if a contract is then concluded on this basis, vacant possession as proprietors is an essential condition of the contract; and the purchasers would then be entitled to conclusive evidence that the head lease had been terminated, whether by irritancy or by renunciation. This point appears to be in doubt at the moment, judging from the copy correspondence provided with the memorial and, that being so, there certainly is no reason at all why a purchaser should take the risk that the head lease has not been effectively brought to an end. In other words, the seller is obliged to provide adequate evidence that there is no adverse interest still subsisting in the tenants under the head lease.

All that the seller's agents have so far produced would seem to be a purely *ex parte* statement on their part that the lease has been terminated; but, against that, there is a letter from the principal tenants' agents maintaining that the lease is still in force. In these circumstances, if a contract for sale and purchase is concluded between the proprietor and the memorialists, then, at the examination of title stage, the point would be raised by the agents for the memorialists and evidence of due termination of the lease would be called for.

One acceptable form of such evidence would be a formal renunciation by the tenants under the head lease in favour of the present proprietor. Strictly speaking, for that renunciation to be valid, the consent of the sub-tenants should be taken; but of course the sub-tenants would have no reason for refusing their consent, once missives had been concluded for the purchase of the subjects.

If the matter is still disputed when the contract for sale and purchase is concluded and if the principal tenants still maintain that the lease is in force, then the memorialists' agents should require the seller to produce a decree of declarator of irritancy as evidence that the principal lease has been duly terminated.

In the circumstances, I would not accept any lesser evidence than either the renunciation or the decree of declarator.

I think this answers the question though not directly. If the matter proceeds without formal evidence of termination of the lease, there is a risk that the lease has not been duly irritated and that the principal tenants are still entitled to enforce their rights thereunder. In that event, if the purchasers proceed, complete the contract for sale and purchase, take a disposition from the seller containing absolute warrandice which they record, and are then asked to pay rent to the tenants, they would undoubtedly have a claim for damages against the selling proprietor but possibly only if the missives contain a nonsupersession clause which is carried forward and kept alive by an appropriate clause in the disposition in their favour. This would allow the memorialists then to refer back to the provisions in the missives dealing with entry and possession and on that footing damages could be claimed. Clearly, however, this is an unsatisfactory position and my advice would be not to agree to settlement of the transaction until acceptable evidence has been produced that the head lease was indeed duly terminated.

2   Provided that the contract is framed in the terms suggested above, and that the agents then insist on appropriate evidence of termination of the lease at the examination-of-title stage, there is no risk of the memorialists as purchaser, subject, of course, to the usual rules for examination of the seller's title.

If, on the other hand, the memorialists proceed to take a disposition and if it then transpires that the head lease has not been duly terminated, the resulting situation would be as follows.

(*a*) The memorialists would have a valid and unchallengeable title as proprietors of the golf course.

(*b*) Their title to the golf course would be subject to the rights of the tenants under the head lease, which would undoubtedly transmit against and be binding on the memorialists as singular successors of the seller under the Leases Act 1449.

(*c*) The memorialists could maintain themselves in possession by virtue of their own sub-lease from the principal tenants, which would not be affected by the transfer of ownership of the golf course to the memorialists. This would, of course, involve payment of rent by the memorialists to the principal tenants. Those payments of rent would be recoverable from the seller and his universal successors under the warrandice obligation in the disposition in favour of the memorialists in the manner described above. However, claims under warrandice are in their nature personal claims only and are unsecured. Accordingly, if the seller went bankrupt, or sold the remainder of the estate and went abroad, or died intestate without known heirs (to give some typical illustrations of the risks), then for practical purposes the entitlement to damages under warrandice would be valueless.

Manual, para 26.25.

(NB: There are no opinions relating to Chapter 27 of the Manual.)

CONTRACTS OF SALE AND PURCHASE

48   *Consensus in idem*

Missives – effect of withdrawal of qualification – action of implement –
action of reduction

Date: August 1990

Memorial
A development company sold one refurbished flat in a block to the memorialist. The developers intended to restore and sell the remaining flats in the block. However, they failed to do so and the flats deteriorated. The developers then approached the memorialist and offered to sell the two remaining flats. Missives were drawn up for vacant possession. However, the top-floor flat had a tenant. The agreement was amended to sell the second-floor flat only.

A formal offer was submitted by the memorialist, which in turn was qualified by the developers. The memorialist sent a further qualifying letter with a minor adjustment. This was withdrawn by formal letter holding the bargain to be concluded. The developers refused to implement the missives arguing that the contract had fallen as a result of the memorialist's qualification. It was then discovered that the flat had subsequently been disponed to a director of the development company.

The following questions were asked:

1   Whether the decision in *Rutterford Ltd* v *Allied Breweries Ltd* 1990 SLT 249 correctly applied the *ratio decidendi* of *Wolf and Wolf* v *Forfar Potato Co* 1984 SLT 100.

2   What is the legal significance, if any, of the fact that the developers originally approached the memorialist with a view to selling the property?

3   What is the current practice with regard to the withdrawal of qualifications and the acceptance of prior missives?

4   What is the legal meaning of the phrase 'for immediate acceptance only' in missives?

5   What is the likely success of the action for reduction and specific implement of the missives?

Opinion
1   In my opinion, the decision in *Rutterford Ltd* v *Allied Breweries Ltd* does correctly apply the *ratio decidendi* in *Wolf and Wolf* v *Forfar Potato Co*.

Further, in the Inner House decision in *Findlater* v *Maan* 1990 SLT 465, the decision in *Wolf and Wolf* was distinguished on special grounds; and I think it is quite clear from the opinion of the Lord Justice-Clerk that the *ratio* in *Wolf and Wolf*, as applied by Lord Caplan in *Rutterford*, was approved. Lord Murray and Lord Morton both agreed with the Lord Justice-Clerk, without comment. In the result, it seems to me fairly clear that the *ratio* of the decision in *Wolf and Wolf*, and the general principles on which that decision was based, must now be taken as applying generally to contracts of sale and purchase of heritage although, of course, *Wolf and Wolf* was concerned with the sale of corporeal movables.

2   I would attach no significance whatever to the fact that the sellers in this case originally approached the purchaser with a view to the sale of the property, if indeed that is the case. We are here dealing with sale and purchase of heritage. It follows that, once the formal offer to purchase had been made, that formal offer superseded and excluded all prior communings which cannot have any bearing on the resulting position as between the parties.

3   The custom and practice in the profession [at the time] in relation to the withdrawal of qualifications and the acceptance *de plano* of prior missives was as expressed by the sheriff principal whose opinion was referred to in the rubric in *Findlater* v *Maan* at p 465L. I think, therefore, that the profession generally would have regarded the withdrawal of a qualification made by one or other of the parties and the substitution in lieu thereof of an unqualified acceptance as validly completing a binding contract. Certainly, in my experience, this practice has been regularly adopted at least in this area for several years past without challenge. The decision of the sheriff in *Findlater* v *Maan*, reported in 1988 GWD 31–1328, seemed to me at the time to run counter to the view generally held within the profession.

Significantly, Professor Halliday in his *Conveyancing Law and Practice* does not refer to *Wolf and Wolf*, which is not cited at all; nor does he refer to the rule as expressed in Gloag on *Contract* on which that decision proceeded.

It may be that the reason for the divergence between professional practice and the views expressed by Gloag arises out of the statement in Gloag that an offer falls; if it is refused, or, if the refusal is not peremptory but is combined with a request for better terms, then the original offer is gone and the parties seeking better terms cannot fall back on an acceptance of the original offer. At least to some extent, that view still persists in the three decisions referred to above. So, in *Wolf and Wolf*, the rubric refers to 'the making of a qualified acceptance and counter offer'. The Lord Justice-Clerk, at p 103, refers to 'the counter offer', not merely 'the qualified acceptance'. Lord Robertson, at p 105, refers, somewhat ambiguously, to the rejection of the original offer and the making of a new offer and, a little further down, he refers to material conditions in the qualified acceptance which rendered it a new offer rather than an acceptance (presumably subject to qualifications) of the original offer. Likewise, and again ambiguously, he refers, at p 106, to the qualified acceptance as a refusal of the offer and as a new offer. This leaves open the question whether every qualified acceptance is automatically and of necessity the refusal or rejection of the original offer and constitutes in every case a new offer; or whether there may be certain qualified acceptances which do not amount to a new offer and are not refusals or rejections of the original. This is particularly relevant in the context of Lord Robertson's comments on the introduction of material conditions into the qualified acceptance.

In the sequence of negotiations which regularly occurs in concluding a bargain for the sale and purchase of heritage, there is normally an initial offer of some complexity met not by a rejection or refusal but by an acceptance subject to certain qualifications which may be on very minor matters. Is such an acceptance now deemed to be a refusal or rejection of the original offer and a seeking of better terms? Clearly, in some cases, it may be; but is this so in every case?

In *Rutterford Ltd* the sequence of formal letters followed that pattern, with an initial offer, an acceptance subject to qualifications, and further acceptances with further qualifications. Lord Caplan seemed disposed to hold each of these qualified acceptances as constituting a fresh offer. His comments at p 252G and H seem to indicate that this result follows in every case where there is a qualified acceptance and so the question whether the qualified acceptance contains material conditions or not, is irrelevant. At p 252L he states: 'A party who receives an offer knows that he must accept it, refuse it outright, or replace it with a counter proposal.' There is no room here for the intermediate case of a qualified acceptance with a request for modified terms, as opposed to a rejection or refusal. Instead, apparently, the two amount to one and the same thing; and, in every case, necessarily involve replacing the original offer with a new or counter offer.

In *Findlater v Maan*, in the rubric at p 466C, ambiguity is again introduced by reference to a party making a statement that 'a qualified acceptance and counter offer' and a statement that 'the letter of 28th March 1988, as a qualified acceptance, fell to be regarded as a counter offer'. It is not clear from the report whether the court took the view that this was the inevitable result of every qualified acceptance or whether it only applied to those qualified acceptances which could be classified as counter offers; but I think probably the former is the better view. That certainly seems to be implied in the comments of the Lord Justice-Clerk at p 468 A and B; but he introduces some doubt, again, on the same page at I and J by referring to a qualified acceptance 'as constituting a counter offer'.

4   There is no authoritative definition of the phrase 'for immediate acceptance only'. The standard rule is that an offer for sale and purchase of heritage, unless it contains a specific time limit, falls if not accepted within a reasonable period – see Halliday, *Conveyancing Law and Practice*, para 15–05. Exactly the same rule would apply to a qualified acceptance which, on the basis of the above decisions, now falls to be treated as a new offer in every case.

Presumably, since we are dealing here with a formal offer document, the introduction of a specific clause into the contract that the acceptance (or, better, the fresh offer) is open for 'immediate acceptance only' is intended to modify that rule; although not necessarily so, because contracts of sale and purchase of heritage frequently include, by express provision, conditions which are implied, eg as to marketable title. In the present case, however, taking clause 2 in isolation and standing by itself, it seems to me that the intention was to modify the common law rule by requiring an acceptance within a shorter period than the law would normally allow by implication.

Such a clause serves very little real purpose but none the less is not uncommon in practice. The nearest analogy would seem to be a provision in missives, also not uncommon, for 'immediate entry' which was the subject of judicial comment in *Heys* v *Kimball & Morton* (1890) 17 R 381: 'The term "immediate entry" is not a term, as to the meaning of which it is possible to lay down any general or hard and fast rule. It perhaps means something more than entry within a reasonable time but it does not necessarily mean instantaneous entry or entry within an hour or a day of the conclusion of the contract...' and 'The phrase "immediate entry" is not a phrase that admits of construction.'

5   In my view, the action of implement will almost certainly fail on two grounds.

First, if I read the decision in *Findlater* v *Maan* correctly, although the opinions in that case are strictly *obiter* to the question at issue here, the views there expressed clearly seem to be that every qualified acceptance, no matter how trivial the qualification, represents the refusal or rejection of the offer which it qualifies and the substitution of a fresh offer in lieu thereof. It was therefore not open to the purchaser unilaterally to withdraw the qualifications in his qualified acceptance and to conclude a bargain on the basis of the original offer and the qualified acceptance as he purported to do. On that view of the matter, there is no concluded bargain and therefore no contract to implement.

Secondly, there is a further point here which has not been developed in the answers by the defender in the copy closed record produced with the papers. Their Answer 2 simply narrates the qualified acceptance and the subsequent purported withdrawal, but does not mention that the seller apparently telephoned the memorialist before the purported withdrawal, disclosing the position as to the planning and 'indicating that, in the circumstances, he no longer wished to proceed at present with the sale'. It was in response to that indication of a change of intention that the memorialist then decided to withdraw the qualifications and to accept *de plano*.

In *Thomson* v *James* (1855) 18 D 1 which is the standard authority on offer and acceptance, the parties were contracting for the sale and purchase of land, and so formal contractual documents were required to complete the contract. The actual sequence of events in that case is not relevant here in that, in *Thomson*, a *de plano* acceptance of an offer was posted, and, simultaneously, a letter was posted recalling the offer. The question was whether the acceptance concluded the contract or not. In the course of his judgment, Lord President McNeill states, at p 10, that recall or withdrawal of an offer has no effect until the recall or withdrawal has been communicated or may be assumed to have been communicated, to the other party. In other words, the other party may accept the offer until the offerer 'gives notice – that is, makes known that he withdraws it'. The critical question is, of course, whether withdrawal of the offer in this context requires formal documentation, as does the offer and acceptance; or whether intimation of withdrawal can be communicated by less formal means. Taking Lord President McNeill's judgment as a whole, I read it as implying that withdrawal of an offer if communicated by whatever means, formal or informal, is sufficient to exclude consensus and, as a result, that any subsequent acceptance comes too late. So, again, the Lord President says at the foot of p 10: 'Revocation or recall is an act of the offerer by which he communicates his change of purpose, and withdraws from the offeree the right he had given him to complete the contract. Having communicated his purpose to purchase, the offeree is entitled to regard that purpose as unchanged until a change is communicated.' And on p 11 he says 'if an offerer changes his mind, but does not take the proper steps to have his change of mind conveyed to the offeree ... he may find himself unwillingly bound. ... Mere change of mind on the part of the offerer will not prevent an effectual acceptance – not even although that change of mind should be communicated to a third party or recorded in a formal writing. ... In all these cases, a binding contract may be made between the parties without ... consensus.'

Likewise, Lord Ivory says at p 15 'the inner act of one mind is nothing in its relations and bearing upon another mind; and that, in law, an act of the mind uncommunicated is no act at all'.

I appreciate that none of these *dicta* gives any indication as to the degree of formality required (if any) for the communicating of a change of mind; and, arguably, since we are dealing here with an *obligatio literis*, a change of mind on the part of the offerer should be incorporated in a formal document such as a holograph missive. But the indications in *Thomson* seem to me clearly to envisage communication of a change of mind by any means. That view is in part borne out by an analogous position in relation to mistaken offers couched in suitable form where the mistake may be corrected by a subsequent informal communication to the other side. Once so communicated, it is incompetent for the other side to accept the original formal offer, even although the mode of communicating the error was itself informal. See Halliday, *Conveyancing Law and Practice*, para 15–06 and the references there referred to and, in particular, Gloag on *Contract*. Again, however, there is a lack of direct authority but, in my view, taking these situations together, it seems to me that the courts would be inclined to hold that the deal was effectively off meantime, the acceptance coming too late because it was known to the acceptor by that time that there no longer was consensus.

Even if I am wrong in my view on the action of implement, however, I suspect that the action of reduction may fail. The basis of that action is that the pursuer has a personal right as against the development company and the disponee from them, based on concluded missives, but has no title to the subjects. If, as is alleged, the disponee from the development company was a party to a collusive arrangement with the company whereby he acquired the subjects in the knowledge of the antecedent contract between the development company and the memorialist, then no doubt the conveyance in his favour would be reducible on the general principle as reaffirmed in *Rodger (Builders) Ltd* v *Fawdry* 1950 SC 483. In order to come within the rule established in that case, it is essential that the pursuer can establish knowledge on the part of the disponee from the development company, which may be difficult, although the absence of missives is certainly significant.

Further, even if the pursuer can succeed in demonstrating knowledge, it may well be that, by the time the notice of litigiosity has been registered in the Personal Register, the subjects have been sold and disponed to a *bona fide* purchaser for value who has registered his title without notice of the memorialist's personal claim under the alleged contract. In that event, I do not think that the action of reduction can succeed, since the effect of it would be to dispossess the *bona fide* purchaser for value without notice who has proceeded on the faith of the records to acquire a title to the subjects in which, on the face of it, the disponer was validly infeft. That possibility can, of course, easily be established by updating the office copy Land Certificate, which will disclose whether or not any such third-party rights have been created. It would certainly be prudent to do so before any further avoidable expense is incurred because it seems to me not unlikely that the property may now have been genuinely so disposed of.

Manual, para 28.7.

49   *The need for consensus*

Error in missives – purchaser seeking to withdraw – *consensus in idem* – Law Reform (Miscellaneous Provisions) (Scotland) Act 1985, s 8 – error

Date: November 1990

Memorial
The memorialists, a firm of developers, entered into missives with purchasers for the sale of a newly constructed dwellinghouse 'with a double garage'. The missives were duly executed by both parties. It was then noticed by the developers that reference should be made to a single and not a double garage, as that was what had been erected on the site. The memorialists brought the error to the attention of the purchasers, and sent a letter to the effect that the amendment should be interlineated and signed by both parties. In response the purchasers sought to amend the date of entry as they had been experiencing difficulty in selling their house. The developers offered to meet the bridging payments of the purchasers for one month. The purchasers then sent a formal letter withdrawing from the missives.

The memorialists maintained that there was a legally binding contract. They formally resiled, resold the property and claimed damages. The purchasers maintained that the contract was not legally binding because a copy of it had not been delivered to them and that there was no *consensus in idem*. The memorialists sought an opinion as to whether there was a legally binding bargain.

Opinion

It is undoubtedly the case that, had it not been for the misprint in the narrative to the formal contract, which incorporated a reference to a double garage instead of the single garage erected on the site, there would certainly have been a binding contract between the parties in that:

(i) The contract contains all the necessary elements for a contract for the sale and purchase of heritage.

(ii) It was executed by both parties and the execution in each case was probative, the signatures of all parties being duly attested.

Although the contract was executed in duplicate, a copy does not seem to have been delivered to the purchasers or their agents but, in my opinion, that is quite irrelevant for two reasons:

(1) Delivery is not essential to complete a contract although it is a necessary element in completing unilateral titles in order to bring such unilateral deeds into operation. But the rules of delivery suffer an exception in the case of bilateral contracts where delivery is unnecessary.

I am not impressed by the purchasers' letter in which they seek a more up-to-date opinion on delivery and on the law of contract than a 1970 reference. If they want a more up-to-date reference, I would refer them to McBryde *Contract*, chapter 7 which deals with the principle of delivery, and in particular paragraphs 7-54 and 7-56 which deal with the exception from the general rule in the case of mutual contracts. See also Halliday, *Conveyancing Law and Practice*, para 9-01. There is no suggestion in either of these authors, or in the authorities which they cite, that the rule is limited to contracts relating to moveables only. The exception applies generally to all *mutual* contracts, whether relating to heritage or moveables. See *Robertson's Trs* v *Lindsay* (1873) 1 R 323.

(2) Further, although not actually delivered, the letter from the memorialists to the purchasers' agents intimated that the contract had been executed by the sellers; and subsequent letters from the sellers' solicitors refer to the document as constituting the completed contract.

It is undoubtedly the case, however, that the contract, although otherwise valid in content and form, contains a material error by referring to a double garage when a single garage was already erected on the site and it seems reasonably safe to assume that, if cross-examined on the point, the purchasers would have to concede that what they were expecting to purchase when they signed the contract was the dwellinghouse with the single garage already erected on the site. I assume that they must have inspected the dwellinghouse prior to purchase. If so, they must have seen that a single garage had been erected; and it really is stretching credibility beyond reasonable limits to suggest that they expected the builders to substitute a double garage for the existing single garage without some specific reference to that fact in the contract or in correspondence passing between the parties, of which there seems to be no evidence whatsoever.

In the result, my view is that there was a concluded contract between the parties, and there was *consensus in idem* on one of two alternative bases, namely:

(1) There is a valid and binding contract of sale and purchase between the parties for the site in question, with the dwellinghouse thereon and a double garage erected on the site in lieu of the existing *single* garage, at the price and on the terms and conditions set out in the contract document. This would be the position if the purchasers could satisfy the court in a litigation that they genuinely believed, when signing the contract document, that the builder had agreed to substitute a double garage for the single garage on the site at the same price as offered for in the contract document.

(2) Alternatively, if the purchasers fail to satisfy the court that they genuinely thought a double garage was to be provided, and instead if they admit or if, on a proof, the court is satisfied that they were contracting to purchase the site, with a house and a single garage as erected at the date of the contract document, then there is a valid and binding contract for the purchase of these subjects. However, to complete the formalities, rectification of the contract document in terms of the Law Reform (Miscellaneous Provisions) (Scotland) Act 1985, s 8, would be required, to substitute 'single' for 'double' in the reference to the garage. Such rectification is retrospective, unless the court otherwise directs under s 9(4). I cannot see any grounds on which the court could apply s 9(4) in this case.

In July 1990, the memorialists wrote to the purchasers' solicitors pointing out what they considered to be an error in the description of the garage. On the facts as presented to me, this must already have been obvious to the purchasers, if indeed they noticed the error in the purchase document at all. The sellers' agents suggested that the error be corrected in both documents, and initialled to complete the formalities. I would emphasise that, in July when this letter was written, there already was a concluded and binding contract for the purchase of the site and dwellinghouse with either a single, or a double, garage depending on alternatives (1) or (2) above. The letter cannot possibly be construed as a formal letter unilaterally amending the terms of that bilateral contractual document, which would have been quite incompetent. At best, whether or not the letter was adopted as holograph (and I suspect it was not), it was merely a suggestion for amending a patent error in the documentation. At least, I think it is fairly safe to assume it was a patent error, for the reasons touched on above.

None the less, the purchasers' agents apparently took the view that there was still no concluded bargain and purported to amend the contract by postponing the date of entry. Their letter to the sellers' solicitors to that effect is formal and adopted as holograph and is clearly intended as an amendment to the contract. As such, in my view, it was incompetent since the contract was already concluded, and was not susceptible of unilateral amendment thereafter. I therefore agree with the terms of the letter from the memorialists' solicitors to the purchasers' solicitors pointing out that the amended date of entry was not acceptable, and making what would seem to be generous alternative proposals to meet the difficulties confronting the purchasers. Again, however, these overtures were rejected and instead, in August 1990, there is a purported unilateral withdrawal of the acceptance. On the assumption that there was a binding contract that had no effect.

In the result, notwithstanding the subsequent correspondence between the two firms of solicitors, the bilateral contractual document remains the contractual document either: for the plot, house and double garage; or subject to rectification, for the plot, house and single garage.

It is, in my opinion, a binding contract for one or other of these alternatives; but the fact that there are two possible alternative variants on the contract does not, in my view, exclude consensus. The reason is simply stated. The formal contract document refers to the plot, with house and double garage. The sellers are committed to provide a property which exactly matches that description and includes, in particular, a double garage *unless* they can succeed in establishing common error on the part of both parties on the grounds that both parties thought that the subjects of sale comprised the plot, a dwellinghouse and a single garage, in which event the word double does not reflect the common intention of both parties. On that basis, my view is that a binding contract has been concluded, subject only to clarification on that one point.

Clearly the purchasers took a different view of the matter, but in my opinion they were not entitled to do so. Whichever be the correct construction of the reference to the garage in the contract, the purchasers made no attempt to clarify the position, and instead first purportedly unilaterally amended what was already a binding contract and then, again unilaterally, purportedly withdrew therefrom. In my view, they were not in a position to do either of these things and so remain bound by the contract. In the result they then put themselves in breach of clause 3 and the sellers, after formal notification, formally rescinded the contract and proceeded to resell. A loss on resale was incurred.

It may seem, at first sight, anomalous that the parties are bound by a contract whose terms have not yet finally been established because of the doubt as to whether a single or a double garage was the subject-matter of the contract. In my opinion, however, this is not a factor which would invalidate the contract between the parties or exclude consensus. See McBryde, *Contract*, para 4–29: 'however, a blunder by a draftsman is one of the instances in which extrinsic evidence may be allowed in the construction of a contract'. I think there is no doubt at all that, in this case, we either have a blunder by the draftsman which is subject to rectification or there is a binding contract to provide a dwellinghouse and a double garage.

There have been a number of cases where the parties were at odds as to the identity of the subjects in a contract of sale and purchase of heritage. The best known of these is probably *Anderson v Lambie* 1954 SC (HL) 43. In that case, there was a contract for the sale and purchase of a farm; but the subsequent disposition conveyed not only the farm but a mine as well. The seller then sought to reduce the disposition on the ground that more had been conveyed to the purchaser than he had bargained for. The purchaser maintained that he had always intended to purchase the mine but the court rejected his evidence and held that he had always intended to purchase simply the farm and nothing more. On that footing, in the House

of Lords, the disposition was reduced to allow a corrective disposition to
be granted. Note that, in this and other similar cases, there was a dispute
between the parties as to the meaning of the missives. In particular the
purchaser maintained that the missives gave him both the farm and the
mine whereas the seller maintained that the missives gave him the farm
only. But there is absolutely no suggestion in the arguments, or in the
report in this case which went to the House of Lords that, in the end of the
day, there was no consensus. This is because the seller intended to sell
the farm and the purchaser, notwithstanding his arguments, was held by
the court to have intended to purchase exactly the same thing. Accordingly,
notwithstanding an argument as to the meaning of the missives, there was
a consensus and so there was a binding contract. It would, of course, have
been quite a different matter if the purchaser in *Anderson* v *Lambie* had
satisfied the court that the missives were intended, and could be construed,
as relating both to farm and mine, whereas the seller maintained that the
missives related to the farm alone. If the court had believed the purchaser
and accepted his evidence, then there would have been no consensus
although there might have been a binding contract. The same result is
evident in other similar cases. So, in *MacDonald* v *Newall* (1898) 1F 68,
there was a contract for the sale and purchase of a property known as the
Royal Hotel. The purchaser claimed that the missives covered certain
additional properties which the seller maintained had not been included in
the contract. On proof, the court rejected the purchaser's evidence and
held that the contract covered only what the seller maintained. But again,
notwithstanding the argument between the parties, it finally turned out, on
proof, that they were at one on the subject-matter of the contract and that
there was no question of lack of consensus. Accordingly there was a
binding contract.

The general principle is, however, subject to this qualification that,
where one party in clear and unambiguous terms makes an offer to the
other party who accepts it, the offerer cannot later say that he really meant
something different from what he clearly undertook to do in terms of the
contract. In this case, the contract states unambiguously that a double
garage was included in the sale. This produces the alternative result
referred to above: if the purchaser genuinely believed that he was to get a
double garage, there is a binding contract and the seller cannot now escape
from the bargain on the footing that he really meant a single garage. So,
although there is an apparent lack of consensus, the court would not permit
the seller to escape from the contract because there is no room for argument as to whether a single or a double garage was contracted for. For a
recent illustration of this qualification to the general rule, see *Spook Erection
(Northern) Ltd* v *Kaye* 1990 SLT 676 and the authorities cited there. In
that case, there was a contract for sale and purchase of heritage. At the date
of the contract, the property was let on a ninety-nine year lease; but the
seller was under the mistaken understanding that the property was subject
to a nine hundred and ninety-year lease. That was an error on the seller's
part not induced by the purchaser and the bargain was concluded on that
footing. The seller then sought to reduce the contract on the ground of
essential error and failed. Clearly, the seller was genuinely in error but,

none the less, the terms of the contract were clear and unambiguous; and that genuine error on the part of the seller did not give grounds for reduction of the contract. Lord Marnoch, in his judgment, quoted with approval from the opinion of Lord Dunpark in an earlier similar case *Steel's Trustee* v *Bradley Homes (Scotland) Ltd* 1972 SC 48, 1974 SLT 133: 'It is essential, in the interests of business efficacy, that the ordinary rule should be that an onerous contract ... in plain terms should bind the parties thereto.'

It follows that the original bilateral contract, duly executed by both parties, was valid and binding, and, since the purchasers failed to implement it, they are in breach of contract and liable in damages.

I would make one qualification. The contract, as it stands, requires the seller to provide a double garage. The subjects have since been resold with a single garage only; and that, presumably, produced a lesser price than a house with a double garage would have produced. Accordingly, in calculating damages, it is essential first to determine exactly what the parties were contracting for and to establish whether the purchaser genuinely believed that the reference to the double garage in the contract was truly intended and that he was to get a double garage; or whether he all along understood that he was to get a single garage only and that the reference to the double garage in the contract was a pure draftsman's error. If the parties contracted for a single garage, the damages are as quantified by the sellers. If, however, the purchaser genuinely believed that he was to get a double garage and made his offer, at the offer price, on that understanding, some allowance must be made for that fact in assessing the damages, because the subsequent sale of the house with a single garage produced a lesser price than a house with a double garage would have produced, thereby increasing the claim by an unwarranted amount.

Further reading
Angus v *Bryden* 1992 SLT 884.

Manual, para 28.11.

50 Time of the essence

Concluded missives – deposit – balance unpaid on date due – whether vendors could resile – interpretation of conditions of sale – mutuality principle

Date: April 1989

Memorial
The memorialist purchased a property at an auction. A deposit of ten per cent of the price was paid at that time.

The general conditions of sale (Scotland) provided that the date of entry would be 28 days thereafter. The general conditions further provided that, 'the settlement date is of the essence of the contract and failure by the purchaser to pay the purchase price ... within ten days of the settlement date shall, without prejudice to the vendor's other rights and remedies, entitle the vendor to resile from the bargain.'

The tenth day after the date of entry was a bank holiday. The Monday was also a bank holiday in England. On the Tuesday without any prior intimation of their intention to resile, the vendors' agents faxed to the memorialist's agents a letter advising that their clients were resiling from the bargain.

The vendors' agents had previously indicated that settlement was to be made by means of telegraphic transfer but they had not provided the memorialist's agents with details of that account. Furthermore, they did not provide the memorialist's agents with a settlement figure although one was requested twice before the faxed letter was received.

The memorialist sought answers to the following questions:

1   Were the vendors entitled to resile from the bargain without giving reasonable notice of their intention to do so?

2   In view of the terms of the articles of roup, minute of enactment, special conditions and general conditions of sale (Scotland), were the vendors obliged to return the deposit and would any interest be payable thereon?

3   Were the vendors barred from resiling by the actions of their agents, particularly their failure to provide details of the bank account into which the funds were to be transferred and their failure to advise the memorialist's agents of the amount required to settle?

4   Were there any other points which should be brought to the memorialist's attention?

Opinion
1   In principle, I answer this question in the affirmative. The critical clause here is clause 9 of the general conditions of sale. In terms of that condition, the purchase price falls to be paid in full on the settlement date, defined in clause 8. It is then expressly provided in clause 9 that payment of the full purchase price is of the essence of the contract. If the clause stopped there, I would have no hesitation whatsoever in advising that the sellers were entitled to resile the day after the price was due to be paid. There is, however, a further and somewhat ambiguous provision, which, to some extent, casts doubt on the position of the purchaser, in that the clause then provides that failure by the purchaser to pay the purchase price within ten days entitles the seller to resile. If that further provision were unqualified, I would be inclined to the view that the two provisions would be read together by the court. In the result, the seller would not be entitled to resile unless and until the purchaser failed to pay the price by the second date stipulated. But the further proviso as to the ten-day period of grace is stated to be without prejudice to the seller's other rights and remedies. If that qualification is strictly construed, then it is certainly arguable that failure to pay the price on or before the first due date would entitle the seller to resile the day after without further notice since payment of the price on the first date is made of the essence of the contract; and the subsequent provision as to the later payment is without prejudice to that earlier provision.

In any event, however clause 9 falls to be construed, the purchaser is in serious difficulty, taking this clause in isolation. Ten days after the settlement date was a bank holiday (Good Friday). That being so, it is possible to call in aid the provisions of the Banking and Financial Dealings Act 1971, s 14, in terms of which no person can be compelled to make payment on a bank holiday; and any payment falling to be made on a bank holiday is made if paid on the next following day on which the purchaser can be compelled to make payment. But bank holidays, as defined in the Act, do not appear to include Saturday or Sunday; and further, in Scotland, they certainly do not include Easter Monday, although Easter Monday is a bank holiday in England.

Clause 26 quite clearly provides that the law of Scotland applies to the interpretation of the general conditions; and so, for the purposes of clause 9, the price should have been paid at latest on Easter Monday. The price was not so paid and accordingly, whatever may be the correct construction of clause 9, there can be no doubt in my opinion that the seller was automatically entitled to resile on or after the Tuesday.

That being so, the fax message of Tuesday in terms of which the sellers' solicitors purportedly resile from the bargain, is valid, and effectively rescinds the contract. The ultimatum procedure (which is appropriate in the absence of special provisions making time of the essence) has no application in this case, and the question of 'reasonable notice' does not arise. If the price is not paid on or before the specified date, then the sellers are perfectly entitled immediately thereafter to rescind the bargain as, in my opinion, they have effectively done, so far as the provisions of clause 9 are concerned.

2 In terms of clause 6(iii) of the general conditions of sale, a deposit of ten per cent fell to be paid on the signing of the minute of enactment, and I assume was so paid. The deposit is then to be held by the auctioneer as agent for the vendor. No further provision is made in clause 6 or elsewhere in the general conditions or in the articles as to this deposit. That being so, and in particular since the deposit is expressly stated as representing ten per cent of the purchase price, and if the bargain has been validly rescinded, the deposit is in my opinion repayable in full but without interest, since there is no rule of law which would entitle the purchaser to insist on interest.

If, however, the sellers have validly rescinded the bargain, then they have a claim for damages against the purchaser, and I think they are probably entitled to retain the deposit, at least until such time as the quantum of their claim for damages is ascertained. They would then be entitled to set off whatever amount they claim as damages against the ten per cent, and would be obliged to repay only the balance after deducting that claim.

3 Whether or not time has been made of the essence of the contract, there is a general overriding principle of mutuality the result of which is that the sellers in this case could not insist on implement by the purchaser (and therefore could not found on failure to implement) if they themselves are not in a position to implement their part of the bargain. This rule was

illustrated recently in the familiar case of *Bowie* v *Semple's Executors* 1978 SLT (Sh Ct) 9. The mutuality principle is, I think, the only ground in this case on which the purchaser can hope to succeed.

Whether or not the facts as narrated in the memorial provide sufficient ammunition to the purchaser to allow him to take advantage of this rule is somewhat doubtful. On balance, I have come to the view that he is in a fairly strong position in this sense, that the sellers' agents specified the code of settlement in a letter in which they also refer to production of a state for settlement containing details of the bank account into which payment was to be made. The state for settlement was also to deal with the question of apportionments. As I understand it, the state for settlement has not been produced and details of the bank account have not been provided. On equitable principles, I do not think the court would allow the sellers to take advantage of the provision as to time being of the essence, where the sellers' agents had in effect rendered it impossible for the purchaser to implement his part of the bargain by their actings. However, the purchaser can only succeed on this ground if he is now in a position immediately to settle. Assuming that he is in that position, it is important that the agents should immediately intimate to the sellers that they are holding them to the bargain and that they are holding their agents liable for the purchaser's failure to pay within the specified time limits because of the agents' failure to provide the required information. Further, I think an ultimatum should be given at the same time to the effect that, unless that information is immediately provided so as to allow the purchaser to pay the price in terms of the contract, the purchaser will raise an action of specific implement. The time limit should be very short and, if the information is not provided within the specified time, I would advise that an action of implement be raised immediately. At the same time, the purchaser should register an inhibition on the dependence, to ensure that the sellers do not resell the subjects to a third party who might otherwise acquire a real right in the subjects to the exclusion of the purchaser.

4   The only actings narrated in the memorial which indicate a failure on the part of the sellers to implement their part of the bargain, or at least to make it possible for the purchaser in turn to pay the price, are a failure on the part of the sellers' agents to provide the state for settlement and information as to the bank account. The contract does, however, contain certain other conditions which the seller must be in a position to implement at settlement, failing which they cannot properly rescind the bargain. Thus, in clause 19 of the general conditions, the seller is to deliver or exhibit Land Register reports in statutory form on the settlement date. In fact, I think the seller may have implemented that obligation but this point should be carefully examined.

Further, in clause 23, the price is payable in exchange for delivery of a disposition in favour of the purchaser. I am not advised whether or not the disposition has yet been adjusted and, if so, whether the sellers have intimated to the purchaser that the disposition has been duly executed and that they are in a position to implement this part of the bargain. Again, this point should be checked.

These points apart, there would seem to be no other obligations in the articles themselves, or in the general conditions, on which the purchaser could found, except for the provision to produce writs in clause 18 which I assume the sellers are in a position to implement.

Manual, para 28.20.

51   Prior communings

House built not in accordance with plans – rescission – damages

Date: October 1987

Memorial

The memorialists entered into builders' missives to purchase a dwelling-house. The missives were signed by the memorialists and accepted without qualification by the developers. The memorialists had negotiations with the developers' foreman regarding the layout of the proposed dwellinghouse. When completed the dwellinghouse was substantially different to the plans that had been agreed and signed by the memorialists (although not referred to in the missives).

The developers offered the memorialists £1,000 in compensation and gave a seven-day ultimatum failing acceptance of which the developers would resile.

The memorialists asked whether they were bound to accept the dwelling-house as it had been constructed and whether they had any remedy against the developers.

Opinion

The contract of sale and purchase in this case is constituted by an offer, signed by the purchasers in July 1987 and accepted without qualification by the builders. There is a plan attached to the offer showing the boundaries of the plot and, in general, the positioning of the building thereon. The offer refers to the purchase of plot 6 together with the dwellinghouse and garage (if any) to be erected thereon but does not contain any further particulars as to the type of dwellinghouse or the specifications thereof. The dwellinghouse is again referred to in clauses 7, 8 and 15 of the offer; but again without specifications. In terms of clause 8, the developers reserve the right to vary the materials used in the construction of the dwellinghouse; and, in terms of clause 15, it is to be erected in accordance with plans approved by the local authority. Beyond that, there is nothing in the formal contract document to indicate what type of building was envisaged.

I understand that, prior to completion of the missives, the memorialists had negotiated with the developers for the erection of a modified dwelling-house according to plans and specifications which were prepared by the developers' architects and approved by the purchasers, in accordance with a plan marked A, in May 1987. No subsequent modifications to that plan were agreed by the purchasers.

Since the formal contract document contains no information whatsoever as to the type of dwellinghouse or the specifications thereof, I think it must be legitimate to look behind it and to refer back to the prior negotiations between the parties and in particular to the dwellinghouse agreed on in terms of plan A as a precise specification of the building to be erected in terms of the subsequent formal missives. That being so, the developers have, in my opinion, undertaken to erect a dwellinghouse exactly in accordance with the specification in plan A but have in fact erected a dwellinghouse on quite a different plan. The memorialists went to considerable trouble to negotiate the plan of the dwellinghouse to suit their particular requirements. The dwellinghouse actually erected by the developers frustrates their intentions to a material degree. In the result, I regard the developers' failure to complete the building according to specification as a material breach of contract on their part. I understand that the developers have offered to make an *ex gratia* payment of £1,000, presumably as compensation although it is not specified as such. This certainly confirms the view that the developers are in breach and that the breach is material.

On that view of the matter, the memorialists have two alternative remedies: (1) to rescind the bargain and claim damages; or (2) to proceed with the bargain, accepting the dwellinghouse although it does not conform to the original plan, but claiming damages from the developers for failure to implement their part of the bargain. I think they must now decide which remedy they wish to adopt, and it is difficult for me to advise them as to which would be the better choice.

Two observations may assist.

First, I understand that the developers are threatening to resile from the bargain unless the memorialists settle within seven days. In my view, the developers are not entitled to adopt this attitude, nor to resile from the bargain, because they are themselves in breach. In these circumstances, a seven-day ultimatum seems to me far too short a period to allow the memorialists to decide what course of action they wish to adopt.

Secondly, I am asked to advise as to what might be considered a reasonable figure of compensation, if the memorialists decide to proceed with the transaction. This is not an easy question to answer. The rule in such cases is that, where the developers are in material breach, but the purchaser none the less agrees to proceed with the contract, the purchaser is liable, not for the contract price but for recompense to the extent to which he is *quantum lucratus*. See *Ramsay & Son* v *Brand* (1898) 25 R 1212, although Professor McBryde doubts the soundness of this rule (see McBryde, *Contract*, paras 6–35 and 36). The decision in *Ramsay & Son* v *Brand* has, however, been approved in the House of Lords, at least in relation to lump sum contracts such as this, and I would be surprised if the rule were not applied in this case.

The alternative basis for assessing the sum due by the memorialists if they accept the building, would be the contract price less an amount by way of damages for the developers' failure to implement the contract.

In either case, I would not have thought that the memorialists would be able to achieve any substantial reduction in the contract price. Granted that the dwellinghouse has not been constructed according to the agreed plan and that this is a material deviation which the purchasers are not obliged to accept, the fact remains that a dwellinghouse of substantially the same value has been constructed on the site. In the result, if the purchasers elect to accept the subjects, I would have thought that the suggested *ex gratia* payment of £1,000 was not unreasonable and that they would be unlikely to secure a greater discount if the matter were litigated.

Manual, para 28.21.

52   The exclusion of the actio quanti minoris

Non-supersession clause not repeated in disposition – effect

Date: May 1990

Memorial

The memorialists sold a dwellinghouse to the purchasers. In the missives there was a clause stating that the memorialists should deliver all relevant documentation to the purchasers relating to alterations carried out. No such documentation was delivered at settlement.

Four years later the purchasers sold the property, but were required to carry out remedial work in order to obtain building control consent. The purchasers claimed the sums they had to expend from the memorialists. There was a non-supersession clause in the original missives between the memorialists and the purchaser, but that was not repeated in the disposition.

The memorialists asked whether the purchasers had a valid claim against them.

Opinion

In my opinion, for the reasons set out below, while the purchasers may technically have a claim against the sellers in this case, that claim is not enforceable as a claim for damages and I do not think the purchasers have any other remedy available to them.

In the missives entered into in 1986 there is an express provision in clause 15 of the schedule attached to the offer to the effect that the conditions in the missives, if not implemented at the date of delivery of the disposition, will remain in full force until implemented. There is no time limit on that condition and it is therefore enforceable at least until cut off by the negative prescription, which does not yet, of course, operate in this case. In the subsequent disposition in implement of the missives, however, there is no reference to clause 15 of the schedule, and no provision in the disposition maintaining that clause in operation. I assume from the terms of the memorial that there was no contemporaneous exchange of letters between the agents for the parties maintaining the clause in force.

Two questions arise:

(1) Does the omission to make further provision for the continued operation of clause 15, either in the disposition or by a separate exchange of letters at settlement, now exclude the operation of that clause or does the clause continue in force notwithstanding that omission? Reference is made in the memorial to the decision of Sheriff Principal Caplan (now Lord Caplan) in *Jamieson* v *Stewart* 1989 SLT (Sh Ct) 13 which is, I think, the latest in a series of decisions on this same point. Sheriff Principal Caplan examines the question in some depth in the context of these earlier decisions and comes to the view that, in the circumstances of that case, it was competent to refer to and found on provisions in the missives not implemented by the disposition, notwithstanding delivery of a disposition which contained no provision maintaining the missives in operation. Although the circumstances and the wording in this case are not the same, my view is that the judgment of Sheriff Principal Caplan is correct and would apply in this case. However, until the matter is disposed of in the Inner House, serious doubts must remain and it is not possible to give a categorical answer with assurance.

(2) As an alternative argument, the purchasers here maintain that, even if the clause in the missives is not referred to in the disposition or in a contemporaneous exchange of letters at settlement, none the less the terms of clause 8 of the schedule to the offer are collateral and so its provisions form an exception to the standard rule that the disposition supersedes the missives and that the provisions of that clause remain enforceable notwithstanding settlement.

Clause 8 of the schedule makes two distinct provisions. First, there is a provision to the effect that all necessary permissions and warrants for building, alterations etc have been obtained, which apparently is not the case. This part of clause 8 is almost identical in its terms to the clause considered by the court in *Winston* v *Patrick* 1980 SC 246. In that case, it was argued that this part of the clause was collateral and therefore fell within exception (b) of the three examples given by the Lord Justice-Clerk at p 249 of the report. In *Winston*, the court rejected that argument. Accordingly, in my opinion, it cannot be successfully argued in this case that the first provision in clause 8 is collateral and would therefore survive delivery of the disposition.

The second provision in clause 8 is to the effect that the permissions and warrants are to be exhibited before the date of entry. It might be easier to maintain that this second provision formed a separate and collateral obligation if it was quite distinct and independent of the first part of clause 8. Clearly, however, that is not so because the second sentence of the clause refers to 'said permissions and warrants'. Accordingly, if the first part of clause 8 cannot survive because it is superseded by the disposition, it is difficult to see how the second sentence could survive, in that it refers directly to the provisions of the first part which are now no longer enforceable. In any event, the obligation was to exhibit the permissions before the date of entry which has long since passed. This certainly raises an inference that the parties have departed from that provision in the missives and so it is no longer enforceable.

My opinion is, so far, inconclusive. There is, however, another ground on which I think, for practical purposes, any claim by the purchasers in this case is bound to fail.

The missives were entered into nearly four years ago and the purchasers have been in occupation ever since. It now emerges that the provisions of clause 8 in the missives were not in fact complied with at settlement. If this point had been raised before settlement, the purchasers would not have been obliged to proceed with the bargain. Arguably, if the clause survived the missives, and if the purchasers had raised the point within a reasonable time after settlement, they would also have been entitled to rescind the bargain and resile. But nearly four years have passed since the transaction settled and it seems to me very doubtful whether it is now possible for the purchasers to rescind the bargain. *Restitutio in integrum* is an essential prerequisite to rescission, and *restitutio* could hardly now be possible after that long lapse of time.

In my view, therefore, the only alternative remedy available to the purchasers is a claim for damages based on the sellers' breach of contract. This could only succeed if the clause in the contract can still be founded on, which is doubtful. But I think it is settled that a claim for damages in circumstances where the obligation is *not* collateral is an *actio quanti minoris.* In other words, what the purchasers are seeking here is retention of the subjects with a reduction in the price to take account of the fact that the subjects do not conform to the terms of clause 8 of the schedule to the offer. It is, however, settled beyond argument that, in the sale and purchase of heritage, the *actio quanti minoris* is not a competent remedy and is not available to the purchasers unless expressly provided for in the missives. In this context, I refer the memorialists to an article by Professor K. G. C. Reid in (1988) 33 JLSS 285 where the question is discussed. Since there is no express provision in the missives in this case which would entitle the purchasers to proceed by way of this form of action, they must come within one or other of the two alternative exceptions to the standard rule referred to by Professor Reid, if the are to succeed in a claim for damages:

(*a*) An exception for collateral obligations. But, for the reasons stated above, I do not consider that the obligation in clause 8 to the schedule to the offer is a collateral obligation in this sense.

(*b*) An exception for latent defects. It is said that, where the defect is latent, then a claim for damages may be competent even after settlement. This, of course, assumes that the condition in the contract remains enforceable and, in any event, the defect must be latent. In this case the defect was latent in that the purchasers were apparently not aware at settlement that the conditions of clause 8 were not complied with. But that is something which could and should have been discovered before settlement. The carrying-out of past alterations seems to have been obvious to the surveyors in the survey. It is therefore very doubtful whether the defect could be termed 'latent' for the purposes of this exception. So, as Professor Reid asks at p 287 in the article referred to above, 'how latent must the defect be?' Clearly, the buyer must not actually know of its existence. But to what extent does he have a duty to make enquiries? Usually, of course, he will have the property surveyed, examine the title, inspect the local authority property certificates and so on. But if he does not do these things and if, had he done so, the defect would have been revealed, can the defect still be regarded as 'latent'? In my view, in a case such as this where enquiry would have disclosed the position, it cannot and so the purchasers have no claim.

There is only one reported case directly in point where a claim of this kind has succeeded, namely *Bradley* v *Scott* 1966 SLT (Sh Ct) 25, but that decision has subsequently been severely criticised and would not, I think, now be followed.

Further reading
Taylor v *McLeod* 1990 SLT 194.
Fortune v *Fraser* 1995 SCLR 121.

The Law Commission Report on Three Bad Rules of Contract which has now been implemented in the Contract (Scotland) Act 1997.

Manual, para 28.23.

53   Effect of conditions in contracts whether suspensive or resolutive

Interpretation of missives – whether purchaser could resile

Date: May 1988

Memorial
The memorialists concluded missives for the purchase of a property, conditional on the sellers' obtaining the renunciation of a lease (the relevant clause is narrated below). In order to encourage the sellers to obtain the renunciation, a further formal offer was issued by the memorialists increasing the purchase price. The renunciation was obtained, and the memorialists purported to withdraw their further formal letter and settle on the original missives. The sellers sought to withdraw on the basis that the renunciation had not been obtained in time.

The memorialists asked:

1   Had the original contract been purified and were the sellers thus prevented from withdrawing?

2   As the missives for the conclusion of the renunciation had been completed, should it be implied that they were in a form acceptable to the sellers thereby preventing them from withdrawing on the basis that they were not acceptable?

3   If the sellers did not proceed with the renunciation, could the memorialists waive the suspensive condition in the original contract to allow the transaction to proceed?

4   If so, could it be argued that the sellers would be obliged to proceed with the renunciation?

5   Could the sellers withdraw on any other grounds?

Opinion

Before answering the questions asked in my memorial, I think it is appropriate to summarise the terms of clause 3 of the original offer as modified by the subsequent correspondence.

Omitting matter not relevant to the point at issue, condition 3 of the offer (as amended by the qualifications in the memorialists' letter and clause 5 of the qualified acceptance) reads as follows. (I have divided condition 3 into 3A and 3B for ease of reference).

> '3A   This Offer and ... the Missives shall be essentially conditional upon:
>
> ...
>
> (4) The Seller's obtaining a Renunciation of the Lease.
>
> The terms of this Condition 3A shall be construed as being for the benefit of the Purchasers only, and the Purchasers expressly reserve the right to waive or withdraw this Condition 3A in whole or in part at any time.
>
> 3B   In the event of sub-clause 4 above ... not having been purified before ... August, 1988, the Purchasers shall be entitled to resile ... or ... to grant ... extension of time ...
>
> If the said Renunciation has not been obtained (by ... February, 1988) the Sellers shall be entitled to resile from the Missives.'

I answer the questions put to me briefly, since the matter is urgent and the agents wish an opinion as soon as possible.

1   No. I think the sellers' actings can be explained by reference to the formal letters offering an increased price, although this increased offer never became formally binding on either party. But, even although the sellers' agents may have been acting on the assumption that an increased price had been agreed to, their actings are still perfectly consistent with the terms of the original contract because, although the sellers themselves were entitled to resile if the renunciation was not obtained by ... February, they were not obliged to do so; and, if they did not elect to do so, they still had a further six months within which to obtain the renunciation before the purchasers in their turn could resile under condition 3B.

The memorialists have to bear in mind that, while the later formal letters lay on the table, as it were, it was open to the sellers' agents at any moment to conclude a bargain on those amended terms by simple acceptance of the qualified acceptance from the memorialists. So long as they had that opportunity available to them, I think it would be very difficult, if not impossible, for the memorialists to maintain that, by proceeding to negotiate the required renunciation, and by intimating that the renunciation was virtually completed, the sellers had abandoned their undoubted right to resile as contained in condition 3B.

It might be possible to argue that, by proceeding as they did, the sellers' agents have committed themselves to the contract, not on its original terms but on the terms contained in the original contract as modified by the later formal letters; and indeed I suspect that they were in fact proceeding on the mistaken assumption that a bargain on these modified terms had been concluded. That mistake would not, however, in my view, support an argument by the memorialists that the sellers had committed themselves to the original bargain in its unamended form as concluded by the formal letters in August and September 1987.

2 No. Condition 3 in its final form as summarised above gives the sellers an unqualified right to resile if the renunciation was not obtained by the stated date. It cannot be disputed, I think, that the renunciation was not so obtained. The fact that a renunciation was obtained at a later date is not sufficient by itself to purify the condition; and I do not think the actings of the sellers or their agents in obtaining that renunciation are so totally inconsistent with the terms of the original missives as to bar them now from resiling.

3 The letter from the sellers' agents withdrawing from the missives is not formal and probative; and in any event merely states their view. It is not, in my view, formal intimation that the sellers have resiled. Accordingly, the purchasers can still competently waive condition 3A(4), in terms of their reserved power.

But in terms of condition 3B the sellers have an absolute right to resile if the renunciation has not been obtained by the stated date and that date has now passed. Waiver by the purchaser of condition 3A(4) would not, in my opinion, thereby deprive the sellers of that right. As I read condition 3, the proviso in the last sentence of condition 3A as summarised above does not apply to the provisions of condition 3B. Accordingly, I do not think there is any way in which the purchasers can compel the sellers to proceed with the contract.

It would require some positive and unequivocal act on the part of the sellers or their agents which clearly implied an intention to proceed with the original bargain and to abandon the right to resile to which they became entitled in February, if the purchasers are to succeed in holding the sellers to the bargain. As I construe the contract, the correspondence and the actings of the parties, I do not think the sellers have so committed themselves. Therefore, in my view, they are still entitled to exercise their right to resile as contained in condition 3B of the missives.

4 No, for the same reasons as are stated in answer to question 3.

5 On the facts disclosed in the memorial and correspondence, there would seem to be no other grounds on which the sellers can resile; but the terms of condition 3, being specific and unqualified, are quite sufficient, in my view, to allow them to resile from the bargain at this stage.

Further reading
Requirements of Writing (Scotland) Act 1995.

Manual, para 28.28.

54   *Title*

Reservation of underground right of way – whether sufficient to render
title unmarketable

Date: July 1987

Memorial
The memorialists had acted in the purchase of a property for a client (Mr
A). It subsequently transpired that the titles contained a reservation of an
underground right of way for railway workings with a right of re-entry to
the surface on six months' notice and payment of compensation. It was
argued that the reservation rendered the title unmarketable. Mr A
contracted to sell the property to Mr B, but before the transaction could
settle, a waiver had to be obtained from British Rail. Mr A sought to recoup
his costs from the memorialists.

An opinion was sought on the validity and marketability of the title as it
stood before the minute of waiver was obtained.

Opinion
Solicitors acting for a purchaser of heritable property in Scotland have a
duty to ensure that the title tendered by the seller is marketable. The term
'marketable title' cannot be precisely defined because it depends, in part,
on the nature of the purchase and, in part, on the terms of the missives
themselves. But, generally speaking, a marketable title means a title so clear
as to protect the purchaser not only from actual eviction but from the risk
of any reasonable challenge; a title which is so regular in form and so
correct in all particulars that no-one later dealing with the purchaser, on
sale or for security, will take exception to it on any ground.

It is always a difficult question to decide whether a particular burden or
restriction in the title renders it unmarketable in the absence of special
provisions in the contract. The present case is particularly difficult and is
undoubtedly a borderline one.

The difficulty which arises on this title is that in a feu contract entered
into in March 1906 between a railway company and a developer, the
railway company reserved to itself and its successors a full and perpetual
underground right of way and passage through, *inter alia*, the plot of
ground on which the tenement in question is constructed or any part
thereof for the purpose of the railway undertaking and, in addition, a right
of re-entry in the event of the plots or areas of ground thereby conveyed
being at any time required for any of the purposes of the railway undertaking, subject to notice and to compensation being paid.

The reservation is now more than eighty years old and, as I understand
it, no action has been taken by the railway company to exercise its rights.
This raises the possibility that the reserved rights, being arguably in the
nature of a servitude rather than a right of property, may have been extinguished by the long negative prescription. On balance, I have come to the
view that they would not be held to be so extinguished. In *Smith* v *Stewart*
(1884) 11 R 921, a very similar reservation was held by the court to be

res merae facultatis and accordingly not affected by the negative prescription. In my view, the reserved rights in this case would be held to be in the same category and so have not been extinguished by the mere passage of time. They therefore remain enforceable although the possibility of their being exercised is extraordinarily remote. The question therefore is whether the servitude right of underground passage and the reserved right to enter on the surface in certain circumstances rendered the title unmarketable.

In the recent case of *Armia Ltd* v *Daejan Developments Ltd* 1979 SC (HL) 56, 1979 SLT 147, the question of marketability is discussed with particular reference to a servitude right of access over the subjects of sale. According to Lord Fraser, any undisclosed burden which materially diminishes the value of the property entitles the purchaser to resile on the grounds of unmarketability. Lord Keith applies the same general test but seems to go further where he says that the position is, in substance, that the existence of 'such conditions' has the effect that the seller is unable to convey the full right of property which he agreed to convey. He refers to Lord MacKenzie's opinion in the earlier case of *Urquhart* v *Halden* (1835) 13 S 844 at p 849, but in fact should have referred to Lord Balgray's, on the same page.

There really could be little doubt, in *Armia*, that the servitude in question did materially diminish the value of the subjects, and accordingly, applying that test, the title was held to be unmarketable. The court took the same view in *Urquhart* v *Halden*, where the servitude was considered very onerous. In the present case, it is much more difficult to say that the existence of the underground right of passage and the right to re-enter the surface materially diminished the value of the subjects, in view of the fact that tenements have been erected on this ground for eighty years and have remained undisturbed throughout that period. Further, the reserved right was waived by British Rail, on request, without any apparent difficulty.

On the other hand, the condition is undoubtedly of an unusual kind and is potentially onerous in two respects:

(*a*) if British Rail had decided to exercise their right to construct tunnels underneath the tenement, this might well have resulted in material disturbance and possible damage, by subsidence or otherwise, even although there are compensation provisions in the title; and

(*b*) if British Rail had exercised their right to re-enter the surface of the ground, this again, might have adversely affected the amenity of the tenement to a serious degree.

On first reading my instructions, I was of the view that the rule as re-affirmed in *Campbell* v *McCutcheon* 1963 SC 505 might also be applied to render the title unmarketable in this case. In that case, an urban dwelling-house was sold without reference to minerals in the contract of sale and purchase. When the purchaser discovered that minerals were reserved to the superior, he resiled and was held entitled to do so on the footing that the title was unmarketable, lacking the minerals. But here the *ratio* of the decision proceeded on the basis that, in the absence of special provisions in the missives, the purchaser of heritage by implication offers for the subjects *a coelo ad centrum*; and, if minerals are reserved, the seller cannot give a marketable title to the whole of what the purchaser offered for. On reflection, however, I think that case may be distinguishable for two reasons.

First, we are here not dealing with something corporeal missing from the title in the sense that minerals were missing from the title in *Campbell* v *McCutcheon*, but rather we are here dealing with a title to entire subjects which are subject to a reservation or burden of, possibly, an onerous kind. The question of onerousness was not relevant in *Campbell* v *McCutcheon*. The absence of minerals did not in any way diminish the value of the subjects nor otherwise operate to the disadvantage of the purchaser; instead he was not offered a title to the *whole* of the subjects of offer.

Secondly, what we are dealing with here is the purchase of the first flat in a tenement. Now it may be that, in terms of the contract of sale and purchase, Mr B did also stipulate that he would get from Mr A a right in common to the solum on which the tenement was constructed, in which case *Campbell* v *McCutcheon* is in point. But, as Professor Halliday points out in *Conveyancing Law and Practice*, vol II, para 21–44, the rule in *Campbell* v *McCutcheon* will not necessarily apply on the purchase of an upper flat in a tenement, without special provision in the missives as to the solum, because of the rule in the law of the tenement that the purchase of an upper flat does not by implication carry with it any higher right in the solum than a mere right of common interest. Accordingly, if that were the position (as it may be in this case), the *ad coelo ad centrum* rule is not offended against and so this decision is not in point. On the other hand, if the offer in question was an offer for the flat with a right in common to the solum, then it may be technically possible to distinguish *Campbell* v *McCutcheon* on the basis that what is here reserved is a mere right of passage whereas in *Campbell* v *McCutcheon* what was reserved was a right to the minerals themselves, as *partes soli*. But that is a very narrow distinction indeed because, in either case, the practical result is that, if the reserved right is exercised, a tunnel or shaft will be excavated underneath the surface of the property through which vehicles (be it coal trucks or railway trucks) will thereafter pass to and fro.

With considerable hesitation, therefore, I have come to the view that the title was probably not marketable in this case.

On the other hand, if the matter is to be contested, there is a fairly strong argument in favour of marketability if it can be shown that the presence of the reserved right of access underground and of repossession of the surface did not materially diminish the value of the subjects. The main argument here would be that, eighty years having passed without the right having been exercised, the possibility of its now being exercised is so remote as to be ignored. This argument is strongly borne out by the fact that, without apparent argument, and without any significant consideration being paid, British Rail gave up their reserved right. Accordingly, one might argue that, even standing the reserved right, the value of the property was totally unaffected and therefore, on the test applied by the House of Lords in *Armia Limited*, there was no material diminution in value, and the burden, although unusual, was not sufficiently onerous or objectionable in the circumstances to render the title unmarketable.

The views I have expressed on marketability are not, I am afraid, particularly helpful to the memorialists.

Manual, para 28.42.

55   Contract to remain in full force and effect

Line of culvert – whether misrepresented by seller – remedies for purchaser

Date: June 1984

Memorial

The memorialist purchased a plot of ground from a district council with the intention of building a house. A plan was annexed and referred to in the missives. It showed the route of a culvert through the ground. When the memorialist started the excavation to erect his house, it was discovered that the culvert did not follow the line shown on the map, but rather took a route through the ground which bisected the proposed site of the house. It was not feasible to relocate the house within the plot.

The missives provided that, as far as the district council were aware, the location of any pipes, culverts, drains, sewers, cables or others running through, over or *ex adverso* the feu was as shown on the plan annexed to the missives, but no warranty was given in respect of the existence, absence or location of the pipes, drains, sewers, cables or others. The feu disposition provided that no construction would be permitted in an area within the immediate vicinity of the culvert shown on the plan.

The memorialist asked the following questions:

1   Had there been a misrepresentation by the district council and if so, could the memorialist rescind the contract?

2   Was the position of the culvert warranted?

3   Could the memorialist justify withdrawing from the contract on any other grounds?

Opinion

Undoubtedly, there has been a serious misrepresentation by the district council, both at the missives stage and in the formal title in that, in the missives, and in the subsequent feu disposition, the line of the culvert is very exactly shown on an accurate scaled plan attached to the missives, a copy of which is incorporated in the feu disposition. Further, not only is the plan accurately drawn and scaled but, both on the missives plan and on the title plan, there is a legend: 'All building work to be kept clear of hatch area *which denotes line of culvert.*' As it turns out, the culvert is not on that line, as a result of which the site, as a building plot, becomes infinitely more difficult and expensive to develop than the purchaser was led to believe at the time when he entered into the contract. Were it not for conditions in the contract, some of which are repeated in substance in the feu disposition, I would have had no hesitation whatsoever in advising that the purchaser was perfectly free to resile and probably to claim damages from the district council.

The difficulty which confronts the purchaser is that, in clause 3 of the offer, the district council, when referring to the culvert, go on to state that no warranty is given in respect of the existence, absence or location of *said* pipes, drains, sewers, cables or others. Admittedly, in this exclusion from warranty, there is no reference to culverts. That certainly helps the purchaser in that he can argue that while no warranty is given as to pipes, etc, the position as to the culvert is warranted. Against that, the district council can argue that the words 'or others' at the end of the warranty exclusion are sufficiently wide to cover culverts as well. In addition, under clause 5 of the offer, the purchaser is to be held to have satisfied himself as to the suitability of the feu for his purpose and, on conclusion of the bargain, any risk in relation to suitability passes to him. Further, there is attached to the offer, a schedule of conditions which refers specifically to the culvert and states that the culvert runs through the feu on the defined line. No exclusion or qualification is given in clause first of that schedule of conditions in regard to that specified culvert although, in clause second, there is a general exclusion to the effect that the feu is subject to the existence of all pipes, culverts, etc; that the cost of repair thereof lies with the purchaser if they are damaged; and that the purchaser has to satisfy himself as to the existence of all pipes, culverts, etc.

To a large extent, the content of the missives has been superseded by delivery of the disposition in favour of the purchaser which carries a plan repeating the information in the offer plan although with this technical defect that the culvert area is stated in the feu disposition to be shaded red on the plan and is not so shaded. However, this is a pure technical error which can easily be corrected by reference to the earlier missives plan and I do not think it affects the position one way or the other.

The plan is referred to in the feu disposition for description and there is no limitation or qualification as to warranty so far as the plan is concerned. Therefore, the plan is warranted under the warrandice obligation in the feu disposition. Finally, clause eleven of the offer expressly preserves all those clauses in the contract which are not incorporated in the feu disposition.

In the result, there is a conflict of terms and conditions.

Internally, within the terms of the feu disposition itself, on the one hand, the line of the culvert is exactly defined and is referred to specifically in clause first of the burdens clauses; in clause second of the burdens clauses, there is a general reservation for culverts etc which would include the culvert referred to in clause first but with a proviso that the feuar has to satisfy himself as to the existence of the culvert; and the district council then grant warrandice. That warrandice, in my view, covers all matters of title which would include a reservation of a servitude right for the culvert as well as the boundaries and other particulars of the title itself although warrandice will not cover suitability of the subjects for the purpose of the feuar. The question then is, given that the line of the culvert is warranted under the warrandice obligation, can the district council escape from that warrandice under the more general exclusion or proviso in the burdens clause second.

Over and above the internal difficulties in construing the feu disposition, there is the further difficulty that the conditions of the missives are preserved and, insofar as not implemented by the feu disposition, remain in force. That would certainly cover clause five of the offer in terms of which the feuar should have satisfied himself as to the suitability of the feu for his purpose. Arguably, on the strength of that clause alone, the council can shrug off responsibility for the present situation.

The following factors seem to me material:

(*a*)   at the missives stage and up to and including delivery of the title, the line of the culvert has been very exactly defined on the plan;

(*b*)   it is clearly very material indeed to anyone intending to build on the feu to know exactly where the culvert lies;

(*c*)   for practical purposes, notwithstanding the provisions in clause five of the offer, it really would be quite impracticable for a feuar intending to build to satisfy himself as to the line and position of a culvert under the feu until he has taken possession and started to build which, in the nature of things, involves him in substantial expense;

(*d*)   the information as to the culvert, insofar as it is precise in the feu disposition and on the plan, is warranted subject to the more general escape clauses both in the feu disposition and in the missives.

On balance, in my view, the courts would hold that, notwithstanding the general exclusion clauses referred to above, the district council have materially and significantly misrepresented the position to the memorialist in terms which entitled him to rely on the line of the culvert as defined on the plan attached to the missives and to the feu disposition. I take this view, notwithstanding the more general exclusion clauses. Having defined very precisely the exact line of the culvert which is a fact of very serious significance to the feuar, the council cannot then escape from the consequences of so defining the culvert line under the general limitations or exclusions.

If that conclusion is correct, then at least the feuar is entitled, in my view, to resile on the strength of the misrepresentation.

Whether the misrepresentation is innocent (in which case the feuar has no claim for damages against the council) or negligent is difficult to say without further investigation. I would have thought, however, that the line of the culvert is a fact which should have been known to the district council's engineering section and, in defining the line of the culvert wrongly, they must be held to be guilty of negligence. If so, in addition to a right to resile, the feuar would be entitled to claim damages.

I do not think there are any other avenues open to the memorialist to justify his withdrawing from the contract other than by founding on the specification of the line of the culvert.

Further reading

Winston v *Patrick* 1980 SC 246 on the non-supersession of missives.

Manual, para 28.53.

(NB: There are no opinions relating to Chapter 29 of the Manual.)

STATUTORY TITLES

56   *Gratuitous alienation and unfair preferences*
Arrestment on the dependence – whether effective – whether assignation to be preferred

Date: August 1991

Memorial
The memorialists, B firm, sold a commercial business to another firm, C. Due to the death of the senior partner of B, settlement of the transaction was delayed. C raised an action for implement, failing which damages. The action was sisted and fell at settlement except for the claim for damages arising from the delay in settlement. The memorialists were advised by their agents that there was a strong possibility that when delivery of the price was made, the purchasers would seek to arrest the funds in the hands of the memorialists' agents on the dependence of the action against B. In consequence, the memorialists gave the agents a formal letter of authorisation and instruction to remit the entire free proceeds of the sale to Mrs D who was a friend of the partners of B.

The letter of authorisation was formally executed by the partners of B and witnessed. B's agents formally acknowledged the mandate on the same day.

Settlement was effected by cheque ten days later. On the same day B's agents received an arrestment on behalf of C, seeking to arrest funds on the dependence of the action for damages.

The memorialists asked following questions:

1   Was the assignation and mandate by B of the future funds held by the agents *ex facie* valid?

2   Would the assignation be preferred to the arrestment?

3   Was it right that the free proceeds should be remitted to Mrs D and that it would be wrong for the agents to retain such funds?

4   Was there anything else of which the memorialists and their agents should be aware?

Opinion
1   Yes. Graham Stewart on *Diligence* at p 114, states categorically that it is not necessary that an assignation be contained in a formal writ. If a debtor has by written mandate or authority authorised his creditor to receive payment of certain sums due to him and the mandate has been intimated to the holder of the funds, it is equivalent to an assignation,

constituting the creditor a procurator *in rem suam* and is irrevocable. While Graham Stewart refers to a creditor as assignee in this passage, exactly the same principles, in my view, apply to a *bona fide* assignee whether for value or gratuitously, provided he is acting *in rem suam*.

In the present case, the mandate is formal, being subscribed and attested, and has undoubtedly been intimated to the holder because the holder's acknowledgement is incorporated *in gremio* of the mandate at the foot thereof. The mandate itself contains a positive instruction to the agents to remit to the order of Mrs D through her bankers, and is declared to be irrevocable and may not be withdrawn without her prior consent. It is dated as is the endorsed acknowledgement of intimation.

2   Yes, but with one major qualification. The mandate and acknowledgment of intimation, being both dated substantially earlier than the arrestment, must necessarily take precedence. See Graham Stewart at p 141. In competition with a voluntary assignation of the debt arrested, the criterion of preference is the date of arrestment as compared with the date of intimation of the assignation. Assuming the date of the mandate and the date of intimation to be correctly stated on that document, which I think we can take for granted, the mandate should therefore prevail in a competition with the arrestment.

My hesitation on this point, and the qualification referred to above, arise out of the peculiar facts in this case. It is not suggested in the memorial, and I assume it is not the case, that the payee under the mandate, Mrs D, is a creditor of B; nor, I assume, was she intended to be either an assignee for value or a gratuitous assignee for her own benefit of the sums authorised to be paid to her in terms of the mandate. Instead, the memorial states that Mrs D is a friend of the partners of B without further elaboration, from which I assume that Mrs D is simply acting as a nominee for the purposes of this arrangement which has been set up deliberately with a view to forestalling and excluding the effect of the anticipated arrestment. While there is no doubt whatever that if Mrs D was a genuine creditor of the parties who were truly indebted to her for value or if she was a purchaser for value or a *bona fide* assignee from them of the sum assigned to her for her own use and benefit, she would be protected under the general rule referred to above, I am doubtful whether in the present circumstances, the mandate does have the effect of taking precedence over the arrestment. It certainly would do so if the mandate and intimation had been lodged with a third party who was totally unaware of the circumstances and had no reason to believe that the transaction was anything other than genuine. But it would seem to be the case here that the agents themselves have devised this arrangement with a view to forestalling diligence. The essence of the statement in Graham Stewart, above referred to, is that the payee is *auctor in rem suam*. But, if she is merely acting as nominee, she cannot claim to be acting *in rem suam*; and that fact is known to the agents.

In the case of sequestration and liquidation, there are of course familiar statutory rules which prevent gratuitous alienations defeating the legitimate rights of the creditors of the bankrupt. So far as I am aware, there is no question of bankruptcy in this case but I think the courts would be disposed to apply the same general equitable principle to an arrangement which was manifestly entered into between the parties, acting as it were collusively, with a view to defeating the rights of an arrester.

Put another way, if Mrs D is no more than a nominee or bare trustee for the granters of the mandate, can the agents as holders of the funds properly state, on the strength of the intimated mandate, that they are not holding the proceeds of sale of the business on behalf of the arrestees, if in fact they know that these funds are being held by them to the order of a third party whose sole function is to act as a go-between and bare trustee for the true beneficial owners?

Unfortunately, I cannot quote any direct authority either for or against this proposition and that in itself may be sufficient to prove that my misgivings are unfounded. Graham Stewart, however, has a short section on revocable trusts (p 66) which, in my view, may have some bearing on the position here. The quotation at p 67 from the judgment of Lord Balgray in *Rigby* v *Fletcher* (1833) 11 S 256 underlines my anxiety. Given the knowledge which I believe the agents may have as to the nature and purpose of the mandate, I doubt if they can truly say that they do *not* hold funds for the parties nominated in the arrestment 'or to *any person or persons for their use and behoof*'. The arrester, therefore, in any question as to attaching the funds, cannot be told that the trustee (here Mrs D) is a different and distinct person from the truster (here the parties in the arrestment).

3   Yes, but subject to the qualification in answer 2 above. Since the funds to which the mandate refers have been received, I think the agents are under a positive obligation to remit them in terms of the mandate unless there is some legitimate impediment to their so doing. An effective arrestment would be such an impediment, but the arrestment in this case, being posterior in date to the mandate and its intimation, is postponed to the mandate and therefore effect must be given to the mandate.

Knowledge on the part of the agents would also seem to operate as a legitimate impediment to payment.

4   In a recent decision in *Abbey National Building Society* v *Barclays Bank plc* 1990 SCLR 639, this and certain related questions were discussed in the sheriff court. So far as the mandate in that case was concerned, the sheriff founding on the passage in Graham Stewart above referred to came to the view that a mandate *in rem suam* was effective as if it were an assignation, but that the mandate in that case failed in its purpose on the grounds that the document merely requested the free proceeds to be remitted to a particular account and that the document of request being not *ex facie* irrevocable, was insufficient *per se* to operate as an assignation. These defects in the mandate in the *Abbey National* case do not apply here because the mandate in this case does not merely request. It authorises and peremptorily instructs the agents to make payment and, in contrast to the *Abbey National* mandate, it is expressly declared to be irrevocable without the prior written consent of the payee. In addition, in the *Abbey National* case, the mandate and its intimation were subsequent in date to certain inhibitions as a result of which it failed on that count to establish any

preference. The mandate in this case is clearly distinguishable for the reasons set out above.

Manual, para 30.9.

57   Protection of purchasers

Disposition granted to non-existent company – procedure to follow to cure defect – whether title marketable

Date: November 1989

Memorial
The memorialists, X Ltd, had concluded missives for the sale of a commercial property to B Ltd subject to a subsisting lease. It was discovered that in the disposition granted by A Ltd in 1979 in favour of the memorialists, the memorialist's name was wrongly stated as XY Ltd, a company which did not exist.

In order to produce a valid marketable title, the memorialists proposed that:

(*a*) a corrective disposition be granted by A Ltd in favour of the memorialists narrating the non-existence of XY Ltd;

(*b*) the corrective disposition should contain warrandice by A Ltd but except therefrom the subsisting lease and the period of time after the date of entry under the 1979 disposition;

(*c*) the disposition in favour of B Ltd by the memorialists would contain absolute warrandice;

(*d*) a search establishing that no company had ever been registered with the name XY Ltd would be exhibited to B Ltd;

(*e*) a search in the appropriate Division of the General Register of Sasines would show the above dispositions but no other disposals since 1979, and no other adverse entries;

Given these proposals the memorialists asked the following questions:

1   Would the proposed corrective conveyance result in a valid marketable title being given to B Ltd?

2   If the proposals would not result in a valid marketable title, were there alternative procedures that could be effected?

3   Was there anything else that the memorialists should be aware of?

Opinion
1   The various steps proposed by the memorialists are certainly appropriate and necessary to provide a marketable title for the purchaser. For the sake of completeness, however, I would add that any reasonable purchaser would require not only a search to establish that no such company as XY Ltd exists or existed at any time between 1979 and the

current date but also the usual searches in the Companies and Charges Registers against the true seller X Ltd and also A Ltd. Of course it may be that these searches disclose matter which renders the title unmarketable. That is a remote possibility but none the less it would have to be covered by production of appropriate searches. Likewise, there would have to be a search in the Personal Register against A Ltd for five years prior to the current transaction, notwithstanding that A Ltd were, no doubt, searched against for five years prior to the 1979 disposition. Given these additional precautions, I think any reasonable purchaser would be prepared to accept the title in that form.

Whether the title is marketable is a somewhat different question; and there is an indication in the memorial that we may not here be dealing with a reasonable purchaser, but one who is seeking to find reasons for not settling the transaction. I am not sure whether that implies that the purchaser is seeking to escape from the bargain and I will return to this below. Assuming, however, that the purchaser does intend to go ahead with the bargain but would prefer meantime not to pay the price, then there is an argument that the title presented in the form proposed above is none the less not marketable because there is on the record an *ex facie* valid irredeemable disposition in favour of a company under the name of XY Ltd duly recorded in the Register of Sasines. No doubt that disposition is a nullity because it was granted in favour of a non-existent company but, unless and until it is reduced, it would be difficult to say that the corrective conveyance conclusively cures the original defect in this title. The reason is, of course, that any *ex facie* valid irredeemable probative writ duly recorded must receive effect according to its terms unless and until set aside. That carries with it the inevitable implication that the present infeft proprietor, on the face of the records, is a company known as XY Ltd and there is no subsequent deed divesting that company. Instead, the purchaser would be asked to accept a disposition by the previous infeft proprietor A Ltd, narrating on a purely *ex parte* statement, that XY Ltd never existed and conveying the subjects to X Ltd under its correct name and designation, leap-frogging the intervening *ex facie* infeftment. Given the searches referred to above, a reasonable purchaser would probably be satisfied with that position, possibly supported by indemnity; but I doubt if the title is marketable in the strict sense.

That being so, and if the purchaser proves intractable, then it would be necessary to reduce the disposition by A Ltd in favour of XY Ltd which is on record. The decree of reduction would have to be recorded in terms of s 46 of the 1924 Act and, when so recorded, would expunge the offending disposition from the record.

Unfortunately, however, there is a significant qualification to the foregoing proposition. If the parties proceed by way of an action of reduction to set aside the original disposition of 1979, it seems to me almost inevitable that the decree would be, in form, a decree in absence since the defenders, being non-existent, cannot appear. Such a decree, if obtained in the sheriff court, would not become final until the expiry of twenty years from its date. I find it difficult to see how there could be *personal* service on XY Ltd who must be the appropriate defenders in such an action since it is their title which is being reduced. So far as I am aware, the same rule as to finality of the decree applies in the Court of Session.

If I am right in that view, the purchaser may still object to the title on the footing that the decree of reduction will not become final for another twenty years. In order to exclude that possible argument on the part of the purchaser, it would therefore be desirable, if it is practicable, to devise a form of procedure which would produce a decree *in foro*, the effect of which is that it would become final on extract.

Alternatively, the memorialists, having reduced the disposition, may seek to rely on the decision in *Sibbald's Heirs* v *Harris* 1947 SC 601. In that case, a title was tendered in which one of the links in title was a decree of general service. The purchaser objected to the title on the footing that the decree might be reduced at any time within the twenty-year period; and undoubtedly in this sense the purchaser was right in that a decree of service is open to reduction on the grounds mentioned in that case, namely on the subsequent emergence of a will, as in *Pettigrew* v *Harton* 1956 SC 67, or by the emergence of another previously undisclosed but prior claimant, as in *Stobie* v *Smith* 1921 SC 894. In *Sibbald's Heirs*, however, Lord President Cooper, with the agreement of the other three judges in the First Division, roundly rejected the purchaser's argument as to the reducibility of the decree in fairly scathing terms. Certainly, if the purchaser were to raise the point, I would first draw his attention to the decision in that case and in the earlier case of *McKay's Executrix* v *Schonbach* 1933 SC 747 which was referred to in Lord President Cooper's judgment, and seek to persuade him that objection to the title on this ground was unreasonable, and that the title was marketable.

Against that, however, the purchaser can quite legitimately point to the provisions of the Conveyancing Amendment (Scotland) Act 1938, s 6 which exempts from any subsequent challenge a decree of declarator of irritancy for the benefit of *bona fide* purchasers for value. But that section is limited in its effect only to declarators of irritancy and does not apply generally to decrees of reduction. There is no equivalent statutory provision for reductions, although the Conveyancing (Scotland) Act 1924, s 46 was almost certainly intended, in my view, to have that effect. But, if that was the intention, it has failed in its purpose as a result of the decision in *Mulhearn* v *Dunlop* 1929 SLT 59. If it was thought necessary to legislate for finality of decrees in this way, that is a clear indication that a decree of reduction, being outwith the scope of this legislation, is not sufficient in itself to provide a marketable title.

Accordingly it might be better to consider whether it is possible to achieve the desired result by a different route. In particular, I wonder whether it would be feasible to proceed by way of rectification of the disposition under the Law Reform (Miscellaneous Provisions) (Scotland) Act 1985, s 8 on the footing that the 1979 disposition patently did not, and could not, have accurately expressed the intention of the disponers since nobody would intend to dispone property to a non-existent disponee. I am not familiar with the procedure which an action under this section takes but presumably it would be competent for X Ltd, as the true purchasers in 1979, to raise an action for rectification directed against the disponers

A Ltd; for A Ltd, by arrangement, to enter appearance, and possibly to appear and nominally defend; and for decree then to be granted rectifying the 1979 disposition, so that the deed reads as if it were a disposition in favour of X Ltd. The advantage of so proceeding is that the decree would be, I think, equivalent to a decree *in foro*, and therefore final on extract. On recording of the decree, the 1979 disposition would be deemed to be a disposition in favour of the correct company under its correct name. This would also incidentally avoid the necessity for the corrective disposition by A Ltd and associated searches, although that is a minor incidental benefit.

Alternatively or in addition to one or other of the foregoing procedures for rectification of the 1979 deed, and if the purchaser still refuses to accept the title, I would be fairly confident that, in these circumstances, the seller could obtain decree in an action of implement against the purchaser.

I am invited to give this opinion on the assumption that there is a binding contract. But, in the preamble to the questions posed in the memorial, I am asked to take into account the possibility that the purchaser may be seeking to find some valid reason for not settling the transaction. If the problem is merely postponement of settlement as opposed to escaping from the bargain, my views are set out above.

On the other hand, if the possibility is that the purchaser will seek to escape altogether from the bargain, then there is an alternative ground of objection which, arguably, might allow the purchaser to resile. The missives have been concluded between XY Ltd and B Ltd. But the selling company does not exist. According to McBryde, *Contract*, para 9–12, the identification of one of the parties to a contract is material, at least if personal identity is essential. In the present case, the selling solicitors have in fact contracted to sell on behalf of a non-existent person and this might in itself render the contract void. See McBryde at paras 9–82 *et seq.*

The memorialists will be familiar with the decision in *Lin Pac Containers (Scotland) Limited* v *Kelly* 1982 SC 50 where exactly this point was raised. In that case, however, the company who contracted under the wrong name had already resolved by special resolution to change their name to the new name under which they contracted; and, only three days later, a certificate of incorporation on change of name was issued in the new name. In these circumstances, Lord Stott held that the contract was not invalid because it was executed in a company name 'to which the pursuers were not legally entitled *until three days later*'. But even in these circumstances, according to Lord Stott, the point, although technical, was not free from difficulty.

In the present case, there never was a company XY Ltd, and that fact is certainly sufficient to distinguish this case from *Lin Pac Containers.*

On the other hand, I would have thought it difficult in the circumstances for the purchaser to find any arguable ground on which he has been prejudiced by contracting with the company in the wrong name; and, that being so, I would have thought that an attempt by the purchaser to escape from the contract on this ground must fail.

Manual, para 30.12.

58 Rectification of defectively expressed documents

Missives – extent of subjects conveyed – error – reduction

Date: September 1988

Memorial
Missives were entered into between an angling club (the memorialists) and a seller (Mr A) for the purchase of river fishings. The offer was amended by the agents for Mr A so that the description of the subjects read 'and the fishings of salmon and other fishes in the river ... and including also the sea fishings'. After much debate and some uncertainty as to exactly what the amended offer was intended to convey, the angling club accepted it.

Two years later Mr A sought reconveyance of the sea salmon fishings on the ground that they had been conveyed in error. The following questions were asked:

1 Did the conveyance carry the right of sea salmon fishings?

2 If the conveyance did carry the sea salmon fishings, could it be reduced by way of an action of reduction at the instance of Mr A?

3 If the conveyance did not carry the sea salmon fishings, would an action of reduction be successful?

Opinion
1 Yes. The facts in this case are simple and straightforward; and the formal documents which constitute the contract produce no ambiguity or difficulty of construction.

In the original offer of October 1986, the subjects of offer were carefully defined both by way of a detailed written description and by reference to the title and plan with which, at the date of the offer, the agents were clearly familiar. The description in the offer seems to me perfectly clear and unambiguous. However, in the qualified acceptance an entirely new description was introduced into the contract in substitution for the description in the original offer. In terms of clause 1 of the qualified acceptance, the subjects of sale are to comprise the subjects as so described in that clause of new 'and not as described in your said offer'. Accordingly, the description in the original offer is entirely superseded and excluded from the contract.

The substituted description is by reference to the original title of 1928 under exception of two areas subsequently sold in 1959 by the then proprietor. I have seen copies of both the dispositions of these areas, with copy plans, and they do not materially affect the issue.

Comparing the description in the original offer with the substituted description in the qualified acceptance, it would seem that both describe substantially the same subjects, but with some possible differences in detail. For example, in the offer, the memorialists stipulated for an exclusive right of fishing for brown trout, which they possibly would not obtain under the description in the qualified acceptance because the right to fish for brown trout is a pertinent of the riparian proprietor, even although the right of salmon fishing is vested in a different owner and carries with it the right to fish for trout. The owner of the salmon fishings and the riparian owner, if different, exercise their respective rights of trout fishing concurrently. Further, in the original offer, there was a general reference to the right to fish for salmon, sea trout and brown trout over the lands and water *presently enjoyed by the seller* in general terms. In contrast, in the description in the qualified acceptance, which is by reference to the title, the right of fishing includes certain fishings specified in considerable detail together with the right of fishings *generally pertaining to the lands* therein aftermentioned, of which the subjects disponed in that disposition formed part, and including also the sea fishings at the mouth of the river.

The memorialists, in consultation with their agents, carefully considered the substituted description in the qualified acceptance in detail and, having done so, decided that it would give them substantially what they had offered for (possibly less, possibly more) and on that basis, decided that it was acceptable. Accordingly, after that careful consideration, the agents were instructed by the memorialists in good faith to conclude the bargain and to accept the new description of the subjects of purchase introduced in the qualified acceptance without further modification.

In the result, the contract concluded between the parties contained a description of the subjects under reference to the title deeds (the terms of which were already known to the memorialists' agents) which was introduced into the contract on the initiative of the seller's agents and the terms of that description were carefully considered and discussed before the memorialists finally agreed to it. In particular, I would emphasise:

(*a*) that there was not, at any stage in the negotiations (and, in the circumstances, there really could not have been) any element of error on the part of the seller or his agents which was induced by the purchasers, since the description in the offer was replaced with a wholly fresh description by the seller's agents, acting entirely on their own initiative and without prior consultation with the purchasers or their agents.

(*b*) that the description in the 1928 disposition (which is repeated in brief in the qualified acceptance) is clear, detailed and unambiguous in its terms, and really leaves very little room for argument as to what is and what is not included in the subjects of sale. In particular, the disposition referred to for description in the qualified acceptance expressly and explicitly includes sea fishings at the mouth of the river in those terms.

The contract so concluded then proceeded to settlement. The disposition granted by the seller in 1986, implementing the missives, exactly reflects in detailed terms the shorter description contained in the qualified acceptance. To that extent, therefore, the disposition exactly mirrors and implements the missives as drafted, and, *prima facie*, accurately expresses the common intention of the parties as expressed in the missives. The disposition, in its turn, specifies, in explicit and categoric terms, that the subjects disponed to the memorialists include the sea fishings at the mouth of the river. I emphasise this point for three reasons.

(*a*) In *Anderson v Lambie* 1954 SC (HL) 43, on which the seller's agents apparently rely almost entirely in their argument, the missives simply stated that the subjects of sale comprised 'the farm of Blairmuckhill, near Harthill ... at present occupied by Hugh Miller & Sons'. No detailed description, and in particular no attempt to define boundaries etc, was included in that offer. This is in contrast to the detailed descriptions first in the offer, and then in the qualified acceptance in the present case.

(*b*) In *Anderson* v *Lambie*, the disposition in implement of the missives conveyed not only the subjects as described very briefly and inadequately, in the missives but also some thirty-seven acres which contained a coal mine. Here, the disposition exactly implements the missives.

(*c*) There is a general presumption, in law, that a person, when he signs a deed, has read it; and, by implication, has understood it. This is, to some extent, an artificial rule when dealing with complicated legal documents, of which the layman may well not entirely understand the full legal implications. In this case, however, the document is relatively straightforward. Mr A has signed the disposition which quite clearly states that he dispones to the memorialists an area of ground extending to 86.48 acres together with the fishings of salmon and other fishes in the river and including also the sea fishings at the mouth of the river. That is a perfectly simple, clear-cut statement; and I think Mr A would find it extraordinarily difficult to explain how he signed a deed in these terms, if he did not intend to transfer the sea fishings.

These three points quite clearly distinguish the case of *Anderson* v *Lambie* from the present case; and, in addition, there are other and more important distinguishing features which are referred to below.

Following on the recording of the disposition in their favour, the memorialists now have a recorded title to, *inter alia*, the sea fishings at the mouth of the river insofar as the disponer's predecessor in title had right thereto; and therefore the memorialists are the heritable proprietors of those salmon fishings unless and until the disposition in their favour is reduced, or rectified.

The sellers now claim that they never intended to sell or dispone the sea fishings at the mouth of the river, notwithstanding the plain terms of the disposition although they concede that this is the effect of that disposition. But, given the plain terms of the missives, of the disposition in implement thereof, and of the antecedent titles, I am bound to say that the argument put forward in support of that contention seems to me unconvincing.

The facts in *Anderson* v *Lambie* were totally different from the facts in this case; and in my opinion the decision in *Anderson* v *Lambie* has no application to the circumstances here.

In *Anderson* v *Lambie*, the subjects were described in the offer in very general terms; and, thereafter, a conveyance was granted which, later, admittedly conveyed to the purchaser substantially more ground than he had bargained for in the original contract. The court accepted that both seller and purchaser had intended to sell and purchase 197 acres comprising the farm of Blairmuckhill; and had never intended to include in the sale the additional thirty-seven acres comprising the coal mine. Owing to an error on the part of the conveyancers dealing with the title, the clear intention in the missives was therefore not properly implemented by the disposition which, instead, transferred a substantially larger area of ground to the purchaser than either party in that contract had originally intended and than was contracted for in the missives.

In this case, the facts are quite different. First of all, the description of the subjects in the missives is clear, explicit and unambiguous. Secondly, the disposition in implement of those missives exactly reflects the contents thereof and conveys to the purchasers exactly what the parties had agreed upon in the missives, as being the subject-matter of the contract.

I emphasise, once again, that there cannot be any suggestion in this case of any element of fraud on the part of the purchasers or their agents; nor can there be any suggestion whatsoever of any element of misrepresentation on their part, either deliberate, innocent or negligent. The purchasers have acted in good faith throughout.

The seller now claims, at this late stage and in the face of plainly contradictory documents, that he never intended to sell the sea fishings at the mouth of the river and he maintains, on that ground, that the disposition in favour of the purchasers should be reduced.

In my opinion, there is absolutely no justification whatsoever to support that argument. Given that the seller may have been under essential or material error as to what was covered by the description in the qualified acceptance, that error was a unilateral error exclusive to him, not shared by the purchasers and not in any way induced by the purchasers in the prior negotiations. In the case of *Anderson* v *Lambie,* the court was satisfied, on proof, that the error was common to both parties. In my opinion, that cannot be the position here.

In considering how a formal document should be construed, the question is not what one or other of the parties intended by the words which he used in the contract but what is the true meaning of those words as construed by the court. Contracts cannot be arranged by what people think in their innermost minds. They are made and enforceable according to what is actually said therein. Applying that rule to the present case, there really cannot be any room for argument as to what the seller held out that he was selling because, in the description which his own agents used, to the exclusion of the description included in the offer by the memorialists, the seller refers to his title which is clear and unambiguous in its terms. In particular, it refers explicitly to the sea fishings at the mouth of the river. Whatever the purchasers' intention may originally have been, they were perfectly entitled to take that description at its face value and to rely on it as describing what the seller wished to sell. Having carefully considered the terms of that description and its implications, they accepted it in good faith as defining the subjects of sale and concluded the bargain on that basis.

If there is error at all in this case, it must be a unilateral error on the part of the seller alone. That, in my view, renders the decision in *Anderson* v *Lambie* inapplicable because, if the purchasers were not in error, the error cannot have been *mutual* and that was fundamental to the decision in that case.

On the question of unilateral error, I would refer to two leading and recent authorities on the law of contract, namely McBryde, *Contract,* chapter 9 and Walker, *Contract* (2nd edn), chapter 14. Both these recent and authoritative works deal with the question of error in great detail. I select only limited quotations from these two chapters to underline what I consider to be the impregnable position in which the memorialists now find themselves.

McBryde states, at p 182, under reference to leading decisions both in the Inner House and in the House of Lords:

'This error was entirely his own error. It was not an error which anyone had done anything to induce. He is not in these circumstances entitled to an issue of essential error in order to prove that he made this error and so set aside his obligation....' *Bennie's Trustees* v *Couper* (1890) 17 R 782 at 785.

'But essential error, to form a ground of reduction, must be error induced by misrepresentation or undue concealment on the part of the person in whose favour the deed sought to be reduced was granted.' *Dornan* v *Allan & Son* (1900) 3 F 112 at 117.

Professor McBryde then expands on these *dicta* at pp 182–184.
His views are confirmed and re-enforced by Walker, p 250.

'Unilateral essential error does not invalidate a contract nor does it justify rescission of the contract or reduction by the court, always assuming that the error was not induced by the misrepresentation of the other contracting party. It is essential in the interests of business efficacy that the ordinary rules should be that an onerous contract reduced to writing in plain terms should bind the parties thereto.' *Steel's Trustee* v *Bradley Homes (Scotland) Ltd* 1972 SC 48, 1974 SLT 133.

Walker then quotes the *dictum* from *Bennie's Trustees* v *Couper* quoted above.

The only case which, in my view, might at first sight assist the seller in the present situation is the decision in *Steuart's Trs* v *Hart* (1875) 3 R 192. But in that case the equities were very heavily against the purchaser; and I do not think the decision helps the seller in this case for two reasons.

First, in *Steuart's Trustees*, there was a substantial element of deliberate concealment, and positive inducement on the part of the purchaser which led the seller into error. Indeed, the purchaser's actings came very close to fraud. See the Lord Ordinary's note at p 198: 'The letters by the defender's agent contain ... representations which were calculated, and which appear ... to have been intended to mislead the sellers ...'. In contrast, there is no suggestion of anything of this kind in the present case.

Secondly, in any event, *Steuart's Trustees* is an old decision, relatively speaking. It has been the subject of considerable criticism over the years and it is dismissed by Walker, at p 251, as being a decision which 'cannot now be regarded as rightly decided'. Lord Dunpark in *Steel's Trustee* disagrees with Walker on this point, at p 57. But he accepts that *Steuart's Trustees* is not a case of pure uninduced error, such as we have here. See also the comments of Lord President Clyde (in the Outer House) in *Brooker-Simpson* v *Duncan Logan (Builders) Ltd* 1969 SLT 304.

For this combination of reasons, I consider that the memorialists are entitled to the fishings in question, that their title thereto is valid and unchallengeable, and that any action of reduction raised at the instance of the seller should be defended.

I might add that, in any event, reduction is probably not now the appropriate remedy; and, instead, the parties would be better advised to proceed under the Law Reform (Miscellaneous Provisions) (Scotland) Act 1985, ss 9 and 10. But in my opinion, if the seller attempts either to reduce the disposition in favour of the purchasers or to have it rectified that attempt will fail.

2   No, for the reasons set out in answer 1.

Further, in my view, it would not be competent for Mr A to seek rectification of the disposition under the Law Reform (Miscellaneous Provisions) (Scotland) Act 1985, ss 8 and 9, because the power of the court under these sections to rectify a document is limited to those cases where the document fails to give effect to the common intention of the parties. That is not the case here. It may be that the seller was under a misapprehension as to the implications of the missives, and therefore of the disposition; but that cannot be said of the memorialists who carefully considered the implications of the substituted description introduced into the missives by the seller's agents, fully understood the implications thereof, and agreed in good faith to go ahead with the contract on the basis of that substituted description. So far as the memorialists are concerned, the missives and the disposition do implement their intention.

For these reasons, my view is that the seller has no legal remedy, either by way of reduction or by way of application to the court for rectification under the 1985 Act, s 8; and, if he does proceed by either of these methods, my view is that he will fail. He may then, of course, have a remedy against his own agents for having failed to carry out his instructions but that does not affect the title or the rights of the memorialists.

3   Question 3 has been superseded by the answers to questions 1 and 2.

Further reading
Angus v *Bryden* 1992 SLT 884.
McCallum v *Soudan* 1989 SLT 522.

Manual, para 30.14.

TRANSMISSION ON DEATH

59   *Protection of purchasers*

Precatory trust – link in title – Succession (Scotland) Act 1964

Date: December 1985

Memorial
The memorialists, Mr and Mrs A, concluded missives for the purchase of a property. The seller, Mrs B, was uninfeft. The property was last vested in Mrs C, the mother of Mrs B, who had died testate. In terms of her will, Mrs C bequeathed the property to Mrs B on condition that the property was made available to Mrs C's two sons for their annual holidays, and that it should not be sold out of the family, but should ultimately pass to Mrs C's grandchildren.

The memorialists were concerned that a precatory trust had been established for behoof of Mrs C's grandchildren. They asked the following questions:

1   Could the memorialists rely on the Succession (Scotland) Act 1964, s 17, and acquire a valid title from Mrs B notwithstanding the statutory provisions relating to good faith?

2   If not, did the provisions of Mrs C's will establish a precatory trust and was there any further difficulty considering that at least one grandchild was a minor?

3   Was it safe to proceed using the docquet as a link in title on the basis that Mrs B was a person entitled to the subjects in terms of s 15(2)(c) of the Succession (Scotland) Act 1964?

Opinion
1   Yes. I observe that, in the will, there is a direct bequest of the dwelling-house to the daughter, Mrs B. Admittedly, that direct bequest is followed by a condition, but the condition is laid upon Mrs B and not upon her executor. Looking to the wording of the clause, I do not think the executor had any option but to transfer the property to Mrs B in implement of the specific legacy in that clause; and I do not think the will imposes any duty on the executor in turn to impose a condition on Mrs B. In any event, even if the condition was imposed, it is necessarily personal and could not bind or affect a singular successor, even one who had notice of it.

Accordingly, the docquet transfer on the confirmation in favour of Mrs B is, in my view, perfectly valid and effective as a link in title and can be relied upon absolutely by a purchaser, using the protection of s 17 of the

1964 Act, if that were required. If the will had not been exhibited to the purchasers' agents along with the titles, that would have been a sufficient answer to all the questions put to me by my instructing agents. Unfortunately, the will has been brought to their notice and, to that extent, I agree that they may no longer be in good faith. But the effect of lack of good faith is not in relation to the confirmation and the implement of the clause by the docquet transfer, but in relation to the trust imposed on the disponee, Mrs B.

I take the view that the executor was bound to transfer the property to her and I doubt whether he was entitled to impose any condition on her in the process of that transfer. On the other hand, Mrs B is under a personal obligation to make the house available for the benefit of the two sons. To that extent, she acts not only for her only beneficial interest but as trustee. But, in relation to that trust, which is a trust on Mrs B, the provisions of s 2 of the Trusts Act 1961 would apply. In terms of that section, any transaction (here, sale by Mrs B) entered into by a trustee (here, Mrs B in relation to the trust imposed on her under the clause of the will) cannot be challenged by any other party on the grounds that the transaction (here, sale by Mrs B) is at variance with the terms of the purposes of her trust.

Even if I am wrong in that view and even if the executor, when transferring the property to Mrs B, should have imposed on her the explicit condition that she was to make the house available for the two sons, they are in any event willing to consent to the sale. Their consent, in my view, effectively eliminates any possibility of challenge on a sale by Mrs B.

I do not regard the final sentence of the clause stating that the house is not to pass out of the family, but should ultimately pass to Mrs C's grandchildren, as imposing any trust whatever. That sentence merely places on record an expressed wish by the testator but is in no way binding as a trust condition, whether precatory or otherwise. Accordingly, so far as title is concerned, that can be wholly ignored.

2   Question 2 is superseded by my answer to question 1.

3   Yes; but I would certainly recommend that the two sons be taken as consentors for whatever interest they may have in order to avoid any future question on the title.

Manual, para 31.26.

(NB There are no opinions relating to Chapter 32 of the Manual.)

EXAMINATION OF TITLE

60 Conditions in the contract

Inhibitions – whether possible to provide clear searches – procedure to
render title marketable

Date: June 1989

Memorial

A building society was in the course of selling a property, having called up
the standard security in their favour. The interim report showed an
inhibition which had been registered before the recording of the standard
security and the disposition in favour of the sellers. The transaction settled.
The purchaser's solicitors became concerned that, since the inhibition had
been registered before the recording of the standard security, the inhibitor
could reduce the title even after it had been recorded in the name of the
purchasers. They contended that the selling solicitors could not give a clear
search in terms of their letter of obligation given the existence of the inhibition. An opinion was sought as to whether this was the case.

Opinion

In my opinion, as the personal register stands at the moment and on the
information so far provided, the selling solicitors are unable to implement
their obligation to deliver clear searches. The reasons can be summarised
thus.

The search in the personal register discloses an inhibition registered
against Mr A in May 1987. This clearly antedates the standard security
in favour of the building society. I expect that this inhibition also antedates the conclusion of the contract by Mr A to purchase the subjects,
in which case that inhibition can be disregarded and has no effect under
the Titles to Land Consolidation (Scotland) Act 1868, s 157. In terms
of that section, an inhibition cannot affect heritage 'to be acquired' by
the inhibited party. However, looking to the very long delay between the
date of delivery of the disposition and the date of its recording it is just
possible that there was a similar delay between completion of the
contract and delivery of the disposition, and this point should certainly
be checked and cleared. Indeed, I think it is arguable that, standing that
inhibition, the title is not marketable and the selling solicitors cannot
give a clear search.

More seriously, there is also an inhibition registered in December 1987.
Admittedly, this inhibition was registered subsequent to the date of delivery
of the standard security but several months before the standard security
was recorded. As a result, on the face of the records, the standard security

is caught by the inhibition and so anything flowing from the heritable creditor under that security is liable to be set aside by the inhibiting creditor. In fact, this will not occur and there is no real risk in that, on the papers provided, it seems perfectly clear that the standard security, although recorded in March 1988, was in fact dated August 1987 and was delivered almost immediately after that date as security for the building society loan. Accordingly, by the time the second inhibition was registered, the granting of the standard security was not a future voluntary act by the inhibited debtor. None the less, this does not appear on the face of the record: and, taking the record alone, there is an inhibition registered in December 1987 and a standard security recorded March 1988 under which the creditor has now exercised his power of sale. That power of sale, on the face of it, is therefore struck at by the inhibition and, in the absence of any further evidence as to the circumstances surrounding the standard security, the inhibiting creditor could challenge the sale by the building society. Again, there is no practical risk because the standard security itself was granted for full consideration long before the second inhibition was registered. None the less the title is not marketable.

In both cases, it is up to the selling solicitors to satisfy the purchaser, in one way or another, that these two inhibitions do not in fact invalidate the sale by the building society.

All the remaining inhibitions were registered after the date of recording of the standard security in favour of the building society and cannot affect the exercise by the society of their powers. See *Newcastle Building Society* v *White* 1987 SLT (Sh Ct) 81.

In view of the terms of their letter of obligation, it is really up to the selling solicitors to decide how best to set about clearing the record. So far as the purchaser is concerned, however, there really only are two acceptable methods, namely: (1) a discharge of the relevant inhibition by the creditor concerned; or (2) recall by way of petition to the court. In the circumstances, I would have thought that the selling solicitors can quite easily clear the record by one or other of these two methods.

Another option is indemnity for an amount sufficient to cover both debts, plus interest thereon and expenses.

Finally, when it comes to encashing the building society cheque on completion of the new loan, if the record has not been cleared by that date, the agents would have to disclose the position to the building society and take their specific instructions as to whether or not the loan cheque can be encashed.

Manual, para 33.2.

61 Pre-emption

Right of pre-emption – whether enforceable – Conveyancing Amendment
(Scotland) Act 1938

Date: December 1991

Memorial
A right of pre-emption was created over the whole of the property disponed
in 1976 in favour of A. The right of pre-emption was constituted as a real
burden in a disposition in terms of which the disponee bound himself,
before selling the subjects, to offer to resell the whole or any part to B or
his successors as proprietor or proprietors of the remaining part and
portion of the land.

Parts of the subjects changed hands. The question arose as to whether
the right of pre-emption remained enforceable.

Opinion
We have here a right of pre-emption constituted as a real burden by way
of disposition, not feu charter. There is no equivalent feudal principle
which prevents the transmission of the benefit of a right, whether it be a
building condition or restriction, a servitude, or a real burden of any other
kind to two or more creditors, each of whom may enforce that burden as
against the burdened proprietor for the time being. Indeed, this is in fact
a familiar situation where a single property is subject to a real burden or
restriction in the title, and is subdivided. I think it is now generally
accepted that, on such subdivision, the disponee of each individual part
acquires by implication a *jus quaesitum tertio* to insist on implement of the
conditions in the original common title as against the proprietor of
another part of the subdivided whole. See *Lees* v *North-East Fife District
Council* 1987 SLT 769.

The right of pre-emption in this case was created over the whole of the
subjects disponed by the 1976 disposition in favour of A. The right of pre-
emption is constituted as a real burden in that disposition under which the
disponee binds himself, before selling the subjects thereby disponed or any
part thereof, that he will offer to resell the same to B or his successors as
proprietor or proprietors of the remaining part and portion of the original
subjects. That remaining part of the subjects is clearly identified by the
titles and no problem arises on that account.

I would make four observations on this right of pre-emption.

(1) It is, undoubtedly in my view, duly constituted as a real burden on
the whole of the subjects conveyed by the above-mentioned disposition and
every part thereof. Accordingly, notwithstanding the provisions of the
Conveyancing Amendment (Scotland) Act 1938, s 9, as amended, my view
is that, on a sale of part of the property, the provisions of that section would
apply to the part so sold; but, whether or not the right of pre-emption was
taken up on the occasion of a part-sale, that would not extinguish or
discharge the right of pre-emption *quoad* the remaining unsold part. This,
I think, is clearly provided for in the clause of pre-emption by the phrase
'before selling the subjects ... or any part thereof'.

(2) It is now settled, I think, beyond argument that a clause of pre-emption of this kind, provided it is clear and unambiguous, may be validly imposed as a real burden on a disponee by feu charter or by disposition; and in my opinion the pre-emption in this case has been validly imposed on the whole of the subjects conveyed by the above-mentioned 1976 disposition and every part thereof.

(3) I think it is also clear from the wording, although this point may not have been positively envisaged by the draftsman, that the right of pre-emption was created for the benefit of B or his successors as proprietor or proprietors of the remaining parts of the farm. It seems to me perfectly clear from this wording that, where there are two or more proprietors of the remaining part of the subjects for whose benefit the pre-emption was created, each of the several proprietors is entitled to exercise the right.

(4) I do not think that, by selling part of the creditor area, B rendered the right of pre-emption unenforceable on the footing that this made the burden ambiguous or uncertain in the technical sense; and accordingly, in my view, the presumption for freedom does not mean, in this case, that the right has ceased to be exercisable.

As I understand it from the titles, there have been subsequent transactions involving transmissions of parts of the property but, on the information so far provided, it seems quite clear that the property now in question was originally conveyed by the 1976 disposition referred to above and has remained in the ownership of A since the date of the recording of that disposition; and he still remains infeft therein.

In 1979 and 1981, B conveyed two parts of the creditor area having the benefit of the pre-emption to C, but apparently no reference was made to the pre-emptions, and no attempt was made to exclude C from the benefit thereof in the conveyances in his favour.

In 1984, a further and more substantial portion of the original creditor area was conveyed, not to A as an individual but to A and D as trustees for a firm. Had these subjects been conveyed to A as an individual, a question of *confusio* might have arisen; but it is clear on the authorities that *confusio* cannot operate unless the creditor in the obligation is the same person acting in the same capacity as the debtor in that obligation. *Confusio* does not apply to the 1984 disposition in that the subjects thereby conveyed were conveyed to A and D as trustees for a firm whereas A, albeit one of the trustees, owned the property in question on a separate title in his own name.

By the 1989 disposition, the trustees for the firm as such trustees and A as an individual conveyed substantial areas of ground to B but there was excluded from that conveyance the field in question which remained in the ownership of B. For the reasons outlined above, it does not seem to me that these various transactions have the effect of extinguishing or discharging the right of pre-emption.

I am forced to the conclusion that the right of pre-emption still subsists as a real burden on the subjects in question and accordingly, if they are now to be sold, in whole or in part, then such whole or part must first be offered to the creditors in the pre-emption whoever they may be. These creditors are clearly identified in the original 1976 disposition as being B and his successor as proprietors of the remaining parts of the subjects. B still retains his original ownership of part of the subjects under the 1976 disposition in his favour and accordingly, in my view, he at least is a creditor in the right of pre-emption. The area hatched blue on the plan provided, which shows that part of B's property conveyed to the firm of Z in 1984, has since been reacquired by B and, since there was no *confusio* on the granting of either of these conveyances, B is also entitled to exercise the pre-emption, by virtue of his reacquisition of that area.

In addition, however, B has given off two areas in 1979 and 1981 to C without making any arrangement as to the future exercise of the pre-emption. That being the position and since C (or his successors) clearly qualifies as being one of the proprietors of the subjects originally conveyed to B in 1976 and therefore included in the creditor area in relation to the right of pre-emption imposed on A, C or his successors are also entitled to exercise the right.

Clearly, this is a matter which really ought to have been adjusted in 1979 and 1981 when these two areas were conveyed away but, in the absence of any specific provision in the two dispositions in favour of C, I cannot see any alternative.

Accordingly, it is my view that the persons now entitled to exercise the right of pre-emption are B, at least in his capacity as owner of two of the fields, along with C and his successors as proprietors of the 1979 and 1981 subjects. Therefore, it seems that, before he can sell the subjects in question, A is bound to offer the field to B and to C or his successors infeft in the subjects acquired by him in 1979 and 1981 as disclosed by a search.

The only point which causes some difficulty is your reference to approaches to the C family to see whether or not they wished to exercise the right of pre-emption 'in connection with other proposed sales'. For reasons explained above, the fact that they did not exercise their right of pre-emption on the occasion of the 1989 sale, seems to me quite irrelevant because that sale did not include the area in question and my view is that the right of pre-emption applies to the whole original subjects and to each individual part thereof unless and until the right is either exercised or discharged. Whether or not there have been any actings which I would qualify as an offer to sell part or the whole of the subjects in question to B or his successors which they positively turned down or failed to take up within the specified time limit is not clear from your letter, but I would assume from the general terms of it that the approach to the C family in relation to 'proposed sales' (if these proposed sales related to the field in question) were informal and were informally dealt with, in which case, in my view, B and his successors have not discharged or lost their pre-emptive right over these subjects.

There are therefore two competing parties, each of whom apparently wishes to exercise the right of pre-emption in respect of the affected subjects. I can find no precedent, either directly, or by analogy, to determine on what basis this conflict between C and his successors on the one hand and B on the other can be resolved if the parties cannot agree. The 1976 disposition requires A to offer to resell the same to B or his successors as proprietor or proprietors of the remaining subjects. I do not think anything can be made out of the use of the word 'resell', since the benefit of the right of pre-emption is conferred, not merely on B individually, but on his successors as such proprietors.

Accordingly, A must, I think, make a formal offer to sell the part of the subjects remaining in his ownership which he now wishes to dispose of both to B or his successors and to C; and at the same time he should indicate to each offeree that a similar offer has been made to the other party. It will then be for B and C or his successors to determine between them how, either jointly or severally, they are to exercise the right; and, failing agreement, they must either submit the matter to arbitration or refer to the court for a determination of their respective rights *inter se*.

Manual, para 33.13.

62 Redemption and reversion

Redemption – whether personal or enforceable against singular successors – interpretation

Date: July 1993

Memorial
The question arose as to whether a right of redemption reserved to the disponers in a disposition in favour of A, recorded in the General Register of Sasines in January 1989 was duly constituted as a real burden. If so, whether it remained enforceable against C Ltd to whom the subjects were disponed by A by disposition recorded in the General Register of Sasines in April 1992.

Opinion
There is no doubt that the right of redemption in the disposition in favour of A was personally enforceable as against A on the basis of contract. Although the disposition is a unilateral writ, it is an accepted rule that, as between original disponer and disponee, it is none the less contractual in effect so that any conditions therein can be enforced on a purely contractual basis. The right of redemption was so enforceable because the requirements for an enforceable contractual condition are less strict than for a real condition or real burden. So, in this case, a clause of redemption which is limited in time (here five years) and which requires an outside reference to a third party arbiter for the determination of the price, is undoubtedly enforceable because the contract *as a contract* contains within its terms a definite method of ascertaining the price which satisfies the rules as to price in a *contract* relating to heritage. See *McLeod's Executor* v *Barr's Trustees* 1989 SLT 392.

The property has, however, transmitted to a singular successor and as a result the foregoing rule ceases to apply. Instead, the condition is enforceable in a question with C Ltd only if it qualifies either as a real condition of the grant, or as a real burden in the strict or narrow sense.

In applying the rules which operate to determine whether a condition in a title is either a real condition or a real burden, I have come to the view without much difficulty that the right of redemption in this case will not qualify under either head and is therefore unenforceable in a question with a singular successor. The reasons can be shortly stated thus:

(1) We are dealing here with a disposition, so there cannot be any question of the right of redemption being constituted as a condition of tenure. But, although the condition is constituted in a disposition, that may produce substantially the same effect if the condition satisfies the rules for real conditions. Indeed, the classic case which lays down the ground rules for real conditions and real burdens, namely *Tailors of Aberdeen* v *Coutts* (1834) 13 S 226, was a case involving conditions imposed by a disposition. Substantially the same rules apply to such conditions whether imposed by feu charter or by disposition.

To qualify as a real condition in this sense, one of the essential common law requirements is that the condition should be of its nature permanent. So, in *Corbett* v *Robertson* (1872) 10 M 329 a proposed restriction on erecting other buildings on or making other use of a piece of land during a period of ten years from and after the date of entry was held not appropriate as a real condition. Menzies in his *Lectures on Conveyancing* (1900), p 577 states as one of the essentials for a real condition that there must be an element of permanency. The point is well illustrated in the further case which Menzies cites in that context, namely *Magistrates of Edinburgh* v *Begg* (1883) 11 R 352.

In any event, even if a burden limited in time can be made a real condition in the wider sense, I very much doubt whether, in this case, the right of redemption is sufficiently precise in its terms to qualify under the rule which applies both to real conditions and to real burdens. That rule requires precision and involves the strictest rules of construction in considering whether or not such conditions are enforceable. The reason is that, in the ordinary case, if a singular successor is to be bound by a real condition or a real burden in the title, he must be able to ascertain within the four corners of the deed *exactly* what his liability will be. So, in *Aberdeen Varieties* v *Jas F. Donald (Aberdeen Cinemas)* 1940 SC (HL) 52 (which was finally decided on a different ground) one of the grounds on which the Court of Session was disposed to reject a condition as real in this sense was that the condition referred to an Act of Parliament for the definition of certain types of use, without setting out the detail within the four corners of the deed. This was held to disqualify the condition as real. More recently, in *Lothian Regional Council* v *Rennie* 1991 SLT 465, a burden purportedly imposed as a real condition was held to be imprecise, and so unenforceable, on the grounds that the exact requirements purportedly imposed on the disponee were not precisely stated in the body of the deed. The same criticism can be levelled at the burden here in that the redemption price is not stated as a sum of money in pounds sterling but has to be referred for determination to a single arbiter, who must take into account various indeterminate factors, as set out in the redemption clause. On this second ground, I would be very doubtful whether the clause would qualify as a real condition. See, for example, most recently *David Watson Property Management* v *Woolwich Equitable Building Society* 1992 SLT 430 and especially the opinion of Lord Mackay at p 434 J and K, where he stresses that indefinite sums of money cannot transmit as real conditions.

For this combination of lack of permanency and lack of precision, the clause fails, in my view, as a real condition.

(2) Alternatively, a burden may transmit and be enforceable against a singular successor as a real burden even although it does not meet all the requirements of a real condition. This distinction is drawn in *Magistrates of Edinburgh* v *Begg*. In particular, the requirement of permanency which is an essential of a real condition, has no place in determining whether or not a real burden is valid. In the strictest sense, a real burden implies the imposition of payment of a sum of money as a burden on the subjects disponed and, in the nature of things, lacks any element of permanency because once payment is made, it is discharged. But one of the requirements for such a real burden is that the sum must be precisely stated. As with a real condition this requires, in my view, the statement of a precise sum of money imposed as a real burden on the subjects. This requirement of the real burden in the narrow sense is demonstrated by the decision in *Magistrates of Edinburgh* v *Begg*. In that case, the feu charter required the vassal to pay to the superior a proportion of the expense of making up the road as and when the same was completed by the superior. The court came to the view, on the grounds there stated, that this condition could not properly be made a condition of the grant, ie a real condition in the sense above described; and it failed to qualify as a real burden simply because the exact amount was not stated on the face of the deed. Therefore, in a question with a singular successor, the proportion of the cost was not recoverable by the superior. This principle is reaffirmed by Lord Mackay in *David Watson Property Management*.

On exactly the same grounds, it seems to me that the right of redemption here must necessarily fail because the redemption price is not stated as such but, instead, there must be reference to an arbiter who in turn must take into account a variety of variable factors to determine the amount payable.

Accordingly, since the property has transmitted to a singular successor, the creditors in the right of redemption cannot enforce it as against A because he is no longer the owner; and they cannot enforce it against a singular successor because the condition fails to qualify as a real condition or a real burden.

Following on the decision in *Magistrates of Edinburgh* v *Begg*, it became standard practice when imposing obligations of this kind so to frame the burden that an exact sum of money was stated as a real burden on the subjects conveyed, possibly with an added provision for limiting the amount payable by reference to extraneous factors such as a calculation of the due proportion of the cost of the work or, here, the redemption price. See *Encyclopaedia of Scottish Legal Styles* (1935) vol 5, p 187 and the preceding style on p 186 where a similar formula is adopted for redemption at a valuation price. Likewise, Burn's *Practice* (4th edn), p 241, end of clause (Sixth). If that device had been adopted here, the clause of redemption would have qualified as a real burden in the narrow sense but, in the absence of any such provision, it fails in its purpose.

This may seem a very strict rule, but in practice it is a rule which was always familiar to conveyancers in particular in relation to heritable securities prior to the passing of the 1970 Act. Apart from specialties introduced in the Debt Securities (Scotland) Act 1856, which have no relevance here, a bond and disposition in security was only valid if the exact sum was stated in pounds sterling; and that form of security could not be used to secure future or fluctuating debt even although there might be provisions inserted in the bond for exactly determining the sum due, for example by reference to a certificate under the hand of an officer of the company or whatever. As a result, the *ex facie* absolute disposition came to be used in practice as the normal form of security because that limitation did not apply to that form of security.

The Conveyancing and Feudal Reform (Scotland) Act 1970 has, of course, overcome this limitation by express statutory provision, but only in the context of the standard security. The provisions of the Act have no application whatsoever to a clause of redemption to which, therefore, the old rules as to precision apply. In fact, if it had occurred to the parties at the time, this right of redemption could have been secured to the creditor in the burden by the use of a standard security, thereby taking advantage of the relaxations in the 1970 Act.

The clause of redemption in its terms does not prohibit transmission by A of the whole or part of the subjects. It simply requires a reconveyance from him or his successors on being given notice within the time limit. On general principle, 'successors' in this context can apply only to universal successors; the obligation cannot bind singular successors unless it is real, which in my view it clearly is not. Therefore, a conveyance by him to a singular successor cannot offend against the terms of the clause even although, as a result, the clause may then become ineffective. But that is not because of any action by A in contravention of any prohibition in the deed. Further, this being a disposition, there is no effective irritancy clause and so there is really no effective way in which the parties could be compelled to reverse the transaction. Since the obligation cannot be enforced in a question with the singular successor for the reasons given above obligation cannot be enforced as against C Ltd, nor is there any redress against A.

Naturally, I agree with counsel who states that a right of redemption, created in a deed executed after 1974, is exercisable only within twenty years of the date of its creation. But s 12 of the Land Tenure Reform (Scotland) Act 1974 has no effect whatever on the quality of the burden and in particular does not have the effect of altering the strict common law rules which apply to the effective constitution of real conditions and real burdens and are set out above. Accordingly, there is no justification for his statement that the redemption in this case, because it is in terms enforceable up to five years from the date of entry, is therefore enforceable under the 1974 Act in a question with a singular successor.

Manual, para 33.14.

63   *Occupancy rights of non-entitled spouses*

Matrimonial Homes (Family Protection) (Scotland) Act 1981 –
conveyance for no consideration – documentation required

Date: May 1988

Memorial

The memorialist (Mrs A) was considering purchasing a property. The
seller (Mrs B) failed to exhibit the documentation required by the
Matrimonial Homes (Family Protection) (Scotland) Act 1981. Mrs B had
acquired the flat in 1987 as a gift from her mother, Mrs C, for no consideration. No matrimonial homes documentation had been prepared at that
time. Mrs C argued that as she had given the flat for no consideration, she
was under no obligation to exhibit any form of documentation. The effect
was that Mrs B could not exhibit the required documentation. Opinion was
sought on this point.

Opinion

The argument put forward by the agents for Mrs B in this case is ingenious
and, insofar as it goes, it is undoubtedly correct to the extent that a donee
cannot look a gift-horse in the mouth. If Mrs C chose to convey her flat to
her daughter Mrs B (as she did in 1987) she certainly would not be under
any obligation, as donor, to grant any form of documentation relating to
the Matrimonial Homes Act or in any other connection. In other words, as
donor, she could grant or withhold the disposition as she pleased; and she
could give with it, or not give with it, such additional documentation as she
saw fit to grant. I therefore agree with the agents for Mrs B, that Mrs B was
not entitled to insist on obtaining an affidavit (or renunciation, if
appropriate) at the date of the original disposition in her favour.

That, however, does not relieve Mrs B of her obligation, in turn, to
satisfy a purchaser from her that there are no occupancy rights arising out
of some previous dealing. Possibly, this may put Mrs B in a difficulty, but
that is a difficulty which, as a donee, she could not require the donor to
resolve for her. None the less, that does not exonerate her in a question
with the present purchaser. A dealing includes any voluntary transaction
affecting or relating to a matrimonial home; and, if an occupancy right is
created by virtue of that dealing, the right subsists and transmits against
successors in title. See Nichols and Meston, *The Matrimonial Homes
(Family Protection) (Scotland) Act 1981* (2nd edn), p 48. Accordingly, if at
the date of the gift of the flat by Mrs C to Mrs B, the flat was a matrimonial home for Mr and Mrs C, Mr C might have claimed occupancy rights
as a non-entitled spouse and these rights would have been enforceable by
him, not only against Mrs B but also against any disponee from her.

There is, however, another ground on which, in my view, an affidavit
is unnecessary and indeed inappropriate. I think it is generally accepted
that any occupancy rights of a non-entitled spouse automatically terminate on the death of the entitled spouse. Certainly this is the view taken
by Nichols & Meston at p 18 of their book. Since Mrs C is now

deceased, any occupancy rights which might have been created for the benefit of Mr C during her lifetime have automatically come to an end and can no longer be enforced either against Mrs B or against a disponee from her. It is therefore irrelevant for the purchaser to seek an affidavit or, as an alternative, indemnity against the enforcement of such occupancy rights because, by necessary implication, they cannot any longer be enforced.

I think this disposes of the question at issue.

Manual, para 33.69.

(NB There are no opinions relating to Chapter 34 of the Manual.)

TRANSACTIONS WITH COMPANIES

64   Capacity

Purchase of flat from company – no title obtained – company dissolved –
application to Queen's and Lord Treasurer's Remembrancer – procedure

Date: June 1987

Memorial

A flat was purchased from a company (A Ltd) during the 1960s. Payment
of the price was made by instalments with the intention that when the last
payment had been made, the purchaser would be given a title. The last
payment was made in the early 1970s, but no title was obtained. A Ltd was
dissolved. The purchaser died, and the memorialist wanted to know the
correct procedure to cure the defect to allow for administration of the
estate.

Opinion

I apologise for the delay in replying to your letter. I had hoped to be able
to devise a reasonable solution to the problem but I am afraid, without
success.

The legal position is fairly simply stated. The property in question, to
which the purchaser undoubtedly had the beneficial right, is presumably
still vested in A Ltd who, no doubt, have a recorded title thereto. The
company has been dissolved and struck off the register. In consequence,
the subjects have vested in the Crown as *bona vacantia*. Thus far, the
position is clear cut. The problem is how best, if at all, to obtain a title to
these subjects from the Crown. In all these matters, the Crown acts
through the office of the Queen's and Lord Treasurer's Remembrancer
whose office is in Exchequer Chambers.

Under the Companies Act 1985 an application to the Queen's and Lord
Treasurer's Remembrancer is competent with a view to obtaining a title to
subjects which belong to the deceased. There would seem to be three
alternative procedures available.

(a) The deceased's executors could apply to the Crown for a notice of
disclaimer under s 656 of the 1985 Act. If a disclaimer is granted, then,
under s 657(5), the executors would apply to the court for an order
vesting the subjects in the executors as representing the deceased who
himself was beneficially entitled to the property. Under s 657(6), such
a vesting order operates as a title by itself without any further
conveyance or assignation. The disadvantage to this procedure is that it
involves not only an application to the Queen's and Lord Treasurer's

270

Remembrancer but also an application to the court which would be both time consuming and expensive.

(*b*) It was formerly possible to apply to the Queen's and Lord Treasurer's Remembrancer for a direct deed of gift in terms of which the Crown, vested in the property as *bona vacantia*, simply conveyed the subjects to the person beneficially entitled without any further disclaimer procedure or application to the court. I am not sure whether he is still prepared to adopt this procedure in appropriate cases but a preliminary enquiry would seem to be justified because, if he is prepared so to act, this is obviously the simplest way of obtaining title.

(*c*) Finally, it would seem to me in the circumstances quickest, cheapest and probably equally as effective for the executors simply to agree with a prospective purchaser that he would take the title as it stands on a conveyance by the executors in his favour supported by an appropriate indemnity. Since the property has clearly been in the possession of the deceased for more than twenty years and the company has probably been struck off for ten years or more, there really cannot be any significant risk of challenge to the title of the executors; and I would have thought that an indemnity policy could be fairly quickly and cheaply obtained. Again, however, before embarking along this line, preliminary enquiry of an insurance company would seem appropriate to establish the terms on which a policy might be obtained.

Whatever course is adopted, I think it would first be necessary for the executors to confirm to the property if this has not already been done so that they at least have a colourable title as executors to the beneficial interest of the deceased in the subjects.

Manual, para 35.4.

INDEX